UNVEILLING 'RARE' USAGES IN THE HISTORY OF ENGLISH

FUJIO NAKAMURA

PROFESSOR OF ENGLISH PHILOLOGY AND LINGUISTICS

AICHI PREFECTURAL UNIVERSITY

EIHŌSHA

TOKYO

2016

UNVEILLING 'RARE' USAGES IN THE HISTORY OF ENGLISH

Published by Eihōsha & Co. Ltd.
Dai-ichi Iguchi Bldg., 2-7-7 Iwamoto-cho,
Chiyoda-ku, 101-0032 Tokyo

© 2016 Fujio Nakamura

This publication is in copyright. Subject to statutory exception, no part of
this publication may be reproduced without the prior written permission of
the publisher.

First published 2016

ISBN 978-4-269-77054-6

Contents

Preface	xi
List of Figures	xiii
List of Tables	xv
Acknowledgements	xxiii

Chapter I
Introduction: Contribution of Non-Literary Texts to the History
    of English Research — 1

1.1. Purpose of the Present Study — 1

1.2. Significance of Analyses of Particular Text Types Such as
Private Diaries and Personal Letters: Discovery of Sundry Evidence
Leading to the Correction of Historical English Facts — 3

    1.2.1. Quotations Indicating the Initial Phase of Linguistic Change — 4
        1.2.1.1. Words or Phrases — 4
        1.2.1.2. Syntax — 6
        1.2.1.2.1. Concurrence of the Marginal Auxiliary *Need To*-
        infinitive and the Auxiliary *Do* — 7
        1.2.1.2.2. Progressive with Passive/Causative/Modal *Have* — 8
        1.2.1.2.3. Passive Progressive — 10
    1.2.2. Quotations Showing Linguistic Conservatism — 14
    1.2.3. Quotations Filling in the Chronologically Awkward Gap — 15
        1.2.3.1. *Be busy* **Verb-***ing* — 15
        1.2.3.2. Progressive of *Have* **Meaning** "drink, eat, etc" + Obj,
        Progressive of *Have* + Action Noun, and Progressive of *Have*
        + O + Adjectival/Adverbial/V-*ing* — 16
    1.2.4. Quotations Unveilling Rare or Unknown Usages — 18

Contents

1.2.5. Quotations Reflecting a Writer's Own View of the English Language during his or her Lifetime   20

1.3. Summary of Chapter I   23

Chapter II
Diachrony of the Third Person Singular Present *Don't*:
Transition from *He Don't Know* to *He Doesn't Know*   25

2.1. Period and Chronological Order in which Negative Contractions Became Established and Diffused, and Purpose of the Present Chapter   26

2.2. Diachrony of the Third Person Singular Present *Don't*   35

    2.2.1. Seventeenth- to Twentieth-century Diaries and Correspondence   35

        2.2.1.1. General Chronological Trends: The Period of the Wane of the 'Normal' Use of the Third Person Singular Present *Don't* in the Texts Examined   36

        2.2.1.2. Examples of the Third Person Singular Present *Don't* in the Texts Examined   37

        2.2.1.3. Syntactic and Stylistic Properties of the Third Person Singular Present *Don't* in the Texts Examined   40

        2.2.1.4. Users of the Third Person Singular Present *Don't* in the Texts Examined   42

    2.2.2. *Oxford English Dictionary*[2] on CD-ROM   44

        2.2.2.1. General Chronological Trends: The Period of the Wane of the 'Normal' Use of the Third Person Singular Present *Don't* in the *OED*[2]   44

        2.2.2.2. Examples of the Third Person Singular Present *Don't* in the *OED*[2]   46

        2.2.2.3. Syntactic and Stylistic Properties of the Third Person Singular Present *Don't* in the *OED*[2]   71

2.3. Summary of Chapter II   73

Contents

Chapter III
Diachrony of Passival Progressive Preceded by Animate/Human Subject: *A drunken boy was carrying (by our constable)* — 77

3.1. Previous Studies and Purpose of the Present Chapter — 77

3.2. Presentation of Examples — 82

  3.2.1. Verbs Taking [±Animate] Prototypical Object — 83
  3.2.2. Verbs Taking [+Animate, -Human] Prototypical Object — 85
  3.2.3. Verbs Taking [+Human] Prototypical Object — 86
  3.2.4. Verbs Taking [+Animate or +Human] Prototypical Object — 89

3.3. Summary of Chapter III and Further Discovery — 89

Chapter IV
Diachrony of Participial Progressive: *Being Going* — 95

Chapter V
Diachrony of *Seem* Meaning 'To Pretend' — 109

5.1. Purpose of the Present Chapter — 109

5.2. One of the Mysteries in Present-day English — 110

5.3. Previous Studies — 113

5.4. New Evidence: Presentation of Examples in the History of English — 113

5.5. A Proposal — 122

5.6. Significance of the Present Study — 123

5.7. Reason Why *Seem* 'To Pretend' Became Archaic or Even Obsolete in Present-day English — 126

5.8. Summary of Chapter V — 127

Chapter VI
Diachrony of Present Participles and Gerunds Followed by *Not* — 129

6.1. Introduction — 129

  6.1.1. Target Constructions — 129

Contents

6.1.2. Post-Position of *Not* against *Ing*-forms in Present-day English   131

  6.1.2.1. References to the Position of *Not* against *Ing*-forms in Present-day English Grammar Books   131

  6.1.2.2. Verification of the Propriety of the Statements in Present-day English Grammar Books—Post-Position of *Not* against *Ing*-Forms in LOB, FLOB, BNC, Brown and Frown Corpora   132

6.1.3. Previous Studies on the History of the Position of *Not* against *Ing*-forms and Purpose of the Present Chapter   143

6.1.4. Texts and Electronic Corpora Examined, and Methodology in Collecting Examples   146

6.1.5. Criteria of Analysis—Inclusion or Exclusion of Examples   148

  6.1.5.1. Inclusion   148

  6.1.5.2. Exclusion   153

6.1.6. Principle of Presentation of Examples in Sections 6.2-6.4   164

6.2. Evidence from Seventeenth- to Twentieth-Century Diaries and Correspondence   165

6.2.1. Variations between Pre- and Post-position of *Not* in Simple Participial Verb-*ing*   165

  6.2.1.1. Examples of Simple Participial Verb-*ing Not*   165

  6.2.1.2. General Chronological Trends   186

  6.2.1.3. Verbs which Occured with Verb-*ing not*   188

  6.2.1.4. Semantic Differences between Pre- and Post-position of *Not*   190

  6.2.1.5. Structural Differences between Pre- and Post-position of *Not*   192

  6.2.1.6. Main Points with Respect to the History of the Negation of the Simple Participles   193

6.2.2. Reasons for the Post-position of *Not* in the Simple Participial Verb-*ing*   194

  6.2.2.1. Positional Freedom of *Not*   194

  6.2.2.2. Avoidance of Semantic Ambiguities   196

  6.2.2.3. Seemingly Resultant Post-position of *not*   197

Contents

vii

6.2.2.4. The Most Plausible Explanation: Reflection of the Mode of Negation in Negative Declarative *Sentences (RNDS theory)* 197

6.2.2.4.1. Evidence Supporting the RNDS Theory: (1) High Percentage of Post-position of *Not* in Compound Participial *Having* PP and *Being* PP 198

6.2.2.4.2. Evidence Supporting the RNDS Theory: (2) Low Percentage of Post-position of *Not* in Compound Gerundive *Having* PP and *Being* PP 215

6.2.2.4.3. Evidence Supporting the RNDS Theory: (3) Lowest Percentage of Post-position of *Not* in Simple Gerundive Verb-*ing* 217

6.2.2.5. Summary of Factors by which the Simple Participial Post-position of *Not* was Induced 220

6.2.2.6. Subsidiary Evidence Supporting the RNDS Theory: Further Features of the Verbs Most Frequently-occurring in Verb-*ing Not* Construction 221

6.2.2.6.1. Aversion to the Auxiliary *do* which Helped Fix the Word Order in Sentences Beginning with Negative Adverbs 221

6.2.2.6.2. Resistance to the Auxiliary *do* in Inverted Conditional Clauses, Tag-questions, Exclamatory Sentences, Coordination with Another Auxiliary and Vicarious Use 224

6.2.2.7. One Problem Involved with the RNDS Theory to be Rectified 225

6.2.3. Summary of Section 6.2 230

6.3. Evidence from Electronic Corpora 233

6.3.1. Variations between Pre- and Post-position of *Not* with Compound Participial *Having* PP 234

6.3.1.1. Helsinki Corpus (Diachronic Part) 234

6.3.1.2. CEECS 235

6.3.1.3. Lampeter 235

6.3.1.4. Newdigate 237

6.3.1.5. CEECS, Lampeter and Newdigate Integrated 238

6.3.1.6. ARCHER 3.1 239

Contents

6.3.2. Variations between Pre- and Post-position of *Not* with Compound Participial *Being* PP   240

6.3.2.1. Helsinki Corpus (Diachronic Part)   240

6.3.2.2. CEECS   241

6.3.2.3. Lampeter   242

6.3.2.4. Newdigate   244

6.3.2.5. CEECS, Lampeter and Newdigate Integrated   247

6.3.2.6. ARCHER 3.1   247

6.3.3. Variations between Pre- and Post-position of *Not* with Simple Participial Verb-*ing*   248

6.3.3.1. Helsinki Corpus (Diachronic Part)   248

6.3.3.2. CEECS   250

6.3.3.3. Lampeter   254

6.3.3.4. Newdigate   260

6.3.3.5. CEECS, Lampeter and Newdigate Integrated   265

6.3.3.6. ARCHER 3.1   266

6.3.4. Variations between Pre- and Post-position of *Not* with Compound Gerundive *Having* PP   269

6.3.4.1. Lampeter   269

6.3.4.2. Newdigate   270

6.3.4.3. Lampeter and Newdigate Integrated   270

6.3.4.4. ARCHER 3.1   271

6.3.5. Variations between Pre- and Post-position of *Not* with Compound Gerundive *Being* PP   272

6.3.5.1. Lampeter   272

6.3.5.2. Newdigate   272

6.3.5.3. Lampeter and Newdigate Integrated   273

6.3.5.4. ARCHER 3.1   273

6.3.6. Variations between Pre- and Post-position of *Not* with Simple Gerundive V-*ing*   274

6.3.6.1. Helsinki Corpus (Diachronic Part)   274

6.3.6.2. CEECS   274

6.3.6.3. Lampeter   275

Contents

6.3.6.4. Newdigate	275
6.3.6.5. CEECS, Lampeter and Newdigate Integrated	276
6.3.6.6. ARCHER 3.1	277
6.3.7. Summary of Section 6.3	279

6.4. Evidence from *OED²* on CD-ROM	279

6.4.1. Variations between Pre- and Post-position of *Not* with Compound Participial *Having* PP	280
6.4.1.1. Examples of Compound Participial *Having not* + PP	280
6.4.1.2. Chronological Trends	282
6.4.2. Variations between Pre- and Post-position of *Not* with Compound Participial *Being* PP	283
6.4.2.1. Examples of Compound Participial *Being not* + PP	283
6.4.2.2. Chronological Trends	289
6.4.3. Variations between Pre- and Post-position of *Not* with Simple Participial Verb-*ing*	289
6.4.3.1. Examples of Simple Participial Verb-*ing not*	289
6.4.3.2. Chronological Trends	305
6.4.3.3. Verbs which Occured with Simple Participial Verb-*ing not*	307
6.4.4. Variations between Pre- and Post-position of *Not* with Compound Gerundive *Having* PP	310
6.4.5. Variations between Pre- and Post-position of *Not* with Compound Gerundive *Being* PP	311
6.4.6. Variations between Pre- and Post-position of *Not* with Simple Gerundive Verb-*ing*	312
6.4.7. Summary of Section 6.4	315

6.5. Users of Post-position of *Not* and Nature of the Documents in which its Examples Occurred	317

6.5.1. LOB, FLOB, BNC; Brown, Frown (Section 6.1)	318
6.5.2. Diaries and Correspondence (Section 6.2)	323
6.5.3. Helsinki Corpus (Diachronic Part), CEECS, Lampeter, Newdigate, ARCHER 3.1 (Section 6.3)	330
6.5.4. *OED²* on CD-ROM (Section 6.4)	339

Contents

6.5.5. Geographical Distribution of Users of Post-position of *Not*	364
6.6. Summary of Chapter VI	368
Conclusion	371
Texts and Electronic Corpora Examined	377
Works Cited	391
Index	401

Preface

This monograph is based upon my doctoral dissertation for which I was conferred with a D. Litt. by the Graduate School of Letters, University of Hiroshima on the third of March, 2016. With the utmost gratitude I acknowledge the supervision, suggestions and comments provided by the members of the Dissertation Committee in the aforementioned institution: Akiyuki Jimura, Professor of English Philology, Graduate School of Letters; Yoshiyuki Nakao, Professor of English Philology, Graduate School of Education; Osamu Imahayashi, Professor of English Philology, Graduate School of Letters; Takashi Yoshinaka, Professor of English Literature, Graduate School of Letters; and Ekiko Kobayashi, Professor of German Literature, Graduate School of Letters. Thanks must also go to Akira Wada, Professor Emeritus of English Philology, Yamaguchi University, who evaluated my dissertation as an external examiner and provided insightful and valuable suggestions.

The monograph consists of six chapters. They are revised and updated versions of material I presented at, amongst others, the International Conference on English Historical Linguistics, the International Conference on Late Modern English, the Societas Linguistica Europaea, the Poznan Linguistic Meeting, the University of Helsinki VARIENG guest lecture, the Cambridge Colloquium, the International Symposium on the Creation and Practical Use of Language Texts, Graduate School of Letters, University of Nagoya, and Modern English Association, Japan.

As demonstrated in this monograph, what are believed to have been 'rare' or 'unknown' usages did in fact occur more frequently than previous research has suggested. Huge quantities of text remain unanalysed. Uncovering more hidden historical facts is one of the most important aims of historical linguistics and linguists, because the explanation of linguistic changes presupposes comprehensive and thorough analyses of synchronic data. It is hoped that the new discoveries in this monograph will contribute to, or stir a controversy in, the historical study of the English language.

List of Figures

Figure 1   Variations between Passival Progressive and Passive Progressive Based upon the Years in which the Examples were Written (a)   11

Figure 2   Variations between Passival Progressive and Passive Progressive Based upon the Years in which the Examples were Written (b)   12

Figure 3   Diagram Showing the History of *Seem* 'To Pretend'   125

Figure 4   The Ascent and Demise of Verbs of 'Pretending' Followed by *To*-infinitive   127

Figure 5   Variations between Pre- and Post-position of *Not* with Simple Participial Verb-*ing*—Diaries and Correspondence   187

Figure 6   Transition of the Frequency of the Post-position of *Not* with Compound Participles and Compound Gerunds—Diaries and Correspondence   200

Figure 7   Transition of the Frequency of the Post-position of *Not* with Simple Gerundive Verb-*ing*—Diaries and Correspondence   218

Figure 8   (Provisional) Frequency of *Do*-negative Declaratives with Verbs Termed "Verbs of Know-group" by Ellegård (1953) and Several Other Verbs in Diaries and Correspondence   229

List of Tables

Table 1   Occurrences of Progressive *Have* in the Texts Examined   9

Table 2   Variations between Passival Progressive and Passive Progressive Based upon the Years in which the Examples were Written   11

Table 3   Variations between Passival Progressive and Passive Progressive with Respect to Verbs which Entered Verb-category in and after 1500   12

Table 4   Occurrences of the Progressive with Transitive *Have*   18

Table 5   Early Occurrences of Negative Contractions: Tabulation from the Descriptions in Brainerd (1989 [1993]: 181-190)   27

Table 6   The Earliest Occurrences of Negative Contractions   28

Table 7   Overall Development of Negative Contractions in the Texts Examined   29

Table 8   Overall Development of Negative Contractions in the *OED²*'s Citations   30

Table 9   Negative Contractions Searched for by the Author in the *OED²*'s Citations   32

Table 10   Overall Development of Negative Contractions in the Electronic British English Texts, with D, Q and Imp Mixed   33

Table 11   Chronological Order in which Negative Contractions Became Established and Diffused, with Special Reference to the Number of Word-final Consecutive Consonants   34

Table 12   Occurrences of *Don't* and *Doesn't* in the Texts Examined, Extracted from Table 7   36

Table 13   Variations between *Doesn't* and 3SG *Don't* in the Texts Examined   36

Table 14   Subjects of 3SG *Don't*—Diaries and Letters   41

List of Tables

Table 15   Types of Clause in which 3SG *Don't* Occurred— Diaries and Letters   41

Table 16   Types of Verb Co-occurring with 3SG *Don't*—Diaries and Letters   41

Table 17   Types of Sentence in which 3SG *Don't* Occurred— Diaries and Letters   41

Table 18   Speech Level of Sentence in which 3SG *Don't* Occurred— Diaries and Letters   42

Table 19   Authentic Users of 3SG *Don't* in the Texts Examined   43

Table 20   Occurrences of *Don't* and *Doesn't* in the *OED²*, Extracted from Table 8   45

Table 21   Variations between *Doesn't* and 3SG *Don't* in the *OED²*   45

Table 22   Subjects of 3SG *Don't—OED²*   72

Table 23   Types of Clause in which 3SG *Don't* Occurred—*OED²*   72

Table 24   Types of Verb Co-occurring with 3SG *Don't—OED²*   72

Table 25   Types of Sentence in which 3SG *Don't* Occurred—*OED²*   72

Table 26   Speech Level of Sentence in which 3SG *Don't* Occurred— *OED²*   73

Table 27   Occurrences of Passival Progressive with [+Animate/Human] Subject   91

Table 28   Occurrences of Participial Progressive in Pepys's Diary (D10)   98

Table 29   Verbs Used in Participial Progressive *Being* + Verb-*ing* in Pepys's Diary (D10)   98

Table 30   Occurrences of *Seem, Seeming* and *Seemingly* with the Notion of 'Pretence' in D10   120

Table 31   Pepys's Use of Verbs of Pretending in D10   121

Table 32   Occurrences of *Pretend To*-infinitive in D10   121

Table 33   Definitions of Verbs Pertaining to Five Bodily Senses and *Resemble*   123

List of Tables

Table 34   Variations between Pre- and Post-position of *Not* against *Ing*-forms—LOB, FLOB; Brown, Frown Corpora   134

Table 35   Variations between Pre- and Post-position of *Not* against *Ing*-forms—BNC   136

Table 36   Methodology in Collecting Examples   147

Table 37   Co-occurrence of *-ing(e)* and *-yng(e)* with *Not(t)*, *Nat* and *Nought*—*OED²*   147

Table 38   Variations between Pre- and Post-position of *Not* Accompanied by Negative Intensifiers—17th- to 20th-century Diaries and Correspondence   149

Table 39   Use of Pre- and Post-Position of *Not* in Documents Written by Non-native Speakers of English   158

Table 40   Examples Collected from Broadly Dated Documents in ARCHER 3.1   162

Table 41   Variations between Pre- and Post-Position of *Not* in American English Documents in ARCHER 3.1—Simple Participial Verb-*ing*   163

Table 42   Variations between Pre- and Post-Position of *Not* in American English Documents in ARCHER 3.1—Simple Gerundive Verb-*ing*   163

Table 43   Variations between Pre- and Post-Position of *Not* in American English Documents in ARCHER 3.1—Compound Participial Perfective *Having* PP and Passive/Perfective *Being* PP   164

Table 44   Variations between Pre- and Post-Position of *Not* in American English Documents in ARCHER 3.1—Compound Gerundive Perfective *Having* PP and Passive/Perfective *Being* PP   164

Table 45   Variations between Pre- and Post-position of *Not* with Simple Participial Verb-*ing*—Diaries and Correspondence   187

Table 46   Verbs Taking Post-Position of *Not* with Simple Participial Verb-*ing*—Diaries and Correspondence   190

List of Tables

Table 47 Variations between Pre- and Post-position of *Not* with Compound Participial *Having* + PP and *Being* + PP—Diaries and Correspondence 199

Table 48 Variations between Pre- and Post-position of *Not* with Compound Gerundive *Having* + PP and *Being* + PP—Diaries and Correspondence 215

Table 49 Variations between Pre- and Post-position of *Not* with Simple Gerundive Verb-*ing*—Diaries and Correspondence 218

Table 50 Verbs Taking Post-position of *Not* with Simple Gerundive Verb-*ing*—Diaries and Correspondence 219

Table 51 Rates of Subject-Verb Inversion according to Clause-initial Adverbs—Bækken (1998: 267-281) 222

Table 52 (Provisional) Variations between *Do*-less and *Do*-negative Declaratives with *Have* in Diaries and Correspondence 227

Table 53 (Provisional) Variations between *Do*-less and *Do*-negative Declaratives with Verbs Termed "Verbs of Know-group" by Ellegård (1953) and Several Other Verbs in Diaries and Correspondence 227

Table 54 Variations between Pre- and Post-position of *Not* with *Doubt*, *Mistake*, *Question*, *Value* and *Love*—Diaries and Correspondence 230

Table 55 Variations between Pre- and Post-position of *Not* with Compound Participial *Having* PP—Helsinki-DP 234

Table 56 Variations between Pre- and Post-position of *Not* with Compound Participial *Having* PP—CEECS 235

Table 57 Variations between Pre- and Post-position of *Not* with Compound Participial *Having* PP—Lampeter 235

Table 58 Variations between Pre- and Post-position of *Not* with Compound Participial *Having* PP—Newdigate 237

List of Tables

Table 59   Variations between Pre- and Post-position of *Not* with Compound Participial *Having* PP—CEECS, Lampeter and Newdigate Integrated   239

Table 60   Variations between Pre- and Post-position of *Not* with Compound Participial *Having* PP—British English Documents in ARCHER 3.1   239

Table 61   Variations between Pre- and Post-position of *Not* with Compound Participial *Being* PP—Helsinki-DP   241

Table 62   Variations between Pre- and Post-position of *Not* with Compound Participial *Being* PP—CEECS   241

Table 63   Variations between Pre- and Post-position of *Not* with Compound Participial *Being* PP—Lampeter   242

Table 64   Variations between Pre- and Post-position of *Not* with Compound Participial *Being* PP—Newdigate   244

Table 65   Variations between Pre- and Post-position of *Not* with Compound Participial *Being* PP—CEECS, Lampeter and Newdigate Integrated   247

Table 66   Variations between Pre- and Post-position of *Not* with Compound Participial *Being* PP—British English Documents in ARCHER 3.1   248

Table 67   Variations between Pre- and Post-position of *Not* with Simple Participial Verb-*ing*—Helsinki-DP   248

Table 68   Verbs Taking Simple Participial Verb-*ing* *Not*—Helsinki-DP   250

Table 69   Variations between Pre- and Post-position of *Not* with Simple Participial Verb-*ing*—CEECS   251

Table 70   Verbs Taking Simple Participial Verb-*ing* *Not*—CEECS   254

Table 71   Variations between Pre- and Post-position of *Not* with Simple Participial Verb-*ing*—Lampeter   254

Table 72   Verbs Taking Simple Participial Verb-*ing* *Not*—Lampeter   255

List of Tables

Table 73   Variations between Pre- and Post-position of *Not* with Simple Participial Verb-*ing*—Newdigate   260

Table 74   Verbs Taking Simple Participial Verb-*ing Not*—Newdigate   261

Table 75   Variations between Pre- and Post-position of *Not* with Simple Participial Verb-*ing*—CEECS, Lampeter and Newdigate Integrated   265

Table 76   Verbs Taking Simple Participial Verb-*ing Not*—CEECS, Lampeter and Newdigate Integrated   266

Table 77   Variations between Pre- and Post-position of *Not* with Simple Participial Verb-*ing*—British English Documents in ARCHER 3.1   267

Table 78   Variations between Pre- and Post-position of *Not* with Compound Gerundive *Having* PP—Lampeter   270

Table 79   Variations between Pre- and Post-position of *Not* with Compound Gerundive *Having* PP—Newdigate   270

Table 80   Variations between Pre- and Post-position of *Not* with Compound Gerundive *Having* PP—Lampeter and Newdigate Integrated   271

Table 81   Variations between Pre- and Post-position of *Not* with Compound Gerundive *Having* PP—British English Documents in ARCHER 3.1   271

Table 82   Variations between Pre- and Post-position of *Not* with Compound Gerundive *Being* PP—Lampeter   272

Table 83   Variations between Pre- and Post-position of *Not* with Compound Gerundive *Being* PP—Newdigate   272

Table 84   Variations between Pre- and Post-position of *Not* with Compound Gerundive *Being* PP—Lampeter and Newdigate Integrated   273

Table 85   Variations between Pre- and Post-position of *Not* with Compound Gerundive *Being* PP—British English Documents in ARCHER 3.1   273

List of Tables

Table 86   Variations between Pre- and Post-position of *Not* with Simple Gerundive Verb-*ing*—Helsinki-DP   274

Table 87   Variations between Pre- and Post-position of *Not* with Simple Gerundive Verb-*ing*—CEECS   275

Table 88   Variations between Pre- and Post-position of *Not* with Simple Gerundive Verb-*ing*—Lampeter   275

Table 89   Variations between Pre- and Post-position of *Not* with Simple Gerundive Verb-*ing*—Newdigate   276

Table 90   Variations between Pre- and Post-position of *Not* with Simple Gerundive Verb-*ing*—CEECS, Lampeter and Newdigate Integrated   276

Table 91   Verbs Taking Simple Gerundive Verb-*ing Not*—CEECS, Lampeter and Newdigate Integrated   277

Table 92   Variations between Pre- and Post-position of *Not* with Simple Gerundive Verb-*ing*—British English Documents in ARCHER 3.1   278

Table 93   Variations between Pre- and Post-position of *Not* with Compound Participial *Having* PP—*OED²*   282

Table 94   Variations between Pre- and Post-position of *Not* with Compound Participial *Being* PP—*OED²*   290

Table 95   Variations between Pre- and Post-position of *Not* with Simple Participial Verb-*ing*—*OED²*   306

Table 96   Verbs Taking Simple Participial Verb-*ing not*—*OED²*   307

Table 97   Variations between Pre- and Post-position of *Not* with Compound Gerundive *Having* PP—*OED²*   311

Table 98   Variations between Pre- and Post-position of *Not* with Compound Gerundive *Being* PP—*OED²*   312

Table 99   Variations between Pre- and Post-position of *Not* with Simple Gerundive Verb-*ing*—*OED²*   313

List of Tables

Table A   American English Texts Examined now available electron-
ically   75

Table B   The Earliest Occurrences of *Doesn't* and its Variants in the
Texts in Table A   75

Table C   Users of the Earliest Examples of *Doesn't* and its Variants
in the Texts in Table A   76

Acknowledgements

Two scholars named Akira guided me to the world of historical English philology and linguistics—Akira Wada and Akira Baba. From the former Akira (then Professor at the University of Yamaguchi), I learnt, as an undergraduate, that the basic requirements of this field of study are linguistic analyses based upon insightful readings and strict interpretations, and that, so as to state even a single word, one has to exert oneself to the utmost in collecting as rich a body of evidence from texts as possible. Under the latter Akira (then Professor at the Graduate School of Literature, University of Okayama), I studied ways of writing academic papers, including my MA thesis, and I also developed a deeper understanding of theoretical frameworks. Their doctrines have since continued to stir my academic blood. While I was a graduate student, I frequented the office of the late Professor Kiyohiko Tsuboi, different as his speciality was from my own. He was a reputable American-literature scholar, and always welcomed and encouraged me. I shall always remember the eternal moment at which Professor Tsuboi, fixing his gaze far upon the US, uttered these words: "I would like you to present your academic achievements to native speakers of English in future, Nakamura-kun". I owe the publication of this monograph to the guidance and encouragement of the aforementioned three professors.

Simultaneously with the conferment of the degree of Master of Arts in 1981, I was provided with a teaching position at Aichi Prefectural University. During these thirty-five years in which I have been on the teaching staff of this university, I encountered and was influenced by quite a few renowned scholars in linguistic circles and at conferences. Through meetings of the Linguistic Circle of Aichi, Gifu and Mie, I encountered Professor Yuji Nakao, University of Nagoya, from whom I learnt the essence of English philology. Through the Modern English Association, I became acquainted with distinguished scholars such as Professor Minoji Akimoto, the late Professor Masachiyo Amano, Professor Sadao Ando, the late Professor Kazuo Araki, Professor Isao Hashimoto, Professor Yoshihiro Hattori, Professor xxiv

Acknowledgements

Michio Hosaka, Professor Osamu Imahayashi, the late Professor Keitaro Irie, Professor Yoko Iyeiri, Professor Akiyuki Jimura, Professor Tomohiro Kawabata, the late Professor Michio Kawai, Professor Shigeo Kikuchi, Professor Osamu Koma, Professor Mitsuru Maeda, Professor Yoshihiko Morita, Professor Ken Nakagawa, Professor Yoshiyuki Nakao, Professor Hideshi Ohno, the late Professor Hayashi Ono, Professor Masanori Toyota, the late Professor Masatomo Ukaji, Professor Shihoko Yamamoto and Professor Hiroshi Yonekura, who provided me with encouragement and insightful suggestions. I am convinced that my skills as a scholar were honed by these associations. I am deeply indebted to them for their support and warm words of encouragement.

Among overseas scholars, I would like to express my gratitude to linguists in the University of Helsinki, especially Professor Terttu Nevalainen, Director of VARIENG, Professor Matti Rissanen, Professor Irma Taavitsainen, and Dr Leena Kahlas-Tarkka for their insightful comments and suggestions. They have always welcomed and permitted me to use the facilities in the VARIENG until late at night whenever I visit them following or preceding my oral presentations in Europe. It was also very kind of Dr Arja Nurmi to teach me ways of manipulating the lexical analysis software WordSmith and WordCruncher, and of Dr Turo Hiltunen to give me detailed explanations and useful advice for using ARCHER 3.1. Without their corpus-linguistic guidance, I could not have written Chapter 6, Section 3. Here I would like to record my appreciation.

Similarly, I would like to record my appreciation for the valuable comments and questions which I received from Professor Mats Rydén, University of Uppsala, and Professor David Denison, University of Manchester, in their offices and even at their homes. Their warm words have always supported my research. Thanks are also due to Professor Ingrid Tieken-Boon van Ostade, University of Leiden, Professor Anthony Warner, University of York, Professor Ilse Wischer, University of Potsdam and Professor Christian Mair, University of Freiburg, who have provided me with helpful comments and encouragement at international conferences in Europe.

Upon reflection, my European conference activities probably date

Acknowledgements

back to the Fourth Cambridge Colloquium on Early Modern English: Language and Style in Early Modern English, held in July 1994, at St. Catharine's College, University of Cambridge. At this meeting I read my paper in English for the first time. Had it not been for the kind guidance of the chair, Professor Sylvia Adamson, I would never have thought to return to international conferences in Europe. I can never thank her enough.

Furthermore, I am also grateful to my colleagues affiliated with the Department of English and the Department of British and American Studies, Aichi Prefectural University: Professor Patrick Hubbuck and Professor Alzo David-West, who not only provided me with useful information on the history of the English language and recent American English respectively but also corrected stylistic errors in the earlier versions of Chapter V and Chapter II and provided useful feedback. My special gratitude is due to Professor Brett Cumming, who read through an earlier version of this monograph and revised the English accordingly. I would like to thank him for his time and energy-consuming work.

With respect to financial aid, I have been receiving continued subsidies from the Japan Society for the Promotion of Science (JSPS) since 2006—Grant-in-Aid for Scientific Research (C), No. 18520385 (2006.4–2009.3), No. 18520385 (2009.4–2013.3), No. 18520385 (2013.4–2016.3) and No. 16K02773003 (2016.4–[2020.3]). It is this fund that has made it possible for me to visit Europe for presentations at international conferences every year. The publication of this monograph was realized with the Presidential Fund for Publication from my home university. I am deeply indebted to the JSPS and Dr and Professor Tadayoshi Takashima, President of Aichi Prefectural University.

In editing this monograph, I received practical and priceless editorial suggestions from Mr Gen Sasaki, President of Eihōsha & Co. Ltd., and its skilled editorial staff, including Mr Kouichi Shimomura and Mr Masao Uji. Their useful advice is highly appreciated.

Last but not least, I am greatly obliged to my late father Hidenosuke, my late mother Iyoko, and three elder brothers, Nobuyuki, Shigenobu and Saburo, who sacrificed their own opportunities of furthering their education

Acknowledgements

so that I might attend university. My utmost thanks are due to Mineko, my wife, Shizuka, my daughter and Hikaru, my son, who supported my academic life. Mineko uncomplainingly allowed me to stay working in my office even on holidays, securing me enough time for research. Thank you for everything.

Tajimi, May 2016
Fujio Nakamura

Chapter I

Introduction:

Contribution of Non-Literary Texts to the History of English Research[1]

1.1. Purpose of the Present Study

When the present author started to learn English at the age of 12, it was of great wonder why the plural form of the noun *roof* is not *reef*, in accordance with the *tooth-teeth* declension. By consulting the *OED* seven years later it was a delight and even relief to know the fact that *reef*, *mans* and *surprisal*, instead of *roofs*, *men* and *surprise*, were used in some stage of the history of English. In the history of English, unexpected usages can occur more often than one expects.

Look at the examples in (1),[2] for instance. None of them are usually permissible in standard Present-day English.

(1) a. Non-counterfactual *would have* PP
  1667 S. Pepys, D10, VIII 218, This did vex me, and I would have gone and I did go to my house, thinking to dine at home;

 b. Parenthetic *I doubt*
  1765 T. Gray, L26, II 678, I am neither sorry, nor glad, for M: (I

---

[1] Chapter I is a combined, expanded and updated version of Nakamura (1998a, 2003a, b, 2007b). With respect to Nakamura (2003a, b), I would like to record my appreciation of the comments which I received gratefully from Professor David Denison, University of Manchester. It was very kind of him to correct my interpretations of several examples. I am also grateful to Professor Matti Rissanen, University of Helsinki, and Professor Olga Fischer, University of Amsterdam, for their encouragement and helpful comments. As to Nakamura (2007b), I would like to express my gratitude to the linguists at VARIENG, University of Helsinki, especially Professor Matti Rissanen, Professor Terttu Nevalainen, Dr Matti Kilpiö, Dr Leena Kahlas-Tarkka and Dr Arja Nurmi for their insightful comments and questions made on the earlier draft.

[2] In each example of this monograph, the year, the name of the writer, the text number, the volume number and the page number are shown in this order before the quotation. For details, refer to "Texts and Electronic Corpora Examined" (pp. 377-389).

doubt) will scarce succeed to his Prebend. | II 702, II 872

c. *have could*

1653 D. Osborne, L4, 29, though the poor fellow made what <u>hast</u> hee <u>coulde</u> to unty his bag, I did nothing but chide him for being soe slow.

d. Causative *do*

1849 T. H. Huxley, D35, 174, Dreamy parables <u>do</u> these waves murmur in one's ears.

The quotation (1a) does not have a counterfactual meaning, contrary to the accepted theory. (1b) shows that, in contradiction to the Present-day English usage, a negative parenthetic clause could be inserted in the medial position of a sentence in Late Modern English. (1c) suggests that the unusual usage of *have could* was used at a personal level by Dorothy Osborne in her letters to Baronet William Temple, diplomat and her near-future husband. The quotation in (1d), the writer of which is a great scientist, born and raised at Ealing and Coventry (*ODNB*), indicates that the causative use of *do* continued to be used even in Late Modern English in spite of the accepted view. At this point, however, it is premature to jump to conclusions: more and more texts reflecting various strata and levels in the development of English must be analysed. It is feasible that, as Rydén (1979: 22) indicates, such constructions are missing from other texts (i) accidentally, (ii) because examples have been overlooked, (iii) because they were not part of the grammar of the time, or (iv) because they were highly idiosyncratic or mere slips of the pen. We are at a complete loss especially when constructions which seem possible for us have not been encountered in the texts.

Historical English linguists have, based upon primarily literary texts, done much to describe and explain both the stability of and change within the English language over time. Even in the early 21st century, however, a considerable amount of evidence leading to the correction of historical English facts in terms of not only lexicon but also syntax can be encountered. This is confirmed from the reading of documents such as private diaries and personal letters which were not intended for publication and

Introduction

have remained largely linguistically unanalyzed. Linguistic phases different from those which are shown in studies carried out based upon the analyses of the language of writers and their literary works can be detected.

For more than thirty-five years the author's time and energy have been devoted to the investigation into the language, exclusively of English diaries and letters, so that a contribution to the history of English research can be made by adding information to the results historical linguists had obtained predominantly through the linguistic analyses of serious literary texts. Though the work has been proceeding slowly, almost 150 volumes of diaries and correspondence written in the 16th to early twentieth centuries have been analysed, with the attention focussed on the use of the progressive, the auxiliary *do*, the auxiliary *have* and the relative pronoun, and on the discovery of examples which antedate or postdate the earliest or latest citations in the *OED*[2]. Letters reflecting popular speech, except for *Paston Letters* and *Cely Letters*, begin to multiply only in the late 16th century, and diaries, according to Matthews (1950), are extant from the 16th century onwards. This is the reason why the texts examined by the present author cover the periods from 1500 onwards. The purpose of the present study consists not so much in showing the linguistic differences in text types as in estimating the contribution of the particular text types of private diaries and personal letters to the history of English.

1.2. Significance of Analyses of Particular Text Types Such as Private Diaries and Personal Letters: Discovery of Sundry Evidence Leading to the Correction of Historical English Facts

In relation to such evidence, this chapter aims to show the contribution of the analyses of the particular text types to the historical study of English, specifically by sorting linguistic data from such documents into the following categories:

(2) (i) Quotations indicating the initial phase of linguistic change
(ii) Quotations showing linguistic conservatism

4

Chapter I

(iii) Quotations filling in the chronologically awkward gap

(iv) Quotations unveilling rare or unknown usages

(v) Quotations reflecting a writer's own view of the English language during his or her lifetime

1.2.1. Quotations Indicating the Initial Phase of Linguistic Change

The first category (2i) consists of quotations, among others, containing negative contractions, the passive progressive, *be near* followed by verb-*ing*, *in order to*-infinitive, the concurrence of *be/have* and the auxiliary *do*, the concurrence of *need to*-infinitive and the auxiliary *do*, *get* + PP, and the progressive with passive/causative/modal *have*.

1.2.1.1. Words or Phrases

Admittedly, the *OED* is an inestimably laborious achievement. We are indebted to it beyond description. It is still, however, open to improvement. Attempts have been, and will be made to check the *OED* documentation. The present writer is also willing to supply possible antedatings and postdatings from the texts examined. It is a great honour to share the joy in improving the *OED*, the heritage publication of our time. The question of how many years earlier or later newly-discovered antedatings or post-datings should be regarded as chronologically relevant cannot fail to be raised in this sort of examination. Schäfer (1980: 35, 44-45), for example, states that antedatings and postdatings below the half-century-tolerance which Dr. Murray set as a realistic goal in the preparation of the *OED* are negligible. This solution of his is incorporated here, and accordingly the citations in (3)-(9) will alter our concept of the history of those particular words and phrases, although they are not absolutely but relatively the earliest since they may be antedated in return in future.

To take an example, the earliest citation of participial adjective *lowering* in the *OED* is of very recent dating (1895 *Daily News*). Earlier by more than two centuries, however, an instance is found in Pepys's Diary, as in (3). Regarding the documentation of participial adjectives in the *OED*,

Introduction

Schäfer (1980: 227; 59 & n. 27) points out that the two participial adjectives in *-ed* and in *-ing* "are assigned main lemmas in the *OED* according to the practical considerations of importance and frequency" and that "it seems that the editors' inclination to assign main lemma status to participial adjectives, particularly pronounced for Letters A and B, decreased in the course of publication".

(3) 1669 Pepys, D10, IX 540, At noon home to dinner, and there find my wife extraordinary fine with her flowered tabby gown that she made two years ago, now laced exceeding pretty, and endeed was fine all over - and mighty earnest to go, though the day was very <u>lowering</u>,

(Nakamura 1986: 166)

Similarly, the examples in (4) can be possible antedatings for the construction of *in order* followed by *to*-infinitive as they are half a century earlier than the earliest citation under *OED²* s.v. order, *n.*, 28b(b) (1711 Steele). Evidence only from Diary 1660-62 appears in (4). Accordingly, the evidence in (4) will alter our concept of the history of *in order to* + infinitive.

(4) 1660 Pepys, D10, I 241, Afterwards to my house and sent all my books to my Lord's <u>in</u> <u>order</u> <u>to</u> <u>send</u> them to my house that I now dwell in. | 1660 Pepys, D10, I 309, 1662 Pepys, D10, III 135, 1662 Pepys, D10, III 190, etc.

(Nakamura 1986: 167)

(5) and (6) shows that the *OED²*'s earliest citation of the relative adverb *whereabout* with the locality sense is more than half a century later than Pepys's use.

(5) 1722 Whiston, *The. Earth*, II 218, At . . . Pekin . . . <u>whereabout</u> probably Noah liv'd immediately before the Deluge.

(*OED²* s.v. whereabout, *interrog.* and *rel. adv., sb.*, 1†b)

(6) 1660 Pepys, D10, I 53, In the afternoon he was at a church in Broadstreet, <u>whereabout</u> he doth lodge.

(Nakamura 1986: 168)

Chapter I

As indicated in (7a), the *OED²*'s earliest citation taken from Walpole is too late for the construction of *be near* followed by a gerund; two examples from Dryden in (7b) are much earlier. They can be further antedated, however, by not only the examples collected from Pepys in (8) but also those coming from 1650s in (9).

(7) a. 1762-1771 H. Walpole, *Vertue's Anecd. Painting*, I. vii. 218, The comeliness of whose person was very near raising him to that throne.

$\qquad$ (*OED²* s.v. near, *adv.*² (and *prep.*), 17c)

   b. 1671 Dryden, *Evening's Love*, 315, our love is drawn out so subtle already, that 'tis [*sic*] near breaking. | 1684 Dryden, *History of the League*, 170, too much mildness, which is so near resembling the godlike attribute of mercy

$\qquad$ (Söderlind 1958 [1976]: 200)

(8) 1664 Pepys, D10, V 314, and to the ale-house with one and was near buying four or five anchors, and learned something worth my knowing of them. | 1665 Pepys, D10, VI 241, And I was near signing to an undertaking for the payment of the whole sum, but I did by chance escape it, | 1667 Pepys, D10, VIII 225, I was very near making a forfeit, but I did command myself . | 1667 Pepys, D10, VIII 553, where I was near being chosen of the Council, but am glad I was not,

$\qquad$ (Nakamura 1986: 166-67)

(9) 1653 D. Osborne, L4, 78, Poore Mrs Fretcheville is neerer being mad then ere she was in her life, | 1653 D. Osborne, L4, 85, I was as neer Laughing Yesterday where I should not; | 1659 S. Pepys, L7, 15, one . . . was very neere having his braines knockt out with a brick batt . . . | 1662 J. Evelyn, D9, III, 318, the bloud was neere breaking the vaines,

As we have seen, the analyses of non-literary texts such as private diaries and personal letters can make a contribution to the historical study of words and phrases, and to the *OED*, "companion to English literature".

1.2.1.2. Syntax

In terms of syntax, the following constructions can be identified as

Introduction

indicating the initial phase of linguistic change: the concurrence of the marginal auxiliary *need to*-infinitive and the auxiliary *do*, the progressive with passive/causative/modal *have*, and the passive progressive.

1.2.1.2.1. Concurrence of the Marginal Auxiliary *Need To*-infinitive and the Auxiliary *Do*

As an instance, according to Visser (1969: 1413, 1416-1418, 1427, 1430, 1435-1436, 1825), the earliest examples showing the concurrence of *use(d)/need/dare/ought to*-infinitive and the auxiliary *do* can be summarised as in (10). However, it is possible to antedate the earliest example with *need to*-infinitive by less than two centuries, as illustrated in (11). This enables us to regard the three marginal modals *use(d)/need/dare to*-infinitive as having begun to take the auxiliary *do* at roughly the same time, that is, in the Early Modern period, while *ought to*-infinitive still shows an aversion to *do* in Present-day English.

(10) a. *use(d) to*-infinitive: (in negative declaratives & questions)
1592 Shakespeare, c1650 Osborne, 1662 Stillingfleet, 1663 S. Tuke, 1677 Wycherley, . . .

b. *need to*-infinitive: (in negative declaratives & questions)
1847-48 Thackeray, 1849 C. Brontë, 1860 C. & A. Williamson, 1866, 1869, 1888, . . .

c. *dare to*-infinitive: (in negative declaratives)
1668 Dryden, 1749 Fielding, 1843 Lytton, 1847 Thackeray, 1850 Hunt, . . .

d. *ought to*-infinitive: (in negative declaratives)
1849 Dickens, 1916 Wells (two instances), 1920 Galsworthy, . . .

(11) Possible antedatings
1663 S. Pepys, D10, IV 353, we have concluded to have him have a lodging elsewhere, and that I will spare him 15*l* of his salary; and if I do not need to keep another, 20*l*. (Nakamura 1997: 118) | 1666 S. Pepys, D10, VII 26, only after I was in the house, heard a great dog bark and so was afeared how I should get safe back again, and there-

8

Chapter I

fore drew my sword and scabbard out of my belt to have ready in my hand - but <u>did</u> <u>not</u> <u>need</u> <u>to</u> <u>use</u> it, but got safe into the coach again. (Nakamura 1997: 118) | 1681 C. Morelli, L5, 119, You <u>doe</u> <u>not</u> <u>need</u> <u>to</u> <u>lodge</u> att a In, . . . (Nakamura 1997: 118) | 1772 J. Wedgwood, L32, 136, <u>Do</u> I <u>need</u> <u>to</u> <u>tell</u> you that he bore his last illness with that fortitude and strength of mind which characterised all his actions. | 1775 J. Wedgwood, L32, 181, Should you like a little of our Tour? you <u>do</u> <u>not</u> <u>need</u> <u>to</u> <u>read</u> it when you have anything better to do.

1.2.1.2.2. Progressive with Passive/Causative/Modal *Have*

With respect to the progressive with *have* + Object + PP or *have* + *to*-infinitive, Denison's citations from 1842 are the earliest for the progressive with passive or causative *have* as shown in (12a), and, as quoted in (12b), the earliest occurrence of the progressive with modal *have*, discovered by Poutsma, comes from 1916 *Punch*. Although Poutsma does not show the year of his *Punch* example, the kindest aid from the Humanities Reference Service, the British Library, has led to specification regarding not only the year of publication of the *Punch* number but also the extra-linguistic context.

(12) a. Progressive with passive/causative *have*
1842 *Blackw. Mag.* LI 388 (*OED*), They *were having their portraits taken* by the photogenic process.

(Denison 1998: 149)

b. Progressive with modal *have*
1916 *Punch*, no. 3900, 232, "Hallo Ethel, so you have started one of those things?" – "Yes, we *'re* all *having to come* to them." ["part of a caption to a drawing" (In the e-mail to Nakamura from the Humanities Reference Service, The British Library)]

(Poutsma 1926: 343)

In actual fact, however, the examples in (12a, b) can be antedated by nearly half of a century, as in (13) and Table 1. Consequently, the quotations from 1790 Woodforde and 1882 Hamilton can be a possible antedating for the progressive of the causative *have* and for the progressive of modal *have*, respectively.

Introduction

(13) Possible antedatings and earlier examples
  a. Progressive with passive/causative *have*
    1790, J. Woodforde, D21, III, 172, After breakfast, whilst the Ladies were having their Heads dressed &c. I walked out into the City and paid the following Bills to my Tradesmen. | 1844 H. Martineau, L47, 97, A friend now here is having the whole lower sash of my window replaced by a single pane of plate glass, . . . (Cited in Denison 1998: 148) | 1851 C. Dickens, L65, VI, 322, For the representation of the new Comedy Bulwer has written for us, to start this scheme, I am having an ingenious Theatre made by Webster's people, for erection on certain nights in the Hanover Square Rooms. | 1851 C. Dickens, L65, VI, 405, I am having him put into a decent suit of morocco, and, when he comes home in his new dress, shall entreat you to give him a place on your shelves for my sake. | 1868 C. L. Dodgson, L55, 115, Somebody told me . . . that you had been having better photographs done of yourselves. | 1872 F. Kilvert, D36, II, 157, She was having the old garden cleared up and contemplated making a gas tar path.
                                                                    (Nakamura 2003b: 69)

  b. Progressive with modal *have*
    1882 E. W. Hamilton, D39, I, 299, It is a little unfortunate that the present Government should be having to make use of that possession. [Textual footnote: "Before EWH [=Edward Walter Hamilton] pencilled emendations of this sentence it read: 'It is unfortunate that the present Government should be making use of that worthless possession.'"]
                                                                    (Nakamura 2003b: 69)

Table 1   Occurrences of Progressive *Have* in the Texts Examined

	With passive or causative *have*	With modal *have*
1775-1799	1	
1800-1824		
1825-1849	1	
1850-1874	4	
1875-1899	4	1
1900-	3	

Chapter I

1.2.1.2.3. Passive Progressive

On the history of the passive progressive, no example antedating the earliest one has been encountered in the texts examined. On the period of its establishment, however, Nakamura (1998b, 2008d) formulates a new theory. The following is the essence of them.

The period around which the passive progressive is thought to have become established has been varied thus far: about 1825 (Curme 1931: 443-44), about 1900 (Visser 1973: 2016-2019) and around mid-19th century (Nakamura 1991: 137). Regrettably, Curme did not provide any evidence for his conclusion. Presenting evidence to prove that it was established much earlier than at the turn of the century as Visser postulates, Nakamura (1998b, 2008d) insists on the regulation of the passive progressive at the common and informal speech level as reflected in private diaries and personal letters in between 1820 and 1850, not later, for the reason below. In Nakamura (1998b), statistics are shown per texts, and in Nakamura (2008d) per fifty years.

The syntactic variants having both progressive and passive sense consisted of: *The house is on repairing* (*a repairing, in repairing*, etc.), *The house is repaired, The house is under repair, The house is undergoing repairs, The house is (up)on the point of / in the act of being repaired, The house is getting repaired* and so on. After showing that the greatest competitor of the passive progressive *The house is being built* was the passival progressive *The house is building*, the rivalry between these two over time is considered. Variations of the passival progressive and the passive progressive per 25 years appear in Table 2, where statistics with '+' indicate those of the case in which the participle involved is a coordinated element, and staistics with '++' those of the case in which the coordinated participle has an independent subject. The figuration of the data in Table 2 is Figure 1. Figure 2 shows the variations of verbs taking passival progressive and passive progressive per 25 years. From Table 2 and Figures 1 and 2, it is evident that 1826-1850 is a turning point; the statistics show a steep decline from the mid-19th century.

Introduction

Table 2 Variations between Passival Progressive and Passive Progressive Based upon the Years in which the Examples were Written

Period	Passival progressive	Passive progressive
-1600	2	0
1601-1625	1	0
1626-1650	5	0
1651-1675	85+ +1	0
1676-1700	43	0
1701-1725	46	0
1726-1750	19+1+1	0
1751-1775	34+4+2	0
1776-1800	43+1	1
1801-1825	55+1	7
1826-1850	44+1+2	22
1851-1875	35	109+7
1876-1900	9	67+1
1901-1925	0	71+1
1926-	0	77+1

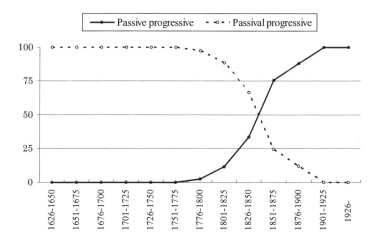

Figure 1 Variations between Passival Progressive and Passive Progressive Based upon the Years in which the Examples were Written (a)—Nakamura (2008d: 46)

Chapter I

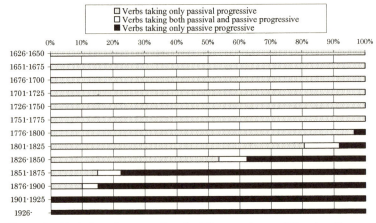

Figure 2 Variations between Passival Progressive and Passive Progressive Based upon the Years in which the Examples were Written (b)—Nakamura (2008 d: 46)

Table 3 demonstrates the behaviour of newly-born verbs.

Table 3 Variations between Passival Progressive and Passive Progressive with Respect to Verbs which Entered Verb-category in and after 1500

Verbs taking passival progressive only		Verbs taking both passival progressive and passive progressive	Verbs taking passive progressive only	
1523 front	1540 power	1515 settle	1529 improve	
1533 allude	1543 gravel	1517 despatch	1535 slaughter	
1552 transcribe	1596 forward		1555 empty	1599 excavate
1561 manage	1597 bet		1560 meditate	
1570 demolish	1599 enlist		1576 review	
c1585 transact	1599 negotiate		1590 admire	
1623 indulge			1600 attack	c1613 foment
			1606 lower	1632 plunder
			1611 reproduce	
		1663 construct	1676 flog	
			1689 test	
			1696 skate	
			1703 bamboozle	
			1750 develop	
			1797 revolutionise	
			1809 lionise	
			1881 ‖ commandeer S. Africa	

Introduction

Table 3 indicates that newer verbs tended to take the new form only, viz.
the passive progressive. All of the people at the time were not speaking or
writing with substantial knowledge of the history of words, even if English
was their first language. However, it is indeed possible to imagine that the
new form of the passive progressive was adopted for verbs that were new
or novel to them. This does not seem to be a mere coincidence, at least to
the present author.

When the sets of evidence above are considered, it can be concluded
that, in such colloquial and popular speech as represented in private diaries
and personal correspondence, it is between 1820 and 1850, not later, that
the passive progressive became dominant among the syntactically and se-
mantically equivalent forms. Although this statement sounds somewhat
mechanical and there are a few exceptions, to people who were born in and
after 1800 the passive progressive was the usual form. Their diaries and
letters were usually written a few decades later after they had grown up,
and therefore it follows that, as far as the present texts examined are concerned, the passive progressive revealed its establishment around the mid-
19th century. As a consequence, it is better to conclude that it was between
1820 and 1850 that the passive progressive became established. Visser
would seem to have been not just overwhelmed by the high frequency of
the passival progressive with the verbs such as *build, do, make, prepare*,
but even influenced by 19th-century grammar books. Visser (1973: 2426-
2429) suggests that, while 18th-century grammarians had tended to con-
demn the passival progressive, 19th-century writers were less censorious
perhaps because it was not quite as unfavourable as a very unpleasant and
clumsy innovation, the passive progressive.

The difference in the results between Visser and the present author
seems to lie in the nature of texts. Although Visser's material examined is
comprehensive and varied, levels of usage are not clearly distinguished.
Furthermore, the main sources of Visser's are serious literary works. In
such a text type, the passival progressive continued to be favoured because
of its vividness. In addition, the more complicated the verb phrase becomes, the more favourably the passival progressive is preferred because

14

Chapter I

the cacophonous repetition of *be* such as *be being, been being* can be avoided. In a sense, the passival progressive and the progressive passive were in complementary distribution, and this can be thought to be a cause of the delay of the polarisation of the progressive passive even after its establishment.

As presented above in 1.2.1 for Category (2i), it may be concluded that, at the common and informal speech level as reflected in private diaries and personal letters, language change in general must have taken place much earlier than has been suggested.

1.2.2. Quotations Showing Linguistic Conservatism

The causative use of *do* in (1d) above belongs to the second category (2ii) "quotations showing linguistic conservatism". Also included in this category is the usage of *I not say*, occurrences showing the gradual extinction of *be busy to* + infinitive, and *do*-less affirmative interrogative sentences such as *How do you?, What say you (to ~)?* and *What think you (of ~)?*

With respect to the history of the negative declarative represented as *I not say*, Partridge (1948 [1953a]: 9) reports that this form was common in 16th century verse. After about 1700, this form disappeared from usage and, in Present-day English, it is chiefly restricted to poetry (Visser 1969: 1532). Visser quotes five examples for Late Modern English, and one example dating from about 1930 for Present-day English. The diaries and correspondence examined for this monograph, however, confirm that this negative form persisted moderately throughout Modern English. The examples never represent substandard English nor subjunctive use. The frequency of the usage in Late Modern English seems to have escaped the attention of linguistic historians. Details, including the negative imperative represented as *Not say*, are discussed in Nakamura (2014, 2015c).

Concerning the construction of *be busy to* + infinitive, this construction was still in occasional use in Samuel Pepys's English, the 17th-century popular speech as shown in (14), even though its earliest and latest citations in the *OED²* date from 1386 Chaucer and c1400 *Destr. Troy. (OED²*

Introduction

s.v. busy, *a.*, †3). Examples only from Pepys' Diary 1660-1663 would suffice.

(14) 1660 Pepys, D10, I 64, To my father's to dinner, where nothing but a small dish of powdered beef and a dish of carrots, they <u>being</u> all <u>busy</u> <u>to</u> <u>get</u> things ready for my Brother John to go tomorrow. | 1660, I 101, 1660, I 112, 1661, II 179, 1663, IV 348, etc.

(Nakamura 1986: 168-169)

The history of *do*-less interrogative sentences is explored in Nakamura (2001, 2007c, d), which conclude that *How do you?*, *What say you (to ~)?* and *What think you (of ~)?* continued to be used moderately until the middle of the 19th century.

1.2.3. Quotations Filling in the Chronologically Awkward Gap

The third category (2iii) "quotations filling in the chronologically awkward gap" includes, for example, quotations with *be busy (in)* + verb-*ing*, *look/smell* + *-ly* adverb and the progressive with transitive *have*. The diaries and correspondence examined in this monograph are materials suitable for compiling instances filling in the chronologically awkward gap.

1.2.3.1. *Be busy* Verb-*ing*

The *OED²*'s earliest citations for the idiomatic *be busy in* + Verb-*ing* date from *c*1680 Beveridge and 1713 Addison and, for the construction of *be busy* + Verb-*ing*, it cites only a modern example (*OED²* s.v. busy, *a.*, 1c). Grammarians think of the latter construction as first used around the mid-19th century. Thus, for example, Jespersen (1931: 171) quotes the earliest instance from 1849-1850 Dickens. To the best of the present author's knowledge, it is only Mossé who shows much earlier instances, as in (15).

(15) a. *be Busy in* + Verb-*ing*
   1529? Latimer, ? *Leicester Correspondence*, 1621 Burton, 1625 Jonson, 1742 Fielding

   b. *be busy* + Verb-*ing*

16

Chapter I

1447 Shillingford, 1597 Deloney, 1660 Pepys, 1798-1805 W. Wordsworth

(Mossé 1938: 117)

This is the reason why the quotations in (16) and (17) result in mere evidence demonstrating the continued use of both constructions. It is worth-
while noticing that the use of the construction without the preposition *in*
exceeds that, with occurrences as early as in Margaret Hoby's and Samuel
Pepys's English.

(16) Examples taken from Pepys's diary (D10)

    a. *be busy in* + Verb-*ing*

    1662 Pepys, D10, III 41, And then to the office again in the afternoon
    to put things in order there, my mind being very busy in settling the
    office to ourselfs, I having now got distinct offices for the other two. |
    1668 Pepys, D10, IX 367, etc.

(Nakamura 1986: 163-164)

    b. *be busy* + Verb-*ing*

    1660 Pepys, D10, I 256, The Comissioners are very busy disbanding
    of the army, which they say doth cause great robbing. | 1660 D10, I
    258, 1661 D10, II 170, 1663 D10, IV 44, 1668 D10, IX 144, etc.

(Nakamura 1986: 164)

(17) Examples of *be busy* + Verb-*ing* taken from Hoby's diary (D2)

    1599 M. Hoby, D2, 65, after dinner, I was buisie dispacting one a
    way to Linton tell:3: a Clock: | 1599 M. Hoby, D2, 90 | 1600 Hoby,
    D2, 95, 99, 106, 107, 111, 118, 132, 133, 141, 141, 145, 148, 148,
    154 | 1601 Hoby, 166, 178, 181, 182, 188

(Nakamura 2003b: 71)

1.2.3.2. Progressive of *Have* Meaning 'drink, eat, etc.' + Obj, Progressive
of *Have* + Action Noun, and Progressive of *Have* + O + Adjectival/Ad-
verbial/V-*ing*

According to Visser (1973: 1966), the progressive of transitive *have*
was "frequently used in Old and Modern English, and . . . very sparingly in
the Middle English period." He cites seven examples from OE and five

Introduction

from the 14th-century English. For Modern English his examples date from c1500, 1837, 1837-39, 1847, 1849-1850, etc. Apart from the discussion about the use in Old English, where there is said to have been little difference in function between the progressive and non-progressive, it is apparent that an awkward chronological gap can be detected in his evidence for Modern English, viz. between c1500 and 1837.

Tabulation of the data for the occurrences of the progressive with transitive *have* in the texts examined appears in Table 4 (p. 18). Just as Warner (1995: 546) has endeavoured to fill in the gap by providing two instances collected from the *OED*—1787 Blake and 1808 Southey—so we can do that as in (18) and Table 4. Since there is still a chronological gap, however, further research remains to be conducted.[3]

(18) a. *have* ('cause a particular effect on / drink / earn / eat / enjoy / experience / hold / keep or put sth in a particular position / keep or feel sth in mind / play / receive / spend / etc.') + O / *have* + action noun

1796 A. Hughes, D20, 91, Day after to-morrow we be having a little partie, . . . | 1797 A. Hughes, D20, 128, John have been abed this three days, having a verrie bad chille, and a fine job we be having to keep him in it. | 1813 J. Austen, L64, 326, We are now all four of us young Ladies sitting round the Circular Table in the inner table writing our Letters, while the two Brothers are having a comfortable coze in the room adjoining. [*coze* "a cosy, friendly talk" (*OED²* on CD-ROM)] | 1821 H. Arbuthnot, D27, 91, I wᵈ not trust Mr. Canning in so responsible a situation; he who, in this country at least, is always intriguing & having some dirty underplot. <coordinated use> | 1829 R. Peel, L45, 115, I have been all morning occupied about your cloak. I mean to give you one of my own choosing, and made to please my fancy. . . . I have ordered Davis to make one, and have been having a long consultation with him about it. | 1830 Marquess of Hertford, L44, 41, The Normanbys were having theatricals and constant hospitality in a most beautiful palace.

---

[3] 1698 J. Lowther, L12, 480 runs as follows: "I am having a plan of the copperas work copied for you." This seems, however, to be part of the editor's précis.

18

Chapter I

b. *have* + O + Adjectival / Adverbial / Verb-*ing*

1795 J. Woodforde, D21, IV, 201, Tho' he has been so ill & so long, yet <u>is</u> continually <u>having</u> Workmen about him & spends great Sums that way, . . . | 1796 A. Hughes, D20, 49, In a day or two we <u>shall</u> <u>be</u> <u>having</u> our harvest home, so we shalle be bussie once more with cooken for a goodlie companie.

Table 4   Occurrences of the Progressive with Transitive *Have*—
Nakamura (2003b: 71)

	have 'drink, eat, etc.' + Obj, *have* + action noun	*have* + Obj + Adjectival / Adverbial / Verb-*ing*
1776-1800	2	2
1801-1825	3	
1826-1850	5	
1851-1875	30	1
1875-1900	27	1
1901-	27	

1.2.4. Quotations Unveilling Rare or Unknown Usages

In the fourth category (2iv) above, quasi-auxiliary *be coming to* + infinitive, the usage of *he don't know*, the construction of the passival progressive preceded by an animate or human subject such as *a drunken boy was carrying by our constable*, the usage of the participial progressive such as *being going*, the usage of *seem* meaning 'to pretend', and the construction of present participles or gerunds followed by *not*, among other examples, are included. As a significant number of examples with the last five have been encountered, they are isolated as the topics of Chapters II, III, IV, V and VI of this monograph respectively. Here in this section only quasi-auxiliary *be coming to* + infinitive is referred to.

To the best of the present author's knowledge, it is only Poutsma (1926: 245) that refers to the quasi-auxiliary *be coming to*-infinitive construction: "*To be coming* appears to be occasionally used in the same function as *to be going*." His evidence consists of only one instance discovered

Introduction

in 1775 Sheridan, *The Rivals*, I.i.213: "Ay, master thought another fit of the gout *was coming to make* him a visit;-so he'd a mind to gi't the slip, and whip! We were all off at an hour's warning." It is clear from (19), however, that this construction was being used at some stages of the history of English. In (19e) in particular, it is worthy of note that the subject is *trial*, [-animate] noun. In all of the examples, *coming* seems to have lost the original meaning of movement and *to* plus infinitive has not a sense of purpose. In respect of the reason why *be coming to*-infinitive did not grammaticalise itself as *be going to*-infinitive did, further research remains to be conducted.

(19) a. 1661 Pepys, D10, II 213, it raining very hard, I went home by Coach, with my mind very heavy for this my expenseful life; which will undo me I fear, after all my hopes, If I do not take up - for now I <u>am coming to lay out</u> a great deal of money in clothes upon my wife, I must forbear other expenses.

b. 1665 Pepys, D10, VI 211, it is said that . . . our Lord Treasurer cannot tell what the profits of Chimny money is; what it comes to per annum - nor looks whether that or any other part of the Revenue be duly gathered as it ought - the very money that should pay the City the 200000*l* they lent the King being all gathered and in the hands of the Receiver, and hath been long, and yet not brought up to pay the City, whereas we <u>are coming to borrow</u> 4 or 500000*l* more of the City - which will never be lent as is to be feared.

c. 1770 T. Gray, L26, III 1121, I <u>am coming to see</u> you, my good Friend, that is, on Monday se'nnight I mean to call on Palgrave for a few days in my way to Blundeston.

d. 1829 J. Ruskin, L51, I 211, If I am now to resign this Labour . . . I <u>am coming to resume</u> a closer a sweeter Intercourse with my Love

e. 1832 S. Palmer, L48, I 59, In the fiery trial which <u>is coming to prove and purify</u> the Church, may he be never daunted or dismayed,

f. 1863 S. Palmer, L48, II 678, I <u>was coming to see</u> your distant Rome this morn[g] . . . you kindly promised to show me but was prevented by the 'Salmon engagement' into which I was unwilling to intrude.

20

Chapter I

If possible, I must try to see your picture but I can seldom get over.

(Nakamura 2003b: 73)

1.2.5. Quotations Reflecting a Writer's Own View of the English Language during his or her Lifetime

The fifth category—in which a writer's feelings about the language of his or her time are disclosed—has personally provided the present author with considerable pleasure. Only a few topics are dealt for this category below.

Comments on usage are to be found in diaries and letters as well as in 17th-18th century grammar-books and in writers with an interest in usage such as J. Dryden, R. Steele and J. Swift. While reading Kubota (1970), an article on Dryden's use of the auxiliary *do*, the present author noticed that diaries and letters could be an important source-book in collecting live information on the usage of the time concerned. As shown in (20), Dryden professes himself to dislike such negative contractions.

(20) Be pleasd therefore, to avoid the words, don't, can't, shan't, and the like abbreviations of syllables, which seem to me to savour of a little rusticity (1691? Dryden, in *The Letters of John Dryden*, ed. Charles E. Ward (New York, 1965), Letter 17)

(Kubota 1970: 21)

The answer to the question why Dryden, the most prominent figure in the literary world of the second half of the 17th century, had to write like that is clear when the drastic increase indicated in Tables 7, 8 and 10 (pp. 29, 30 and 33) is considered. As shown in Table 6 (p. 28), the contracted forms of *don't/won't/can't* originated years before or after 1600 and, as indicated in Tables 7, 8 and 10, it was in the course of the second half of the 17th century that they became well established. (Much earlier examples occur in the *OED²*, but they seem to be based upon modernized texts.) Dryden showed aversion to the sudden increase of these blunt ways of spelling contracted forms, henceforth few examples can be found throughout Dryden's writings.

Introduction

21

As hinted by all of these, descriptions of or feelings on the English language of a person's time in the history of English prove to be important, though not direct, evidence for us.

A few instances in the texts examined appear in (21). In earlier English there were two kinds of plural form available for the noun *cow*: *kine* and *cows*. The *OED²* provides the information that *kine*, originated in Middle English, was the traditional plural form, while *cows* initiated in the 17th century. F. Kilvert's diary as quoted in (21a) indicates that, at least in the west of England and North Wales in the second half of the 19th century, the use of *kine* could be an interesting litmus test distinguishing older generations from younger generations. Next, the description in (21b) indicates that the use of *drave* was old and no longer useful around 1800 among educated people. Furthermore, in (21c), William B. Stevens wonders why *will + not* is not contracted into *win't* as *can + not* and *shall + not* is amalgamated into *can't* and *shan't*. Stevens' linguistic self-introspection indicates that even the educated person, who obtained Doctor of Divinity at Magdalen College, Oxford (*ODNB*), did not have a strong knowledge of the history of his mother tongue. Finally, (21d) reveals that even Oscar Wilde, a distinguished Irish man of letters, who graduated from Trinity College, Dublin and Magdalen College, Oxford (*ODNB*), felt apprehensive of his use of the auxiliary *will* and *shall*.

(21) a. 1872 Kilvert, D36, II 298, Dame Matthews used to live at the Home Farm at Langley Burrell. She was a member of the family, but she must have lived a long time ago, as Mrs. Banks remarked, because she called cows 'kine'

   b. 1800 E. Darwin, in a letter to G. Wakefield, classical scholar and unitarian, L33, 324, I . . . think the word "spoke" more in use amongst polite people, than "spake". I esteem it to be an abbreviation of the word spoken. So broke for broken, etc. In your valuable satire you have written drave for drive; which, if it ever was in use, is long since superannuated.

   c. 1793 W. B. Stevens, D22, 66, We vulgarly say 'It 'aint so' and 'I wont', but the proper contraction from 'It is not' should be 'It isn't'.

22

Chapter I

Perhaps it arose from a barbarous confusion of numbers and 'You are not well' I fear may easily yield 'You arn't', 'You a'nt', 'I cannot', 'I can't', 'I may not', 'I maynt', 'I shall not', 'I shan't'. All this is regular then why should 'I will not' make 'I won't', instead of 'I win't'? The Clowns in this country say--'I canna', 'I shanna' and 'I wonna do 't' for 'I cannot', 'I shall not' and 'I will not do it'.

d. 1894 O. Wilde, L58, 124, I return corrected proofs. The title-page, dedication, play-bill etc. have not yet come . . . I wish the reader would go through the play once and correct any slips in the use of "will" and "shall"—my use of the words is Celtic not Saxon

Descriptions of this nature can be enumerated with relative ease, as shown in (22). Diaries and letters can actually be a source-book for collecting writers' feelings about the language of their time and miscellaneous information, including the reason why Dickens made considerable use of the present tense of the verb in his novels, the origin of 'Lewis Carroll', the nom de plume of Charles L. Dodgson and the process of how he entitled his book as "Alice's Adventures in Wonderland".

(22) a. 1689 J. Evelyn, in a letter to S. Pepys, L7, 207-210: On the corruptions of the English language and proposals

b. 1751 P. D. Stanhope, in a letter to his son, L21, 245: On the use of relative pronouns

c. 1758 T. Gray, L26, II 597: On the use of relative pronouns

d. 1762 T. Fitzmaurice, in a letter to A. Smith, L30, 83, Pray have you seen Dr Louths English Grammar which is just come out? It is talk'd of much. Some of the *ingenious men* with whom this University overflows, are picking faults and finding Errors in it at present. Pray what do you think of it?

e. 1872 Kilvert, D36, II 292-293, The tempest raged with such fury during the evening service that the sermon could scarcely be heard for the uproar and they thought the windows must be blown in. Miss Ellen Fry frightened out of her propriety and Lindley Murray exclaimed aloud ungrammatically but emphatically and with unmistakable meaning, 'I wish I hadn't came'.

Introduction

1.3. Summary of Chapter I

The emphasis has been laid on the necessity of the analyses of non-literary texts, especially documents not intended for public eyes or official use such as private diaries and personal letters, because they are valuable data for the historical study of English in order to fill a gap of our knowledge of the history of English mainly based on literary texts. Yet research into an enormous amount of text remains to be conducted. Uncovering more hidden historical facts for the explanation of linguistic change based on thorough analyses of synchronic data is required for the development of historical English linguistics.

Out of the five categories in (2), Categories (i) and (iv) seem to be currently significant in the history of English research and, accordingly, the present monograph deals with Category (iv). Category (i) will be isolated in another monograph in the not so distant future.

In the main body of this monograph, five varieties of usage that have been believed 'rare' or 'unknown' in the historical study of the English language are selected and unveiled. They are the usage of *he don't know* (Chapter II), the construction of the passival progressive preceded by an animate or human subject such as *a drunken boy was carrying (by our constable)* (Chapter III), the usage of the participial progressive such as *being going* (Chapter IV), the usage of *seem* meaning 'to pretend' (Chapter V), and the construction of present participles or gerunds followed by *not* (Chapter VI), among other examples. These seem to have escaped grammarians' notice in the history of English linguistic research.

Chapter II

Diachrony of the Third Person Singular Present *Don't*:

Transition from *He Don't Know* to *He Doesn't Know*[4]

Chapter II explores the diachrony of the usage of *he don't know*. This usage was used even in non-vulgar English until it was replaced by *doesn't* in the course of the second half of the 19th century. Relative to the rise of *doesn't* around the mid-19th century, the usage of *he don't know* came to be stigmatised as a vulgar and informal usage, developing in that direction up to the early 20th century, when it was ultimately established at the vulgar or non-standard speech level, or current conversational grammar. This chapter also attempts to unravel the mystery of why the employment of *doesn't* was slow in acceptance in American English.

---

[4] Chapter II is a combined and updated version of Nakamura (2012d, 2013, 2015b). I would like to acknowledge my appreciation for the useful comments and questions which I received from Professor Marina Dossena, University of Bergamo, and Professor Gabriella Mazzon, University of Innsbruck. Thanks are also due to Professor Alzo David-West of Aichi Prefectural University, who provided me with useful information on recent American English. Abbreviations used in the Tables are as follows:

D	Declarative
Imp	Imperative
O	Ordinary use with a main verb as in "I remember <u>he doesn't propose</u> going 'till Thursday next" (1749 W. Shenstone, L27, 162)
Q	Interrogative
T	Use in the tag as in "'have you seen Lord Buckingam?' . . . 'Well, he stutters as much as ever, <u>doesn't he</u>?'" (1786 B. Sheridan, D23, 91)
V	Vicarious use as in "if you see Forster pray tell him; I have been expecting him every Saturday since I left town: <u>he promised</u> to come and <u>doesn't</u>." (1855 A. Tennyson, L50, II 135)

Chapter II

2.1. Period and Chronological Order in which Negative Contractions Became Established and Diffused, and Purpose of the Present Chapter

Before the end of the 1980s, there were few full-scale studies with special reference to negative contractions. Only passing comments were available. The accepted view of the first written occurrences of negative contractions was that they originated around the mid-17th century (Jespersen 1940: 429-30; Partridge 1948 [1953a]: 9, 13; Partridge 1964: 176; Barber 1976: 254). They were, however, antedated by Brainerd (1989 [1993]) in a remarkable achievement containing many insightful suggestions. Even though he calls his article "a historical note", it is more than that. Table 5 is tabulated from his descriptions into a statistical table.

Some of the more significant points of Brainerd's study are that, first, concentrating on dramas, he uncovered ample pre-Restoration examples to overturn the view accepted until then, although the earliest examples of *can't* and *won't* discovered by Brainerd can be further antedated by the OED^2 on CD-ROM since we can avail ourselves of the advantage of its CD-ROM's word search function (Nakamura 2012a: 1; see Table 6 on p. 28). Second, Brainerd argued that the contracted forms were not respectable at first, on the grounds that they were deliberately used in comical scenes by 17th-century playwrights. He outlined the progress of contracted *n't* from its first explicit appearance in forms such as *don't, can't, won't* and *shan't* in the early 17th century, through its phase of consolidation in the 18th, to its wide acceptance in the 19th.

Brainerd's uncovering of sufficient pre-Restoration examples has to be highly appreciated. However, there are a few shortcomings in his study. First, Brainerd did not undertake to describe and explain both the stability and change of the negative contractions in post-1680 English on a large scale, perhaps because for him post-1680 was no longer a central period. Second, while *don't, can't, won't* and *shan't* accounted for 156, 118, 104 and 33 examples respectively, his statistics for the other contractions were based on a much more limited number of examples. Thirdly, the development of negative contractions based upon their functions such as the

27

Diachrony of the Third Person Singular Present *Don't*

Table 5   Early Occurrences of Negative Contractions: Tabulation from the Descriptions in Brainerd (1989 [1993]: 181-190)—Nakamura (2012a: 2)

	1620s	1630s	1641	1670s	1680s	1690s	1701-1725	1726-1750	1751-1800	1801-
Don't										
don't	5	"more than" 27	6	45			54			
don't [= does not]				1	1	4		1	1	2
dan't						4				
dorn't										4
dorn't [= does not]										1
dostn't								1		
dustunt [= dost not]								1		
Doesn't										
doesn't								1	1	
dozn't				1						
Didn't										
didn't				3			1	1	1	
den't										5
Can't										
can't	1	22	9	45			39			
caunt						1				
caint										1
cassent [= canst not]								1		
Couldn't										
couldn't								1	1	
cou'd'n't							1			
cudn't										2
coodn't										1
coon't										1
Won't										
won't	1	19	4	49			25			
wo'nt		2								
oon't										1
oan't										1
chawnt [= 'I will not']								1		
chont [= 'I will not']								1		
wuttent [= wilt not]								1		
Wouldn't										
wouldn't				1				1	1	
'oodn't										3
wudsent [= wouldst not]								1		
Shan't										
shan't		6		13			4			
sh'ant		1								
sha'n't		3								
shall n't							1			
shalln't							1			
shon't								1		
shain't										2
chant [= 'I shall not']								1		
shatunt [= shalt not]								1		
Shouldn't										
shopuldn't								1		
shou'dn't				2						
shudn't										1
shoon't										1
chudent [= 'I should not']								1		
Mustn't										
mustn't							1		1	
mussent								1		
Mayn't				1			2			
Mightn't									1	
Daren't										
daren't							2			
dar'n't									1	

Chapter II

declarative, the interrogative and the imperative, was not taken into account at all.

Currently, among the earliest occurrences of principal negative contractions in written documents, the majority of contractions appear for the first time during the 17th century, as Table 6 indicates.

Table 6   The Earliest Occurrences of Negative Contractions—Nakamura (2012b: 1)

	Brainerd (1989[1993])	*OED* [2] (2002)	Nakamura (2011)
don't	?c1625/?c1615	a1643 (Q)	1654 (D, Imp)
doesn't	1674	1774 (D)	1730 (Q)
didn't	1674	1705 (D)	1736 (D)
can't	c1625	**1597 (D)**	1664 (D)
couldn't	1702	**1694 (D)**	1752? (Q)
won't	1621	**1579 (D)**	1662 (D)
wouldn't	1674	1704 (D)	1699 (D)
shan't	1631-32	1664 (D)	1692 (D)
shouldn't	1674	**1628 (Q)**	1833 (D)
mustn't	1702	1741 (D)	1822 (D)
mayn't	1674	**c1631 (D)**	1711 (D)
mightn't	1775	1865 (D)	1883 (D)
daren't	1701	1840 (D)	1859 (D)
needn't	1775	**1748 (D)**	1821 (D)
oughtn't	1836	1884 (Q)	1856 (Q)

Unexpectedly, however, the period of their establishment is varied, as indicated in Table 7. The table indicates that the present-tense group except for *doesn't* was frequently used, being established in the course of the second half of the 17th century, whereas *doesn't* and the preterite-tense group such as *couldn't*, *wouldn't* and *shouldn't* were regulated more than one and a half centuries later, a little before the mid-19th century. The statistics are based on the analyses of 5,774 examples collected from 130 volumes of diaries and correspondence primarily written during from 1600 to 1900.

Whether this is a mere textual coincidence or not, this result was so hard for the present author to believe immediately that the *OED* [2]'s citations were checked next. Based upon the analysis of 13,190 examples, Table 8 (p. 30) shows almost the same distribution as Table 7.

29

Diachrony of the Third Person Singular Present *Don't*

Table 7 Overall Development of Negative Contractions in the Texts Examined—Nakamura (2012a: 5; 2012b: 2)

			1601-1625	1626-1650	1651-1675	1676-1700	1701-1725	1726-1750	1751-1775	1776-1800	1801-1825	1826-1850	1851-1875	1876-1900	1901-1925	1926-1950	1951-	Total
don(')t	D	O			11	50	265	394	213	145	133	323	668	302	47	48	69	2,696
	D	V			1	1			3	1	2	7	7	1	5			
do n't	Q	O				1	30	11	19	14	7	30	40	17	3	2	3	185
do'nt	Q	T					2				1		2	1				
dostn't	Q	V										1						
	Imp	O			3	5	62	78	61	24	37	53	139	54	17	4	5	547
	Imp	V										1	2	2				
can(')t	D	O			4	88	149	259	58	24	24	52	233	154	18			1,087
	D	V				2		3	1			1	11	4	2			
cann't	Q	O					1	1	1	2	2	7	6	5	1	*The results here have not been tabulated.*		26
	Q	T																
	Q	V																
won(')t	D	O			9	25	107	69	37	15	8	35	99	92	14	*For the time being, please substitute*		524
	D	V						4	2			3	4		1			
won't	Q	O					1	4			1	3	4	2		*Table 8, the analysis of*		23
wunt	Q	T					1				1	3	1		1	*the quotations in the OED².*		
	Q	V									1							
shan(')t	D	O				5	12	20	2	4	6	13	21	10	5			102
sha'nt	D	V												4				
sha'nt	Q	O							1				1					2
sh'ant	Q	T																
	Q	V																
doesn't	D	O						2	4		1	5	34	30	10	4	17	111
	D	V											2	1		1		
dosnt	Q	O																11
	Q	T						2				1	3	2				
	Q	V								1			2					
didn(')t	D	O						2	1		2	13	82	41	4	10	39	194
didna	D	V																
dinna	Q	O									1	2	4	6			2	15
couldn(')t	D	O										4	42	30	3			83
	D	V											4					
could'nt	Q	O																9
cou'dnt	Q	T							1			1	4	3				
	Q	V																
wouldn't	D	O						1				5	27	20	4			63
	D	V				1		1					1	2				
would'nt	Q	O											3	1				7
would n't	Q	T											2	1				
	Q	V																
shouldn(')t	D	O										4	12	9				26
should'nt	D	V											1					
	Q	O										2	2	2	*The results here have not been tabulated.*			8
	Q	T													*For the time being, please substitute*			
	Q	V											2		*Table 8, the analysis of*			
mustn't	D	O									1		10	10	*the quotations in the OED².*			22
	D	V											1					
	Q	O																
	Q	T																
	Q	V																
mayn(')t	D	O					1	2				2	2					7
may'nt	Q	O											1					1
mightn't	D	O												1				1
	Q	O																
daren't	D	O										2	2					4
	Q	O																
daredn't	D	O																
	Q	O																
needn't	D	O						1			1		6	7				15
	D	V												2				2
	Q	O																
oughtn't	D	O											1					2
	D	V												1				
	Q	O											1					1

Note for the shaded right‑hand cells: The results here have not been tabulated. For the time being, please substitute Table 8, the analysis of the quotations in the OED².

30

Chapter II

Table 8 Overall Development of Negative Contractions in the *OED²*'s Citations—Nakamura (2012b: 5)

			1576-1600	1601-1625	1626-1650	1651-1675	1676-1700	1701-1725	1726-1750	1751-1775	1776-1800	1801-1825	1826-1850	1851-1875	1876-1900	1901-1925	1926-1950	1951-1975	1976-	Total
don('t / doon't / dunt	D	O				5	36	67	60	70	35	64	219	328	422	374	498	902	311	3,446
		V					1	2	1				3	6	8	9	8	12	4	
	Q	O			1	1	5	10	12	6	10	8	31	49	46	35	69	79	31	468
		T											3	7	9	4	13	29	5	
		V														2	1	2		
	Imp	O				4	12	23	36	25	17	27	140	146	197	178	257	351	95	1,523
		V							2				1		4	4	3	1		
can('t / canna	D	O	2		2	15	21	67	50	30	36	69	100	185	208	193	244	427	148	1,832
		V									1	3	2	7	3	5	11	1		
	Q	O				1	1	2	2	2	2	3	3	5	10	15	22	18	29	140
		T							2				1	1	2	4	3	4	3	
		V													1			1		
won('t / we'n't / willn't / winna / wunna	D	O	12		1	7	22	28	27	29	39	39	76	128	114	110	130	231	83	1,115
		V					2		2	1	1	1	1	2	7	3	5	5	4	
	Q	O						2	3	1		1	2	6	7	6	6	3	12	81
		T											2	4	3	2	5	8		
		V									1			1						
shan't / shanna / shann't / she'na / sha'n't / shinna / sha'nt	D	O				4	8	6	7	8	12	5	12	15	19	6	10	11	3	132
		V					1					1	1	1	1			1		
	Q	O								1								1		2
		T																		
		V																		
doesn('t / dosn't	D	O						1			1	6	21	49	58	140	274	100		669
		V													1	3	4	2		
	Q	O											1	1	2	7	13	12	6	63
		T													2	4	5	7	2	
		V													1					
didn('t / dident / dedent	D	O						1	1	4	3	11	55	88	145	150	251	530	193	1,471
		V										2	1	3	5	5	7	14	2	
	Q	O							1	1	1		17	11	20	22	22	40	7	177
		T											1	2	5	13	10	1		
		V												1	1	1				
couldn('t / couldent / cou'dn't / coudn't	D	O					2				1	5	37	50	81	80	142	263	88	765
		V											1		3	1	6	5		
	Q	O											3	2	1	6	7	19	2	41
		T															1			
		V																		
wouldn('t / wou'dn't / wodn't	D	O						1	2		2	7	46	70	95	104	161	273	77	850
		V										2			1	3	3	3	3	
	Q	O												2	4	8	18	16	4	74
		T											1	2	2	4	6	2		
		V														2	3			
shouldn('t / shou'dnt	D	O							1		1	2	7	17	17	12	18	38	19	138
		V												1	1		2	2		
	Q	O			1		1			1		1	1			1	2	5	3	28
		T														1	1			
		V														1				
mustn('t	D	O						1				2	6	7	12	16	9	7		61
		V														1				
	Q	O											1							3
		T													1					
		V													1					
mayn't	D	O			1		1	1	2			1					1	2		9
	Q	O				1		2			1		1		1					6
mightn't	D	O												1	1		1	6	1	10
	Q	O																		
daren't / dorn't / darn't	D	O											3	1	2	1	1	1	1	10
	Q	O																		
daredn't	D	O												1		1				2
	Q	O																		
needn't	D	O							1		1	2	3	7	14	11	10	7	5	61
	Q	O																		
oughtn't	D	O														2	7	3		12
	Q	O													2					2

Diachrony of the Third Person Singular Present *Don't*

The examples in Table 8 include those written by Americans and other native English speakers and in non-standard English, and text types vary. Thus, classification was next to impossible. Quite a few examples have been excluded from the statistics including (a) uses in quotations in grammar books, (b) uses in titles of writings, (c) uses in titles of songs, (d) uses in proverbs or maxims, (e) nominal or adjectival uses of negative contractions such as "1902 *Monthly Rev.* Aug. 168, Already he was beginning to know the just value of a woman's *won't*, so he gave up the contest" (*OED²*, s.v. won't, a) and (f) uses in modernised editions of Middle English texts. The same citations were counted as one. The auxiliaries and their variants the present author searched in the *OED²*'s citations appear in Table 9 (p. 32).

In order to confirm the result that the preterite-tense group and *doesn't* were not at people's disposal until the mid-19th century, further computer-aided analyses were conducted. The corpora were a heterogeneous assortment of 260 different electronic British English documents, such as biographies, dramas, essays, journals, letters, novels, speeches, travelogues and treatises, randomly selected and downloaded in October 2005 from various university and organisation websites,[5] as well as LOB and FLOB. 19,149 examples gathered from these electronic texts appear in Table 10 (p. 33), where again almost the same distribution as in Tables 7 and 8 can be observed.

---

[5] These are McMaster University (http://socserv2.socsci.mcmaster.ca/), Project Gutenberg (http://www.gutenberg.org/), Rutgers University in Newark (http:// andromeda. rutgers.edu/), University of Michigan (http://www.hti.umich.edu/), University of Oregon (http://darkwing.uoregon.edu/), University of Pennsylvania (http://digital.library. upenn.edu/), University of Toronto (http://eir.library. utoronto.ca/), University of Virginia (http://etext. lib.virginia.edu/) and York University, Canada (http://psychclassics. yorku.ca/). Here I owe them a great debt of gratitude. Their on-line electronic texts were very useful, saving me considerable time in compiling examples before drawing up Table 10.

Chapter II

Table 9 Negative Contractions Searched for by the Author in the OED^2's Citations—Nakamura (2012b: 4)

do	{dee, do, doe, doo(e), du, do'st, doest, doost, dost, dust}+{n't / nt}
	{ don, doon, doun}+{(n)'t / (n)t}
does	{does, doeth, dois, doose, dos, dose, doth, dus}+{n't / nt}
did	{dede, did(d), dide, dode, dud(e), dyd(e), diddest, dides(t), didst, dudest, dydes(t)}+{n't / nt}
can	can(n), con(n), kan+{(n)'t / (n)t} canna
will	{el, ool, ull, vyll, wal, wel(e), welen, well(e). wil(e), will(e), willen, willyn, wol(l), wol(l)e, wol(l)en, woleth, wool(l), woul, wul(e), wull(e), wyl(e), wyll(e), wyl(l)en, wyn, wilt, willt, wilte, wlt, wolt, woot, w'oot, woo't, wot, wult, wut, wylt, wylte}+{n't / nt} we'n't, willn't, winna, won(')t, wunna
shall	{sal(l), sale, salle, sc(e)al, scall, scel(l), schal(l), schall(e), schawl(l), schel(e), schill, schol(l), schul(l), scyl, sell, shal(l), shall(e), shol(l), shul(l), sol, sul, xal(le), sald, salt, scald, scalt, scealt, schald, schalt, schelt, schild, shallt, shalt, shat, shelt, shult, xalt}+{n't / nt} sha'na, shanna, shan(n)'t, sha'n(')t, shinna
could	{cold(e), coold, coud(e), could(e), couth(e), cou'd, culd, koude, kowd}+{n't / nt} couldestn(')t, couldstn(')t
would	{owld, wald(e), weld, wild(e), willed, wo(')d, wold(e), woled, wolld(e), wolt, woo(')d, woold(e), woud(e), would(e), wou'd, wud(e), wuld(e), wu'd, wyld(e)}+{n't / nt}
should	{sald(e), schold(e), schud(e), schulde, sculd, shold(e), shooldc, shoo'd, shoud, should(e), shou'd, sho'd, shuld(e), shullde, shu'd, sold, soud, sould(e), sowld, suld(e), suuld}+{n't / nt}
must	{mast, moist, moost, most(e), must(e), mostest, mustest}+{n't / nt} {mosten, moston, mostyn, musten, mustyn}+{(n)'t / (n)t}
may	{mai(e), may(e), mei, mey, mou, mow(e), mowghe, mowne, mu, maht, maiest, maist(e), mait, mat(e), maucht, maxste, mayest, mayhte, may'st, mayst(e), mayt, mayth, meht, meiht, micht, miht, myht}+{n't / nt} {mawen, moun, mowen, mown}+{(n)'t / (n)t}
might	{macht, mahte, may't, meghte, meith, micht(e), might(e), miht(e), mith, mocht, moght(e), moht, moucht(e), mouct(h)e, mought(e), mouht, mout, mouth(e), mowcht, mowcte, mowt, mowth, mucht, mught, muhte, mycht, myght, myht(e), myt(e), myth(e), mightest, mightist, mihtes, myghttyst}+{n't / nt}
dare	{dar(e), darne, darr, daur, dear(r), der, dor, dore, dorre, dur, durne, durre, durrone, dar'st, darest, darist, darrst, darryst, darst(e), daryst, derst}+{n't / nt} {doren, dorren, duren, durn, durren, durron}+{(n)'t / (n)t}
dared	{dared, darste, daur'd, derste, dirst, dorst(e), draste, drust, durrste, durst(e) }+{n't / nt} {dorsten, dursten}+{(n)'t / (n)t}
need	{nede, neede, neid, neyd, neade, nead, nied, need}+{n't / nt} {neoden, neden, nedyn}+{(n)'t / (n)t}
ought	{acht(e), aght(e), ahhte, ahte, ahut, aucht, aucte, aught(e), auht(e), aute, awcht, awght, awt, eght, hahte, ight(e), iht, ocht, oft, oght(e), ohte, oucht, ought(e), ouhte, out(e), owght(e), owt(e)}+{n't / nt}

33

Diachrony of the Third Person Singular Present *Don't*

Table 10 Overall Development of Negative Contractions in the Electronic British English Texts, with D, Q and Imp Mixed—Nakamura (2012a: 12; 2012b: 6)

Period / Corpus size	1500-1550 1.20MB	1551-1600 1.95MB	1601-1650 1.42MB	1651-1700 12.7MB	1701-1750 12.8MB	1751-1800 13.4MB	1801-1850 27.0MB	1851-1900 18.6MB	1901-1950 8.02MB	LOB 6.67MB	FLOB 7.06MB	
do not	0	46	68	1,082	776	1,080	2,152	1,300	439	279	206	
don't	0	0	1	62	487	674	2,117	3,538	1,738	496	598	
can( )not	0	193	210	1,353	1,284	1,600	2,420	1,398	427	319	241	
can()t	0	0	1	34	245	178	420	923	525	146	228	
will not	1	2	8	17	13	7	11	6	3	104	112	
won()t	0	0	0	1	0	1	2	5	8	108	97	
shall not	2	27	28	228	202	184	438	229	39	26	13	
shan't	0	0	0	0	24	21	41	90	45	5	3	
does not	0	3	2	206	292	543	762	485	299	260	235	
doesn't	0	0	0	0	0	0	28	229	226	107	132	1838→
doth not	0	27	32	56	77	42	13	0	0	0	0	
dothn()t	0	0	0	0	0	0	0	0	0	0	0	
did not	0	21	22	909	1,377	1,154	2,480	2,424	1,226	337	289	
didn't	0	0	0	0	0	2	366	713	399	285	445	1782, 1814, 1816, 1821-22, 1838→
could( )not	0	80	34	1,090	1,528	1,294	2,950	1,833	734	221	151	
couldn't	0	0	0	0	0	0	273	359	215	122	198	1838→
would not	0	53	39	806	1,000	925	1,514	1,388	328	166	117	
wouldn't	0	0	0	0	0	0	320	407	208	107	128	1814, 1838→
should not	0	29	27	251	297	354	595	545	82	87	68	
shouldn't	0	0	0	0	0	0	79	258	111	25	29	1838→
must not	0	11	12	133	121	145	419	229	81	40	18	
mustn't	0	0	0	0	0	0	39	57	42	18	6	1838→
may not	0	47	26	161	204	235	348	180	48	47	81	
mayn't	0	0	0	0	4	1	8	26	10	0	0	→
might not	0	9	2	108	220	111	280	172	42	25	25	
mightn't	0	0	0	0	0	0	10	20	6	3	0	1838→
dare not	0	4	7	83	34	37	98	22	10	4	3	
daren't	0	0	0	0	0	0	3	4	12	0	0	
dared not	0	0	0	1	7	5	105	38	21	4	2	
daredn't	0	0	0	0	0	0	0	1	0	0	0	
need not	0	3	7	85	114	111	256	165	44	38	17	
needn't	0	0	0	0	0	0	70	70	49	9	6	1838→
ought not	0	11	11	63	63	73	92	146	33	8	2	
oughtn't	0	0	0	0	0	0	9	20	12	1	0	1838→

At this point it is confirmed that, as far as written documents are concerned, the discoveries in (23) are indisputable historical facts.

(23) a. The establishment and diffusion of negative contractions was not simultaneous, but varied and gradual according to auxiliaries and their functions, irrespective of their first occurrences. They became established and diffused in the order described in Table 11 (p. 34), where '17-2', for example, represents the second half of the 17th century. Their overall establishment was around 1850. As is well-known, it was in the 19th century that the interrogative permissive *can* as in *Can I go home now?* was regulated, though this process was initiated at a much earlier time. We see a similar linguistic evolution regarding negative contractions.

Chapter II

Table 11　Chronological Order in which Negative Contractions Became Established and Diffused, with Special Reference to the Number of Word-final Consecutive Consonants—Nakamura (2012 a: 5; 2012b: 3)

<table>
<tr><th colspan="3"></th><th><17-2></th><th><18-1></th><th><18-2></th><th><19-1></th><th><19-2></th></tr>
<tr><td rowspan="11">Number of consecutive consonants</td><td rowspan="5">two</td><td>/-nt/</td><td></td><td></td><td></td><td></td><td></td></tr>
<tr><td>don't</td><td>D</td><td>Q/Imp</td><td></td><td></td><td></td></tr>
<tr><td>can't</td><td>D</td><td></td><td></td><td>Q</td><td></td></tr>
<tr><td>won't</td><td>D</td><td></td><td></td><td>Q</td><td></td></tr>
<tr><td>shan't</td><td></td><td>D</td><td></td><td></td><td></td></tr>
<tr><td rowspan="6">three</td><td>/-znt/</td><td></td><td></td><td></td><td></td><td></td></tr>
<tr><td>doesn't</td><td></td><td></td><td></td><td></td><td>D/(Q)</td></tr>
<tr><td>/-dnt/</td><td></td><td></td><td></td><td></td><td></td></tr>
<tr><td>didn't</td><td></td><td></td><td></td><td>D</td><td>(Q)</td></tr>
<tr><td>couldn't</td><td></td><td></td><td></td><td></td><td>D/(Q)</td></tr>
<tr><td>wouldn't</td><td></td><td></td><td></td><td></td><td>D/(Q)</td></tr>
<tr><td></td><td></td><td>shouldn't</td><td></td><td></td><td></td><td></td><td>D/(Q)</td></tr>
<tr><td></td><td></td><td>needn't</td><td></td><td></td><td></td><td></td><td>D</td></tr>
<tr><td></td><td></td><td>/-snt/</td><td></td><td></td><td></td><td></td><td></td></tr>
<tr><td></td><td></td><td>mustn't</td><td></td><td></td><td></td><td></td><td>D</td></tr>
</table>

b. There seems to have been a certain principle in the chronological order of their diffusion: from declaratives to interrogatives (and imperatives in case of *don't*), from the present-tense group (except for *doesn't*) to the preterite-tense group and *doesn't*. The preterite-tense group with word-final treble-consonant clusters /-dnt, -znt, -snt/ (*didn't, couldn't, wouldn't, shouldn't, needn't, mustn't*) and *doesn't* were established more than one and a half centuries after the present-tense group simply with /-nt/ (*don't, can't, won't, shan't*). As evidenced in Nakamura (2012a: 7-9; 2012b: 4), all the writers who confidently included *don't, can't, won't* and *shan't* as part of their grammar hesitated over using *doesn't, didn't, couldn't, wouldn't* and *shouldn't*.

c. The reason why there was more than a century's time lag between the establishment of the present tense group and the preterite tense group and *doesn't* was attributable to phonological reasons: caco-phony, i.e. harsh sounds. The latter contractions had something in common: they had word-final treble consonant clusters /-dnt/ or /-znt/ or /-snt/. Yet no evidence has been found to prove that the contracted preterite-tense group and *doesn't* were stigmatised in 17th- to 18th-century prescriptive grammar books. Grammarians seem not to have referred to *doesn't, didn't, couldn't, wouldn't* and *shouldn't*. Perhaps they were silent because these negative contrac-tions were unnatural or unfamiliar at the time.

Tables 7, 8, 10 and 11 seem to provide hints with respect to the his-tory of constructions with negative contractions such as tag-questions, established a little before 1850 (see Nakamura 2012b), and the establish-ment of *can't help* V-*ing* and its syntactic variants (Nakamura 2012c). The history of the third person singular present *don't* ('3SG *don't*'), the present topic, is no exception.

Thus arises the need to demonstrate how 3SG *don't* was superseded by *doesn't* in Late Modern English and why the regulation of *doesn't* was late in American English. Few full-scale studies with special reference to 3SG *don't* have been undertaken to date; only passing comments are avail-able to the effect that the usage of *he don't know* was permissible, whereas present-day people would more typically say *he doesn't know*.

2.2. Diachrony of the Third Person Singular Present *Don't*

2.2.1. Seventeenth- to Twentieth-century Diaries and Correspondence

The history of 3SG *don't* which occurred in diaries and letters are focussed on first. Texts examined for the present topic are 130 volumes of private diaries and personal correspondence written mostly between 1600 and 1900. As it is hoped that they were written in informal and colloquial English, negative contractions are expected to occur in these diaries and letters just as frequently as in dramas.

36

Chapter II

2.2.1.1. General Chronological Trends: The Period of the Wane of the 'Normal' Use of the Third Person Singular Present *Don't* in the Texts Examined

Extracted from Table 7, Table 12 shows the occurrences of *don't* and *doesn't* in the texts examined. From over three thousand examples of *don't* in Table 12, 3SG *don't* accounts for 44 examples, as represented in Table 13.

Table 12 Occurrences of *Don't* and *Doesn't* in the Texts Examined, Extracted from Table 7—Nakamura (2013: 6)

			1601-1625	1626-1650	1651-1675	1676-1700	1701-1725	1726-1750	1751-1775	1776-1800	1801-1825	1826-1850	1851-1875	1876-1900	1901-1925	1926-1950	1951-	Total
don(')t	D	O			11	50	265	394	213	145	133	323	668	302	47	48	69	2,696
do n't		V			1	1			3	1	2	7	7	1	5			
do'nt	Q	O				1	30	11	19	14	7	30	40	17	3	2	3	185
dostn't		T					2				1		2	1				
		V										1	1					
	Imp	O			3	5	62	78	61	24	37	53	139	54	17	4	5	547
		V										1	2	2				
doesn't	D	O						2	4		1	5	34	30	10	4	17	111
dosnt		V											2	1		1		
	Q	O						2				1	3	2				11
		T								1			2					

Table 13 Variations between *Doesn't* and 3SG *Don't* in the Texts Examined—Nakamura (2013: 6)

			1651-1700	1701-1750	1751-1800	1801-1850	1851-1900	1901-	Total
don't (= doesn't)	D	O		5	9	4	6	7	
	D	V	1		1			1	44
dont (= doesn't)	D	O		1	5	4			
doesn't	D	O		2	4	5	64	31	
	D	V					3	1	
dosn't	D	O				1			122
doesn't	Q	O		2		1	5		
	Q	T			1		2		

Table 12 indicates that *don't*, which appeared in early 17th-century documents for the first time, was regulated as early as the second half of the 17th century. By contrast, *doesn't* was not popularly used until around 1850, even though the first written occurrence was in evidence in a drama written in 1674. It took *doesn't* a little less than two hundred years to become established. This historical fact makes it presumable that *don't* was standard until the regulation of *doesn't* around 1850, and it actually was: as indicated by the shading in Table 13, *don't* was used at first, and then *doesn't* began to be used. However, *don't* was more frequently used than *doesn't*, irrespective of the person and the number of a subject, to conjugate with the third person singular subject as if it were a modal auxiliary like *I can't, you can't* and *he/she/it can't*. It was in the course of the second half of the 19th century that *doesn't* took precedence over *don't*. The first half of the 19th century can be regarded as a period of transition from *he don't know* to *he doesn't know*. Considering the fact that *doesn't* needed a little less than two centuries to become accepted, it was natural that, until its wide acceptance in the mid-19th century, most people, even the educated, had recourse to the non-contracted form of *does not* or else to 3SG *don't*.

2.2.1.2. Examples of the Third Person Singular Present *Don't* in the Texts Examined

All of the examples of 3SG *don't* are quoted in (24), in which counterfactual subjunctive use of *don't* is excluded from the list, and where words with thick underlines represent formal or elevated phases of English and those with wavy lines vulgar or informal ones. For this distinction of word-levels, the present author depended on the *OED²* and present-day English dictionaries such as *OALD⁸* and *LDCE⁵*. Whether this distinction applies to earlier English can be guaranteed by no one. Nevertheless the author could not but resort to this procedure simply because dictionaries of usage with respect to earlier English have not been published. From the quotations in (24), it is evident that formal or elevated words could co-occur with 3SG *don't*.

(24) Quotations of 3SG *don't* tabulated into Table 13
    a. 1651-1700
        1672 C. Lyttelton, L3, I 89, Mʳ Wrenne being so ill he is not able, and some think scarce ever will; and, if he <u>don't</u>, I beleeve Savville will keepe it [= the place of secretary]
    b. 1701-1750
        1739 T. Gray, L26, I 115, we are not vastly curious about his Name, first because it <u>don't signify</u>, 2dly because we know it already: |

Chapter II

1742 T. Gray, ibid., 206, as to the Facts it don't signify two pence, who's in the right; the manner of fighting, & character of the Combatants is all: | 1745 J. Holles, Duke of Newcastle, L22, 163, our insipid political Situation, don't require your presence, till something more particular or material happens, than at present seems likely, for some time. | 1746 T. Gray, L26, I 258, Frattanto I send you a scene in a tragedy: if it don't make you cry, it will make you laugh; | 1747 L. Pitt, L24, 114, he [= Pitt's brother] . . . wishes that Mr Spence, and you, had not only talk^d of coming to See him: but had come this last Summer: for he dont love to expect so great a pleasure: and wait so long for it: as next Summer: | 1748 T. Gray, L26, I 299, The town is an owl, if it don't like Lady Mary, and I am surprised at it: we here are owls enough to think her eclogues [= *Six Town Eclogues*] very bad;

c. 1751-1800

1751 T. Gray, L26, I 342, If Dodsley don't do this immediately, he may as well let it alone. | 1756 T. Gray, L26, II 473, D^r L:, if he is not dead, will recover. mind, if he don't. | 1759 T. Gray, ibid., 619, whether he has or not, don't much signify: | 1760 T. Gray, L26, 680, I have seen a Discourse in Mss. about them . . . with specimens of their writings. this is in Latin, &, tho' it don't approach the other, there are fine scraps aming it. | 1768 T. Gray, L26, III 1009, It don't appear that he knew any thing of your book: | 1784 J. Woodforde, D21, II 122, If at the beginning of taking the Bark it should happen to purge, put ten Dropps of Laudanum into the Bark you take next, if that dont stop it put 10. drops more of Do. in the next Bark you take— | 1784 B. Sheridan, D23, 33, as my Father don't *like* speaking French I forced D. [= D'Ivernois] to speak English in which by the bye he is no way improved. | 1785 B. Sheridan, D23, 43, at these times he [= Betsy's father] dont like going out and I dont like leaving him so we have spent the day at home. | 1785 B. Sheridan, D23, 52, She thinks it necessary to be very wise with us, talks of books which probably she don't understand, and that in vulgar language. | 1786 B. Sheridan, D23, 82, I have promised to dance this Eevening as my Father says he don't understand my turning Old Woman; and our young Oxonian Mr Drake is to have the honor of my hand. | 1788 B. Sheridan, D23, 141, The same set will probably be here tonight and this is the life always when Mrs S— don't go out. | 1796 A. Hughes, D20, 83, At this Carters wiffe do say never her boy do so, but he sayeing if she dont believe, to go quiet to the out hous, and she will see her ladd. | 1796 A. Hughes, D20, 84, Then we to the kitchen where she do start to cry, sayeing she dont know why her ladd do such things and be so wicked, and she verrie troubled. | 1798 J. Woodforde, D21, V 123, Nancy dont like to go, as for my going it is quite out of the Question. . . . | 1800 J. Woodforde, D21, 242, Vegetation don't seem to be advancing as yet but very slowly, very much so indeed.

d. 1801-1850

1823 H. Arbuthnot, D27, 272, Ld Liverpool . . . has lost two or three holes in his stirrup leather this year; &, if he don't mind, he will lose the rest next year. | 1820 J. Clare, L46, 74, I had some time back an invitation to write for the 'Ladies Museum' & promisd the Editor I would but alterd my mind & gave it up as it dont suit my taste to please boarding school Misses & such like paper Vanities | 1821 J. Clare, L46, 88, never mind Lord R.s pencilings in the 'Peasant Boy' what he dont like he must lump as the dog did his dumpling | 1821 J. Clare, L46, 104, Bowles will whine him [= Mr Gilchrist] out at last if he dont mind | 1822 J. Clare, L46, 135, if opportunity dont come too late I will make use of it | 1829 J. Clare, L46, 224, the measure in which he has translated some passages of Dante is very curious but it don't strike me as one well suited for the Epic. | 1836 J. Ruskin, L51, I 348, when you are sitting in the evening solitary and silent, dumpy and melancholy; then imagine to yourself the delights of our drawing room; imagine mamma and Mary, and imagine me, Me, in my corner; if that don't bring you home, if you don't bite at that bait, why, I don't know what will, | 1850 'Shiel', D32, I 375, Ashley amused us by saying he had asked Shiel what he thought would be the effect of all this Popish affair, to which Shiel replied: 'It don't much matter what I think, . . .'

e. 1851-1900

1859 S. Palmer, L48, I 565, His buttered muffins won't sit on his stomach his corns keep on shooting like Enfield rifles—and withal he is miserable and don't know what's the matter with him | 1863 G.

Meredith, L54, I 103, I have taken some trouble with her and really shall begin to think her character weak in this respect, if she <u>don't</u> hand in what I think due, speedily. | 1863 G. Meredith, L54, 112, All this means . . . that I am going to make the spring, and if the ring <u>don't</u> swing I may cling like anything, and just be caught up to a six weeks' Heaven among you, and nothing short of it under your wing. | 1870 'Old James Godsell', D36, I 148, Old James Godsell . . . said 'if the rain <u>don't</u> come soon we shall have no hay nor yet straw'. | 1872 'the old soldier', D36, II 118, I said I thought the tree had better lie where it falls. 'Ah,' said the old soldier, 'I've heard many old people talk about that. When death <u>do</u> call upon <u>we</u> it <u>don't</u> matter what becomes of our bodies.' | 1880 C. L. Dodgson, L55, I 369, I was rather frightened of him for there was only Aunt and me in the house, as the maid <u>don't</u> sleep here.

f. 1901-

1904-5 J. Hawker, D37, 51, It always seemed strange to me that if you see 100 Hares come out of a wood, it <u>don't</u> matter where, we never get them in. | 1904-5 J. Hawker, D37, 55, A Hare is very Sensitive to Smell or Sound. It <u>don't</u> Depend on sight so much. | 1904-5 J. Hawker, D37, 56-57, The fox and stoat are curious Little Chaps. One eats a lot he <u>Don't</u> kill, the other kills a Lot he <u>Don't</u> eat. Many people think the Fox kills a large quantity of Game. He <u>don't</u>. He is too lazy. I never knew many men do much Hard work if they were a bit foxey. | 1904-5 J. Hawker, D37, 59, If you can find a small Plantation within two miles or more of any Preserve, it <u>don't</u> matter if there is only half a dozen trees, so long as there is water near, you will find a Brace or a couple of Brace of Pheasants. | 1904-5 J. Hawker, D37, 76, The Farmer was more Humane, Kinder hearted, and He allowed Privileges the Farmer today <u>Don't</u> allow. | 1904-5 J. Hawker, D37, 80, If I go into a Pub the worse for Drink, this man can't Refuse to Serve me, because if he <u>don't</u> smell much, he has to clear out.

2.2.1.3. Syntactic and Stylistic Properties of the Third Person Singular Present *Don't* in the Texts Examined

In this section, syntactic properties of 3SG *don't* and speech-level of

Diachrony of the Third Person Singular Present *Don't*

the sentences in which 3SG *don't* occurred are sought. Table 14 proves that 3SG *don't* appears to have conveniently favoured a personal pronoun as the subject, and Table 15 that 3SG *don't* occurred in various clause types. From Table 16 it is clear that 3SG *don't* seems to have had no bias towards particular types of verbs or constructions, and from Table 17 it is evident that 3SG *don't* occurred exclusively in the declarative sentence. Table 18 testifies that 3SG *don't* occurred even at a non-vulgar speech level.

Table 14   Subjects of 3SG *Don't*—Diaries and Letters

Subject of 3 sg *don't*	1651-1700	1701-1750	1751-1800	1801-1850	1851-1900	1901-	Total
personal pronoun	1	5	8	6	3	7	30
demonstrative pronoun			1	1			2
substantive		1	5	1	3	1	11
wh- clause (*whether*)			1				1

Table 15   Types of Clause in which 3SG *Don't* Occurred—Diaries and Letters

	1651-1700	1701-1750	1751-1800	1801-1850	1851-1900	1901-	Total
in the conditional *if*-clause	1	2	4	4	3	1	15
in the subordinate clause introduced by		1	6	2	1	3	13
the other subordinate conjunction;		(1)	(3)	(1)	(1)		(6)
nominal *that*;			(2)				(2)
relative clause			(1)	(1)		(3)	(5)
in the superordinate clause		3	5	2	2	4	16

Table 16   Types of Verb Co-occurring with 3SG *Don't*—Diaries and Letters

	1651-1700	1701-1750	1751-1800	1801-1850	1851-1900	1901-	Total
intransitive verb		2	5	4	4	4	19
intransitive verb omitted			1				1
transitive verb		4	9	4	2	3	22
transitive verb omitted	1					1	2

Table 17   Types of Sentence in which 3SG *Don't* Occurred—Diaries and Letters

	1651-1700	1701-1750	1751-1800	1801-1850	1851-1900	1901-	Total
in the declarative sentence	1	6	15	8	6	8	44
in the interrogative sentence							0

42

Chapter II

Table 18 Speech Level of Sentence in which 3SG *Don't* Occurred—
Diaries and Letters

	1651-1700	1701-1750	1751-1800	1801-1850	1851-1900	1900-	Total
Without vulgar words	1	6	13	8	5	8	41
With vulgar words			2		1		3

Sources of Tables 14-18: Nakamura (2013: 9)

2.2.1.4. Users of the Third Person Singular Present *Don't* in the Texts Examined

In connection with the speech level, users of 3SG *don't* are explored. In the texts examined, four examples occurred where the users of which were not identified, as quoted in (25a-c). For example, the quotation (25a) was taken from H. W. Greville's diary. Greville was an Oxford University graduate, an attaché to Paris Embassy, and also an usher at court. The direct quotation in (25a), however, is not Greville's but of a person called 'Shiel'. Judging from the fact that another person 'Ashley' was the seventh Earl of Shaftesbury, who was also an Oxford graduate, it is likely that the person called 'Shiel' is also an educated person. However, for safety's sake, the present author would refrain from commenting on his usage level, as the author could gather no information about 'Shiel' from the Introduction or Index to the Greville's diary or the *ODNB*. The two examples in (25b) were quoted from Diary no. 36. This diary was kept by F. Kilvert, an Oxford University alumnus, who worked as a curate and vicar around the border between England and Wales. The direct speech in (25b), however, was not uttered by Kilvert but of a person 'Old James Godsell' and 'the old soldier' respectively, unknown to readers of D36. The latter speech can be regarded as vulgar English because 'death do' and 'upon we' are used instead of 'death does' and 'upon us'. The quotation in (25c) is a part of a letter sent from 'Mabel' to 'Emily', who are both dolls. Here Dodgson, i.e. Lewis Carroll, seems to have had Mabel utter the usage of 3SG *don't* deliberately.

(25) Users unidentified

   a. 1850 'Shiel', D32, I 375, Ashley amused us by saying he had asked Shiel what he thought would be the effect of all this Popish affair, to

Diachrony of the Third Person Singular Present *Don't*

which Shiel replied: 'It <u>don't</u> much matter what I think, . . .'

b. 1870 'Old James Godsell', D36, I 148, Old James Godsell . . . said 'if the rain <u>don't</u> come soon we shall have no hay nor yet straw' | 1872 'the old soldier', ibid., II 118, I said I thought the tree had better lie where it falls. 'Ah,' said the old soldier, 'I've heard many old people talk about that. When death <u>do</u> call upon <u>we</u> it <u>don't</u> matter what becomes of our bodies.'

c. 1880 C. L. Dodgson, L55, I 369, I was rather frightened of him for there was only Aunt and me in the house, as the maid <u>don't</u> sleep here.

Thus, with the other 40 quotations of 3SG *don't*, the writers are listed in Table 19, based upon the *ODNB*, the Introduction, Notes, Indices or the inside book covers of the texts examined. With the possible exception of two persons, Ann Hughes and James Hawker, Table 19 leads to speculation that even educated people did not care to use 3SG *don't* in the history of English. Moreover, they did not use this usage deliberately. Partridge (1953b: 258) states that 3SG *don't* was "common in good speech until 18th C", although here "18th" should be altered into "19th".

Table 19   Authentic Users of 3SG *Don't* in the Texts Examined

C. Lyttelton 1629-1716	third baronet and politician; Governor of Jamaica, Harwich, Landguard Fort, and Sheerness; knight; Brigadier-general [information taken from the textual note and *DNB*]
J. Holles 1693-1768	Holles, Thomas Pelham-, Duke of Newcastle upon Tyne and first duke of Newcastle under Lyme, Earle of Clare, etc.; LL.D., Clare Hall, Cambridge; chancellor of Cambridge University [*DNB*]
L. Pitt ?-?	Lucy Baskett from whom Dodsley would purchase the copyright of C. Pitt [= L. Pitt's brother, 1699-1748]'s translation of Virgil's Aeneid . . . in 1751; C. Pitt is a great uncle to R. Lowth [textual note]
T. Gray 1716-1771	poet and literary scholar; studied at Eaton College and Peterhouse, Cambridge [*DNB*]
J. Woodforde 1740-1803	diarist and Church of England clergyman; New College, Oxford, BA, MA, BD [*DNB*]
B. Sheridan 1758-1837	Elizabeth Sheridan; R. B. Sheridan's younger sister [inside book cover]
A. Hughes ?-?	a farmer's wife who lived in a remote country farmhouse near Chepstow, Monmouth-shire [inside book cover]

J. Clare 1793-1864	poet, farm labourer, and naturalist. [*DNB*]
H. Arbuthnot 1793-1834	daughter of the Honourable Henry Fane, M.P., second son of the 8th Earl of Westmorland; married the Right Honourable Charles Arbuthnot, M.P.; extreme tory; close friend of the Duke of Wellington and Lord Castlereagh [Introduction to the text and *DNB*]
S. Palmer 1805-1881	landscape painter and etcher; the Palmers were an upper-middle-class family. [*DNB*]
J. Ruskin 1819-1900	art critic and social critic; Christ Church, Oxford. [*DNB*]
G. Meredith 1828-1909	novelist and poet of the Victorian era [*DNB*]
C. L. Dodgson 1832-1898	*pseud*. Lewis Carroll; author, mathematician and photographer; BA, Oxford [*DNB*]
J. Hawker	poacher and autobiographer [*DNB*]

2.2.2. *Oxford English Dictionary*² on CD-ROM

To confirm the validity of what has been demonstrated in 2.2.1, the results of the analyses of the *OED*²'s citations are shown in this section.

2.2.2.1. General Chronological Trends: The Period of the Wane of the 'Normal' Use of the Third Person Singular Present *Don't* in the *OED*²

Excerpted from Table 8, Table 20 indicates the occurrences of *don't* and *doesn't* in the *OED*²'s quotations. From over five thousand examples of *don't* in Table 20, 3SG *don't* accounts for 257 examples, as shown in Table 21. Indicatively, *don't*, which appeared for the first time in early 17th-century documents, was regulated as early as the second half of the 1600s. By contrast, *doesn't* was not popularly used until around 1850, even though the first written occurrence was in evidence in a drama written in 1674. *Doesn't* needed a little less than two hundred years to become established (Table 20).

Table 20 Occurrences of *Don't* and *Doesn't* in the *OED²*, Extracted from Table 8—Nakamura (2013: 11)

			1601-1625	1626-1650	1651-1675	1676-1700	1701-1725	1726-1750	1751-1775	1776-1800	1801-1825	1826-1850	1851-1875	1876-1900	1901-1925	1926-1950	1951-1975	1976-	Total
don(')t doon't dunt	D	O			5	36	67	60	70	35	64	219	328	422	374	498	902	311	3,446
		V				1	2	1				3	6	8	9	8	12	4	
	Q	O		1	1	5	10	12	6	10	8	31	49	46	35	69	79	31	468
		T										3	7	9	4	13	29	5	
		V													2	1	2		
	Imp	O			4	12	23	36	25	17	27	140	146	197	178	257	351	95	1,523
		V						2				1		4	4	3	1		
doesn(')t dosn't	D	O							1		1	6	21	49	58	140	274	109	669
		V											1	3	4	2			
	Q	O										1	1	2	7	13	12	6	63
		T												2	4	5	7	2	
		V													1				

Table 21 Variations between *Doesn't* and 3SG *Don't* in the *OED²*—Nakamura (2013: 11)

			1651-1675	1676-1700	1701-1725	1726-1750	1751-1775	1776-1800	1801-1825	1826-1850	1851-1875	1876-1900	1901-1925	1926-1950	1951-1975	1976-	Total
don't (= doesn't)	D	O		2	7	4	7	6	9	20	36	48	26	33	29	4	236
		V		1	1								1	2			
	Q	O								1			2	2			13
		T								3		1		1	1	1	
		V											1				
dont (= doesn't)	D	O	1				2					1			1		7
		V											1				
	Q	O												1			
doont (= doesn't)	D	O										1					1
doesn't	D	O					1		1	5	21	48	55	139	274	109	663
		V											1	3	4	2	
	Q	O								1	2		7	13	12	6	62
		T									2		4	5	7	2	
		V											1				
doesnt	D	O									1		3	1			5
dosn't	D	O							1								1
	Q	O									1						1

This historical fact suggests that *don't* was in dominance over *doesn't* until the regulation of the latter around 1850. The shaded columns in Table 21 indicate that only *don't* was initially used, while *doesn't* came into use later. However, *don't* was more frequently used than *doesn't*, irrespective of the person and the number of subjects, to conjugate with the third person singular subject as if it were a modal auxiliary. *Doesn't* took precedence over *don't* in the course of the second half of the 19th century. In other words, the second half of the 19th century can be regarded as a transitional period from *he don't know* to *he doesn't know*, half of a century later than in the diaries and letters. Considering that a little less than two

46

Chapter II

centuries elapsed before *doesn't* was accepted, and widely so in the mid-19th century, people (even the educated) naturally used the non-contracted form of *does not* or 3SG *don't*.

2.2.2.2. Examples of the Third Person Singular Present *Don't* in the *OED*[2]

All of the examples of 3SG *don't* are quoted under (26) below. As is the case with the examples illustrated in (24), words with thick underlines represent formal or elevated phases of English and those with wavy lines vulgar or informal ones. This distinction of word-levels is based on the *OED*[2] and present-day English dictionaries such as *OALD*[8] and *LDCE*[5]. Whether this distinction applies to earlier English is not guaranteed. Nevertheless, there was no alternative but to resort to this differentiation simply because usage dictionaries for antecedent English were not published before the 20th century.

In some quotations, especially those quoted from novels, it is clear that 3SG *don't* was used for linguistically colouring the characters. As not more than half of the sources of the quotations containing 3SG *don't* was available for the present author, however, there was no choice but to abandon this attempt to evidence the uses of 3SG *don't* from such perspectives. This is the reason why an analysis of the kind of words which co-occurred with 3SG *don't* was relied upon. As it was possible to collect biographical information about only a limited number of the writers of 3SG *don't*, a user-list as shown in Table 19 (pp. 43-44) was not made.

As the quotations in (26) suggest, in earlier examples there seem to have been few examples of 3SG *don't* which were in vulgar use; on the contrary, formal or elevated words could co-occur with it. Around 1826 to 1850, the number of words with wavy underlines became prominent. This development suggests that 3SG *don't* began to occur in vulgar and non-standard speech around the mid-19th century, when *doesn't* started gaining ground. In some quotations, especially those quoted from novels, 3SG *don't* was clearly used to rhetorically colour the characters.

Diachrony of the Third Person Singular Present *Don't*

(26) Quotations of 3SG *don't* tabulated into Table 21

a. 1651-1675

<Vulgar>

<?British English> 1670 in *Coll. Rhode Isl. Hist. Soc.* (1902) X. 102 Evidence of .. River being more than 11 Miles Long but how Much More <u>dont</u> say. (*OED²* s.v. do, *v.*, A. 2c "The orig. northern form *does* superseded *doth*, *doeth*, in 16–17th c. in general use; the latter being now liturgical and poetic. The form *he do* is now s.w. dial., and *he don't* is vulgar") [Declared to be vulgar in the *OED²* s.v. do, *v.*, A. 2cγ, where this quotation is the earliest example.]

b. 1676-1700

<Non-Vulgar>

<British English> 1682 T. Flatman *Heraclitus Ridens* No. 67 (1713) II. 168 He has found out a new Tory Popish-Plot upon his Puppily Courant; some body or other, if he <u>don't</u> lie, made his Printer tipsie. (*OED²* s.v. puppily, *a*) (*Heraclitus Ridens* is a "political and comic periodical" regarded "as a remote predecessor of the London Punch") | 1689 *Upon King's Voy. to Chatham in Coll. Poems on Affairs of State* 19, I wish this sad Accident <u>don't</u> spoil the young Prince, Take off all his Manhood and make him a Wench. (*OED²* s.v. manhood, *n.* Add, 2c) | 1696 *Lond. Gaz.* No. 3212/4 She seems to cut behind but <u>don't</u>, unless clouterly shod. (*OED²* s.v. clouterly, *adv.*)

c. 1701-1725

<Non-Vulgar>

<British English> 1705 Vanbrugh *Mistake* iv. i, *Jacin.* Have a care he <u>don't</u> rally, and beat you yet tho'; pray walk off. (*OED²* s.v. walk, *v.*¹, 8c) | 1705 Vanbrugh *Confed.* ii. i, You like your neighbour's [wife] better. .. What a pity it is the law <u>don't</u> allow trucking. (*OED²* s.v. trucking, *vbl. n.*¹, a) | 1706 Phillips (ed. Kersey) s.v., A Ship is said *To stay a Weather of a Wake*, when in her Staying she does it so speedily, that she <u>don't</u> fall to the Leeward, but that when she is tacked, her Wake is to the Leeward; which is a sure Sign that she feels

Chapter II

her Helm well, and is nimble of Steerage. When a Ship being in Chace of another, has got as far into the Wind as she, and sails directly after her; the usual Saying is, *That she has got into her Wake.* (*OED²* s.v. wake, *n.²*, 1b) | 1714 *Barrow's Euclid* 517 This method <u>don't</u> suppose the conic surface .. to consist of as many parallel circumferences perpetually increasing from the vertex, or decreasing from the base. (*OED²* s.v. conic, *a.* and *n.*, A, *adj.*, 2) | 1715 De Foe *Fam. Instruct.* i. iv. (1841) Wks. I. 73 I'll cane the rascal if he <u>don't</u>. (*OED²* s.v. cane, *v.¹*, 1)

<?British English> 1703 *Country Farmers' Catech.* in Brand *Pop. Antiq.* (1870) I. 287 My daughter <u>don't</u> look with sickly pale looks, like an unlit Chritmas Candle. (*OED²* s.v. Christmas, *n.*, 4) | 1710 Palmer *Proverbs* 115 A woman of virtue keeps a guard upon her eye, and yet <u>don't</u> affect to look soure, squeamish, and suspicious. (*OED²* s.v. squeamish, *a., adv., and n.*, 6a)

<Vulgar / Informal>

<British English> 1713 R. Nelson *Life Bull* 81 Why, said the Preacher, Solomon <u>don't</u> say so. (*OED²* s.v. do, *v.* B, 29a) [Declared to be vulgar in the *OED²* s.v. do, *v.*, B, 29a]

d. 1726-1750

<Non-vulgar>

<British English> 1741 Mrs. Foley in *Mrs. Delany's Corr.* (1861) II. 164 If your fair sister <u>don't</u> <u>epistle</u> me this post. (*OED²* s.v. epistle, *v.* 2) [epistle, *n.* "*formal* or *humorous*" (*OALD⁸*)] | 1747 *Gentl. Mag.* XVII. 383 Parties may be abolish'd, but the late <u>dissolution</u> of the parliament <u>don't</u> look much like it. (*OED²* s.v. look, *v.*, 10b) [dissolution "*formal*" (*OALD⁸*)] | 1747 H. Glasse *Cookery* ii. 38 Untye your Cucumbers, but take care the Meat <u>don't</u> come out. (*OED²* s.v. untie, *v.*, 1b)

<Vulgar / Informal>

<British English> 1741 Richardson *Pamela* I. 65 He <u>don't</u> know you. (*OED²* s.v. do, *v.* A, 2c) [Declared to be vulgar in

49

Diachrony of the Third Person Singular Present *Don't*

the *OED²* s.v. do, *v.*, A. 2cγ, where this quotation is the second earliest example.]

e. 1751-1775

<Non-vulgar>

<British English> 1751 Smollett *Per. Pic.* (1779) III. lxxviii. 44 'Howsomever, that <u>don't</u> argufy in <u>reverence</u> of his being in a hurry. (*OED²* s.v. argufy, *v.*, 1) [*OED²*, s.v. howsomever, *adv.* Now *dial.* or *vulgar*] [reverence "*formal*" (*OALD⁸*)] | 1753 *Scots Mag.* Mar. 127/2 The eviction or destruction of a thing mortgaged, <u>don't extinguish</u> the debt. (*OED²* s.v. eviction, 1) [extinguish "*formal*" (*OALD⁸*)] | 1753 *Chambers' Cycl.* Suppl. s.v. *Stopper*, It serves, when they are hoising the main-yard, to stop it, that it <u>don't</u> run out too fast. (*OED²* s.v. run, *v.*, B, 77e(b)) | 1771 Smollett *Humph. Cl.* 3 June, She <u>don't</u> yet know her letters .. but I will bring her the A B C in gingerbread. (*OED²* s.v. gingerbread, 1)

<⁰British English> 1755 Croker *Orl. Fur.* xxv. lxix, Entwining bearbind <u>dont</u> more knots unite. (*OED²* s.v. bearbine, -bind)

<American English> 1754 Edwards *Freed. Will* ii. v. 53 If Liberty <u>don't</u> <u>consist in</u> this, what else can be <u>devised</u> that it should <u>consist in</u>. (*OED²* s.v. devise, *v.*, 10) [consist in sth "*formal*" (*OALD⁸*)]

<Vulgar / Informal>

<British English> 1762 *Gentl. Mag.* 38 It <u>don't</u> regard the present war. (*OED²* s.v. do, *v.*, B, 29a) [Declared to be vulgar in the s.v. do, *v.*, B, 29a] | 1763 Colman *Deuce is in Him* Prol., If our author <u>don't</u> produce Some character that plays the deuce; If there's no frolick, sense, or whim, Retort! and play the dev'l with him! (*OED²* s.v. deuce², *colloq.* or *slang.*, b²)

<American English> 1774 P. V. Fithian *Jrnl.* (1900) 202 A Sunday in Virginia <u>dont</u> seem to wear the same Dress as our Sundays to the Northward. (*OED²* s.v. do, *v.*, A. 2c) [Declared to be vulgar in the *OED²* s.v. do, *v.*, A. 2cγ, where this quotation is the third earliest example.]

f. 1776-1800

Chapter II

<Non-vulgar>

<British English>   1777 Sheridan *Trip Scarb.* i. ii, If the devil
don't step between the cup and the lip. (*OED²* s.v. cup, *n.*, 12a.
Proberbs and Phrases) | 1780 Mrs. Thrale *Let. to Johnson* 10
June, Mr. Thrale seems thunderstricken, he don't mind anything. (*OED²* s.v. thunderstricken, *a.*, 2) (cf thunderstruck *"formal"* (*OALD⁸*))

<American English>   1781 J. Adams in *Fam. Lett.* (1876) 403
Burgoyne don't seem to be affronted that his [= Cornwallis's]
nose is out of joint. (*OED²* s.v. nose, *n.*, 9b) (affront sb/sth
"formal" (*OALD⁸*))

<Source of author/text unidentified>   1782 E. N. Blower *Geo.
Bateman* II. 174 The child don't like to lugger folks. (*OED²*
s.v. lugger, *v. Obs.*) | 1800 Hoyle & Jones *Hoyle's Games Im-
proved* 308 The Game of All-Fours. .. If the eldest [hand]
don't like his cards, he may, for once in a hand, say, *I beg*,
when the dealer must either give a point or three more cards
to each .. player. (*OED²* s.v. beg, *v.*, 2h)

<Vulgar / Informal>

<Source of author/text unidentified>   1781 G. Parker *View Soc.*
ii. 133 About Darkey [*i.e.* twilight], or when Oliver don't
widdle [*footn.* The Moon not up]. (*OED²* s.v. whiddle, *v.
slang.*) [*OED²* s.v. darky, darkey, 1. *slang.*]

g. 1801-1825

<Non-vulgar >

<British English>   1803 G. Colman *John Bull* iii. ii. 35 If he
don't behave himself, I'll come in and thump him blue.
(*OED²* s.v. thump, *v.*, 1a) | 1811 Byron *Hints fr. Hor.* 734 note,
If she don't take a poetical twist, and come forth as a shoe-
making Sappho. (*OED²* s.v. twist, *n.*¹, 21a) | 1818 Byron *Ep.
Murray* iii, The pompous rascallion, Who don't speak Italian
Nor French, must have scribbled by guesswork. (*OED²* s.v.
guess-work)

<Source of author/text unidentified>   1815 *Zeluca* I. 393 See,
see—he's going to shirk Lady Kitty—he pretends he don't

Diachrony of the Third Person Singular Present *Don't*

see her coming up. (*OED²* s.v. shirk, *v.*, 3a, Now *rare* or *Obs.*)
| 1819 *Blackw. Mag.* IV. 566 One don't sift Such trifling
doggrel strains with eye severish. (*OED²* s.v. severish, *a.*)

<? Vulgar / Informal>

<British English>   1804 *Something Odd* II. 89 He don't believe
there is a devil. *Apropos* of his nigrific Majesty [etc.]. (*OED²*
s.v. nigrific, *a. nonce-wd*)

<Source of author/text unidentified>   1802 M. Charlton *Wife &
Mistress* I. xii. 273 He ['cross Lord John'] don't vally what he
says to young or old, man or woman—its all the same to old
gruffy! (*OED²* s.v. gruffy, *a.* and *n.*; *a. (pron., adv.)*, A, *Adj.*,
8) [*OED²* s.v. gruffy, *a.* and *n. Obs.*, B. *n.* "A nickname for a
gruff person, a 'cross patch'"] [*OED²* s.v. vally, dial. variant
of FELLOE, VALUE)

<Vulgar / Informal>

<British English>   1803 J. Kenney *Raising Wind* ii. i. 24 What a
fine seal; and I'll be shot if it [*sc.* a letter] don't feel like a
bank note. (*OED²* s.v. shoot, *v.*, 31, *slang* or *vulgar.*)

<American English>   1813 J. K. Paulding *John Bull & Br. Jon.*
ii. 9 The old saying that a man don't know when he is well off.
(*OED²* s.v. do, *v.*, A, 2cγ) [Declared to be vulgar in the *OED²*
s.v. do, *v.*, A. 2c, where this quotation is the fourth earliest
example.]

h. 1826-1850

<Non-Vulgar>

<British English>   1835 Dickens *Sk. Boz, River*, Why don't
your partner stretch out? (*OED²* s.v. stretch, *v.*, 20c) | 1839 H.
Ainsworth *Jack Sheppard* iii, If he don't tip the cole without
more ado, give him a taste of the pump, that's all. (*OED²* s.v.
pump, *n.*[1], 1b) | 1840 Marryat *Poor Jack* vi, The sparmacitty
don't take the harpoon quite so quietly as the black whale
does. (*OED²* s.v. whale, *n.*, 1b) | 1847 Lever *Knt. Gwynne*
xviii, He [a horse] starts, or shies, or something of that sort—
don't he? (*OED²* s.v. start, *v.*, 5b) | 1848 Dickens *Dombey* v,
She don't gain on her papa in the least. (*OED²* s.v. gain, *v.*[2],

Chapter II

9d) | 1849 Dickens *Dav. Copp.* xx. (C.D. ed.) 178 That shows
the advantage of asking, <u>don't</u> it. (*OED²* s.v. ask, *v.*, 7)

<British Colony of Nova Scotia> 1837–40 Haliburton *Clockm.*
(1862) 79 If that <u>don't</u> happify your heart, then my name's not
Sam Slick. (*OED²* s.v. happify, *v.*) | 1837 Haliburton *Clockm.*
Ser. i. xxiii, She <u>don't</u> wait any more for him to walk lock and
lock with her. (*OED²* s.v. lock, *n.*², 13) | 1847 Haliburton *Old
Judge* I. ii. 44 It <u>don't</u> do to hang a feller for his looks, after
all, that's a fact; for that crittur is like a singed cat, better nor
he seems. (*OED²* s.v. singed, *ppl. a.*¹, b) [*OED²* s.v. critter
"Widespread dial. and jocular var. creature"] | 1843 Hali-
burton *Attaché* I. xii. 218 Preacher there <u>don't</u> preach morals,
because that's churchy. (*OED²* s.v. churchy, *a.*, 1)

<American English> 1837 Miss Sedgwick *Live & let Live*
(1876) 190 A looking-glass that <u>don't</u> make you look as if
your face was all agee. (*OED²* s.v. agee, *adv. Sc.* and *dial.*) |
1848 Lowell *Fable for Critics* 598 He <u>don't</u> sketch their
bundles of muscles and thews illy. (*OED²* s.v. illy, *adv.*) |
1850 Mrs. Stowe *Uncle Tom's C.* vi. 35 'Old lady <u>don't</u> like
your humble servant, over and above,' said Haley. (*OED²* s.v.
above, *adv.* and *prep.*, A. *adv.*, 7)

<? Vulgar / Informal >
<British English> 1838 Dickens *Nickleby* (1839) xxix. 288
Why, he <u>don't</u> mean to say he's going! .. <u>Hoity toity</u>! non-
sense. (*OED²* s.v. mean, *v.*¹, Appended from Additions 1997,
1g; hoity-toity, *n., a., adv., int.*, D. *int.*) [hoity-toity, *adj. "old-
fashioned, informal"* (*OALD⁸*)] | 1839 F. Trollope *Dom. Man-
ners Amer.* xxix. 271 Well! if that <u>don't</u> beat creation! (*OED²*
s.v. creation, 4b, *U.S. colloq.*)

<British Colony of Nova Scotia> 1840 Haliburton *Clockm.* Ser.
iii. v, It <u>don't</u> seem to hang very well together <u>nother</u>. (*OED²*
s.v. nother, *adv.*¹ and *conj.*, *Obs.* exc. *dial.*, 4)

<Vulgar / Informal>
<British English> 1837 Marryat *Dog-Fiend* xxxvi, I'm <u>jiggered</u>
if he <u>don't</u> tell a lie. (*OED²* s.v. jigger, *v.*², *slang* or *colloq.*)

Diachrony of the Third Person Singular Present *Don't*

<British Colony of Nova Scotia> 1836 Haliburton (Sam Slick) *Clockmaker* Introd., It <u>don't</u> seem to me that I <u>had ought</u> to be made a fool on in that book. (*OED²* s.v. ought, *v.* , 7c, "Been obliged (*vulgar Eng.*")

<American English> 1835 R. M. Bird *Hawks of Hawk-Hollow* I. xi. 143, I wonder she <u>don't</u> sing; for a speaking voice, she has the richest *soprano*. (*OED²* s.v. do, *v.*, A, 2c) [Declared to be vulgar in the *OED²* s.v. do, *v.*, A. 2cγ, where this quotation is the sixth earliest example.] | 1837 *Southern Lit. Messenger* III. 86, I say, <u>darkie</u>, the old man keeps good liquor, and plenty of belly timber, <u>don't</u> he? (*OED²* s.v. old man, 1h) [*OED²* s.v. darky, darkey, *slang*] [*OED²* s.v. belly-timber, *Obs. exc. dial.*] | 1837 R. M. Bird *Nick of Woods* I. xvi. 220 If that <u>don't</u> make me eat a niggur, may I be tetotaciously <u>chaw</u>ed up myself! (*OED²* s.v. teetotaciously, *adv. U.S. dial. Obs.*) [*OED²* s.v. chaw, *v.*, now *vulgar*] | 1850 Seaworthy *Nag's Head* v. 35 'It <u>don't</u> seem to <u>gee</u>!' said Isaac, as he was trying to adjust the stove. (*OED²* s.v. gee, *v.¹ slang*)

<Source of Author/Text Unidentified> 1831 Fonblanque *Eng. under 7 Administ.* (1837) II. 100 God <u>don't</u> suffer them now. (*OED²* s.v. do, *v.*, A, 2c) [Declared to be vulgar in the *OED²* s.v. do, *v.*, A. 2cγ, where this quotation is the fifth earliest example.] | 1833 A. Greene *Life & Adv. D. Duckworth* II. 66 He <u>don't know beans</u>. (*OED²* s.v. bean, *n*, 6e, Slang phrases: *not to know beans* (U.S.))

i. 1851-1875

<Non-vulgar>

<British English> 1855 Kingsley *Westw. Ho!* i, And who <u>don't</u> agree, let him choose his weapons, and I'm his man. (*OED²* s.v. man, *n.¹*, 4k) | 1855 Kingsley *Westw. Ho!* i, See if he <u>don't</u> tell you over the ruttier as well as Drake himself. (*OED²* s.v. ruttier) | 1861 Mayhew *Lond. Labour* III. 73 'The galantee show <u>don't</u> answer, because magic lanterns are so cheap in the shops.' (*OED²* s.v. galanty show) | 1861 Mayhew *Lond. Labour* III. 204 [Street-photographer *loq.*] A lady <u>don't</u> mind taking her bonnet off .. before one of her own sect.

Chapter II

(*OED*[2] s.v. sect, *n.*[1], 1d) | 1861 S. Brooks *Silver Cord* viii.
(1865) 44 Or perhaps your memory <u>don't</u> serve you as well
as it did. (*OED*[2] s.v. serve, *v.*[1], 26a) | 1863 Reade *Hard Cash*
II. 246 That <u>don't</u> <u>dovetail</u> nohow. (*OED*[2] s.v. nohow, *adv.*
(*and a.*), 1b) [dovetail, "*formal*" (*OALD*[8])] | 1865 Dickens
Mut. Fr. ii. vii, The yard gate-lock should be <u>looked to</u>, if you
please; it <u>don't</u> catch. (*OED*[2] s.v. look, *v.*, 21c) [look to sth,
"*formal*" (*OALD*[8])] | 1875 *Punch* 18 Sept. 113/2 It <u>don't</u> mat-
ter a rap whether it's rough or fine. (*OED*[2] s.v. rap, *n.*[2], 1c)

<[?]Australian English>   1865 H. Kingsley *Hillyars & Burtons* lii,
'Well! if this <u>don't</u> bang wattle gum', began Gerty. (*OED*[2] s.v.
wattle, *n.*[1], 4d)

<American English>   1856 P. Cartwright *Autobiogr.* 192 (De
Vere), If he <u>don't</u> get his soul converted God will damn him
as quick as he would a Guinea Negro. (*OED*[2] s.v. Guinea, 1a)
| 1858 in Herndon *Life A. Lincoln* (1892) II. 115 The idea put
forth by Judge Douglas, that he '<u>don't</u> care whether slavery is
voted down or voted up.' (*OED*[2] s.v. vote, *v.*, 7) | 1862 Lowell
Biglow P. Ser. ii. ii. 22 Ef your soul <u>Don't</u> sneak thru shun-
pikes so 's to save the toll. (*OED*[2] s.v. shun, *v.*, 9, shun-pike
U.S.) | 1862 R. H. Newell *Orpheus C. Kerr Papers* 1st Ser.
360 He's not an economical man if he <u>don't</u> destroy his life-
insurance policy. (*OED*[2] s.v. life, *n.*, 17) | 1866 'Mark Twain'
Lett. from Hawaii (1967) 250 This Injun <u>don't</u> seem to know
anything but 'Owry ikky', and the interest of that begins to let
down after it's been said sixteen or seventeen times. (*OED*[2]
s.v. let, *v.*[1] , 32b) | 1873 'Mark Twain' & Warner *Gilded Age*
xxvii. 249 A man wants rest, a man wants peace—a man
<u>don't</u> want to rip and tear around *all* the time. (*OED*[2] s.v. rip,
v.[2], 9b)

<Source of Author/Text Unidentified>   1857 Costello *Million-
aire Mincing L.* 60 (Hoppe) That <u>don't</u> look like a come-off.
(*OED*[2] s.v. come-off, *n.*, 3)

<[?] Vulgar / Informal>

<British English>   1852 Dickens *Bleak Ho.* iv, It <u>don't</u> come out
altogether so plain as to please me, but it's <u>on the cards</u>.

Diachrony of the Third Person Singular Present *Don't*

(*OED²* s.v. card, *n.*², 2e) [on the cards (*BrE*) . . . (*informal*)
likely to happen (*OALD⁸*)] | 1854 Thackeray *Newcomes* II. 48,
I will take a back~hander, as Clive don't seem to drink.
(*OED²* s.v. back-hander, 2) [backhander . . . (*BrE, informal*) |
1857 Dickens *Dorrit* i. xxx, She don't know what she means.
She's an idiot, a wanderer in her mind. (*OED²* s.v. wanderer,
1a) | 1869 Trollope *He Knew* xv. (1878) 83 It don't mean
much, only just idle talking and gallivanting. (*OED²* s.v. gallivanting, *vbl. n.*) [gallivant . . . *v.* . . . *informal* (*LDCE⁵*)]

<American English>   1857 Holland *Bay Path* xxiv. 285, I like
your spunk, but it don't count in a fight with crazy folks and
fools. (*OED²* s.v. spunk, *n.*, 5a) [spunk, "*informal*" (*OALD⁸*)]

<Vulgar / Informal>

<British English>   1854 Dickens *Hard T.* vi, Tight-Jeff or Slack-
Jeff, it don't much signify; it's only tight-rope and slack-rope.
(*OED²* s.v. jeff, *n.*¹ *Circus slang.* "A rope") | 1854 W. Collins
Hide & Seek ii. x. (1904) 259 It don't do me no good: it only
worrits me into a perspiration. (*OED²* s.v. worrit, *v.*, *colloq.*,
1b) | 1855 Kingsley *Westw. Ho!* viii, If it don't ate so soft as
ever was scald cream, never you call me Thomas Burman.
(*OED²* s.v. scald, *a.*²) | 1861 Hughes *Tom Brown at Oxf.* xii.
(1889) 110 I'm not going to peach if the proctor don't send
again in the morning. (*OED²* s.v. peach, *v.*, 2 "Now chiefly
slang or *colloq.*") | 1861 Hughes *Tom Brown at Oxf.* xii, One
don't like to go in while there's any chance of a real row ..
and so gets proctorized in one's old age for one's patriotism.
(*OED²* s.v. proctorize, *v.*) [*OED²* s.v. row, *n.*², "A slang or colloquial word . . . in common use from *c*1800. Noted by Todd
(1818) as 'a very low expression'"] | 1863 Dickens in *All Year
Round* (Christmas No.) 7/2 'Well!' I says, 'if this don't beat
everything!' (*OED²* s.v. beat, *v.*¹, 10a) | 1868 *All Year Round*
10 Oct. 431 As for your being a furrener, it don't matter
shucks. (*OED²* s.v. shuck, *n.*², Chiefly *dial.* and *U.S.*, 2b)

<American English>   1855 *Yale Lit. Mag.* XX. 192 (Th.), What-
ever he knows of Euclid and Greek, In Latin he don't know
beans. (*OED²* s.v. bean, *n*, 6e, Slang phrases: *not to know*

Chapter II

beans (U.S.)) | 1857 *San Francisco Call* 19 Apr. 2/3 He <u>don't</u> appear to care <u>nothing</u> for <u>nobody</u>—he's 'as independent as a hog on ice!' (*OED²* s.v. hog, *n.*¹, 11a, *U.S. colloq.*) | 1855 F. M. Whitcher *Widow Bedott Papers* xiv. (1883) 54 They say when she <u>ain't</u> a <u>spinnin'</u> street yarn, she <u>don't</u> dew <u>nothin'</u> but write <u>poitry</u>. (*OED²* s.v. street, *n.*, 4f. *U.S.*) | 1852 Mrs. Stowe *Uncle Tom's C.* viii, You've got to <u>fork over</u> fifty dollars, flat down, or this child <u>don't</u> start a peg. (*OED²* s.v. peg, *n.*¹, 4) [*OED²* s.v. fork, *v.*, 5. *transf.* (*colloq.* or *slang.*) | 1862 O. W. Norton *Army Lett.* (1903) 120 It <u>don't</u> take ten thousand acres here to support one family. (*OED²* s.v. do, *v.*, A, 2c) [Declared to be vulgar in the *OED²* s.v. do, *v.*, A. 2cγ, where this quotation is the seventh earliest example.] | 1869 Mrs. Stowe *Oldtown Folks* xxxvii. 483 Your minister <u>sartin</u> <u>doos</u> slant a leetle towards the Arminians; he <u>don't</u> quite <u>walk the crack</u>. (*OED²* s.v. crack, *n.*, 7c) | 1869 Mrs. Stowe *Old Town Folks* l, If she <u>don't</u> do <u>nothin'</u> more 'n take a walk 'longside on him .. , why, I say, let <u>'er</u> rip. (*OED²* s.v. rip, *v.*², 9a) | 1872 E. Eggleston *End of World* xxiii. 158 Clark township <u>don't</u> want <u>none</u> of <u>'em</u>, I'll be <u>dog-oned</u> [*sic* Nakamura] if it do. (*OED²* s.v. dog-gone, *U.S. slang*, C)

j. 1876-1900

<Non-vulgar>

<British English>

1876 'Ouida' *Winter City* vi. 125 She <u>don't</u> care a hang what anybody says of her. (*OED²* s.v. hang, *n.*, 5) | 1880 L. Wingfield *In her Maj. Keeping* II. i. xii. 51 It <u>don't</u> matter to me a buttonshank. (*OED²* s.v. button, *n.*, 12a) | 1881 C. M. Yonge *Lads & Lasses Langley* ii. 64 'Well, it <u>don't</u> sting like the other,' said Frank, .. as if he thought stinging a good quality in beer. (*OED²* s.v. sting, *v.*¹, 4b) | 1881 *Leic. Gloss.* 249 The summer wet <u>doon't</u> sog in deep. (*OED²* s.v. sog, *v.*, 1b) | 1877 J. M. Bailey *Folks in Danbury* 40 (Th.), [The lamp] <u>don't</u> give more light than a fire-bug. (*OED²* s.v. fire, *n.*, B. 5c) | 1882 Mrs. J. H. Riddell *Daisies & B.* II. 239 'Hat covers his family, <u>don't</u> it?' 'He has no one belonging to him I ever heard of.' (*OED²* s.v. hat, *n.*, 5c) | 1884 H. Smart *Post to Finish* II. xvi. 251 He <u>don't</u> warrant my calling for

Diachrony of the Third Person Singular Present *Don't*

'pop' [champagne]. (*OED²* s.v. pop, *n.*¹, 5 *colloq.*) | 1885 T. A. Guthrie *Tinted Venus* viii. 93 Haven't you missed out a lot, sir? .. because it <u>don't</u> seem to me to hook on quite. (*OED²* s.v. hook, *v.*, 5a) | 1890 Stockton in *Century Mag.* Feb. 543/1 The story <u>don't</u> step up to the mark. (*OED²* s.v. mark, *n.*¹, 12c) [up to the mark (*BrE*) (*NAmE* up to snuff) (*OALD⁸*)] | 1893 *Wiltsh. Gloss., Liberty*, to allow anything to run loose. 'It <u>don't</u> matter how much it's libertied', the more freedom you give it the better. (*OED²* s.v. liberty, *v.*) | 1897 W. Rye *Norfolk Songs* 25 'He <u>don't</u> like working between meals' is a succinct description of a lazy man. (*OED²* s.v. meal, *n.*², 2a) | 1899 B. Harraden *Fowler* 83 He <u>don't</u> like that little viper gentleman any more than I. (*OED²* s.v. viper, 5c)

<⁷British English>   1880 C. B. Berry *Other Side* 244 The ship is so beamy that she <u>don't</u> heel over much. (*OED²* s.v. over, *adv.*, 1c)

<American English>   1876 H. James in *Atlantic Monthly* XXXVIII. 693/2 A silly young girl and a heavy, overwise young man who <u>don't</u> fall in love with her! That is the *donnée* of eight monthly volumes. I call it very flat. (*OED²* s.v. donnée) | 1883 'Mark Twain' *Life on Mississippi* xliii. 440 It's human nature—human nature in grief. It <u>don't</u> reason, you see. 'Time being, it don't care a dam. (*OED²* s.v. time, *n.*, 2) | 1883 'Mark Twain' *Life on Mississippi* xliii. 440 It's human nature—human nature in grief. It don't reason, you see. 'Time being, it <u>don't</u> care a dam. (*OED²* s.v. time, *n.*, 2) | 1886 *Leslie's Monthly* Feb. 203/1 Old Sampson <u>don't</u> like the Summer <u>gentry</u>. (*OED²* s.v. summer, *n.*¹, 4f, *U.S.*) | 1893 *Harper's Mag.* Jan. 214/2 It's just a phonograph. .. It <u>don't</u> seem to be exactly in order. Perhaps the cylinder's got dry. (*OED²* s.v. cylinder, *n.*, 2c) | 1897 *Scribner's Mag.* Sept. 305/1 And it <u>don't</u> cut no ice with you whether folks call you <u>inconsistent</u> or not. (*OED²* s.v. ice, *n.*, 2c) | 1898 F. P. Dunne *Mr. Dooley in Peace & War* 38 'They'll kill him with kindness if he <u>don't</u> look out,' said Mr. Hennessy. (*OED²* s.v. kill, *v.*, 7d) | 1898 R. B. Townshend in *Westm. Gaz.* 19 Nov. 2/1 It <u>don't</u> seem to 'phase' him in the very slightest. (*OED²* s.v. phase "erroneous

Chapter II

spelling of FAZE *v.*, to discompose, disturb") [*OED*² s.v. faze, *v.* orig. *U.S.*] [faze . . . *informal* (*LDCE*⁵)]

<?American English>   1882 G. W. Peck *Peck's Sunshine* 24 If he don't put on an old driving coat and go out on the road occasionally. (*OED*² s.v. driving, *vbl. n.*, 3)

<Vulgar / Informal>

   <British English>   1884 W. E. Norris *Thirlby Hall* xxv, It don't do to let them get the whip~hand of you, according to my experience. Put that in your pipe and smoke it, Master Charley. (*OED*² s.v. pipe, *n.*¹, 10d) [Put/stick that in your pipe and smoke it *spoken* (*LDCE*⁵)] | 1885 *Sporting Times* 11 Apr. 1/4 Too bad, too bad! after getting fourteen days or forty bob, the bally rag don't even mention it. (*OED*² s.v. bally, *a.* and *adv. slang*) | 1886 Elworthy *W. Somerset Word-bk.* s.v., He don't never give no quest 'thout he's right 'pon it. (*OED*² s.v. quest, *n.*¹, 6) | 1886 *W. Somerset Word-bk.* s.v., Well, I be zorry vor to zee a widow umman a-stress'd; but her can't never 'spect to bide there, not if her don't pay no rent. (*OED*² s.v. stress, *v.*²) [*OED*² s.v. spect, *v.*², 2, "Repr. (chiefly U.S.) non-standard pronunc. of (*I*) *expect* or *suspect*"] | 1888 Fenn *Dick o' the Fens* 381 He don't wear as I should like to see un. He's wankle. (*OED*² s.v. wankle, *a. Obs.* exc. *dial.*) [*OED*², s.v., un, un¹, . . . 'him'] | 1890 P. H. Emerson *Diary* 25 Nov. in *On Eng. Lagoons* (1892) xxii. 100 Rum night this, hefty weather, don't it blow and snow. (*OED*² s.v. hefty, *a.* orig. *dial.* and *U.S.*, 1 "Weighty, heavy; hard, grievous") [*OED*² s.v. rum, *a.*² *slang*. . . . Odd, strange, queer. Also, bad, spurious. 1774→] | 1891 Clark Russell *Marriage at Sea* ii, We're going to get a breeze . . ; nothing to harm .. if it don't draw westerly. (*OED*² s.v. westerly *adv.*, 1) [*OED*² s.v. breeze *n.*², 3b. Slang phrases: . . . *to get (have) or put the breeze up* . . .] | 1893 *Temple Bar Mag.* XCVII. 21 It don't concern you who takes up the bets. (*OED*² s.v. take, *v.*, , B. 93h) | 1896 *Warwickshire Gloss.*, This teapot don't teem well. (*OED*² s.v. teem, *v.*² Chiefly *dial.* and *techn.*, 1c) | 1896 B. L. Farjeon *Betrayal J. Fordham* iv. 299 It don't make black white, 'cause I'm a wrong 'un. (*OED*² s.v. wrong 'un *slang*, 2) [*OED*² s.v. cause, 'cause, *conj.*

Diachrony of the Third Person Singular Present *Don't*

Obs. exc. *dial.* 2. "Since *c*1600 often written *'cause*; now only *dial.*, or *vulgar*; also spelt *cos, coz, cuz, case,* etc."] | 1897 'Ouida' *Massarenes* xxxii, 'One don't pipe one's eye when one comes into a fortun'", said the wheelwright. (*OED²* s.v. pipe, *v.*¹, 7 "*to pipe one's eye or eyes* (orig. *Naut. slang*; 1789→): to shed tears, weep, cry") | 1897 Kipling *Capt. Cour.* i, Old man's piling up the rocks. Don't want to be disturbed I guess. (*OED²* s.v. rock, *n.*¹, 2e. *U.S. slang . . . to pile up the rocks,* to make money.) | 1897 R. Stuart *In Simpkinsville* 110 The little talkin' machine inside it has got out o' fix .. an' it don't say 'papa' an' 'mama' any more. (*OED²* s.v. talking, *ppl. a.*, 2a . . . *talking machine* (chiefly *U.S.*)) | 1897 Kipling *Capt. Cour.* i, 'The West don't suit her. She just tracks around with the boy and her nerves, trying to find out what'll amuse him, I guess'. (*OED²* s.v. track, *v.*¹, 3a; 1590→; Now *U.S. slang*) | 1899 R. Whiteing *No. 5 John St.* ix. 94 What price grammar? It don't seem to teach people to keep a civil tongue in their 'ead. (*OED²* s.v. price, *n.*, B. 6) [what price. . .? (*BrE, informal*) (*LDCE⁵*)] | 1900 *Daily News* 6 Nov. 9/1 The prisoner .. said, 'It don't matter whether I get a sixer or a stretch'. (*OED²* s.v. sixer *colloq.*, 2 *slang* "Six months' hard labour. Also, six month' imprisonment") [*OED²* s.v. stretch, *n.*, 7. *slang.* b. "A term of hard labour; twelve months as a term of improsonment [*sic*]"] | 1900 *Eng. Dial. Dict.* (S. Nott.), 'A dont like pluckin this fowl; it's all pen-feathers'. (*OED²* s.v. pen-feather, 2)

<American English> 1877 B. Harte *Story of Mine* 85 That .. don't fetch me even of he'd chartered the whole shebang. (*OED²* s.v. shebang, *N. Amer. slang*, 1b) | 1878 Mrs. Stowe *Poganuc P.* iii. 24 Come to heft him, tho', he don't weigh much 'longside o' Parson Cushing. (*OED²* s.v. heft, *v.*¹, 2) | 1878 Mrs. Stowe *Poganuc P.* i, He don't believe in keeping none of them air prayer-book days. (*OED²* s.v. them, *pers. pron.*, B. 5 "As demonstr. adj. = THOSE. Now only *dial.* or *illiterate*", a) | 1885 Howells *Silas Lapham* (1891) I. 65 I'll be the death of that darkey .. if he don't stop making on such a fire. (*OED²* s.v. make, *v.*¹, 90a) [*OED²* s.v. darky, darkey, 1.

Chapter II

slang] | 1888 *Gd. Words* 470 You see stranger .. Uncle Sam don't care a dime for you and me being robbed, but it's a cussedly different thing, touching the mails. (*OED²* s.v. cussed, *a.* "orig. *U.S.* . . . Vulgar pronunciation of CURSED") | 1890 *Dialect Notes* I. 69 When it rains and wets our old rooster, He don't look like he useter. (*OED²* s.v. useter . . . Repr. an informal or uneducated pronunc. of *used to*) [*OED²* s.v. rooster Chiefly *U.S.* and *dial.*] | 1892 J. C. Duval *Early Times in Texas* vi. 82 'Well, I declar, boys,' said he, 'ef this don't beat all natur.' (*OED²* s.v. nature, *n.*, 13d, "*all nature*, everything, everyone, all creation . . . *U.S. colloq.*") | 1892 *Dialect Notes* I. 211 *Wallop*, .. 'My food don't set well. I kind o' wallop it up.' (*OED²* s.v. wallop, *v.*, Add: 7 *dial.* and *colloq.*) | 1893 *Harper's Mag.* Feb. 458 Jest so it don't tas'e hoppy, I ain't pertic'lar; but from hoppy bread deliver me! (*OED²* s.v. hoppy, *a.*[1], 1) | 1896 Ade *Artie* xiv. 129 I'll bet that guy up in your place don't know nothin' on earth except how to hold down his measly job. (*OED²* s.v. hold, *v.*, 35c . . . orig. *U.S. colloq.*) [*OED²* s.v. measly, *a.*, 4. *slang*. Poor, contemptible, of little value] | 1898 E. N. Westcott *David Harum* 14 Mis' Perkins don't hev much of a time herself. (*OED²* s.v. time, *n.*, 6)

k. 1901-1925

<Non-vulgar>

<British English> 1921 J. Buchan *Path of King* xiv. 276 It's curious that a man who don't use tobacco or whisky should be such mighty good company. (*OED²* s.v. use, *v.*, 11a(b)) [John Buchan, 1st Baron Tweedsmuir]

<American English> 1910 Churchill *Mod. Chron.* iii. x, It don't amount to shucks, as we used to say in Missouri. (*OED²* s.v. shuck, *n.*[2], Chiefly *dial.* and *U.S.*, 2) | 1913 J. London *Valley of Moon* I. x, Honest to God, Saxon, he don't like all his horses as much as I like the last hair on the last tail of the scrubbiest of the bunch. (*OED²* s.v. honest, *a.*, 4d) | 1916 *San Francisco Call & Post* 28 Nov. 12 'Don't Mr. Jenks know a lot of people?' 'They're all phonies.' (*OED²* s.v. phoney,

Diachrony of the Third Person Singular Present *Don't*

phony, *a.* and *n.*, B. *n.*) | 1919 F. Hurst *Humoresque* 184 So
many times it comes up in the scenarios and the picture-
plots .. how money don't always bring happiness. (*OED²* s.v.
scenario, *n.*, 1b) | 1923 L. J. Vance *Baroque* xxvii. 174 [It]
don't listen reasonable to me. (*OED²* s.v. listen, *v.*, 4. . . . *U.S.*)

<Source of Author/Text Unidentified>   1924 A. J. Small *Frozen
Gold* i. 14 A fight, he says—and he don't know what a mouthful he's said. (*OED²* s.v. mouthful, b. . . . *to say a mouthful*, to
make a striking or important statement . . . *colloq.* (orig. *U.S.*)

<Vulgar / Informal>

<British English>   1909 J. Masefield *Tragedy of Nan* i. 21 You
better watch out she don't tread a thy corns. (*OED²* s.v. watch,
v., 4g) | 1910 *Punch* 9 Feb. 104/3 It don't look as if I'm goin'
to 'ave a job this arternoon. 'Owever, no matter. There's
always the work'us. (*OED²* s.v. always, *adv.*, 3) | 1911 *Cham-
bers's Jrnl.* Feb. 170/1 'Ought to prove a tidy job for us,
though,' he muttered with some anxiety, 's'long as she don't
take to submarinin' first.' (*OED²* s.v. submarine, *a.* and *n.*,
Hence, submarine, *v.*) | 1913 A. Lunn *Harrovians* ii. 31 'Is he
Irish?' 'He don't seem to know. Father who's pipped was
Irish. His mother's pipped too.' (*OED²* s.v. pip, *v.*³, *colloq.* or
slang, 2) | 1918 A. Huxley *Let.* 28 June (1969) 157, I only
hope that this letter will reach you, though your loss will not
be very great if it dont. (*OED²* s.v. do, *v.*, A, 2c) [Declared to
be vulgar in the *OED²* s.v. do, *v.*, A. 2cγ, where this quotation
is the eighth earliest example.] | 1904 in Eng. Dial. Dict. V.
506/2 Yer needn't come slawmin 'ere, for a don't believe yer.
(Notts.) (*OED²* s.v. slaum, *v. dial.*) [*OED²* s.v. yer¹ "repr. a
dial. or vulgar pronunc. of YOU"]

<Australian English / New Zealand>   1914 A. A. Grace *Tale of
Timber Town* xix. 88 Go on chiacking—poke borak—it don't
hurt me. (*OED²* s.v. chi-hike, *n.*, Hence chiacking, *vbl. n.*)
[*OED²* s.v. borak, *Austral.* and *N.Z. slang* . . . in *to poke (the)
borak*, to make or poke fun] | 1916 C. J. Dennis *Moods of
Ginger Mick* 89, I can see ole Ginger .. Grinnin' a bit to
kid 'is wound don't pain. (*OED²* s.v. kid, *v.*⁴ *slang*) | 1920 B.

Chapter II

Cronin *Timber Wolves* x. 185 Maybe they're all right, but it don't do to run risks. Tell some of them blobs they'll need to walk to Green Valley next time they get a thirst up, if they don't act reasonable. (*OED[2]* s.v. blob, *n.*[1], 3c. . . . *colloq.* and *slang* (chiefly *Austral.*))

<British Guyana English>   1914 W. J. Locke *Fortunate Youth* xiii, Lets 'em have it bing-bang in the eye. Don't he, Jane? (*OED[2]* s.v. bing, *n.*[3] and *int.*, Also, bing-bang *colloq.*)

<American English>   1902 A. H. Lewis *Wolfville Days* xi. 152 He don't own no real business to transact; he's out to have a heart-to-heart interview with the great Southwest. (*OED[2]* s.v. heart, *n.*, 51c) [transact . . . *formal* (*LDCE[5]*)] | 1903 G. S. Wasson *Cap'n Simeon's Store* v. 86 It don't look right for nobody .. to take and hang on to them tormented ole witchbridles so-fashion! (*OED[2]* s.v. so, *adv.* and *conj.*, B. 7a, so-fashion *adv.*, In this or that manner. *U.S. dial.*) [*OED[2]* s.v. ole, ol, *a.* A representation of a *colloq.*, *dial.*, and Black English pronunc. of OLD *a.*] [*OED[2]* s.v. witch, *n.*[2], c, witches bridle "an iron collar and gag formerly used as an instrument for torture in Scottish witch-trials"] [torment . . . *formal* (*LDCE[5]*)] | 1905 B. Tarkington *In Arena* 22 I'm going to clear this town of fraud, and if Gorgett don't wear the stripes for this my name's not Farwell Knowles! (*OED[2]*, s.v., stripe, *n.*[3], 1d, *pl.* A prison uniform . . . *U.S. slang*) | 1906 E. Dyson *Fact'ry 'Ands* v. 56 Come off! She don't look where I live. (*OED[2]* s.v. come, *v.*, B. 65c, *U.S. slang*) | 1906 H. Green *At Actors' Boarding House* 359 They're goin' to mix it up. The little un'll win out, see if she don't. My eye! dames is allus fightin'. (*OED[2]* s.v. mix, *v.*1h, Slang phr. . . . So *to mix it up*: to figh vigorously) [un, un[2], "dial. f. ONE *pron.*"] | 1909 *Sat. Even. Post* 1 May 5/1 He's an old dope, which he don't look like, or he's on. (*OED[2]* s.v. dope, *n.*, 3. *colloq.* (orig. *dial.*). A stupid person, a simpleton, a fool. Also (*U.S. slang*), a person under the influence of, or addicted to, some drug) | 1912–13 W. C. Handy *Memphis Blues*, Mr. Crump don't 'low no easy riders here. (*OED[2]* s.v. easy, *a.* and *adv.*, A. *Adj.*, 14c. *easy rider* (*U.S. slang*)) | 1914 *Sat. Even. Post* 4 Apr. 10/2 That kid don't want

no handouts. He gets setdowns. Yes, siree, bo; every time.
Setdowns in the kitchen. (*OED²* s.v. set-down, 3. *U.S. slang*)
[*OED²* s.v. bo, *n. slang*. Chiefly *U.S.*] | 1916 *Dialect Notes* IV.
278 Look at that mullet-head of a Sam Smith. He don't know
beans. (*OED²* s.v. mullet-head, 2) (*OED²* s.v. bean, *n*, 6e,
Slang phrases: *not to know beans* (U.S.)) | 1916 C. J. Dennis
Ginger Mick 28 Why don't ole England belt 'em in the slats?
(*OED²* s.v. slat, *n.*¹, 4c. *pl*. The ribs. *slang* (orig. and chiefly
U.S.) | 1920 'B. L. Standish' *Man on First* 127 It don't take
the shine off your little performance. You were there with the
berries. (*OED²* s.v. berry, *n.*¹, 1c. *slang* (*U.S.*). A dollar;..) |
1922 B. A. Colonna *Hist. Company B, 311th Infantry* 78 If he
did not sign he did not get paid and often when he does sign
he don't get paid. So 'sanferriens'. (*OED²* s.v. san fairy ann,
slang) | 1924 *Cosmopolitan* Nov. 104/2 It don't sound kosher
to *me*! (*OED²* s.v. kosher, *a. (n.)*, A. *adj.*, c. . . . *colloq.*)

<?American English> 1921 R. D. Paine *Comr. Rolling Ocean* vi.
105 He don't get by with his blow-hard stuff, but I'll have to
say he is entertaining. (*OED²* s.v. blow-hard, *a.* and *n. colloq.*
(orig. *U.S.*), A. *adj.*) [*OED²* s.v. get, *v.*, 64 get by . . . *colloq.*
(orig. *U.S.*)]

l. 1926-1950

<Non-vulgar>

<British English> 1942 H. C. Bailey *Dead Man's Shoes* xiv. 63
'A new married man with a lovely wife spends half the night
with a police inspector he meets by chance! That's not the
stuff to give the troops.' .. 'No, it don't sound natural.' (*OED²*
s.v. stuff, *n.*¹, 7f. *that's the stuff (... to give the troops)*: that is
what is particularly appropriate to the situation, that is what is
required.) | 1946 A. Uttley *Country Things* v. 64 He loves me.
He don't. He'll have me. He won't. He would if he could, But
he can't. (*OED²* s.v. love, *v.*¹, 2d) | 1947 'N. Shute' *Chequer
Board* 4 She don't half carry on about the beer I drink. (*OED²*
s.v. carry, *v.*, 52e)

<American English> 1926 F. Scott Fitzgerald *Great Gatsby* ix.
209 It just shows you, don't it? .. Jimmy was bound to get

Chapter II

ahead. (*OED²* s.v. show, *v.*, 25d) | 1937 *Sun* (Baltimore) 28 Apr. 6 (Advt.), Now Mike don't be calling *me* a panty waist. (*OED²* s.v. panties, *n. pl.*, 3b. . . . panty-waist *U.S.*, (*a*) a sissy, a coward) | 1938 J. Stuart *Beyond Dark Hills* iii. 59 John's got a bad boy. He'll go to the pen if he don't mind out—that boy will. (*OED²* s.v. mind, *v.*, 10d) [*OED²* s.v. pen, *n.*¹, 2c. A prison; a cell in a prison. orig. *U.S.*] | 1938 E. Pound *Let.* 9 Jan. (1971) 305 If letter via *Criterion* don't reach him, I will indaginare his ubicity. (*OED²* s.v. ubicity *rare*. Whereabouts) [Nakamura was not able to identify the Modern spelling of 'indaginare'.] | 1941 L. G. Blochman *See You at Morgue* (1946) ix. 61 Don't your Old Lady make gefüllte fish any more for Shabbath dinner? (*OED²* s.v. gefüllte fish)

<Vulgar / Informal>

    <British English> 1932 Wodehouse *Hot Water* vi. 112 Back home .. a cop .. don't hardly even notice it if you sock him on the beezer. (*OED²* s.v. beezer, 2. . . . Nose. *slang*) [*OED²* s.v. cop, *n.*⁵, *slang*] | 1933 D. L. Sayers *Murder must Advertise* x. 165 That don't prove nothing. .. Not without you know 'ow long it took Mr. Tompkin to shoot 'is mouth off. (*OED²* s.v. shoot, *v.*, 23g. *slang* (orig. *U.S.*). *to shoot off one's mouth* to talk indiscreetly or abusively, . . .) | 1936 J. Curtis *Gilt Kid* ii. 23 She don't do so bad, I should cocoa. (*OED²* s.v. cocoa, *v.* "In phr. *I should cocoa* (Rhyming slang), I should say so. Freq. used ironically." | 1939 H. G. Wells *Holy Terror* i. ii. 41 Seems he don't like the idea of this new war that's coming. .. *We* had a dose. (*OED²* s.v. dose, *n.* , 2b) | 1939 *What Immortal Hand* xiv. 151 If she's gone and got herself tangled up with a lot of rye mushes she don't want to have nothing to do with a gaol-bird like me. (*OED²* s.v. rye, *n.*³ *slang*. . . . rye mush, a gentleman.) | 1950 A. Baron *There's no Home* i. 16 'It don't 'alf pong,' he observed. (*OED²* s.v. pong, *v.*² *colloq.*) | 1950 A. Baron *There's no Home* v. 57 This ol' street may niff a bit, but it don't smell as bad as the water out of polluted wells. (*OED²* s.v. niff, *v.*² *slang*)

    <?Australian English> 1944 K. Levis in Murdoch & Drake-Brockman *Austral. Short Stories* (1951) 423 Some nitwit of a

Diachrony of the Third Person Singular Present *Don't*

loot's in charge that <u>don't</u> know a bush track from Pitt Street. (*OED²* s.v. loot, *n.³ U.S. Mil. slang*, Shortened from Amer. pronunciation of LIEUTENANT) [*OED²* s.v. nitwit, *colloq.* A stupid person, a person of little intelligence.]

<American English> 1926 *Flynn's* 16 Jan. 638/2 Some <u>stiffs</u> <u>uses</u> <u>mud</u> but <u>coke</u> <u>don't</u> need any <u>jabbin'</u>, <u>cookin'</u>, or flops. You can hit it <u>an'</u> go. (*OED²* s.v. jab, *v. colloq.* or *dial.*, e. . . . So jabbing *vbl. n. slang* (orig. *U.S.*)) ?[stiff = *a., n.,* and *adv.*, 4. *slang.* a. A penniless man; a wastrel] ?[mud = *n.¹*, 2d. Opium. *U.S. slang*] [coke = *n.²*, Slang (orig. *U.S.*) abbrev. of COCAINE (in its use as a drug)] | 1928 C. McKay *Home to Harlem* vi. 56 Jake is such a fool <u>spade</u>. <u>Don't</u> know how to handle the <u>womens</u>. (*OED²* s.v. spade, *n.²*, 3a. . . . *slang* (orig. *U.S.*)) | 1929 W. Faulkner *Sound & Fury* 49 He <u>don't</u> like that rissy dress. (*OED²* s.v. prissy, *a. (*and *n.) colloq.* (orig. *U.S.*)) | 1929 W. D. Edmonds *Rome Haul* ii. 24 Jeepers! A cat would <u>n't</u> stand <u>no</u> show at all. *Ibid.* 30 Spinning swore. 'I'll bet that's right. <u>Jeepers</u> Cripus! How can they expect us to help a marshal if he <u>don't</u> let us know who he is?' (*OED²* s.v. jeepers, *int. slang* (orig. *U.S.*)) | 1931 W. Faulkner *Sanctuary* xvii. 156 If it was a <u>stall</u>, <u>dont</u> common sense tell you I'd have invented a better one? (*OED²* s.v. stall, *n.²*, 4a. . . . *slang*) | 1932 W. R. Burnett *Silver Eagle* i. 7 'He <u>don't</u> even pack a <u>heater</u>.' '<u>Don't</u> what?' 'He <u>don't</u> carry a gun.' (*OED²* s.v. heat, *n.*, 12b. *slang* (orig. *U.S.*) . . . also *heater*) [*OED²* s.v. heater, 1b. *slang*. A gun] | 1934 J. M. Cain *Postman rings Twice* vi. 59 A thing like that <u>don't</u> happen to a dumb <u>cluck</u> like him every day. (*OED²* s.v. cluck, *n.*, 5. *U.S. slang*) | 1934 M. C. Boatright *Tall Tales from Texas* 30 He's a good-natured bird and <u>don't</u> git <u>ringy</u> about it. (*OED²* s.v. ringy, *a.¹*, 2. *N. Amer. slang*) [*OED²* s.v. git, *slang*] | 1935 D. Lamson *We who are about to Die* xi. 193 Witnesses, juries, pay-off, fixin's—<u>don't</u> matter what it is. .. There <u>ain't</u> <u>nothin'</u> he won't do, <u>long as</u> you got the potatoes. (*OED²* s.v. pay-off, 2) | 1936 M. Mitchell *Gone with Wind* i. i. 11 <u>Don't</u> it look to you <u>like</u> she would <u>of</u> asked us to stay for supper? (*OED²* s.v. look, *v.*, 10a. . . . *(it) looks like.* it seems likely (*colloq.*, chiefly *U.S.*)) [*OED²* s.v. like, *a.*,

Chapter II

adv. (conj.), and *n.*[2], B. *adv.* (quasi-*prep.*, *conj.*), 6. "Used as *conj.*: = 'like as', as. Now generally condemned as vulgar or slovenly, though examples may be found in many recent writers of standing." | 1938 M. K. Rawlings *Yearling* ii. 17 Why, you leetle ol' penny piece, you. You're good money, a'right, but hit jest don't come no smaller. Leetle ol' Penny Baxter. (*OED*[2] s.v. penny, B. 12) | 1938 E. Pound *Let.* 6 May (1971) 313 'Sardinia is Barbagia' don't seem either English or Wop. (*OED*[2] s.v. wop, *n.*[2] and *a. slang* (orig. *U.S.*), A. *n.*, b. The Italian language) | 1939 J. Steinbeck *Grapes of Wrath* ii. 14 A guy that never been a truck skinner don't know nothin' what it's like. (*OED*[2] s.v. skinner[1], 7. . . . *N. Amer.*) | 1939 J. Steinbeck *Grapes of Wrath* xx. 371 Sheriff gets seventy-five cents a day for each prisoner, an' he feeds 'em for a quarter. If he ain't got prisoners, he don't make no profit. .. This fella today sure looks like he's out to make a pinch one way or another. (*OED*[2] s.v. pinch, *n.*, 1d) [*OED*[2] s.v. fella, fellah, "representing an affected or vulgar pronunciation of FELLOW *n.* 9] | 1940 R. Chandler *Farewell, my Lovely* xxxvi. 276 It stands to reason that he had an in with the city government, but that don't mean they knew everything he did or that every cop on the force knew he had an in. (*OED*[2] s.v. in, *n.*, 3a) | 1943 *N.Y. Times* 9 May ii. 5/6 He's got a band that don't need a five o'clock needle like some other bands. (*OED*[2] s.v. needle, *n.*, 3b(b) . . . *slang* (orig. *U.S.*)) | 1945 T. Shor in Mencken *Amer. Lang.* (1948) Suppl. II. 695 A square don't know from nothin' and a creep is worse'n a jerk. (*OED*[2] s.v. know, *v.*, 1b(b) Phrases: . . . *(not) to know from nothing* (*U.S.*): to be totally ignorant (about something)) [*OED*[2] s.v. square, *n.*, 16. Slang uses] [*OED*[2] s.v. creep, *n.* 1d. A stealthy robber; a sneak thief; esp. one who works in a brothel. *Criminals' slang.* (orig. *U.S.*).] [jerk, *n.*[1], 5. *slang.* (orig. *U.S.*). Someone of little or no account; a fool, a stupid person] | 1946 S. J. Perelman in *New Yorker* 5 Jan. 21/3 Our nineteen-year-old son, which he's home from Yale on his midyears and don't suspicion that his folks are rifting. (*OED*[2] s.v. suspicion, *v. dial.* and *colloq.* (orig. *U.S.*), a) | 1947 A. Miller *All my Sons* i. 12 Now go out,

Diachrony of the Third Person Singular Present *Don't*

and keep both eyes peeled. .. A policeman <u>don't</u> ask questions. Now peel <u>them</u> eyes! (*OED²* s.v. peel, *v.*¹, 3e. *to peel one's eyes*. to keep one's eyes peeled) [*OED²* s.v. peeled, *ppl. a.*¹, 4b. *fig*. Of the eys: Open, on the alert: in phr. *to keep (one's) eyes peeled*. *colloq*. (orig. *U.S.*)] | 1949 N. Algren *Man with Golden Arm* 60 He *wants* to carry the <u>monkey</u>, he's <u>punishin'</u> <u>hisself</u> .. <u>'n</u> <u>don't</u> even know it. (*OED²* s.v. monkey, *n.*, 14b. . . . hence *monkey* = addiction to, or habitual use of, drugs. *slang*)

<Source of Author/Text Unidentified> 1946 K. Tennant *Lost Haven* (1947) i. 15 A man <u>what</u> <u>don't</u> profit from all a woman's telling and hiding the bottles <u>ain't</u> worth the trouble. (*OED²* s.v. do, *v.*, A, 2c) [Declared to be vulgar in the *OED²* s.v. do, *v.*, A. 2cγ, where this quotation is the latest example.]

m. 1951-1975

<Non-vulgar>

<British English> 1951 J. B. Priestley *Festival at Farbridge* i. ii. 55 Oh phooey, Benny. .. This <u>don't</u> count as a drink. (*OED²* s.v. phooey, *int. (n.)*) | 1960 *News Chron*. 16 Feb. 6/6 She <u>don't</u> want to stand rabbiting away about colourful <u>denizen</u>s. (*OED²* s.v. rabbit, *v.*¹, 6) [denizen ". . . *formal* or *humorous*" (*OALD⁸*)] | 1960 J. Stroud *Shorn Lamb* v. 56 'Dear mr mall,' it said '.. if she says she <u>don't</u> want donald, we will have him, yours respectfully.' (*OED²* s.v. respectfully, *adv.*, b)

<Australian> 1953 T. A. G. Hungerford *Riverslake* vi. 130 'Sling, Stefan!' When the Pole looked at him <u>uncompre-hending</u>ly Murdoch whipped a ten-pound note out of the bundle and handed it to the ring-keeper. 'He <u>don't</u> know,' he explained. 'It's the first time he's played.' (*OED²* s.v. sling, *v.*¹, 9) [uncomprehending "*formal*" (*OALD⁸*)]

<New Zealand> 1960 N. Hilliard in C. K. Stead *N.Z. Short Stories* (1966) 241 He's East Coast, he <u>don't</u> know the *hapus* up our way. (*OED²* s.v. hapu)

<American English> 1960 A. Lomax *Folk Songs N. Amer.* 257 I'll eat when I'm hungry and drink when I'm dry, If moonshine <u>don't</u> kill me, I'll live till I die. (*OED²* s.v. moon- shine,

Chapter II

n., 4)

<Vulgar / Informal>

   <British English>   1958 G. Barker *Two Plays* 18 'Why won't he come?' 'Simply because he <u>don't</u> want to.' '<u>Fair enough</u>. Fair enough. Let's get the dinghy.' (*OED²* s.v. fair, *a.* and *n.²*, A. *adj.*, 10f) [fair enough . . . *informal, especially BrE* (*LDCE⁵*)] | 1968 E. McGirr *Lead-lined Coffin* ii. 51 Joe Silverman <u>don't</u> like <u>his neck being breathed down</u>. <u>Nossir</u>. (*OED²* s.v. nossir, Chiefly *U.S. colloq.*) [breathe down sb's neck ". . . *informal*" (*OALD⁸*)] | 1973 'B. Mather' *Snowline* vi. 75 Watch it. .. The Swami <u>don't</u> dig <u>taking the mike out of</u> the gods. (*OED²* s.v. mike, *n.⁶*. In slang phr. *to take the mike out of* = to take the micky out of) | 1974 M. Ingate *Sound of Weir* viii. 62 'Would you say that he is very feeble?' 'Stronger than he lets on if you ask me. He <u>don't</u> need <u>t'</u> walk like that.' (*OED²* s.v. let, *v.¹*, 36a) | 1974 Wodehouse *Aunts aren't Gentlemen* xvii. 145 'Nasty slinking-looking <u>bleeder</u>.' .. 'He <u>don't</u> half <u>niff</u>.' (*OED²* s.v. niff, *v.² slang. intr.* To have a disagreeable smell) [*OED²* s.v. bleeder, 3. *low slang.* A very stupid, unpleasant, or contemptible person]

   <?British English>   1958 R. Storey *Touch it Light in Plays of Year* XVIII. 376 *Ted.* That farmer <u>don't</u> like us, sir. Ever since that bomb fell on his cowshed. *Og.* He thought it should have fallen on you? *Syd.* It <u>had our name on it</u> all right. (*OED²* s.v. name, *n.*, 1g) [have your/sb's name on it ". . . *informal*" (*OALD⁸*)] | 1962 G. Callingford *Third Party Risk* iii. 42 Might buy <u>'erself</u> .. brushed nylon if she <u>don't</u> fancy the see-through. (*OED²* s.v. see-through, *a.* and *n.*, B. *n.*, 2) | 1974 P. Cave. *Mama* (new ed.) x. 80 It makes you realise what a <u>pissy</u> little island we live on, <u>don't</u> it? (*OED²* s.v. pissy, *a. coarse slang*)

   <Australian English>   1951 Cusack & James *Come in Spinner* iv. 32 If people <u>have got any tickets on themselves</u>, Blue <u>don't</u> get <u>nowhere</u> with them. (*OED²* s.v. ticket, *n.¹*, 5c "*to have tickets on oneself* and varr. . . . *Austral. slang*")

   <Trinidad English>   1952 S. Selvon *Brighter Sun* viii. 157 Look at <u>yuh</u>, <u>yuh</u> nasty dog! <u>Yuh</u> suspect she horning <u>yuh</u>! <u>Yuh</u>

Diachrony of the Third Person Singular Present *Don't*

ain't have no shame? Dat poor gul don't even look at any odder man but you. (*OED²* s.v. horn, *v.*, 2)

<Guyana English> 1958 J. Carew *Wild Coast* iii. 44 He don't have juice in his back to fill up a mopsy with delight. (*OED²* s.v. mopsy, 2)

<American English> 1952 E. Ferber *Giant* xx. 334 You want to look out, Bick, she don't get tromped the way they're milling around today. (*OED²* s.v. tromp, *v.*) [tromp "*NAmE, informal*" (*OALD⁸*)] [mill around/about (sth) . . . *informal* (*LDCE⁵*)] | 1955 W. Gaddis *Recognitions* ii. i. 308 His analyst says he's in love with her for all the neurotic reasons in the book. It don't jive, man. (*OED²* s.v. jive, *v.*, *slang* (orig. *U.S.*) 1b) | 1962 'K. Orvis' *Damned & Destroyed* ix. 61 My boss don't go for guys that goof like that. So he bounced me fast. I'm through pushing. (*OED²* s.v. pushing, *vbl. n.*, a) [goof ". . . *informal, especially NAmE*" (*OALD⁸*)] | 1967 W. Murray *Sweet Ride* x. 168 He got busted last week and he don't take that too kindly. Guess he figured you was heat. (*OED²* s.v. heat, *n.*, 12b, *slang* (orig. *U.S.*)) | 1967 C. Major in A. Chapman *New Black Voices* (1972) 299 How come so many Of us niggers Are dying over there In that white Man's war They say more of us Are dying Than them peckerwoods & it just Don't make sense. (*OED²* s.v. peckerwood, b, *slang*) | 1968 A. Young in A. Chapman *New Black Voices* (1972) Drew's got an alto [horn]... Drew dont hardly touch it, he too busy woodsheddin his drums. (*OED²* s.v. woodshed, *v. Mus. slang*) | 1969 C. Burke *God is Beautiful, Man* (1970) 29 If he don't come back his old man will get sick and kick off too. (*OED²* s.v. kick, *v.*¹, 11. kick off. c. "To die. *slang* (orig. *U.S.*)") | 1969 C. Burke *God is Beautiful, Man* (1970) 80 And it don't really make no difference if you're one or two. 'Cause with God, you're always number one. (*OED²* s.v. number, *n.*, 5d) [*OED²* s.v. cause, 'cause, *conj. Obs.* exc. *dial.* 2. "Since *c*1600 often written *'cause*; now only *dial.*, or *vulgar*; also spelt *cos, coz, cuz, case*, etc."] | 1970 R. D. Abrahams *Positively Black* ii. 45 I'm one motherfucker that don't mind dying. (*OED²* s.v. mother, *n.*¹, 17a, mother-fucker *coarse slang* (orig. and chiefly *U.S.*),

Chapter II

a base, despicable person) | 1972 J. Gores *Dead Skip* (1973)
viii. 52 White meat don't turn me on. I got Maybelle and four
cute kids to home. (*OED²* s.v. home, *n.*[1] and *a.*, A. *n.*, 14. to
home. *dial.* (also *U.S.*) = At home] [*OED²* s.v. white meat,
whitemeat, 2. *slang.* (chiefly *U.S.*). White women considered
as sexual partners or conquests] [*OED²* s.v. turn, *v.*, 75. turn
on. c. To excite, interest, fill with enthusiasm; to intoxicate
with drugs, to introduce to drugs; to arouse sexually. . . . *slang*
(orig. *U.S.*)] | 1972 G. V. Higgins *Friends E. Coyle* xviii. 108
She don't own no pants. .. Wears them panty hose. (*OED²* s.v.
panties, *n. pl.*, 3) [*OED²* s.v. them, *pers. pron.*, B. 5. As
demonstr. adj. = THOSE Now only *dial.* or *illiterate*] | 1972 J.
S. Hall *Sayings from Old Smoky* 133 'His head is full of
stump water.' That is, 'He don't use his brain.' .. Possibly
'stump water in the head' meant originally that the person had
been affected by magic, that is, was 'teched in the head', or
dazed. (*OED²* s.v. stump, *n.*[1], 19. stump water *U.S.*) | 1973
Guardian 14 Apr. 10/3 Chuck Berry don't drink either but he
gets hopped. (*OED²* s.v. hopped, *a.*, 2a. Stimulated by, or
under the influence of, a narcotic drug. . . . *U.S. slang*)

<Source of Author/Text Unidentified> 1973 *Time Out* 2–8 Mar.
13/2 Nah, she don't know. (*OED²* s.v. nah². a representation
of a colloq. or vulgar pronunciation of NO *adv.*³)

n. 1976-

<Vulgar / Informal>

<British English> 1984 A Carter *Nights at Circus* iii. i. 199 Not
that the 'wagon salon' isn't very pleasant, if it don't give you
the willies. (*OED²* s.v. willies, *n. pl. slang* (orig. *U.S.*) | 1985 I.
Handl *Sioux* vii. 90 You, Ouisti, y'all will got to hold it naow,
Grand M'sieu he don't stop for nothing on the road. (*OED²*
s.v. naow, *adv.*[1] [Repr. colloq. or vulgar pronunc.] | 1991 M.
Kilby *Man at Sharp End* 261 'Well it's fairly obvious that
you can't go back to the plant, innit?' agreed his platinum
blonde flatmate Deirdre. 'Well I mean to say . . it stands to
reason like .. don't it?' she added. (*OED²* s.v. mean, *v.*[1], Appended from Additions 1997, 1h; *I mean to say*: used paren-

Diachrony of the Third Person Singular Present *Don't*

thetically or as an exclamation, usu. to emphasize the speaker's sincerity or concern. *Brit. colloq.*) [*OED²* s.v. innit, vulg. form of *isn't it*]

<²Jamaican English>   1978 *Observer* 21 Aug. 11/1 The police are simply the sharp and visible end of 'Babylon': white society and all its frustrations. 'There is nothing going on that is right,' said Derrick. 'Babylon <u>don't</u> really have <u>nothing</u> to offer <u>I</u>.' (*OED²* s.v. Babylon, *n.*, Appended from Additions 1993, 2. *Black* (chiefly *Jamaican*) *English.... spec.* the police, a policeman; (white) society or the Establishment)

<American English>   1976 'Trevanian' *Main* (1977) x. 205, I warn him, but he <u>don't</u> listen. And you .. tell me he's got himself <u>reamed</u>. (*OED²* s.v. ream, *v.*³, Appended from Additions 1993, 5a; *U.S. coarse slang*)

2.2.2.3. Syntactic and Stylistic Properties of the Third Person Singular Present *Don't* in the *OED²*

Upon analysis, 3SG *don't* users appear to have conveniently favoured a personal pronoun as the subject (Table 22), and 3SG *don't* occurred in various clause types (Table 23). In addition, 3SG *don't* seems to have had no bias towards a particular type of verbs or constructions (Table 24). Evidently, 3SG *don't* occurred almost exclusively in declarative sentences. Interrogative 3SG *don't* occurred in 14 examples, half of which were used in tag-questions (Tables 25 and 23). Notably, 3SG *don't* occurred even at the non-vulgar speech level before the mid-19th century. After *don't* was replaced by *doesn't* during the second half of the 19th century, 3SG *don't* developed up to the early 20th century, when it was finally established at the vulgar or non-standard speech level in British English. In American English, 3SG *don't* not only has been used in vulgar speech, but also seems to have been a residual form even in non-vulgar English (Table 26). The syntactic and stylistic properties of 3SG *don't* in *OED²* quotations are almost identical as those in diaries and letters which are presented in 2.2.1.3. (pp. 40-42).

Chapter II

Table 22 Subjects of 3SG *Don't—OED²*

Subject of 3sg *don't*	1651-1675	1676-1700	1701-1725	1726-1750	1751-1775	1776-1800	1801-1825	1826-1850	1851-1875	1876-1900	1901-1925	1926-1950	1951-1975	1976-	Total
personal pronoun		2	3	1	4	1	6	15	20	35	23	21	19	4	154
demonstrative pronoun						1		3	4	2		2			12
indefinite pronoun *one*							1		1	1					3
substantive	1	1	5	3	4	5	1	6	10	13	8	16	12	1	86
wh-clause (nominal relative *who*)							1		1						2

Table 23 Types of Clause in which 3SG *Don't* Occurred—*OED²*

Type of the clause in which 3sg *don't* occurs	1651-1675	1676-1700	1701-1725	1726-1750	1751-1775	1776-1800	1801-1825	1826-1850	1851-1875	1876-1900	1901-1925	1926-1950	1951-1975	1976-	Total
in conditional *if*-clause		1	1	1	2	2	3	5	8	6	2	3	3	1	38
in the subordinate clause introduced by	1	3	1	1	1	3	2	4	3	5	5	2			31
the other subordinate conjunction;						(1)									(4)
nominal *that*;		(1)	(2)				(2)	(1)		(1)		(1)	(1)		(9)
nominal *if*;									(1)		(1)				(2)
adverbial *that*;			(1)	(1)	(1)					(1)	(1)				(5)
relative clause								(1)	(1)	(1)	(1)	(2)	(4)	(1)	(11)
in superordinate clause	1	1	4	2	6	3	3	14	24	41	24	30	25	3	181
in the tag								3		1		1	1	1	7

Table 24 Types of Verb Co-occurring with 3SG *Don't—OED²*

Type of the verb co-occurring with 3sg *don't*	1651-1675	1676-1700	1701-1725	1726-1750	1751-1775	1776-1800	1801-1825	1826-1850	1851-1875	1876-1900	1901-1925	1926-1950	1951-1975	1976-	Total
intransitive verb		1	4	1	4	3	2	8	18	26	13	15	12	2	109
intransitive verb omitted		1						1			1			1	4
transitive verb	1	1	3	3	5	3	7	13	18	24	15	20	18	2	133
transitive verb omitted				1				2		1	2	4	1		11

Table 25 Types of Sentence in which 3SG *Don't* Occurred—*OED²*

Type of the sentence in which 3sg *don't* occurs	1651-1675	1676-1700	1701-1725	1726-1750	1751-1775	1776-1800	1801-1825	1826-1850	1851-1875	1876-1900	1901-1925	1926-1950	1951-1975	1976-	Total
in the declarative sentence	1	3	8	4	9	6	9	20	36	50	28	35	30	4	243
in the interrogative sentence								4		1	3	4	1	1	14

Diachrony of the Third Person Singular Present *Don't*

Table 26   Speech Level of Sentence in which 3SG *Don't* Occurred—*OED²*

		1651-1675	1676-1700	1701-1725	1726-1750	1751-1775	1776-1800	1801-1825	1826-1850	1851-1875	1876-1900	1901-1925	1926-1950	1951-1975	1976-
Without vulgar words	BrE		3	5	3	4	2	3	6	8	12	1	3	3	
	?BrE			2		1					1				
	Austral. / NZ									1				2	
	Nova Scotia								4						
	AmE					1	1		3	6	9	5	5	1	
	?AmE										1				
	Unidentified						2	2		1		1			
?Vulgar / ?Informal	BrE							1	2	4					
	Nova Scotia								1						
	AmE									1					
	Unidentified							1							
With vulga/informal words	BrE			1	1	2		1	1	7	17	6	7	5	3
	?BrE	1											3		
	Austral. / NZ											3		1	
	?Austral.												1		
	Nova Scotia								1						
	Trinidad														
	Guyana											1	1		
	?Jamaican														1
	AmE					1		1	4	8	11	13	22	13	1
	?AmE												1		
	Unidentified						1		2				1	1	

Sources of Tables 22-26: Nakamura (2013: 23-24)

2.3. Summary of Chapter II

Based on the diachronic analyses of *doesn't* and 3SG *don't* samples collected from not only 130 volumes of diaries and correspondence but also the *OED²*, the following conclusions can be drawn, as far as written documents are concerned:

(27) a. Usage of 3SG *don't* was superseded by *doesn't* in the course of the second half of the 19th century. Until that time, the construction was not confined to vulgar English. Partridge (1953b: 258) states that 3SG *don't* was "common in good speech until 18th C, but now regarded as vulgar." "18th", however, should be altered into "19th".

b. The usage of 3SG *don't* was acceptable even in non-vulgar English until the end of the 19th century. *Doesn't* took more than 150 years to be accepted, despite its first written occurrence in 1674. Even educated people naturally resorted to the non-contracted form of *does not* or to 3SG *don't* until the wide acceptance of *doesn't* around

Chapter II

the mid-19th century.

c. There were no syntactic environments unique to 3SG *don't*, except for two following cases: 3SG *don't* occurred predominantly with the personal pronoun subject *he/she/it*, almost exclusively in the declarative sentence.

d. Relative to the rise of *doesn't* around the mid-19th century, 3SG *don't* began to be stigmatised as a vulgar and informal usage, developing in that direction up to the early 20th century, when it was finally established at the "vulgar" (*OED²* on CD-ROM, s.v. do. *v.*, 2c) or "non-standard" (Denison 1998: 195) speech level, or "current" "conversational grammar" (Biber, *et al.* 1999: 1123).

e. In American English, the usage of 3SG *don't*, which was brought about by immigrants in the early 17th century, developed roots as a normal usage. Mencken (1919 [1977]: 542), for example, states that the negative contraction of *do* was usually *don't*, and that *doesn't* was seldom heard. Among Southerners, he continues, 3SG *don't* rose "to the level of cultured speech". Trask (2004: 199) also writes that "the form *doesn't* scarcely exists in vernacular speech" in west New York. Thus, it was a century later, i.e. in the course of the second half of the 20th century, that *doesn't* was established (Bloomfield and Newmark 1963: 26), except for Southern dialects and the west part of the State of New York (Mencken 1919 [1977]: 542; Trask 2004: 199). Perhaps Americans gradually became conscious of the components of *don't*.[6]

---

[6] Contrary to Mencken, who was born and reared in Baltimore, Maryland, I obtained divergent findings; *doesn't* seems to have commenced in use a little before the mid-19th century in the Eastern United States, in areas facing the Atlantic Ocean to the north-east of Baltimore, including the states of Massachusetts, New Jersey and New York. These areas are relatively close to Britain. The corpora were texts written between 1771 and 1920 now available electronically (Table A). Consisting of 194 different documents, such as autobiographies, essays, letters, novels, speeches and treatises, they were randomly selected and downloaded in October 2005 from the websites of various universities and organisations: The Constitution Society (http://

Diachrony of the Third Person Singular Present *Don't*

www.constitution.org/), Project Gutenberg (http://www.gutenberg.org/), University of Missouri-Kansas City (http://www.law.umkc.edu/) and University of Virginia (http://etext.lib. virginia.edu/). The earliest occurrences of *doesn't* and its variants in the corpora above seem to suggest that *doesn't* began to be used a little before 1850 in the Eastern United States (Table B). On the writers, see the information in Table C. In order to settle whose findings, Mencken's or mine, reflect the actual linguistic situation in 19th- and early 20th-century American English, further research on the history of the variation of *doesn't* and 3SG *don't* is needed.

Table A   American English Texts Examined now available electronically

Period	No. of documents	Corpus size	Writers including
18-2	11	5.59MB	B. Franklin, T. Jefferson, G. Washington
19-1	84	18.4MB	J. F. Cooper, N. Hawthorne, E. A. Poe, C. M. Sedgwick
19-2	46	384 KB	H. Alger, C. W. Chesnutt, A. Lincoln, F. R. Stockton
20-1	53	424 KB	B. T. Washington, E. Wharton

Table B   The Earliest Occurrences of *Doesn't* and its Variants in the Texts in Table A

Text	Functions of *doesn't*			
	DO	DV	QO	QT
1823 J. F. Cooper, *Pioneers*			1	
1835 C. M. Sedgwick, *Home*	1			
1841 J. F. Cooper, *Deerslayer*	24		1	
1845 E. Sargent, *Fleetwood*	3	1	1	
1868 H. Alger, *Struggling Upward*	1			
1899 W. Chesnutt, *The Bouque*	1			
1900 E. Wharton, *April Showers*	2			
1902 E. Wharton, *The Mission of Jane*				1
1905 E. Wharton, *The Best Man*	1			
1906 E. Wharton, *In Trust*	2			
1910 E. Wharton, *The Legend*	1			

76

Chapter II

f. *Doesn't* was rarely used in British English until the mid-19th century, and accordingly, this negative contraction was unnatural and unfamiliar to people who immigrated to the United States before that time. This seems to be one of the reasons why Americans continued to resort to 3SG *don't* as a normal usage, and consequently, employment of *doesn't* was postponed in American English.

Table C   Users of the Earliest Examples of *Doesn't* and its Variants in the Texts in Table A

James F. Cooper 1789-1851	born in Burlington, New Jersey; first major American novelist, author of the novels of frontier adventure known as the Leatherstocking Tales, featuring the wilderness scout called Natty Bumppo, or Hawkeye (http://global.britannica.com/EBchecked/topic/136268/James-Fenimore-Cooper)
Catharine M. Sedgwick 1789-1867	born in Stockbridge, Mass.; early American writer whose internationally popular fiction was part of the first authentically native strain of American literature. Sedgwick was a daughter of Theodore Sedgwick, lawyer, congressman, and later senator and judge of the state Supreme Court (http://global.britannica.com/EBchecked/topic/532171/Catharine-Maria-Sedgwick)
Epes Sargent 1813-1880	born in Gloucester, Mass.; well-known American author, editor, and psychical investigator; graduated from Boston Latin School and joined the editorial staff of the Boston Daily Advertiser (http://www.answers.com/topic/epes-sargent-1)
Horatio Alger 1832-1899	born in Chelsea, Mass.; one of the most popular American authors in the last 30 years of the 19th century and perhaps the most socially influential American writer of his generation; at Harvard University he distinguished himself in the classics and graduated in 1852 with Phi Beta Kappa honours (http://global.britannica.com/EBchecked/topic/14993/Horatio-Alger)
Charles W. Chesnutt 1858-1932	born in Cleveland, Ohio; first important black American novelist; principal (1880–83) of State Colored Normal School (now Fayetteville State University) (http://global.britannica.com/EBchecked/topic/109652/Charles-W-Chesnutt)
Edith Wharton 1862-1937	born in New York and died near Paris, France; American author best known for her stories and novels about the upper-class society into which she was born; came of a distinguished and long-established New York family; educated by private tutors and governesses at home and in Europe, where the family resided for six years after the American Civil War (http://global.britannica.com/EBchecked/topic/641481/Edith-Wharton)

Chapter III

Diachrony of Passival Progressive

Preceded by Animate/Human Subject:

A drunken boy was carrying (by our constable)[7]

3.1. Previous Studies and Purpose of the Present Chapter

Of the following syntactic homonyms available to express both passive and progressive ideas during the period surveyed, the passival progressive seems to have been the most prevalent until the passive progressive became established around 1820-50 (Nakamura 1998b: 3-15, 2008d: 46): (a) Passive progressive: *The house is being repaired*, (b) Passival progressive: *The house is repairing*, (c) *be* + Preposition + *-ing*: *The house is on (a, in,* etc.) *repairing*, (d) *be* + Past Participle: *The house is repaired*, (e) *be* + Preposition + Substantive: *The house is under repair*, (f) Active progressive: *The house is undergoing repairs*, (g) *The house is (up)on the point of / in the act of being repaired*, (h) *be becoming / getting / growing* PP: *The house is getting repaired*, and (i) Others: e.g. 1650 J. Evelyn, D9, III 14, having a mind to see *what doings was among the Rebells*. It is an accepted theory that the passive progressive came into existence and its use was accelerated partly through semantic and syntactic defects of active progressive with passive meaning *the house is building*. One of the restrictions on the passival progressive is that the subject was virtually limited to inanimate one. This chapter, however, seeks to demonstrate that the passival progressive with an animate or human subject was not as uncommon as has been believed and, accordingly, that this restriction on the subject seems not to have been strictly applied in usage.

---

[7] Chapter III is a revised and extended version of Nakamura (1989, 1991, 1998a, 2002). I would like to thank Peter Lang and Professor Jacek Fisiak, the publisher and the editor of Nakamura (2002) respectively. It was very kind of them to give me their permission and consent to reprinting this article with minimum alterations as Chapter III of the present monograph.

Chapter III

Some attention has been paid to the passival (or activo-passive) progressive with [+Animate or Human] surface subject. Poutsma (1919) seems to be the first to have defined the nature of the subject of the passival progressive as [-Human], although, interestingly, the description concerned was deleted in Poutsma (1926: ch. LVII "The Participles"). No one knows the reason for his deletion, but he might have had the same feeling as the present author. Quoting those two examples taken from 1666 Pepys and 1864-65 Dickens, he states as follows:

(28) It will have been observed that among the above quotations there are none in which the active present participle in a passive meaning is connected with a word denoting a person. The following are the only instances that have come to hand:

Coming home to-night, a drunken boy *was carrying* by our constable to our new pair of stocks. Pepys, Diary, 12/4, 66.

Being a boy of fourteen, cheaply *educating* at Brussels when his sister's expulsion befell, it was some little time before he heard of it. Dick., Our Mut. Friend, I, Ch. II, 21:

(Poutsma 1919: 133)
(deleted in Poutsma 1926: ch. LVII)

To this effect, Baugh (1951 [1976]: 353) remarks that the "subject was practically and virtually expected to be [-animate]". Visser (1973: 2017) emphasizes the scarcity of co-occurrence of the passival progressive with a human subject by means of a supplementary remark made after the quotation: "(exceptionally) with human beings as subject".[8] More recently, this view is supported by Denison (1993, 1998) and Rissanen (1999: 218), as shown in (29). While carefully writing that there is "a slight risk of circularity here, since only the most prototypical examples may be recorded as passival" in note 48 of his 1998 work, Denison states as in (29b):

(29) a. the 'passival' active is always used with an inanimate subject, or at

---

[8] It is quite unknown, at least to me, why Visser made such a supplementary remark only to the two citations taken from 1839 Lord Shrewsbury and 1850 Ch. Kingsley, since there are apparently more with this construction in his examples of the passival progressive (see (30) below).

Diachrony of Passival Progressive Preceded by Animate/Human Subject

least one that could not be mistaken as Agentive.

(Denison 1993: 390)

b. the surface subject is nonhuman or at least clearly nonagentive . . .

(Denison 1998: 149)

c. In Middle and Early Modern English the active progressive was used to express the passive . . . There is, in fact, little risk of confusion between the active and passive meaning (the transitive or the intransitive use), as the subject is normally animate in the former case and inanimate in the latter:)

(Rissanen 1999: 218)

From the references in the previous studies shown above, it is evident that an animate or human subject rarely co-occurred with the passival progressive in the history of English. This rarity is confirmed by the total number of examples grammarians have collected so far: for the construction with *be*, they have collected no more than 18 varieties of verbs (or 15 unless the quotations from 1908 A. Bennett, 1928 S. Maugham, 1937 M. Allingham and 1967 A. Wilson are regarded as instances of the present target structure) together with 19 (or 15) examples. For the use without *be*, they have discovered two further varieties of verbs. Their quotations appear chronologically in (30), though a few of them seems to be used in the active voice.[9]

---

[9] Out of the examples compiled by Visser through his strenuous efforts (1973: 2010-2019), the following types of quotations have been excluded because, in (a), the *ing*-forms seem to have been transferred to the participial adjective, as shown in the *OED²*; 'beholding' in (b) should be regarded as a variant of 'beholden', as shown in the *OED²*; the two participles in (c) can be appositive; 'taking' in (d) can be construed as a variant of 'taken'; 'getting' in (e) seems to be a verb of movement; 'blinding' in (f) seems to lack in passivity. Although the quotation (g) is a passival progressive, 'the horses' here stands for a coach [-animate]. Incidentally, Dryden's use of (e) and 'beholding' in (b) does not seem to be documented as the passival progressive in Söderlind (1951 [1973]: 74-101).

(a) 1340 *Ayenbite* 169, Asemoche ase he is wor betere þanne ich, zuo moche ich am yeldinde. | 1605 W. Shakespeare, *Macbeth* V. viii, 38, Macduff is missing. | 1847 W. M. Thackeray, *Vanity F.* 305, poor Amelia would be little wanting for company this day. | 1937 M. Allingham, *Dancers in Mourning*,

80

Chapter III

(30) Evidence in previous studies: a total of 18 (or 15) verbs together with
19 (or 15) instances

<With *be*>

*c*1475 Ordinances Household Edw. IV, whyles the Kinge specially
shal be asservinge [N.B._Nakamura to asserve "To serve, attend to (a
person)" (*OED²*, s.v. asserve, *v. Obs.*, 1a)] (Visser 1973: 2011) |
*c*1475 The Romans of Partenay, Anon After the preste were send-
ing, (Visser 1973: 2011) | 1523-5 Lord Berners, he was anoynt-
ynge. (Visser 1973: 2012) | 1663 S. Pepys, *Diary*, IV 101, a
drunken boy was carrying by our Constable to our new pair of
stocks (Aronstein 1918: 16) (Poutsma 1919: 133) | 1685 C. Cotton
(trans. of Montaigne, Essays), whilst he was whipping, (Visser
1973: 2013) | 1704-7 Earl of Clarendon, some regiments of foot

253, The young girl was missing for three days. | 1948 J. Tey, *The Franchise
Affair* 18, the girl had been missing for three weeks.
(b) 1470-85 Malory, *Wks.* 646, mesemyth ye ar muche beholdynge to this
mayden. | 1476-88 *Cely Papers* no. 15, The mor ys done for hym the mor ys
he beholdyng. | Ibid. no. 90, I am beheldyng to hym for hys labur. | 1482
Stonor, *Lett.* no. 306; 1565 Th. Stapleton, *A Fortresse of the Faith* 15; 1681 J.
Dryden, *Spanish Friar*, V. ii.; 1860 G. Eliot, *Mill on the Floss*, I, VI.
(c) *c*1400 *Visions of Tundale*, 522, Now he was in fyre brenand, And now in
colde ise fresand.
(d) *c*1475 *The Romans of Partenay* 1753, Many were slayn . . . The Ausoys
takying all And slayn don-right. | ibid. 4920, full faste thay fle, Thay sore
doubted lest taking [thay] should be.
(e) 1681 J. Dryden, *Spanish Fryar* II. i, In my conscience, when she was getting,
her mother was thinking of a riddle.
(f) 1937 M. Allingham, *Dancers in Mourning* 54, [apropos of a motor car ac-
cident:] 'I was blinding, you know,' he said suddenly. 'Didn't see her until I
was over her' | Ibid. 56, 'didn't you see her fall?'—'no, I keep telling you,'
Sutane sounded sulky. 'I was blinding. Naturally I was looking at the road.'. . .
'I tell you', Sutane was obstinate. 'I was blinding with my eyes on the road
and my mind on those damned invitations.
(g) 1852-53 C. Dickens, *Bleak House*, IV 153, entreating me to . . . refresh myself while the horses were making ready.
(h) 1393 W. Langland, *P. Pl.* C IX 103, he is holding, ich hope, to haue me in hus
masse. | 1465 *Paston Lett.* no. 510, I pray you lete hym be thankynde therfor.
In addition, the four examples in (30), which Visser collected from 20th-century
texts, also seem to be controversial, except that of 1909 J. Galsworthy.

were <u>levying</u> for his service. (Visser 1973: 2015) | 1724 D. Defoe, his native country, where <u>his children</u> <u>were</u> <u>breeding up</u>. (Visser 1973: 2015) | 1773 O. Goldsmith, <u>The horses</u> <u>are</u> <u>putting to</u>. (Visser 1973: 2015) | 1787 W. Beckford, or whether <u>she</u> <u>was</u> <u>taking</u> to account by some disappointed votary, (Visser 1973: 2015) | 1834 F. Marryat, <u>the shark</u> <u>was</u> <u>hauling</u> [= was being carried] on board. (Visser 1973: 2017) | 1839 Lord Shrewsbury, We must have a new race of <u>zealous English missionaries</u> such as <u>are</u> now <u>bringing up</u> at Oxolt. (Visser 1973: 2017) | 1847 C. Brontë, 'And the carriage?' '<u>The horses</u> <u>are</u> <u>harnessing</u>.' (Jespersen 1931: 207) | 1850 Ch. Kingsley, But <u>are</u> there <u>six labourers' sons</u> <u>educating</u> in the universities at this moment? (Visser 1973: 2017) | 1859 Dickens, <u>the jury</u> <u>were</u> <u>swearing in</u>; (Jespersen 1931: 208) | 1908 A. Bennett, How <u>is</u> <u>that Mrs. Gilchrist</u> <u>shaping</u> as a nurse? (Visser 1973: 2018) | 1909 J. Galsworthy, <u>Ye</u> <u>were not</u> <u>needing</u> to come for your wife, Mr Underwood. We are not rowdies. (Visser 1973: 2018) | 1928 S. Maugham, <u>My friend Brown</u> <u>was</u> <u>transferring</u> from the F.D. to the diplomatic service and had been promised a post at Lisbon. (Visser 1973: 2019) | 1937 M. Allingham, your man Lugg. <u>He</u> <u>is</u> <u>shaping</u> as well as can be expected. (Visser 1973: 2019) | 1967 A. Wilson, His Home Cinemas was going ahead, old Fison was recovering and, if he didn't <u>young Fison</u> <u>was</u> <u>rearing</u> to get in on the thing. (Visser 1973: 2019)

<without *be*>
1601 W. Shakespeare, women are angels <u>woing</u>. [= while they are being wooed] (1919 Poutsuma: 133) | R. B. Sheridan, I met a wounded peer <u>carrying off</u>. (Jespersen 1931: 208) | 1838-9 C. Dickens, as if he were some extraordinary wild animal then <u>exhibiting</u> for the first time. (Visser 1973: 2017) | 1864-65 C. Dickens, Being a boy of fourteen, cheaply <u>educating</u> at Brussels when his sister's expulsion befell, (1919 Poutsuma: 133)

However, the problem is that almost the same number of instances as discovered so far has been encountered in the present texts examined, as shown in 3.2. Even though people could avail themselves of the active voice, without the passival progressive it would have been inconvenient

Chapter III

for verbs tending to take an animate or human object only, such as *educate*, *fat* "To make fat, fatten; usually, to feed (animals) for use as food . . . *to fat up*" (*OED²* s.v. fat *v*. 3. *trans*.), *nurse* "To wait upon, attend to (a person who is ill)" (*OED²* s.v. nurse *v*. 5a), *plague* "In weakened sense (chiefly *colloq*.). a. To 'torment', trouble, vex, tease, bother, annoy" (*OED²* s.v. plague *v*. 2), *put to* "To attach (a horse, etc.) to a vehicle" (*OED²* s.v. put, *v*.[1] 53, put to †c. *trans*. (c)), and *wean* "To accustom (a child or young animal) to the loss of its mother's milk; to cause to cease to be suckled. a. with obj. a child. . . . b. with obj. a young animal" (*OED²* s.v. wean *v*. 1 *trans*.). When these newly-discovered examples are taken into account, the generalisation about the restriction on the subject of the passival progressive seems to be sweeping. Thus, 3.2. attempts to unveil the history of the passival progressive preceded by an animate or human subject to demonstrate that this usage was not rare in the history of English.

3.2. Presentation of Examples

A transitive verb, depending on the verb itself or under a certain meaning of the verb, can take either a [±animate], [+animate & -human], [+human], [+animate or +human], or [-animate] noun as an object. Under each category excepting the last, examples of the passival progressive are exemplified below.[10]

---

[10] The following types of quotations have been excluded because, in group (a), the meat is referred to rather than the animal itself; 'the horses' in (b) stand for a coach; in (c) a book written by the man is referred to rather than the man himself; in group (d) 'the Navy' and 'the fleet' are considered as a single undivided body [-animate] rather than a collection of individuals:

(a) 1796 A. Hughes, D20, 50, after the hare hav been cookeing 1 hower and a half; | 1801 D. Wordsworth, D24, 58, We walked out while the Goose was roasting— | 1821 A. Watkin, D30, 93, Went in the evening to look at the ox and sheep which were roasting at Salford Cross. | 1874 F. Kilvert, D36, II 405, this gigantic spit was turned round while the ox was roasting whole.

(b) 1834 J. Skinner, D25, 491, whilst the horses were getting ready for our return to Camerton, Boodle taught me some of the moves of the Chess men with which I was unacquainted, . . .

(c) 1922 Lady Gregory, D42, I 327, But Methuselah is selling very well in-

Diachrony of Passival Progressive Preceded by Animate/Human Subject

3.2.1. Verbs Taking [±Animate] Prototypical Object

As shown in (31a), the *OED²* shows that the phrasal verb *put to* had a transitive use with 'a horse, etc.' ([+animate]) or, in transferred use, 'an engine' ([-animate]) as an object. (31b) makes up its passival progressive:

(31) a. "To attach (a horse, etc.) to a vehicle (cf. 10e); *trans.* (an engine) to a train."

(*OED²* s.v. put, *v.*¹ 53. put to †c. *trans.* (c), 1768→1862)

[Cf. To harness (a draught animal) *to* a vehicle; to place *in* the shafts of a cart, etc. (Ibid. 10e, 1565→)]

b. 1821 P. Hawker, D29, I 213, he offered us coffee, and showed us his very handsome house &c. while the horses were putting to.

Similarly, it is possible for *educate* to take both human (32a, b, c, e) and animate (32d) objects and inanimate objects (32e). (33) is a passival progressive of *educate* with a prototypically human object.

(32) a. "To bring up (young persons) from childhood, so as to form (their) habits, manners, intellectual and physical aptitudes."

(*OED²* s.v. educate v. 2, 1618→)

b. "To instruct, provide schooling for (young persons)."

(Ibid. 2b, 1588→)

c. "To train (any person) so as to develop the intellectual and moral powers generally."

(Ibid. 3, 1849→)

d. "To train (animals)."

(Ibid. 4b, 1850→)

---

deed especially in America, and I told him he must go to lecture there.
(d) 1673 R. Southwell, L8, I 34, His Majesty and R. H. returned this day from the Navy, which is refitting as fast as may be; some say they may require a fortnight's time to be in order. | 1673 R. Yard, L8, I 43, Whilst the fleet is refitting at the buoy of the Nore, . . . | 1673 H. Ball, L8, I 115, his Majesty, Royall Highness, my Lord Arlington, Mr. Speaker, and divers persons of quality, went down to the fleete, which has been ever since fitting out, . . .

Chapter III

e. "To train, discipline (a person, a class of persons, a particular mental or physical faculty or organ), so as to develop some special aptitude, taste, or disposition. Const. *to*, and *inf.*"

(Ibid. 4, 1841-4→)

(33) 1825 J. Skinner, D25, 282, <u>a number of young men</u> <u>are</u> now <u>educating</u> for the priesthood.

Further examples are listed in (34).

(34) <with *be*>

a. 1660 Pepys, L5, 19, There was one sent to mee this morning from Sir Anthony Cooper to lett mee know that <u>severall</u> <u>were</u> <u>putting in</u> for your Lordships lodgings, and that hee did desire to know your intentions concerning them, whether to keepe them or part with them.

b. 1667 S. Pepys, D10, VIII 98, Great preparations there are to fortify Sheernesse and the yard at Portsmouth, and <u>forces</u> <u>are</u> <u>drawing</u> down to both those places, and elsewhere by the seaside.

c. 1680 R. Josselin, D8, 631, <u>we</u> <u>were</u> <u>gathering</u> [= were being caused to assemble in one place] for the captives of Algiers, god blesse our worke.

d. 1773 J. Wedgwood, L32, 142, <u>Holland</u>, who <u>has been</u> some years <u>training up</u> as a fireman, Glosser, Color man, Plinther, Packer, &c &c, left us on Thursday and begun to pack ware on his own account to travel the Country with as a Hawker.

e. 1808 J. Austen, L64, 210, Mrs. Tilson's remembrance gratifies me, & I will use her patterns if I can; but poor Woman! how <u>can</u> <u>she</u> <u>be</u> honestly <u>breeding</u> again?—I have just finished a Handkf. for Mrs. James Austen, . . .

f. 1820 J. Skinner, D25, 146, whilst <u>the horses</u> <u>were</u> <u>changing</u> at Cross Hands I made the best of my way to the camp . . .

g. 1836 C. Darwin, D34, 424, All the fragments of the civilized world, which we have visited in the southern hemisphere, all appear to be flourishing; <u>little embryo Englands</u> <u>are</u> <u>hatching</u> in all parts.

Diachrony of Passival Progressive Preceded by Animate/Human Subject

<without *be*>[11]
h. 1689 J. Evelyn, D9, IV 622, Forces <u>sending</u> to Ireland, that K<ing>-dom being in great danger, <u>by</u> the E. of Tyrconnells Armie, . . .

3.2.2. Verbs Taking [+Animate, -Human] Prototypical Object

The verb *bait* "To give food and drink to (a horse or other beast), *esp.* when upon a journey; to feed" (*OED²* s.v. bait *v¹* 5. *trans.*, 1375→) takes exclusively an animate and non-human object excepting figurative uses. The examples in (35a) represent the passival progressive of *bait* with a prototypically [+Animate, -Human] object. Likewise, the verb *fat* "To make fat, fatten; usually, to feed (animals) for use as food. Also *to fat up*" (*OED²* s.v. fat *v.* 3. *trans.*, 13..→) basically requires that an animate and non-human object should best follow it, although it can take an inanimate object under the *OED²*'s definition 5 ('to enrich (the soil) with nutritious and stimulating elements; to fertilize') since 1562.

(35) a. 1813 P. Hawker, D29, I 82, While <u>the tandem horses</u> <u>were</u> <u>baiting</u> I hired a post horse . . . | 1817 J. Skinner, D25, 101, Whilst <u>the horse</u> <u>was</u> <u>baiting</u> we called upon Mr. Griffith, . . . | 1823 J. Skinner, D25, 245, While <u>the horses</u> <u>were</u> <u>baiting</u> at Wells we had time to visit the cathedral and the exterior of the Bishop's palace, . . . (Cf. 1832 J. Skinner, D25, 441, At Blagdon we stopped to <u>bait the horses</u>, . . .)

b. 1782 J. Woodforde, D21, II 44, Mr. Custance told me this morning that he had a few Days ago <u>about 80 Turkies, geese, Ducks, and Fowls</u> stolen from [him] in one night—many of <u>them</u> that <u>were fat-ting</u>.

The verb *bait* also has an intransitive use: 'Said of horses or other beasts: To take food, to feed, *esp.* at a stage of a journey' (*OED²* bait *v.¹* 6. (*refl.*

---

[11] The quotation below has been excluded because 'tearing' is not a progressive participle without *be*. The underlined part is thought of as meaning 'a hedgehog which was pulled asunder by force'.

1875 F. Kilvert, D36, III 212, He said scalps with hair still on them were left lying about and that he himself had seen <u>a hedgehog</u> <u>tearing</u> at the arm of a body which still had flesh upon it.

86

Chapter III

and) *intr.*, c1386→). When Skinner's practice as quoted under "Cf." in (35a) is taken into consideration, however, the prototypical construction of 1817 and 1823 J. Skinner in (35a) is understood to be *We were (²I was) baiting the horse(s)*. The quotation in (35b) exemplifies the passival pro-gresssive, not the active progressive with the intransitive use 'grow or become fat' (*OED²* s.v. fat *v.* 2. *intr.* a1225→), since Woodforde refers to many of the turkeys, geese, ducks and fowls that were being fattened or raised by Mr Custance so that they could be used for food.

3.2.3. Verbs Taking [+Human] Prototypical Object

The verb *plague* "In weakened sense (chiefly *colloq.*). a. To 'tor-ment', trouble, vex, tease, bother, annoy (*OED²* s.v. plague *v.* 2, 1594→)" takes nothing but a human object. The example in (36a) represents a pas-sival progressive of *plague* with a prototypically [+Human] object. Simi-larly, (36b) is an example of the passival progressive of the verb *nurse* "To wait upon, attend to (a person who is ill) (*OED²* s.v. nurse *v.* 5a, 1736→)", which takes exclusively a human prototypical object.

(36) a. 1828 J. Skinner, D25, 326, The workmen are plaguing and, if spoken to, insolent. (Cf. 1828 J. Skinner, D25, 327, but I am satisfied, if Skuse does not plague me . . .)

b. 1843 S. Pamer, L48, I 419, and I wish I could come to Bayswater to witness the happiness of you all—but I am nursing to regain health for tomorrow— . . .

Evidently, (36a) is not an active progressive because, according to the *OED²*, the verb *plague* itself has neither intransitive use nor participial adjective use. Nor is (36b) an active progressive with the intransitive use 'To perform the duties of a sick-nurse.' (*OED²* s.v. nurse *v.* 5c. *intr.*, 1861→).

Similarly, the verbs *enlist, indulge, muster* and *pour*, the definitions concerned of which are listed in (37a-d), take a prototypically human ob-

Diachrony of Passival Progressive Preceded by Animate/Human Subject

ject. The quotations in (38a-d) make up their passival progressives.[12]

(37) a. To enrol on the 'list' of a military body; to engage as a soldier.
    (*OED²* s.v. enlist *v*. 1. *trans.*, 1698-9→)

b. To give free course to one's inclination or liking; to gratify oneself, take one's pleasure. Const. *in* . . .
    (*OED²* s.v. indulge *v*. 1. *transitive* b. *refl.*, 1659→)

c. To collect or assemble (*primarily* soldiers) for ascertainment or verification of numbers, inspection as to condition and equipment, exercise, display, or introduction into service. . . .
    (*OED²* s.v. muster *v*.[1] 2. *trans.*, c1420→)

d. *transf.* and *fig.* To send forth as in a stream; to send forth, emit, discharge copiously and rapidly. a. With material object: To send forth (persons) in a stream (also *refl.*); to discharge in rapid succession or simultaneously, as missiles; to cause (money or any commodity) to flow or pass in a constant stream; to bestow profusely.
    (*OED²* s.v. pour *v*. 3, 1599→)

(38) a. 1854 H. W. Greville, D32, II 146, But, alas! we are ill able to afford such victories, and our army has need of double the number of its present exhausted, harassed, and overworked force. The press is now crying out for reinforcements, and every available man is being

---

[12] These four verbs also have an intransitive use, which makes matters complicated:

a. To have one's name inscribed in a list of recruits; to engage for military service. Also *transf.* and *fig.*
    (*OED²* s.v. enlist *v*. 4. *intr.* for *refl.*, 1776→)
b. (ellipt. for *indulge oneself in*, 1b): To give free course to one's inclination for; to gratify one's desire or appetite for; to take one's pleasure freely in (an action, course of conduct, etc., or a material luxury). . . . Also with *indirect passive*.
    (*OED²* s.v. indulge *v*. intransitive. 7. *indulge in*, 1706→)
c. Of an army, etc.: To come together for inspection, exercise, or preparation for service.
    (*OED²* s.v. muster *v*.[1] 2c. *intr.* for *refl.*, c1450→)
d. *transf.* and *fig.* Of persons or things: To run or rush in a stream or crowd; to come or go in great numbers, continuously, or in rapid succession; to stream, to swarm.
    (*OED²* s.v. pour *v*. 7, 1573-80→)

Chapter III

sent off. Recruiting and volunteering are going on with great enthusiasm; <u>150 men</u> per day <u>are</u> <u>enlisting</u> at Liverpool alone.

b. 1857 H. W. Greville, D32, III 47, <u>Lord Ellenborough</u> <u>has been</u>
<u>indulging</u> in unfair and unseemly attacks upon the Indian Govern-
ment, offering absurd advice, and advancing facts without foundation.

c. 1864 S. Palmer, L48, II 712, People have a notion, gorgeous and
glowing like those leaves you 'lifted off,' of a moral millennium just
beginning to rise softly like summer dawn. A curious time for it,
when almost all the periodical press is *influentially* . . . infidel, and
<u>the powers of good and evil</u> <u>are</u> even now <u>mustering</u> for the battle.

d. 1854 H. W. Greville, D32, II 152, It is probable that the terms of
this treaty will, when known, disappoint the public, but on the Ex-
change it was believed that peace would be signed in three months,
and that it was impossible the Emperor could hold out against all
the great Powers of Europe. It is reported that Prussia has adhered to
this treaty. <u>Reinforcements</u> <u>are</u> <u>pouring</u> into the Crimea—where . . .
nothing has been done on either side beyond entrenching and forti-
fying their respective positions. | 1861 H. W. Greville, D32, III 373-
374, Absolute war has broken out between North and South; all
communication by post or telegraph is suspended. Maryland, which
has hither . . . been considered loyal to the Government, has seceded.
A murderous onslaught was made in Baltimore . . . on the troops
going through to Washington. These were New England regiments
and a large body of Pennsylvanians—the latter unarmed, expecting
to find their accoutrements in Washington. Of course this has ex-
cited a tempest of rage and indignation throughout the North.
<u>Troops</u> <u>are</u> <u>pouring</u> into Philadelphia night and day, and are now
being despatched by sea to Washington instead of through Balti-
more.

The two quotations in (39a), though lacking in the form of the verb
be, can be regarded as pertaining to the passival progressive, since the verb
hang means (39b), not (39c):[13]

---

[13] In the following quotation, it is not clear whether Gill saw the very moment the

Diachrony of Passival Progressive Preceded by Animate/Human Subject

(39) a. 1673 J. Evelyn, D9, IV 21, His servant . . . seeing his Master hanging, brake in before he was quite dead, . . . | 1769 N. Nicholls, L26, III 1064, You remember the fifty men hanging by a rope . . .

    b. To fasten up or suspend on a cross or gibbet, as a mode of capital punishment; †a. formerly, *spec.* to crucify; b. now, *spec.* to put to death by suspension by the neck.

                                     (OED^2 s.v. hang *v.* 3, c1000→)

    c. Of a person: To be suspended *on* or *upon* a cross, gibbet, gallows, etc.; to suffer death in this way; esp. as a form of punishment. Also as an imprecation: cf. 3c [= 'To commit suicide by hanging']. Now usu. in phr. *to go hang*, to go and be hanged; to 'go to the devil' to be dismissed or rejected; freq. *let* (*it*, etc.) *go hang*.

                       (OED^2 s.v. hang *v.* 10 *spec.* a, c1000→)

3.2.4. Verbs Taking [+Animate or +Human] Prototypical Object

OED^2's sense 1 of *wean* requires that the object should be animate or human: "To accustom (a child or young animal) to the loss of its mother's milk; to cause to cease to be suckled. a. with obj. a child. . . b. with obj. a young animal." (OED^2 s.v. wean *v.* 1 *trans.*, a. c960→, b. 1481→). The quotation in (40) is its passival progressive, since the underlying construction is *Mrs. Jeanes is weaning Charlotte, her daughter*.

(40) 1791 J. Woodforde, D21, III 271, Sent Mrs. Jeanes, for her little puny Daughter Charlotte who is now weaning, a Spring Chicken this Evening by Briton.

3.3. Summary of Chapter III and Further Discovery

Tabulation of the data in (30), (31b), (33), (34), (35), (36), (38),

---

Loughnane boys were being hanged or Gill saw their dead bodies hanging or pendulous from the scaffold after the execution:

1920 Lady Gregory, D42, 211, He knew the Loughnane boys—"One of them may have been a bit in it, but the other was as innocent as myself. It is said they were hanged, and that Gill saw them hanging when he went in over the stile, but that he went back on it and was afraid to say it."

90

Chapter III

(39a) and (40) is represented in Table 27.[14]

Based on the evidence presented above in 3.2, it is likely that the usage of passival progressive with an animate or human subject was used by more different people including the educated and the upper class, and with more different verbs than has been believed, from around 1600 to 1820-50, when the passival progressive was superseded by the passive progressive (1.2.1.2.3 and Nakamura 1998b). This usage spread to the extent that it is not to be regarded as a mere idiosyncrasy or exception. At this point, the constraint involved in the passival progressive's decline will need to be reconsidered. Animate or human nouns could be agentive surface subject in some stages of English history to some extent, at least in informal and common English. Although a distinct line occasionally can hardly be drawn between transitive and intransitive verbs as indicated by the question marks in Table 27, it is still an undisputable fact that the passival progressive with an inanimate or human subject occurred far more often than has been thought. This frequency perhaps overwhelmed historical linguists such as Poutsma when he deleted the description of the subject constraints on the passival progressive in reproducing the description concerned from Poutsma (1919) into Poutsma (1926). It is quite reason-

---

[14] A few progressives with intransitive verbs might have been mixed among the citations above; especially, those of (34d, e, 38b-d) are questionable. I regret to recognise that those quotations are not easily categorised as being either of the active progressive or of the passival progressive. The verbs involved are those which can be transitive as well as intransitive. In such cases, context takes on even greater importance. Accordingly, an effort has been made to provide evidence to show that they seem to be the passival progressive in terms of context as well as *OED*[2]'s definition. After all, we would be able to add 18 (or 13) verbs, together with 21 (or 15) examples, to those 18 (or 15) verbs together with 19 (or 15) instances listed in (30) above which are copied from previous discoveries.

Incidentally, although 'taking' in the following quotation is a passival participle, it lacks the idea of progressiveness:

1867 M. Arnold, L53, 365, There was a great evening party afterwards, and Tom and his wife came. They put up the boys beautifully, and the pupils taking to them immediately, as young men generally do to boys, Tom and Dick were in great bliss.

Diachrony of Passival Progressive Preceded by Animate/Human Subject

Table 27　Occurrences of Passival Progressive with [+Animate/Human] Subject

a. With *be*

Verb	Previous studies	Nakamura	Verb	Previous studies	Nakamura
anoint	1		muster		1
asserve	1		need	1	
bait		3	nurse		1
breed up	1	1	plague		1
bring up	1		pour		$^?2$
carry	1		put in		1
change		1	put to	1	1
draw		1	rear	$^?1$	
educate	1	1	send	1	
enlist		1	shape	$^?2$	
fat		1	swear in	1	
gather		1	take	1	
harness	1		train up		1
hatch		1	transfer	$^?1$	
haul	1		wean		1
indulge		$^?1$	whip	1	
levy	1				

Without *be*

carry off	1		hang		2
educate	1		send		1
exhibit	1		woo	1	

able for Denison (1998: note 48) to state that "the generalisation seems to hold good for a great many examples". But now it would seem that significant numbers of counterexamples have been presented.

　　In this regard the construction of the passival progressive followed by a *by*-agent should be mentioned here. As shown in (41a, b), this con-

Chapter III

struction has been rare in the history of English; previous studies show that only five examples have been discovered with this construction, including the examples in (41c).

(41) a. The agent *by*-phrase rarely accompanied the passival progressive.

(Y. Olsson 1961: 176)

b. "In all instances of the passival, the agent would have been human if expressed (which, incidentally, it rarely is . . .)"

(Denison 1998: 149)

c. 1660 S. Pepys, *Diary*, I 113, they told us for certain that the King's statue *is making by* the Mercers Company (who are bound to do it) to set up in the Exchange. | 1807 J. Austen, *Letters*, 178, Our Garden *is putting* in order, *by* a Man who bears a remarkably good character, has a very fine complexion & asks something less than the first.

(Visser 1973: 2013)

To these five, however, 14 more verbs together with 21 more examples collected from the texts examined can be added. This usage was used even by the educated and the upper class such as Harriet Arbuthnot, John Evelyn, Thomas Gray, John Lowther, Samuel Pepys, James Woodforde and Robert Yard. Since the agent consisted of new information in 20 out of 21 instances, the writers had to put the agent towards the end of the sentence with the preposition *by* accompanying it. Here also the constraint on the passival progressive should be reconsidered. Some examples are shown in (42).

(42) 1662 J. Evelyn, D9, III 327, to see a new vessel building there by some of our Society. | 1698 J. Lowther, L12, 556, I have a scheem making by a great master, | 1711 D. Defoe, L14, 311, Of The Project Pushing on by Sir Pat. Johnston | 1788 R. Burns, L37, 85, you shall see them in print in the *Scots Musical Museum*— a work publishing by a friend of mine in this town. | 1820 H. Arbuthnot, D27, I 31, Castlereagh detailed to me in confidence the intrigues which have been recently carrying on by Wilberforce, by Lord Kenyon & by all the Saints to persuade the King to change his ministers | 1821 J. Skinner, D25, 161, to see the new Parsonage House building by Mr. Ham-

mond, | 1823 P. Hawker, D29, 269, Got to Keyhaven, and proceeded to Lymington to inspect two new punts <u>building</u> for me <u>by</u> Inman.

(Nakamura 2000: 26-31)

It is an accepted theory that the passive progressive came into existence through the ambiguity of the passival progressive; for example, Jespersen (1931 [1970]: 210), who looks upon the passival progressive with an animate or human subject as liable to be misunderstood in some combinations, and Scheffer (1975: 44). There are not so many progressives with an animate or human subject the status of which remains to be decided whether it is active or passive, however. Curiously enough, Scheffer (1975: 260-261) states quite to the contrary, in the very book referred to above, that "the old argument that they (one of them being the passival progressive) could cause ambiguity is conspicuously little supported by proof". The present author shares this opinion. It is not meaning but voice that can be ambiguous, and voice is a concern not of people in those days but of linguists.

The rareness of the co-occurrence of an animate or human subject with the passival progressive would not seem to be because this usage was unrecognised as part of grammar by people living between 1600 and 1820-50, but simply because it has been encountered with extreme infrequence.

Chapter IV

Diachrony of Participial Progressive: *Being Going*

It is described that the participial progressive, which first appeared in
Middle English, is clumsy and, in effect, very rare throughout the history
of the English progressive (Jespersen 1931 [1970]: 205; Poutsma 1926:
329; Visser 1973: 1955 & n. 1; Scheffer 1975: 22.2). In Samuel Pepys's
Diary, however, no less than 34 instances, or 4.8% of the whole use of the
progressive, have been discovered, as shown in (43). The simple participial progressive is the usual construction with 27+1 examples, and the perfective participial progressive is also found in 6 examples.

(43) a. *Being* + Verb-*ing*
  (i) Main clause + *ing*-clause
      1660 S. Pepys, D10, I 302, And dined at home, where my father
      came and dined with me – who seems to take much pleasure to
      have a son that is neat in his house, I being now making my new
      door into the entry, which he doth please himself much with. |
      1661 S. Pepys, D10, II 14, And then was much troubled my wife
      was not come, it being ten a-clock just now striking as I write this
      last line. | 1661 S. Pepys, D10, II 128-29, This day the Portuguese
      Embassador came to White-hall to take leave of the King, he
      being now going to end all with the Queene and to send her over.
      | 1662 S. Pepys, D10, III 198, So to Deptford, and took my Lady
      Batten and her daughter and Mrs. Turner along with me, they
      being going through the garden thither. | 1662 S. Pepys, D10 III
      244, Lay pretty long in bed; and then up and among my workmen
      – the Carpenters being this day laying of my floor in my dining-
      room, | 1662 S. Pepys, D10, III 248-49, and to supper and bed,
      my pains being going away. | 1662 S. Pepys, D10, III 276, and
      there sat all the morning, Mr. Coventry and I alone, the rest being
      paying off of ships. | 1663 D10, IV 1, which I perceive I shall be
      able to do with great confidence, being now beginning to be pretty
      well-known among them. | 1664 S. Pepys, D10, V 280, Up; pretty

Chapter IV

well again, but my mouth very scabby, my cold being going away | 1666 S. Pepys, D10, VII 20, But we parted, resolving to meet here at night, my Lord Brouncker being going with Dr. Wilkins, Mr. Hooke, and others to Collonell Blunts | 1666 S. Pepys, D10, VII 70, There met Mr. Coventry coming out, going alone with the Commissioners of the Ordinance to the water-side to take barge, they being going down to the Hope. | 1666 S. Pepys, D10, VII 76, and after dinner we walked to the King's play-house, all in dirt, they being altering of the Stage to make it wider | 1666 S. Pepys, D10, VII 90, who is become a good serious man and I hope to do him good, being sending him a muster-maister of one of the squadrons of the fleet. | 1666 S. Pepys, D10, VII 108, And so back again alone to Hales and there met my wife and Mercer – Mrs. Pierce being sitting, and two or three idle people of her acquaintance more standing by. | 1666 S. Pepys, D10, VII 193, Thence to my Lord Bellaces to take my leave of him, he being going down to the North | 1666 S. Pepys, D10, VII 199, and there find my aunt Wight with my wife, come to take her leave of her, being going for the summer into the country. | 1666 S. Pepys, D10, VII 362, Thence home and with my brother to dinner, my wife being dressing herself against night. | 1666 S. Pepys, D10, VII 367, Creed and I did step [in] (the Duke of York being just going away from seeing of it) at Pauls, | 1666 S. Pepys, D10, VII 374, And so I delivered it to Mr. Chevins, and he to Sir W. Coventry in the Cabinet, the King and Council being sitting – where I leave it to its fortune, | 1667 S. Pepys, D10, VIII 37, The Parliament is not yet up, being finishing some Bills. | 1667 S. Pepys, D10, VIII 523, He desirous to get back into the House, he having his notes in his hands, the lawyers being now speaking to the point of whether treason or not treason. | 1668 S. Pepys, D10, XI 217, it puts me to great trouble and I know not how to get out of it, having no good excuse, and too late now to mend, he being coming home.

[Coordinated use]
1665 S. Pepys, D10, VI 278, And thither comes Sir Jer. Smith and Sir Chr. Mings to see me, being just come from Portsmouth and going down to the fleet.

Diachrony of Participial Progressive: *Being Going*

(ii) *Ing*-clause + main clause

1661 S. Pepys, D10, II 149, He <u>being</u> <u>going</u> with a venison in his panyards to London, I called him in and did give him his breakfast with me. | 1661 S. Pepys, D10, II 159, From thence about 2 a-clock to Mrs. Wheately's, but she <u>being</u> <u>going</u> to dinner, we went to White-hall and there stayed till past 3. | 1663 S. Pepys, D10, IV 181, But <u>being</u> <u>going</u> to bed and not well, I could not see him.

(iii) S + *ing*-clause + V

1664 S. Pepys, D10, V 347, because he, <u>being</u> now <u>beginning</u> to be called on offices, resolves not to take the new oath,

(iv) V+ *ing*-clause + S

1667 S. Pepys, D10, VIII 62, This morning came up to my wife's bedside, I <u>being</u> up <u>dressing</u> myself, little Will Mercer to be her Valentine. [Nakamura_This example can be in appositive use.]

b. *Having been* + Verb-*ing*

(i) Main clause + *ing*-clause

1660 S. Pepys, D10, I 99, he was then drunk, <u>having been</u> all night <u>taking</u> his leave at Gravesend the night before, | 1666 S. Pepys, D10, VII 53, and then my wife comes home, <u>having</u> <u>been</u> <u>buying</u> of things. | 1667 S. Pepys, D10, VIII 229, since which they have never been great friends, Pen <u>having</u> by degrees <u>been</u> continually <u>growing</u> higher and higher, | 1667 S. Pepys, D10, VIII 483, Here most of our discourse is of the business of the Parliament, who run on mighty furiously, <u>having</u> yesterday <u>been</u> almost all the morning <u>complaining</u> against some high proceedings of my Lord Chief Justice Keeling, | 1667 S. Pepys, D10, VIII 492, Sir W. Penn tells me he was gone to bed, <u>having</u> <u>been</u> all day <u>laboring</u>, and then not able to stand, of the goute.

(ii) *Ing*-clause + main clause

1662 S. Pepys, D10, III 180, And Will <u>having</u> <u>been</u> <u>making</u> <u>up</u> books at Deptford with other clerks all day, I did not think he was come home; but was in fear for him, it being very late, what was become of him.

Chapter IV

Tabulation of the data, presented in Tables 28 and 29, reveals that the position of the participial progressive relative to the governing clause is fairly fixed: the former tends to follow the latter, and that the verb of highest frequency is *go*.

Table 28   Occurrences of Participial Progressive in Pepys's Diary (D10)

a. *Being* + Verb-*ing*

SV - *being* Verb-*ing*	22+1
being Verb-*ing* - SV	3
S *being* Verb-*ing* V	1
V *being* Verb-*ing* S	1
Total	27+1

b. *Having been* + Verb-*ing*

SV - *having been* Verb-*ing*	5
having been Verb-*ing* - SV	1

Table 29   Verbs Used in Participial Progressive *Being* + Verb-*ing* in Pepys's Diary (D10)

go (12+1 times)
begin dress sit (2)
alter come finish lay make pay send speak strike (1)

It is uncertain why the construction in question was frequently used in Pepys's 'Diary. Ota (1956: 77), referring to Bergeder (1914), writes that it is due to the diary-style written while Pepys was busy. This may sound plausible in view of Pepys's diary-writing habit; about the composition of his diary, Matthews, one of the two editors of D10, infers in the Introduction to D10 (Latham and Matthews, p. xcvii-cvi) as follows:

(44) Much of the diary was written at Pepys's office, for secrecy as some have thought; but the diarist sometimes preferred to work on it in his home, and sometimes he did so elsewhere, abroad ship, in lodgings, in several places in the country. . . . The appearance of most of the manuscript, the regularity and even spacing of the symbols and lines, the straightness of the lines, the even colour of the ink over large sections,

Diachrony of Participial Progressive: *Being Going*

> the neat disposition of the daily entries on the pages, all suggest that
> this is in fact largely a fair copy. . . . The logic of these details suggests
> five possible stages in the composition of the diary. . . .

However, according to the same editor, Pepys "sometimes read over entries he had recently made in the diary-book and revised them." (Latham and Matthews, p. cii) Then the question is raised of why Pepys did not re-write the participial progressive into the verb-*ing* alone in this particular case, even though he could have done so. In this point Bergeder's is not thought to be a decisive view; instead, the construction now in question is far from an inadvertent expression resulting from his busy life. The present author would rather look at the matter in a positive way as described below.

As to the development of the participial adverbial construction, it is assumed that the participle used as the predicate appositive gradually came to be possessed of an adverbial function. This use was already established in Pepys's time. During 1660-1685 the so-called absolute participle reached maturity as an anglicised usage (Jespersen 1940 [1970]: 45-46). Naturally, it is frequently used in Pepys's diary. The advantages of the participial con-struction lie in the following aspects: it conveys the undifferentiated senses such as time-relation, causality, explanation, concession and condition, while the basic idea is that of attendant circumstances (Söderlind 1958 [1976]: Ch. XII). Being descriptive, a present participle employed as a predicate appositive is preferable to a usual finite clause and a gerund after a preposition except in cases where the logicality is lost, and makes the depiction more graphic and dynamic (Curme 1931: 258). Such impressive-ness being weighed, a loose participial construction is much more suitable for the addition of the idea of time-relation, explanatory specification and so on, than the fixed construction of a preposition + gerund or a finite clause in general. Therefore, in this particular case, a participial progres-sive clause is added after the governing clause in 82% of all the participial progressives in Pepys's diary (see Table 28a, b). Moreover, when the parti-cipial construction and the progressive are blended into one, the synthetic form, i.e. the participial progressive, conveys Pepys's dynamic connotation of the action in progress, the planned future event or the arrangement far

Chapter IV

better than the verb-*ing* alone. Because Pepys set these connotation before everything, he needed to use the participial progressive irrespective of such clumsiness stemming from successive participles as pointed out by Bolinger (1979).[15]

Thus far, Pepys's use of the participial progressive in D10 has been focussed. This usage is also encountered, however, in other diaries and letters written during the 17th-19th centuries. It is not Pepys's idiosyncrasy. As shown in (45), the form of *being* + Verb-*ing* occurred in 63+3 examples written by 20 different individuals (45a), and the form of *having been* + Verb-*ing* in 16 examples used by 10 individuals (45b).

(45) a. *Being* + Verb-*ing* (63+3 examples)

   1625 J. Glanville, D3, 93, But the Councell being now riseing made not anie order nor gave anie directions att all touching this busines. | 1630 J. Rous, D4, 55, About Michaelmas the king's Whelpe, that (as it seemeth) Lynne men had obteined this summer to garde theire fleete, being returning, tooke a Dunkerke by the way, | 1644 J.

---

[15] It is my simple query as a non-native speaker of English why the double participial *ing*-forms were felt to be clumsy in spite of the fact that those below could be evidenced in many examples. Phonetically, there seems to be little difference between *being going* (*to the work*) and, for example, *being willing* (*to do the work*).

1625 J. Glanville, D3, 106, The 12 shipps were his Ma[tes] shipp the Rainebowe, 3 of our horse shipps, 2 of our prizes (the third being missing) and 6 other shipps, | 1666 J. Milward, D6, 38, the bill had a second reading concerning giving directions to the country | 1667 J. Milward, D6, 114, from doing anything | 1667 J. Milward, D6, 116, in execution for preventing robbing by the high-way. | 1668 J. Milward, D6, 188, not having anything | 1668 J. Milward, D6, 190, the saying being taken notice of, | 1783 J. Woodforde, D21, II 65, Betty, my Upper Maid stayed at home being Washing Week. | 1790 J. Woodforde, D21, III 180, It being exceeding cold and windy, | 1793 J. Woodforde, D21, IV 77, It was rather beyond the Line of being pleasing. | 1793 J. Woodforde, D21, IV 88, It was charming walking this Morn' so very calm. | 1801 D. Wordsworth, D24, 62, through hurrying driving clouds | 1776 A. Smith, L30, 201, in as good order as it is capable of being during the continuance of that morbid state.

For some, the double consecutive use of *that* was not clumsy as in the following:

W. Wordsworth, D24, 212, W. Wordsworth's unpublished poem "Tinker", What is that that's coming?

Diachrony of Participial Progressive: *Being Going*

Evelyn, D9, II 162, Vaucluse so much renound for the solitude of the learned Petrarch, we beheld from the Castle; but could not goe to visite it, for want of time; being now taking Mules, & a guide for Marcelles: | 1645 J. Evelyn, D9, II 333-34, Being now approching the [hill] as we were able with our Mules, we alighted, | 1645 "A New Tricke to Take Townes, etc.", D5, 220, the walls of the Priory within Carbine shot of the Gate, being then standing gave an advantage there to lodge the Forlorne party of Fire-locks.

1673 J. Evelyn, D9, IV 22, being one day discoursing with him, | 1679 H. Savile, L11 (in a letter to Lord Ambassador Jenkins), 104, This is not onely the greatest but onely newes I can send y^r Ex^{cy}, who will pardon my brevity, beeing just taking coach for St. Germain's. | 1679 S. Pepys, L6, 88, Till which, as being just now going to attend his Majesty . . . I bid you farewell, | 1680 J. Evelyn, D9, IV 235-36, Came the *Duke of Norfolck* to visite me, and lay this Night at my house, being the next day going towards *Dover* & Embark for Flanders: | 1682 J. Evelyn, D9, IV 298, I gave Almighty God thanks for his gracious preservation hitherto, being now advancing in yeares apace: | 1683 S. Pepys, D11, 389, Up on my Lord's business and papers, and so on the quarter-deck. Finding my Lord going to send a ship before us to call at Cadiz, we being now, every hour, expecting to make the south Cape, I went down and wrote a letter to Mr. Gough there, | 1683 S. Pepys, D11, 431, The timber in Pole Fort, being now taking up, towards destroying the Fort, proves more rotten than it would in another place in a great deal longer timw. | 1687 J. Evelyn, IV 563, Our Viccar proceeded on his Text 119 *Psal*: 68 shewing the transitorynesse of all worldly things . . . being now going to his Living at London during the Winter: | 1690 J. Evelyn, D9, V 36, I then tooke leave of the Marquis de Ruvigny and his Mother, being myselfe leaving the Country to winter in London, with my family: | 1690 R. Davies, D13 141, I visited the Earl of Meath, and dined with Captain Stearn, that regiment being just going into the trenches to relieve Lieutenant-General Douglas; | 1694 W. Gilpin, L12, 127, The post being waiting for me I am forced to break off, and leav other matters to the next. | 1699 A. Charlett, Master of University College, Oxford, L7, I 173, I went to tell him that being going into the country, I must leave his grandson

Chapter IV

to keep house. | 1699 J. Jackson, L7, I 199, Not, I thank God, that this is like to be our case, the wind continuing in the same corner still, and I being just now (one a clock) going on board again, | 1699 J. Wallis, Savilian Professor of Geometry at Oxford, L7, I 188, Mr Glyd having been for some while with me, and being now returning to London, is willing to bring you a letter from me. | 1699 J. Wallis, Savilian Professor of Geometry at Oxford, L7, I 210, My daughter Blencow . . . tells me that, knowing nothing of the eclipse before, but being then writing a letter (about a-clock) finding the light of the sun look somewhat dim, looked out to see what the matter was, and found it to be an eclipse. | 1699 S. Pepys, L5, 281 (in a letter to J. Dryden), as being just stepping into the Ayre for 2 Days.

1701 J. Evelyn, D9, V 469, I also visit<ed> the Co: of Sunderland, Earle of Kent . . . and some other friends being myself preparing for the Country in few days: | 1701 J. Jackson, L7, II 182, I am in hopes it may, fireworks being certainly preparing in the Retiro, and triumphal arches for other places. | 1705 D. Defoe, L14, 105, they might live like Christians, Neighbourd, and Gentlemen with their Brethren who Differ in some Cases and not Two Partyes being Eternally Cutting One Anothers Throates on Chimeras of a Presbyterian Govornmt which I Dare Undertake to Convince Men of their sence and Candor No Dissenter in his witts Can Desire, | 1705 W. Nicolson, D15, 332, The Commons being Reading the Bill for the Land-Tax a third Time, the Lords waited for its comeing up till after four; | 1706 D. Defoe, L14, 160, The Gentlemen kept me So late the last post night that I Closed your Letter in Some Confusion, the post being just goeing Elce I had sent this paper back that night. | 1709 E. Young, L17, 194, he had received your Account, and being Just going out of Town Comanded me to acquaint you. | 1712 W. Nicolson, D15, 587, An Appeal being hearing, I left it; | 1749 G. B. Dodington, D16, 4, The same morning I receiv'd a very civil letter from Mr Pelham . . . acquainting me that he would come to me, on Monday the 13th, in the morning, before he went to Court, being then just going into the country.

1756 J. Hawkesworth, L24, 236, being then coming to do it, and though nothing had supervened that might justify his preventing Lodowick and le Noy from meeting, | 1777 S. Johnson, L61, II 14,

Diachrony of Participial Progressive: *Being Going*

This information, when I wrote, I could not give you; and being going soon to Lichfield, think it necessary to be left behind me. | 1779 J. Woodforde, D21, I 259, A Clergyman . . . went with me in the Diligence from Bath he being going to see a Friend at Weymouth | 1782 J. Woodforde, D21, II 22, he shall not be at Mattishall for the two first Sundays, being going from Home on Sunday on the above melancholy Occasion | 1783 J. Woodforde, D21, II 56, Advanced this Evening to Js. Smith, himself and Son being hedging and ditching for me 0. 10. 6. | 1785 J. Woodforde, D21, II 182, Jack went with me—Will being brewing. | 1785 J. Woodforde, D21, II 187, Will: Coleman dined with our Folks to day, he being here preparing the Vessels for brewing to Morrow. [Nakamura _?appositive] | 1785 J. Woodforde, D21, II 202, Colin Roupe told us that the Baloon which Major Money went up in, went 7 Leagues on the Sea, and that Major Money was 5 Hours up to his Chin in the Sea before he was taken up, and then by chance, a Boat very providentially being returning by him. | 1785 J. Woodforde, D21, II 203, Mr. Custance called on us this morning, stayed but a very short Time with us, being going to Peachmans | 1785 J. Woodforde, D21, II 204, Mrs. Davy also and Nancy vexed me rather to night, being going to Morrow to Norwich in Bucks Cart, and talking of buying such a Number of things for the House &c. &c. | 1785 J. Woodforde, D21, II 221, Supper being just going in for the Family I joined them, and there met with the best Supper I ever met with at an Inn. | 1787 J. Woodforde, D21, II 346, Soon after Dinner Nancy and Betsy Davy returned with Ben as they came to Witchingham to Mr. Jeanes's to spend a few days with Mrs. Jeanes, Mr. Jeanes being going to Norwich for 2 or 3 Days. | 1787 J. Woodforde, D21, II 351, None from Weston House, their Coach being mending. | 1790 J. Woodforde, D21, III 191, Mr. Love the Painter dined with our Folks to day in Kitchen, he being painting my Weather-cock. | 1790 J. Woodforde, D21, III 203, Mr. and Mrs. Custance are at present under great disagreeableness, Mr. and Mrs. Alldis, the Butler and Housekeeper being going away from the. | 1790 J. Woodforde, D21, III 218, Nancy did not make her Appearance being dressing. | 1790 J. Woodforde, D21, III 220, I sent a Note to Weston House this morning to desire the favour of Sir. Edmund and Lady Bacon, with Mr.

Chapter IV

and Mrs. Custance's Company to Tea this Afternoon, Sr. Edmd. being going away from Weston House to Morrow Morn'. | 1791 J. Woodforde, D21, III 253, but Nancy being dressing would not make her appearance. | 1791 J. Woodforde, D21, III 315, Mr. Mann called on me this Morning and as he cannot wait on me to Morrow, he being going to Gressenhall Fair then, paid me his Annual Composition for Tithe the Sum of 36. 10. 0. | 1793 J. Woodforde, D21, IV 39, At Reading there were two young Gentlemen by name Jolliffe taht got up on the top of the Coach, being going home from School for the Vacation. | 1793 J. Woodforde, D21, IV 84, We did not get out of our Carriage being going farther. | 1794 J. Woodforde, D21, IV 101, Mr. Carbould we met as we were going to Hungate-Lodge, he being going to Weston House. | 1794 J. Woodforde, D21, IV 112, Mr. Custance made us a Morning Visit to take his leave of us, being going to Bath very soon. | 1794 J. Woodforde, D21, IV 122, About 11. o'clock Mr. and Mrs. Jeans called here with her eldest Daughter, they being going to make Mrs. and Miss Mellish a Morning Visit. | 1796 J. Woodforde, D21, IV 272, Mr. Corbould overtook us near Mouses House and went with us, he being going to dine there. | 1796 J. Woodforde, D21, IV 272, we had to dress ourselves (being going to Mr. Mellish's to dinner) | 1796 J. Woodforde, D21, IV 275, Gave my Boy, Tim Tooley, being going to Norwich to Morrow to get some Cloaths 0. 5. 0. | 1796 J. Woodforde, D21, IV 288, Old Mr. Corbould soon after called on us, he came to take Leave, being going to Norwich in the Afternoon | 1796 J. Woodforde, D21, IV 299, Willm. Hardy & Brother James, Masons, being repairing Weston Chancel in the outside, I walked up to them about two o'clock and stayed there till near three, | 1799 J. Woodforde, D21, V 202, Mrs. Bodham, with a Mrs. Dade & Daughter from Yarmouth . . . went by our House this Morning in Mrs. Bodhams little Whiskey, their [*sic*] being going to dine at Boston with Mr. Dade who boards there.

1802 D. Wordsworth, D24, 106, I made a vow that we would not leave this country for G. Hill Sara and Tom not being going to the Wolds. | 1802 J. Woodforde, D21, V 377, Mr. Dade being going to Cambridge soon, desired me to get a supply for him if I could at Weston Church on Sunday April 4th or the 11th. | 1825 H. Arbuthnot, D27, what was meant by the report of a ship being preparing at

Diachrony of Participial Progressive: *Being Going*

Portsmouth to take the Duke to India.

[Coordinated use]
1707 D. Defoe, L14, 198, the Latter part will be worse than the beginning and I shall be Sincerely affraid of it, Severall of the Best men being gone or Goeing, Some into the Country, some to England. | 1793 J. Woodforde, D21, IV 36, No Service at Church to day, part of the Church being at present unroofed & undergoing repairs. | see also 1783 J. Woodforde, D21, II 56 on p. 103.

b. *Having been* + Verb-*ing* (16 examples)

1644 J. Evelyn, D9, II 199, we were conducted to the third heaven if any be on Earth, the famous *Mausoleum* or Chapel where the *Dukes* are Inhum'd, it having now ben an hundred yeares building & not yet quite finished, | 1666 J. Evelyn, L5, 27, I have not enjoy'd one minutes repose since my returne . . . having ben ever since soliciting for a little monye to preserve my miserable flock from perishing: | 1679 H. Savile, L11, 83 (in a letter to Viscount Halifax), the Dane and Brandenburgh envoyes having been posting who should ride fastest hither,

1711 D. Defoe, L14, 309, I have Since my last had Occasion of doeing I hope Some little Service here, The Commission of the assembly haveing been Sitting for this Week past; | 1747 R. Hurd, L29, 167, Colley Cibber, having <try'd> been trying his Hand for these many Years, but with slender Success, at Poetry, is now at last . . . resolv'd to turn Critic, ["Deletions are incorporated in the text, within angle brackets wherever possible." (Introduction to L29, p. lxxxi)]

1794 J. Woodforde, D21, IV 160, Mr. Stoughton of Sparham about 3. o'clock this Afternoon brought us a brace of Partridges . . . having been shooting at Weston all the Morning,

1801 J. Woodforde, D21, V 344, Mr. Collison of Deerham having been shooting at Weston to day, sent us two brace of Partridges this Afternoon—very hadsome of him indeed. | 1828 J. Skinner, D25, 362, this morning we had done breakfast ere he came to the table, dripping with rain, having been walking backwards and forwards in the garden during the heavy storm. | 1812 P. Hawker,

Chapter IV

D29, I 43, Having been only from a quarter past eleven till three to-day filling my bag, I returned to Bradford at the latter hour, in good time to despatch some birds to town. | 1814 P. Hawker, D29, I 106, Left Longparish for Lymington, with the intention of embarking immediately for France, having only been waiting for a fair wind to make a second excursion to that country. | 1842 E. FitzGerald, L49, I 340, Aubrey de Vere having been hunting for Tennyson in the same way. | 1848 E. FitzGerald, L49, I 625, I also have finished Thucydides—today: having been a year and a half reading what has taken you but two months or so. | 1850 E. FitzGerald, L49, I 692, so many Ministers of the Church of England . . . having been so long and so loudly proclaiming the essential Unity of the Church of England with that of Rome;

1864 G. Meredith, L54, I 161, on the last evening of my stay here, I write to you, having been intending the thing from the day of my arrival. | 1868 G. Meredith, L54, I 193, I have carried about this piece of Club paper for a fortnight, having been intending to commence a letter to you there, and unable either to do that or to go on with it since. | 1866 A. C. Swinburne, L56, I 58, having been fighting my battles in the *New York Tribune* he means to continue apropos of the *Notes*, of which I have sent him a copy.

As evidenced above, in contradiction to the remarks by Jespersen (1931 [1970]: 205), Poutsma (1926: 329), Visser (1973: 1955 & n. 1) and Scheffer (1975: 22.2) that the participial progressive was very rare throughout the history of the English progressive, this construction has been proved to be not necessarily rare.[16]

---

[16] In Chapter IV, the following quotations have been excluded from my discussion because, in (a), 'taking' is used as 'taken' and, in (b), 'sweating', 'stirring', 'arguing' and 'threatening' are participial adjectives and 'shooting' is in the appositive use:

    (a) 1797 J. Woodforde, D21, V 36, Being taking extremely ill on 12th. May 1797 declined entering any thing in this Book.

    (b) 1663 S. Pepys, D10, IV 247, In this walk, being all bewildered and weary and sweating, Creed, he lay down upon the ground; | 1673 H. Ball, L8, I 72, neither that nor this can give your Excellency much newes, little being noe stirring here. | 1739 J. Wesley, L23, 283, Almost as soon as we went out of

Diachrony of Participial Progressive: *Being Going*

Incidentally, the gerundive progressive has been rarely encountered in diaries and correspondence as in (46).

(46) Gerundive progressive

1682 S. Pepys, L5, 134, by reason of the Kitchin-yachts' not being yet coming; | 1701 J. Evelyn, L7, II 239, But how, deare Friend, am I fallen into a sermon instead of a letter, which should account for my having ben so long groveling in the country! | 1701 J. Jackson, L7, II 178, The Jesuits vent an intelligence from their correspondents of my Lord Portland's being coming to congratulate the King upon his Accession to the Crown, but it meets with little credit. | 1756 E. Gibbon, L, 37, I don't doubt of their being translating into English. | 1865 M. Arnold, L53, 309, freeing them from the necessity of being always standing upon their toes, crowing.

---

town the minister sent or went to each of the members, and, being arguing and threatening, utterly confounded them, so that they were all scattered abroad. | 1798 J. Woodforde, D21, V 159, Willm. Custance called on us this Morning being out shooting & brought us a fine Hare.

In addition, the following quotations, in which older form of the progressive *be* + Preposition + Verb-*ing* is reflected, were also excluded from my analyses:

1651 R. Josselin, D8, 244, my noble friends the Mr Harlakends. and one of their wives with mee eating a tansy, and a nesse of creame, wee being in preparing for London. | 1797 J. Woodforde, D21, V 76, Mr. Hambleton Custance gave us a Call this Morning, but did not stay any time scarce with us, being a shooting.

Furthermore, the construction of *there being* + Subject + Verb-*ing* was also excluded from my discussion.

1726 D. Eaton, L20, 87, there being a bitch going proud, the hounds were frequently quarrelling

Chapter V

Diachrony of *Seem* Meaning 'To Pretend'[17]

5.1. Purpose of the Present Chapter

Dealing with a history of *seem* 'to pretend', this chapter will unravel the mystery of why the *OED²*'s *seem*-derivatives—such as *seemer, seeming, seemingly* and *seemingness*—have the concept of 'active, deliberate show or pretence', unlike the verb *seem*. This fact seems to have escaped grammarians' notice in the field of historical English linguistics.

Previous to the discussion of the verb *seem* meaning 'to pretend', the meaning of 'pretend' is defined. This verb has historically had various meanings. According to the *OED²*, no less than ten meanings are still in use, and the two main meanings are 'to profess or claim' as in the definitions 4a and 13c, d and 'to declare falsely with intent to deceive' as in the definitions 3b and 7a, c, d, 15a. As not only the *OED²* but also contemporary dictionaries including *AHD³* (1992), *COD¹⁰* (1999), *LDCE⁵* (2009),

---

[17] Chapter V is a combined, expanded and updated version of Nakamura (2007e, 2010). Here, I am deeply grateful to Peter Lang, the publisher, and Professor Merja Kytö, Professor John Scahill and Professor Harumi Tanabe, the editors of Nakamura (2010) respectively, who granted permission to republish this paper with minimum alterations as Chapter V of the present monograph. I would also like to acknowledge my appreciation of the kind words which I received from Professor Minoji Akimoto, and of useful comments and questions which I received from Professor Ilse Wischer, University of Potsdam, Professor Hans H. Hock, University of Illinois at Urbana-Champaign, Professor Pieter A. M. Seuren, University of Max Planck Institute for Psycholinguistics, and Professor Brigitte L. M. Bauer, University of Texas. I would also like to record my appreciation for the helpful comments and questions made on the earlier draft of that paper by Linguists at VARIENG, University of Helsinki, especially by Professor Matti Rissanen, Professor Terttu Nevalainen, Dr Matti Kilpiö, Dr Leena Kahlas-Tarkka and Dr Arja Nurmi. I am also grateful to Professor Christian Mair, University of Freiburg, for his useful comments and encouragement. Thanks are also due to Professor Patrick Hubbuck of Aichi Prefectural University, who corrected stylistic errors of the earlier version of this paper and provided useful feedback.

Chapter V

MWCD¹² (2013) and *OALD⁸* (2010) state, these two senses are typically the leading current senses of *pretend*. In order to avoid confusion, the verb *pretend* is used exclusively as signifying the first definition in contemporary dictionaries, that is, 'to feign to be or do' in this chapter.

Regarding the texts examined, letters reflecting popular speech begin to multiply only in the late 16th century, and diaries, according to Matthews (1950), are extant from the 16th century onwards. This is the reason why the texts examined cover the periods from 1500 onwards.

5.2. One of the Mysteries in Present-day English

A glimpse of the derivatives of *seem* listed in (47) and (48) shows that *seemer* (47a), gerundive *seeming* (47b), participial *seeming* (47c), *seemingly* (48a) and *seemingness* (48b) have the sense of 'pretence', whereas no such notion is detected in (47d-h) and (48c-g).

(47) Primary derivatives of *seem, v.*
   a. seem·er [f. SEEM *V.²* + -ER¹.] "One who seems, or makes a pretence or show."
      1603 Shakes. *Meas. for M.* I. iii.; 1647 Trap *Comm. 1 Cor.;* 1875 Jowett *Plato* (ed. 2) III. 297 When the guardians of the laws and of the government are only seemers and not real guardians.
      (*OED²*, s.v. seemer *sb.*)

   b. seem·ing [f. SEEM *V.²* + -ING¹.] "External appearance considered as deceptive, or as distinguished from reality; an illusion, a semblance."
      1576 Gascoigne *Steele Gl.*; 1603 Shakes. *Meas. for M.* III. ii.; 1816 Byron *Sketch*; 1891 F. Thompson *Sister-Songs* (1895) 35 Even so Its lovely gleamings Seemings show Of things not seemings.
      (*OED²*, s.v. seeming *vbl. n.*, 3)

   c. seem·ing [f. SEEM *V.²* + -ING².] "Apparent to the senses or to the mind, as distinct from what *is*."
      a1557 *Tottel's Misc.*; 1653 H. More *Antid. Ath.*; 1700 Dryden *Sigism. & Guisc.*; 1766 Goldsm. *Vic. W.*; 1857 H. Miller *Test. Rocks*; 1875 Jowett *Plato*; 1883 R. W. Dixon *Mano* II. iv. 74 We

Diachrony of *Seem* Meaning 'To Pretend'

came upon him riding loftily, Clad in his knightly arms without disguise, No seeming pilgrim now. . . .

(*OED*[2], s.v. seeming *ppl. a.* 3)

d. †seem·able [f. SEEM *V.*[2] + -ABLE. Cf. SEMBLABLE.]

(*OED*[2], s.v. †seemable, *a.*)

e. seem·ble   obs. form of SEEMLY *a.*

(*OED*[2], s.v. seemble)

f. seem·less [f. SEEM *V.*[2] (assumed to be the source of SEEMLY *a.*) + -LESS.]

(*OED*[2], s.v. seemless, *a.*)

g. seem·ly, *a.* [a. ON. *sómilig-r* . . . see SEEM *V.*[2] and *-LY*[1].]

(*OED*[2], s.v. seemly, *a.*)

h. seem·ly, *adv.* [a. ON. *sómiliga* . . . see prec. and -LY[2].]

(*OED*[2], s.v. seemly, *adv.*)

(48) Secondary derivatives of *seem*, *v.*

a. seem·ing·ly [f. SEEMING *ppl. a.* + -LY[2].] "To external appearance, apparently. (Distinguished from but not necessarily opposed to *really*.) †b. ? *nonce-use*. ? So as to seem real. *Obs.*"

1602 *Kyd's Sp. Trag.* iii. xii. A. 123 Canst paint a dolefull crie? *Paint.* Seemingly, sir.

(*OED*[2], s.v. seemingly, *adv.*, 2)

b. seem·ing·ness [f. SEEMING *ppl. a.* + -NESS.] "The quality or fact of seeming to be something; unreal pretence; plausibility."

1640 G. Abbott *Job Paraphr.*; 1644 Digby *Nat. Bodies*; 1647 Trapp *Comm. Matt.*; 1830 Lamb *Let. to Rev. J. Gillman* 8 Mar., In the silken seemingness of his nature there is that which offends me.

(*OED*[2], s.v. seemingness 1)

c. seem·li·head [f. SEEMLY *a.* + -HEAD.] (*OED*[2], s.v. seemlihead)

d. †seem·li·hood [f. SEEMLY *a.* + -HOOD.] (*OED*[2], s.v. †seemlihood)

e. †seem·li·ly, *adv.* [f. SEEMLY *a.* + -LY[2].] (*OED*[2], s.v. †seemlily, *adv.*)

f. seem·li·ness [f. SEEMLY *a.* + -NESS.] (*OED*[2], s.v. seemliness)

g. †seem·li·ty [f. SEEMLY *a.* + -TY.] (*OED*[2], s.v. †seemlity)

Chapter V

It is true that the use of *seem* to mean the notion of active, deliberate show or pretence is thought to be uncommon in Present-day English, as the notion is not clearly defined in contemporary dictionaries. *Seemer* is not so much as listed as a vocabulary entry in these contemporary dictionaries. The meaning pertaining to active, deliberate show or pretence, however, is defined in large-scale American dictionaries such as *Webster's International Dictionary*, *The Century Dictionary* and *The Random House Dictionary*.

Unexpectedly, however, no definition demonstrating that the verb *seem* pertained to the sense of active deliberate show or pretence is detected in the definitions of *seem, v.*[2] in the *OED*[2]. This verb was an inert verb in origin. The senses are all non-active except for the second definition (49a) and, although the third and the fourth definitions (49b, c) might be thought to raise a possibility of pretence, there is no guarantee of this, as follows:

(49) a. *refl.* and *intr.* To vouchsafe, deign. . . . *Obs.*

(*OED*[2], s.v. seem, *v.*[2] †2)

b. With n., adj., or phrase as complement: To appear to be, to be apparently (what is expressed by the complement).

(*OED*[2], s.v. seem, *v.*[2] 3)

c. With infinitive: To appear *to be* or *to do* something.

(*OED*[2], s.v. seem, *v.*[2] 4)

Incidentally, it is a matter of fact that, as shown in (50), functionally-shifted uses of the verb *seem* have no notion of pretence.

(50) a. [a. ON. *sém-r:* see SEEM *V.*[2]] Seemly, proper, fitting.

(*OED*[2], s.v. †seem, *a. Obs.*)

b. [f. SEEM *V.*[2]] Seeming, semblance, appearance.

(*OED*[2], s.v. seem, *n.* ? *Obs.* or *dial.* (chiefly *Sc.*))

Thus it is natural to question why the verb *seem* in the *OED*[2] does not have the meaning 'to pretend', whereas some of its derivatives have the sense of 'pretence'. The derivatives may have newly acquired this concept independently and individually in the course of time. The present

Diachrony of *Seem* Meaning 'To Pretend'

author, however, would like to oppose this idea. It is absolutely unnatural so long as *seem*-clusters derived from *seem*. Instead, suppose the verb *seem* had had the meaning 'to pretend' unnoticed in the history of English. This supposition may unravel the mystery above with relative ease. In fact, as shown later, this usage did exist in the history of English. Evidence suggests that the use of *seem* to mean 'pretend' seems to have been overlooked in hunting for its citations.

5.3. Previous Studies

Among other studies, no less than two direct references to the usage now in question have been noticed. The first, Schmidt (1875 [1971]: 1022), reports that *seem* clearly had the sense of 'pretend' in Shakespearian English: "3) to appear, to be seen, to show oneself or itself: . . . Hence = to assume an air, to pretend to be". He presents 7 examples, four of which occur with the *to*-infinitive, two with the substantive and one with an adjective, taken from Shakespeare's *MM* I.iv.32, *AYL* V.ii.86, *WT* IV.iv.157, *AWW* III.vi.94, *Mac.* I.ii.47, *Mac.* I.v.30, *Per.* I.i.121. The other, Wright (1905 [1981]: 317), with respect to the late 19th-century Southern dialect of Isle of Man, quotes "1889 T. E. Brown, *The Manx Witch, and Other Poems*, 39, Feelin nothin, or seemin we didn" under the definition "4. To pretend". All of these facts will raise the possibility that the verb *seem* meaning 'to pretend' might have continued being used in not only Early but also Late Modern English. The next section establishes that this was an undeniable fact.

5.4. New Evidence: Presentation of Examples in the History of English

As quoted in (51)-(56), a considerable number of instances have been encountered in the texts examined. With such repeated occurrences it is not reasonable to overlook this usage as a mere slip of the tongue and the pen. This meaning of *seem* should not be ignored as peripheral.

The quotations in (51) and (52) are all taken from D10, Samuel Pepys's diary. The examples in (51) were noticed by Latham and Matthews,

Chapter V

editors of D10. The editors include this usage in "Select Glossary", as "SEEM: to pretend".[18] In the first citations in (51a, b, c, d), for example, the following parts reinforce this particular sense of *seem* respectively: "but . . . for mirth sake", "Bradly (the rogue that had betrayed us) and one Young, a cunning fellow", "though I am confident many in their hearts were against it", and "but is not".

(51) Examples of *seem* 'to pretend' noticed by the editors of D10

---

[18] The five examples below are those which were noticed by the editors but which were excluded from this monograph. I still feel that the verb *seem* in these quotations means just 'to show', not 'to pretend', even though the first-person subject may induce us to interpret the verb *seem* as 'to pretend'.

1660 S. Pepys, D10, I 123-124, the commanders all came on board, and the council set in the coach (the first council of war that hath been in my time), where I read the letter and declaration; and while they were discoursing upon it, I seemed to draw up a vote; which being offered they passed. | 1664 S. Pepys, D10, V 176, My wife made great means to be friends, coming to my bed's-side and doing all things to please me; and at last I could not hold out, but seemed pleased and so parted; and I with much ado to sleep, but was easily wakened by extraordinary great rain; and my mind troubled the more, to think what the soldiers would do on board tonight in all this weather. | 1667 S. Pepys, D10, VIII 52, Up, and by water to the Temple; and thence to Sir Ph. Warwickes about my Tangier warrant for tallies, and there met my Lord Bellasses and Creed and discoursed about our business of money; but we are defeated as to any hopes of getting anything upon the Pole=bill - which I seem but [am] not much troubled at, it not concerning me much. | 1669 S. Pepys, D10, IX 485, Here we stayed talking till 10 at night, where I did never drink before since this man came to the house; though for his pretty wife's sake, I do fetch my wine from this, whom I could not nevertheless get para see tonight - though her husband did seem to call for her. So parted here, and I home and to supper and to bed. | 1669 Pepys, S. Pepys, D10, IX 546, Thence with my wife abroad with our coach, most pleasant weather, and to Hackny and into the marshes, where I never was before, and thence round about to Old ford and Bow; and coming through the latter home, there being some young gentlewomen at a door and I seeming not to know who they were, my wife's jealousy told me presently that I knew well enough, it was that damned place where Deb dwelt; which made me answer very angrily that it was false, as it was; and I carried back again to see the place, and it proved not it, so I continued out of humour a good while at it, she being willing to be friends, as I was by and by, saying no more of it.

Diachrony of *Seem* Meaning 'To Pretend'

a. With 1st person subject + *to*-infinitive (4 examples)

1661 S. Pepys, D10, II 68, Sir Wm, telling me that old Edgeborow, his predecessor, did die and walk in my chamber - did make me somewhat afeared, but not so much as for mirth sake I did seem. | 1661 S. Pepys, D10, II 195-196, But Lord, to hear how she talks and how she rails against my uncle would make me mad. But I seemed not to be troubled at it; | 1661 S. Pepys, D10, II 208 | 1667 Pepys, D10, VIII 68

b. With 1st person subject + Adjectival (2 example)

1661 S. Pepys, D10, II 182, and then going toward the Court= house, met my Uncle Thomas and his Son Tho., with Bradly (the rogue that had betrayed us) and one Young, a cunning fellow who guides them. There passed no unkind words at all between us, but I seemed fair and went to drink with them: I said little till by and by that we came to the Court - which was a simple meeting of a company of country rogues, with the Steward and two Fellows of Jesus College, that are lords of the towne. | 1669 Pepys, D10, IX 511, Thence home; and there, after a while at the office, I home; and there came home my wife, who hath been with Bateliers late and been dancing with the company; at which I seemed a little troubled, not being sent for thither myself; but I was not much so, but went to bed well enough pleased.

c. With non-1st person subject + *to*-infinitive (3 examples)

1660 S. Pepys, D10, I 123-124, the commandersa ll came on board, and the council set in the coach (the first council of war that hath been in my time), where I read the letter and declaration; and while they were discoursing upon it, I seemed to draw up a vote; which being offered they passed. Not one man seemed to say no to it, though I am confident many in their hearts were against it. | 1663 Pepys, D10, IV 111-112, Another book I bought, being a collection of many expressions of the great Presbyterian preachers upon public occasions in the late times, against the King and his party (as some of Mr. Marshall, Case, Calamy, Baxter, &[c.]), which is good reading now, to see what they then did teach and the people believe, and what they would seem to be now. | 1666 Pepys,

D10, VII 232, But Lord, to see the dissembling of this widow; how upon the singing of a certain Jigg by Doll, mrs. martin's sister, she <u>seemed</u> to be sick, and fainted and God knows what, because the Jigg which her husband (who died this last sickness) loved.

d. With non-1st person subject + Adjectival (1 example)
1668 Pepys, D10, IX 174, Up, and with Sir J. Mennes to my Lord Brouncker and with him, all of us, to my Lord Ashly to satisfy him about the reason of what we do or have done in the business of the tradesmen's certificates, which he <u>seems</u> satisfied with, but is not; but I believe we have done what we can justify, and he hath done what he cannot, in stopping us to grant them; and I believe it will come into Parliament and make trouble.

The examples in (52)-(54) below were discovered by the present author. The verb *seem* in the quotations is an active, not inert, verb with the meaning of deliberate show or pretence. In the quotations in (52a), the following parts reinforce this particular sense of *seem*: "but I was not pleased at all", "that I bought the other day, which is the same with that", and "though I saw on Saturday last". In (52b), the meaning of pretence is reinforced by "though in my mind I think it too much", "but am no friend to the man's dealings with us", "but I am glad of it", "though I did it only to see what she would do", "but I hear she is too gallant for me and am not sorry that I misse her", "though I know him to be a rogue and one that hates me with his heart", "though I do not grudge it her", and "but know not how to order the matter whether they shall come or no". Furthermore, "but . . . they do not in their hearts trust one another" and "but make the King and these great men buy it dear before they have it" in (52c) and "but . . . he is heartily troubled" and "but is not" in (52d) induce one to interpret the verb *seem* as to 'pretend'. Signalling the usage presently in question, they are linguistic indicators promoting the interpretation of *seem* as an active, not inert, verb with the meaning of deliberate show or pretence. Even if such a linguistic indicator does not co-occur with the verb *seem*, which of the examples with *seem* have the notion of pretence can be contextually explained in most cases.

Diachrony of *Seem* Meaning 'To Pretend'

(52) Further examples of *seem* 'to pretend' in D10 discovered by the present author

a. With 1st person subject + *to*-infinitive (10 examples)
1661 S. Pepys, D10, II 237, So home after sermon, and there came by appointment Dr. T. Pepys, Will Joyce, and my brother Tom and supped with me; and very merry they were and I <u>seemed</u> to be, but I was not pleased at all with their company. | 1663 Pepys, D10, IV 124, In the evening Deane of Woolwich went home with me and showed me the use of a little Sliding ruler, less than that I bought the other day, which is the same with that but more portable; however, I <u>did</u> <u>not</u> <u>seem</u> to understand or even to have seen anything of it before. | 1668 Pepys, D10, IX 326, and thence my wife and Mercer and W. Hewer and Deb to the King's play-house, and I afterward by water after them, and there we did hear the Eunuch (who it seems is a Frenchman, but long bred in Italy) sing; which I <u>seemed</u> to take as new to me, though I saw on Saturday last but said nothing of it. | 1661 S. Pepys, D10, II 108 | 1662 S. Pepys, D10, III 284 | 1663 Pepys, D10, IV 184-185 | 1663 Pepys, D10, IV 395 | 1664 Pepys, D10, V 159 | 1665 Pepys, D10, VI 20 | 1666 Pepys, D10, VII 331

b. With 1st person subject + Adjectival (14 examples)
1661 S. Pepys, D10, II 212, So to the Wardrobe, where I found my Lady hath agreed upon a lace for my wife, of 6*l*., which I <u>seemed</u> much glad of that it was no more, though in my mind I think it too much, and I pray God keep me so to order myself and my wife's expenses that no inconvenience in purse or honour fallow this my prodigality. | 1662 S. Pepys, D10, III 165-166, after dinner comes in a Jugler, which showed us very pretty tricks. I <u>seemed</u> very pleasant, but am no friend to the man's dealings with us in the office. | 1663 Pepys, D10, IV 154, So home and read to my wife a Fable or two in Ogleby's Æsop; and so to supper and then to prayers and to bed - my wife this evening discoursing of making clothes for the country; which I <u>seem</u> against, pleading lack of money, but I am glad of it in some respects, because of getting her out of the way from this fellow, and my own liberty to look after my business more then of late I have done. | 1663 Pepys, D10, IV 158, So I

Chapter V

waked by 3 a-clock, my mind being troubled; and so took occasion by making water to wake my wife, and after having lain till past 4 a-clock, <u>seemed</u> going to rise, though I did it only to see what she would do; and so going out of the bed, she took hold of me and would know what ayled me; | 1664 Pepys, D10, V 261-262, Mr. Hill came to tell me that he had got a gentlewoman for my wife, one Mrs. Ferrabosco, that sings most admirably. I <u>seemed</u> glad of it; but I hear she is too gallant for me and am not sorry that I misse her. | 1664 Pepys, D10, V 312, Up betimes, and down with Mr. Castle to Redriffe, and there walked to Deptford to view a parcel of brave Knees of his, which endeed are very good. And so back again - home - I <u>seeming</u> very friendly to him, though I know him to be a rogue and one that hates me with his heart. | 1666 Pepys, D10, VII 298, Thence away by coach and called away my wife at Unthankes, where she tells me she hath bought a gown of 15*s* per yard; the same, before her face, my Lady Castlemaine this day bought also - which I <u>seemed</u> vexed for; though I do not grudge it her, but to incline her to have Mercer again - which I believe I shall do, but the girl, I heare, hath no mind to come to us again - which vexes me. | 1667 Pepys, D10, VIII 25, At noon to dinner; and there comes a letter from Mrs. Pierce, telling me she will come and dine with us on Thursday next with some of the players, Knipp, &c., which I was glad of but my wife vexed, which vexed me; but I <u>seemed</u> merry, but know not how to order the matter whether they shall come or no. | 1661 S. Pepys, ibid., II 75 | 1662 S. Pepys, ibid., III 250 | 1663 Pepys, ibid., IV 316 | 1663 Pepys, ibid., IV 416-417 | 1664 Pepys, ibid., V 358 | 1669 Pepys, ibid., IX 450-451

c. With non-1st person subject + *to*-infinitive (5 examples)

1667 Pepys, D10, VIII 596-597, He doth suggest that something is intended for the Duke of Monmouth, and it may be against the Queene also. . . . That my Lord of Buckingham, Bristoll, and Arlington <u>do</u> <u>seem</u> to agree in these things; but that they do not in their hearts trust one another, but do drive several ways, all of them. | 1668 Pepys, D10, IX 360-361, And he tells me, therefore, that he doth believe that this policy will be endeavoured by the Church and their friends: to <u>seem</u> to promise the King money

Diachrony of *Seem* Meaning 'To Pretend'

when it shall be propounded, but make the King and these great men buy it dear before they have it. | 1661 S. Pepys, ibid., II 75 | 1666 Pepys, ibid., VII 381 | 1667 Pepys, ibid., VIII 352

d. With non-1st person subject + Adjectival (5 examples)

1666 Pepys, D10, VII 24, He <u>seems</u> pleased, but I perceive he is heartily troubled at this act and the report of his losing his place, and more at my not writing to him to the prejudice of the Act. | 1668 Pepys, D10, IX 189, Here I did kiss the pretty woman newly come, called Pegg, that was Sir Ch. Sidly's mistress - a mighty pretty woman, and <u>seems</u>, but is not, modest. | 1663 Pepys, ibid., IV 334 | 1666 Pepys, ibid., VII, 415 | 1667 Pepys, ibid., VIII 298

(53) Examples of *seeming, ppl. a.* with the sense of pretence in D10 (8 examples)

1660 S. Pepys, D10, I 234, We found all well in the morning below-stairs, but the boy in a sad plight of <u>seeming</u> sorrow; but he is the most cunning rogue that ever I met with of his age. | 1664 Pepys, D10, V 279, To the Tangier Committee; and there I opposed Collonell Legg's estimate of supplies of provisions to be sent to Tangier, till all were ashamed of it and he fain, after all his good husbandry and <u>seeming</u> ignorance and joy, to have the King's money saved - yet afterward he discovered all his design to be to keep the furnishing of these things to the officers of the Ordnance. | 1665 Pepys, D10, VI 79, Up, and betimes to Mr. Povy, being desirous to have an end of my trouble of mind touching my Tangier business, whether he hath any desire of accepting what my Lord Ashly offered, of his becoming Treasurer again. And there I did, with a <u>seeming</u> most generous spirit, offer him to take it back again upon his own terms; but he did answer to me that he would not, above all things in the world - at which I was for the present satisfied; | 1663 Pepys, ibid., IV 158 | 1666 Pepys, ibid., VII 306 | 1667 Pepys, ibid., VIII 75 | 1668 Pepys, ibid., IX 148 | 1669 Pepys, ibid., IX 534

(54) Examples of *seemingly, adv.* with the sense of pretence in D10 (4 examples)

120

Chapter V

1665 Pepys, D10, VI 13, Povy, Creed, and I stayed discoursing, I much troubled in mind <u>seemingly</u> for the business; but indeed, only on my own behalf, though I have no great reason for it, but so painful a thing is fear. | 1667 Pepys, D10, VIII 77, A sorry dinner, not anything handsome nor clean but some silver plates they borrowed of me. My wife was here too. So a great deal of talk, and I <u>seemingly</u> merry - but took no pleasure at all. | 1667 Pepys, ibid., VIII 44 | 1667 Pepys, ibid., VIII 352

The meaning of deliberate show or pretence is best revealed in its use with the progressive as in (55), because it is only with verbs of dynamic senses that the progressives are permitted excepting in some dialects.

(55) 1666 Pepys, D10, VII 415, I down into the Hall, and there the Lieutenant of the Tower took me with him and would have me to the Tower to dinner; where I dined - at the head of his table next his lady - who <u>is</u> comely, and <u>seeming</u> sober and stately, but very proud and very cunning, or I am mistaken - and wanton too.

Table 30 is a tabulation of the data for *seem*, *seeming*, and *seemingly* with the notion of 'pretence' in D10, Pepys's diary. Table 30 reveals that even non-first person subjects were permitted with the usage now in question, and that *to*-infinitive as well as an adjectival could follow the verb *seem*, and that participial *seeming* and adverbial *seemingly* had the meaning of pretence as well.

Table 30 Occurrences of *Seem*, *Seeming* and *Seemingly* with the Notion of 'Pretence' in D10

Seem, *v.*				Seeming, *ppl. a.*	Seemingly, *adv.*
1st Person Subject		Non-1st Person Subject			
+ *to*- infinitive	+ Adjectival	+ *to*- infinitive	+ Adjectival		
14	16	8	6	8	4

Here arise simple questions: Did Pepys not have the verb *pretend* and its synonyms in his vocabulary? Was this usage Pepys's idiosyncrasy? Far from it; Table 31 answers the first question. He often used *pretend to* +

Diachrony of *Seem* Meaning 'To Pretend'

infinitive though less frequently than *seem*.

Table 31   Pepys's Use of Verbs of Pretending in D10

affect to + infinitive	1*	*dissemble to* + infinitive	0
assume to + infinitive	0	*feign to* + infinitive	2
counterfeit to + infinitive	0	*pretend to* + infinitive	14
* *affect to seem* Adj			

Table 31 suggests that, in Pepys, the verb *seem* meaning 'to pretend' was being used side by side with *pretend to* + infinitive, and that other synonymous verbs were infrequent. It might be partly because the verb *pretend* could not take an adjectival and partly due to the verb *pretend* having the two main meanings, 'to feign' and 'to profess or claim' that Pepys preferred the verb *seem*, as in Table 32.

Table 32   Occurrences of *Pretend To*-infinitive in D10

Sense of *pretend*	1st Person Subject	Non-1st Person Subject	Total
'to feign'	8	6	14
'to profess or claim'	1	12	13

The second question above will be answered by the examples in (56). This usage of *seem* meaning to 'pretend' was employed by other people as well.[19]

(56) a. 1748 P. D. Stanhope, L21, 65, The more you know, the modester you should be . . . Even where you are sure, <u>seem</u> rather doubtful; represent, but do not pronounce, and if you would convince others, <u>seem</u> open to conviction yourself.

---

[19] The two quotations below have been excluded, because I have not felt certain that the verb *seem* means 'to pretend' rather than just 'to show':

1679 Viscount Halifax, L11, 89, yet I hope you will not impute more to yourself in it than is necessary in the place you are in, that you may not draw a disadvantage upon yourself by <u>seeming</u> to resent too much what hath been done to you | 1748 P. D. Stanhope, L21, 67, Never <u>seem</u> wiser, nor more learned, than the people you are with.

Chapter V

b. 1748 P. D. Stanhope, L21, 109, if a flippant woman, or a pert cox-comb, lets off anything of that kind [= indirect or mean attacks], it is much better not to <u>seem</u> to understand, than to reply to it.

c. ?1772/?1773 P. D. Stanhope, L21, 381, Be wiser and better than your contemporaries, but <u>seem</u> to take the world as it is, and men as they are,

d. 1799 W. B. Stevens, D22, 486, I did not show his Lordship my dis-gust, believing if there should ever be any chance of his giving You another or a better, it will be more easily obtained by Not <u>seeming</u> to be displeased.

The notion of deliberate show or pretence is best revealed in the two im-perative uses in (56a, c), because it is only with verbs of dynamic senses that the imperatives are permitted. These examples are not context-depend-ent uses, in contrast to those in (51)-(54). The length of the quotations talks. It is to be noted that the authors of the examples in (56) as well as (51)-(55) are all educated people; Samuel Pepys, Philip D. Stanhope (that is, the Fourth Earl of Chesterfield) and William B. Stevens were so-called Ox-bridge wits in those days. It may be concluded that *seem* 'to pretend' must have been a part of the usage at least in the 17th and 18th centuries.

Thus, at the common and informal speech level as reflected in pri-vate diaries and personal letters, linguistic phases different from those which are shown in studies carried out based upon the analyses of literary language can be detected. As has been shown up to now, in Early Modern English *seem* was clearly used as an active verb referring to deliberate show on the part of the agent subject and, in the course of Late Modern English, it went out of use and came to be restricted only to the modern use in which *seem* describes the effect on our perceptions of appearances, at least in Britain.

5.5. A Proposal

This is the reason why it is thought to be necessary to formulate in the *OED²*'s *seem*, possibly between sense 4 and sense 5, a new definition

Diachrony of *Seem* Meaning 'To Pretend'

as in (57).

(57) †To feign an action, character or the like; make oneself seem (*to* do or *to* be); assume an air; pretend. *Obs. rare.* exc. *dial.* ?Now *U.S.*?

It is true that, whereas both active and inert senses are described with five verbs of bodily sensation in almost all contemporary dictionaries, as shown in Table 33, a contextual process-meaning of the verb *resemble*, that is, 'to become like' (as in the progressive sentence *My wife is resembling her mother more and more as the years go by*) is usually not defined.

Table 33   Definitions of Verbs Pertaining to Five Bodily Senses and *Resemble*

	AHD [3] (1992)	COD [10] (1999)	LDCE [5] (2009)	MWCD [12] (2013)	OALD [8] (2010)
see	±Active	±Active	±Active	±Active	±Active
hear	±Active	±Active	±Active	±Active	±Active
smell	±Active	±Active	±Active	±Active	±Active
taste	±Active	±Active	±Active	±Active	±Active
feel	±Active	±Active	±Active	±Active	±Active
resemble	+State	+State	+State	+State	+State

In the case of the verb *seem*, however, it is necessary to describe a definition as proposed in (57) in semantic relation to its derivatives *seemer*, *seeming*, *seemingly* and *seemingness*.

5.6. Significance of the Present Study

In 5.4, exertions have been made to have this rare usage which has remained unnoticed see the light of day. If this attempt is approved, the greatest merits are, above all, the two points in (58b, c) in addition to (58a).

(58) a. Uncovering of a rare or unknown usage

b. Accountability for the *seem*-derivatives pertaining to the 'gene' of pretence

Chapter V

c. Accountability for the residual use of *seem* 'pretend' in American English

(i) "To appear; to make or have a show or semblance."
(N. Webster, *An American Dictionary of the English Language* [1828; rpt. New York and London: Johnson Reprint, 1970], sense 1)

"To make pretense; to assume an appearance."
(*Webster's New International Dictionary of the English Language* [1909; rpt. Springfield: G. & C. Merriam; Tokyo: Maruzen, 1910], sense 4)

"To make pretence of being; to pretend or feign. Either you are ignorant, or *seem* so craftily. *Shak.*"
(*Webster's New International Dictionary of the English Language*, Second Edition, Unabridged [Springfield: G. & C. Merriam Co., 1934], sense 5)

"To pretend to be: FEIGN. Either you are ignorant, or ~ so craftily—Shak."
(*Webster's New International Dictionary of the English Language*, Unabridged [Springfield: G. & C. Merriam Co., 1961], sense 2a(2))

(ii) "To appear; be seen; show one's self or itself; hence, to assume an air; pretend."
(*The Century Dictionary* [New York: The Century Co., 1914], sense 3)

(iii) "To give the outward appearance of being or to pretend to be: He only seems friendly because he wants you to like him."
(*The Random House Dictionary of the English Language* [New York: Random House, 1966], sense 5)

One merit is, as shown in (58b), that by all of this thinking we can more naturally and easily account for the *seem*-derivatives' pertaining to the concept of 'pretence' rather than by the inference drawn from the definitions of the *OED²*. Even after the "parent", that is, the verb *seem*, abandoned this sense in the end, the "children", namely primary derivatives, and the "grandchildren", secondary derivatives, retained the DNA, that is the sense of deliberate pretence. *Seemer, seeming, seemingly* and *seemingness* are, as it were, fossils.

The other merit is, as shown in (58c), that the route of the development of *seem* 'pretend', survived in American English, is elucidated.

Dictionaries of contemporary English, British, American, Australian, Canadian or South-African do not provide such a definition as one of the senses. The definition now in question is documented only in a few American dictionaries with considerations given to lexical history, that is, the editions of *Webster's International Dictionary*, *The Century Dictionary*, *The Random House Dictionary*, as in (58c (i)-(iii)). Although in such American dictionaries, the citation is either not presented or is a very old quotation coming from Shakespeare, the editions of *Webster's International Dictionary* have consistently documented the definition now in question.

All this makes it possible to infer one process concerning the route of the development of *seem* 'to pretend', as diagrammed in Figure 3.

Figure 3 Diagram Showing the History of *Seem* 'To Pretend'

As far as the evidence is concerned, the use of *seem* with the notion of deliberate show or pretence originated in Elizabethan English, was still in use in Modern English and gradually went out of use in the course of the 19th century in British English, while in American English it has or seems to have survived since its emigration. We often find old British pronunciation and usage surviving in American English, including the use of *fall* 'autumn' and *be sick* 'be ill', the pronunciation of *clerk*, and the retention of the preposition *from* in the construction of *save/stop/prevent* + Obj + *from* Verb-*ing*, although, as to the last, it was towards the end of the 20th century that the *from*-less construction would seem to have superseded the *from*-construction, as pointed out by Christian Mair (2006). The usage of

Chapter V

seem meaning 'to pretend' is thought to be one of the cases in which past British English usages are retained in American English. The question of the situation regarding current English in Canada, Australia, New Zealand, South Africa, India, for instance, arouses the present author's interest.

5.7. Reason Why *Seem* 'To Pretend' Became Archaic or Even Obsolete in Present-day English

Finally, the reason why *seem* 'to pretend' became archaic or even obsolete in Present-day English is briefly mentioned.

First, as an internal factor, it is conceivable that *seem* was an inert verb in origin, and did not accord with active meanings. The OED^2's senses are all non-active. The definitions in (59) might be thought to raise a possibility of active meaning, but there is no guarantee of this.

(59) a. 'to vouchsafe, deign' (OED^2, s.v. seem, $v.^2$ †2)   *a*1300
      b. 'to think, deem, imagine' (OED^2, s.v. seem, $v.^2$ †9a)   *c*1386→1627
      c. 'to think fit' (OED^2, s.v. seem, $v.^2$ †9b)   *c*1450→1610

Second, the interpretation of *seem* as deliberate pretence tended to be context-dependent, so the binary use of *seem* might have been felt to be clumsy. Third, an external factor can be applicable as the reason. As shown in Figure 4, the verb *pretend* became fully established in the course of Early Modern English and, furthermore, from 1600 onward, a number of synonymous verbs began to be adopted from foreign languages. It is true that, strictly speaking, they have not exactly the same use as each other. It is probable, however, that *seem* 'to pretend' became no longer useful, although *seem* had the advantage of being directly followed by adjectivals, while others did not. This may have prolonged the use of *seem* 'to pretend' to some extent. In any event, the verb *seem* must have played a role in bridging the gap during the transition period, until *pretend* and other related verbs gained ground.

Whether the verb *seem* had the sense of pretence in Middle English should also arouse our interest. As far as Middle English dictionaries are concerned, at least, we can find no such definition. Incidentally, with re-

Diachrony of *Seem* Meaning 'To Pretend'

spect to the verbs *appear* and *look*, no example which has the sense of active deliberate show or pretence seems to have been reported in the history of English. However, given the common expression "appearances can be deceiving", perhaps a study comparable to this one might yet uncover them.

	1400	1500	1600	1700	1800	1900	2000
pretend 1412→	————————————————————————————
counterfeit 1548-1639	———————
feign 1563→	————————————————————
assume 1602→	—————————————————
affect 1603→	—————————————————
dissemble 1634-1660	—
(seem) 1590-1889	————————————

Figure 4   The Ascent and Demise of Verbs of 'Pretending' Followed by *To*-infinitive

Sources: *OED²*, s.v. pretend, *v.*, 3b; assume, *v.*, 8; counterfeit, *v.*, 4†b; affect, *v.*¹, 6b; feign, *v.*, 9b; dissemble, *v.*¹, †5†c.

5.8. Summary of Chapter V

Based upon the aforementioned evidence, we can conclude the following. The verb *seem* meant 'to pretend' in Modern English. This accounts for not only some *seem*-clusters pertaining to the notion of pretence but also the residual presence of *seem* 'to pretend' in present-day American English. Since this usage has been noticed by Schmidt (1875 [1971]), Wright (1905 [1981]) and Latham and Matthews (1970-1983), the present author's proves not to be a completely new discovery in the truest sense. What the present author has done in this paper is to have this rare usage, hitherto unnoticed, see the light of day by providing an abundance of further evidence.

129

Chapter VI

Diachrony of Present Participles and Gerunds Followed by *Not*[20]

In this chapter, a diachrony of participles and gerunds followed by *not* is elucidated. In the introduction (6.1), target constructions, their use in the 20th-century English, the purpose of the present chapter and criteria of analyses are dealt with, and results of analyses of diaries and correspondence are detailed (6.2). So as to confirm the results in 6.2, those in five electronic texts—Diachronic Part of Helsinki Corpus (Helsinki-DP), CEECS, Lampeter, Newdigate, ARCHER 3.1—are shown (6.3). Next, results based on the *OED²* on CD-ROM (which is different in nature from the normal linguistic corpora above) are provided (6.4). Finally, users of participles and gerunds followed by *not* and properties of the texts in which this usage occurred are explored (6.5).

6.1. Introduction

6.1.1. Target Constructions

Theoretically, the target constructions now in question are those in which participial or gerundive *ing*-forms are followed by the negative particle *not* and, based upon their grammatical functions (whether they are participial or gerundive) and their forms (whether they are in the simple or the compound forms), they are classified into eight categories in (60): (a) simple participial Verb-*ing not* vs. *not* Verb-*ing*, (b) compound participial

---

[20] Chapter VI is a combined, expanded and updated version of Nakamura (1998a, c, 2000, 2003a, b, 2005, 2007a, b, 2008a, b, c, 2009, 2015a, d). Here, I would like to acknowledge my appreciation of the useful comments, questions and encouragements which I received from Professor Anthony Warner, University of York, Professor Ilse Wischer, University of Potsdam, Professor Christian Mair, University of Freiburg, Professor Bartosz Wiland, University of Poznan, Dr Wojciech Guz, John Paul II Catholic University of Lublin, Dr Steven Coats, University of Oulu, Professor Yoshiyuki Nakao, Hiroshima University and Professor Emeritus Akira Wada, Yamaguchi University.

Chapter VI

passive *being not* PP vs. *not being* PP, (c) compound participial perfective *being not* PP vs. *not being* PP, (d) compound participial perfective *having not* PP vs. *not having* PP, (e) simple gerundive Verb-*ing not* vs. *not* Verb-*ing*, (f) compound gerundive passive *being not* PP vs. *not being* PP, (g) compound gerundive perfective *being not* PP vs. *not being* PP and (h) compound gerundive perfective *having not* PP vs. *not having* PP.

(60) Target constructions

a. Simple participial Verb-*ing not*
1660 S. Pepys, D10, I 215, To bed, <u>having not</u> time to write letters;

b. Compound participial passive *being not* PP
1660 S. Pepys, D10, I 322, In the morning to Alderman Backwells for the Candlesticks for Mr. Coventry; but they <u>being not done</u>, I went away;

c. Compound participial perfective *being not* PP
1661 S. Pepys, D10, II 114, But they <u>being not come</u>, we went over to the Wardrobe

d. Compound participial perfective *having not* PP
1660 S. Pepys, D10, I 5, There, <u>having not eat</u> anything but bread and cheese, my wife cut me a slice of brawn which I received from my Lady,

e. Simple gerundive Verb-*ing not*
1789 J. Woodforde, D21, III 94, When at last in great haste there came one—and the reason of its <u>being not</u> here before, was, that Raven at the Kings Head to whom I had sent a Note, had entirely forgot it.

f. Compound gerundive passive *being not* PP
1775 J. Woodforde, D21, I 168, I went down to Sister Clarke's this morning and made her a visit, she is not at all pleased in <u>being not invited</u> to the Christening yesterday—

g. Compound gerundive perfective *being not* PP
1699 S. Pepys, L7, I 202, Between my comeing thus farr and the sealeing it, your 3d most unwellcome notice of your <u>being not gone</u> the 17th is come to hand.

131

Diachrony of Present Participles and Gerunds Followed by *Not*

h. Compound gerundive perfective *having not* PP
1713, J. Swift, L16, II 670, Having not used riding these 3 years, made me terrible weary; yet I resolve on Monday to sett out for Holyhead, as weary as I am.

6.1.2. Post-Position of *Not* against *Ing*-forms in Present-day English

6.1.2.1. References to the Position of *Not* against *Ing*-forms in Present-day English Grammar Books

In Present-day English, it is an accepted theory that the negative particle *not* is positioned before the non-finite verb forms, as shown in (61a-c), although there are some differences in connotation between these three grammar books.

(61) References to the position of *not* in Present-day English grammar

a. *not* in reality stands *before* the real verbal element, the part containing the verbal meaning, i.e., infinitive or participle, just as other sentence adverbs stand before infinitive or participle and just as older *ne* as a sentence adverb stood before the real verb.

(Curme 1931: 137)

b. In negative nonfinite clauses, the negative particle is generally positioned before the verb or the *to* of the infinitive:

(Quirk et al. 1985: 994)

c. Secondary verbal negation differs from the others in two respects. First, it never introduces the auxiliary verb *do*. Second, it is always analytic: negative verb-forms are all primary except for the *don't* of imperatives. In all cases, then, secondary verbal negatives are formed by placing *not* as premodifier of the VP,

(Huddleston and Pullum 2002: 803)
(The present author's underlining)

Since no further books and articles dealing with this usage in detail appear to have been published, the present author has conducted research based on five electronic corpora of contemporary English, namely LOB, FLOB and BNC representing British English, and Brown and Frown representing

132

Chapter VI

American English. This has been in an attempt to enquire into the propriety of the statements of the grammar books in (61), to know how much extent 'in reality' in (61a) and 'generally' in (61b) indicate and whether *not* is in 'all cases' positioned before *ing*-forms as described in (61c).

6.1.2.2. Verification of the Propriety of the Statements in Present-day English Grammar Books—Post-Position of *Not* against *Ing*-Forms in LOB, FLOB, BNC, Brown and Frown Corpora

In this section, the propriety of the statements in contemporary English grammar books in (61) is verified by analysing LOB, FLOB, BNC, Brown and Frown corpora. In these corpora, three examples which seemingly have the form of *ing*-forms followed by *not* have been encountered, as in (62). However, *not* in the quotations in (62) does not negate the preceding *ing*-form but the following words *directly*, *so great* and *new* respectively.

(62) a. 1961 R. Sherwood, "The United Kingdom and the European Common Market", *Peace News*, 6-7, LOB F15, Coal and steel production being <u>not</u> directly military matters, and France being moreover the biggest of the six contracting parties, acceptance of a supra-national authority did not in this case offend French susceptibilities.

b. 1961 O. Prescott, "Books of the times", *The New York Times*, p. 33, Brown C03, Field Marshal Slim has abridged it for the benefit of "those who, finding <u>not</u> so great an attraction in accounts of military moves and counter-moves, are more interested in men and their reactions to stress, hardship and danger".

c. 1991 P. Quinn, "Second Hand WOES", *Making Music*, no. 61, 18-19, FLOB E12, The minute you buy something, it becomes 'used', and its value drops dramatically - even if you never take it out of its box - it has the stigma of being '<u>not</u> new'.

Contrastively, the following three examples in (63) exemplify the

Diachrony of Present Participles and Gerunds Followed by *Not*

ing-form + *not* construction.[21] Although the *ing*-form in (63a) is a compound gerund governed by the preposition *by*, it seems to have less nominal force because of the distance between them. This applies to the *ing*-form in (63c), which is governed by the preposition *of*.

(63) a. 1961 V. Gaul, "Ayrshire's Little Castle", *Scottish Field*, 55-56, LOB F29, Some of the painting, which took four years to complete, was ruined by the lime of the thick walls having not yet dried out, and Scott repainted part in zinc.

   b. 1961 G. Green, *The Heartless Light*, 166-170, Brown K12, She answered him precisely, missing not a beat in her scrutiny of the financial reports.
   ["Without missing a beat: if you do something without missing a beat, you do it without showing that you are surprised or shocked" (*LDCE⁵*, miss, *v.*, 15)]
   ["*fig.* (orig. and chiefly *N. Amer.*). In negative constructions, as **not to miss a beat** and variants: to react effectively and unfalteringly, esp. in demanding circumstances, or when making a transition from one activity to another; . . ." (*OED²*, beat, *n.*[1], Draft partial entry June 2002, b)]

   c. 1991 D. Jacobson, *Hidden in the Heart*, 120-25, FLOB K14, It was indistinguishable, this pride, from the conviction of being utterly ignorant of what was going to happen to me and caring not at all what that might turn out to be.

The text category of (63a) is, according to LOB, "List of Text Samples", popular lore. The *ing*-form in this example is a gerund governed by the preposition *by* but, as a compound perfective form, it has less nominal connotation. The present author has attempted to identify Victoria Gaul, the writer of this example, in vain. The example is quoted from a novel entitled "Ayrshire's Little Castle" which ran in the narrative part of the *Scottish Field*. The *ing*-form in (63b) is a simple gerund. Its text category is gen-

---

[21]Regarding my judgement on *ing*-forms co-occurring with negative intensifiers as in (63b, c), it may be predicted that some grammarians will consider that they should be excluded from the discussion. I would, however, like to make an opposite judge-

Chapter VI

eral fiction, and the example is placed in the descriptive part. The writer, Gerald Green(berg) (1922-2006), was born in New York, graduated from Columbia College, and was an American novelist and film director <https://www.goodreads.com/author/show/214742.Gerald_Green>. The quotation in (63c) is also used in the narrative part of a general fiction. The *ing*-form in this example is a simple gerund governed by the preposition *of* but, perhaps due to the distance between *of* and *ing*-form, it has less nominal force. The writer of this example, Dan Jacobson was born in Johannesburg, graduated from Witwatersrand University, worked as a professor of English at University College London and, as a novelist, won prizes including the Somerset Maugham Award <http://literature.britishcouncil.org/dan-jacobson>.

Consequently, sorted according to the forms and functions of *ing*-forms, the occurrences of pre- and post-position of *not* against *ing*-forms in the LOB and FLOB corpora, together with those of the Brown and Frown corpora, are represented in Tables 34a-c. These tables indicate that, in any construction, whether it is participial or gerundive, simple or compound, the post-position of *not* is rarely used in these corpora.

Table 34　Variations between Pre- and Post-position of *Not* against *Ing*-forms—LOB, FLOB; Brown, Frown Corpora

a. Simple Verb-*ing*

	V-*ing*	
	Participle	Gerund
	Pre : Post	Pre : Post
LOB (1961)	63 [40] : 0 [0]	31 [20] : 0 [0]
FLOB (1991,1992)	51 [37] : 0 [0]	40 [27] : 1 [1]
cf. Brown (1961)	59 [49] : 1 [1]	38 [30] : 0 [0]
Frown (1991,1992)	24 [22] : 0 [0]	38 [30] : 0 [0]

Notes to Table 34a:
[a] 'Pre' and 'Post' represent 'pre-position of *not*' and 'post-position of *not*' respectively.
[b] "63 [40]", for example, indicates that 63 examples, together with 40

ment as described in 6.1.5.1 (pp. 148-149).

Diachrony of Present Participles and Gerunds Followed by *Not*

varieties of verbs, occurred in the form of participial *not* + Verb-*ing* in LOB Corpus.

b. Compound Passive *being* + PP

	being + PP	
	Participle	Gerund
	Pre : Post	Pre : Post
LOB (1961)	1 : 0	2 : 0
FLOB (1991,1992)	0 : 0	1 : 0
cf. Brown (1961)	1 : 0	0 : 0
Frown (1991,1992)	0 : 0	1 : 0

c. Compound Perfective *having* + PP

	having + PP	
	Participle	Gerund
	Pre : Post	Pre : Post
LOB (1961)	3 : 0	4 : 1
FLOB (1991,1992)	2 : 0	2 : 0
cf. Brown (1961)	4 : 0	3 : 0
Frown (1991,1992)	0 : 0	2 : 0

In contrast with these four corpora, the BNC shows different aspects. Tables 35a-d (p. 136) indicate that the post-position of *not* occurs in every construction: simple participial/gerundive Verb-*ing*, compound passive participial/gerundive *being* + PP and compound perfective participial/gerundive *having* + PP. Particularly in the compound perfective participial *having* + PP (Table 35d) and the simple participial Verb-*ing* (Table 35a), predominantly with *being*, quite a few examples with the post-positioned *not* have been encountered.

Chapter VI

Table 35　Variations between Pre- and Post-position of *Not* against *Ing*-forms—BNC

a. Simple Participial Verb-*ing*

be	have	know	feel	look	wish
Pre : Post	Pre : Post	Pre : Post	Pre : Post	Pre : Post	Pre : Post
329　12	113　2	330　1	27　2	117　2	81　1

Other Verbs/Constructions which take the post-position of *not*

(i) With Negative Intensifiers (e.g. *a* (*single*) + N, Superlative Degree Words, *at all*)
   take (2); absorb, include, feel, share, show (1)

(ii) With *not* A *but* B Construction
   be (4); look, take (2); amount, claim, face, give, go, indicate, invite,
   involve, launch, mean, reside, see, serve, start, stress, use, want, wear (1)

b. Simple Gerundive Verb-*ing*

be	Other Verbs which take the post-position of *not*
Pre : Post	With *not* A *but* B Construction
566　2	ask, be, favour, give, have, speak, stroke (1)

c. Compound Passive *being* + PP

being + PP	
Participle	Gerund
Pre : Post	Pre : Post
112+2　1	227+9　1

Note to Table 35c:

A statistical number prefixed with '+' indicates that of the case in which the verb involved is an element coordinated by means of *(n)or/ and*, like *respected* in the following: "1991 K. Sevenoaks, *Counselling older people*, BNC-CE1, This in turn makes the parents feel unhappy about being a burden, and <u>not</u> <u>being</u> loved <u>and</u> <u>respected</u> in the way they had expected."

d. Compound Perfective *having* + PP

having + PP		
Participle	Gerund	Undiscriminating
Pre : Post	Pre : Post	Pre : Post
109+1　20	146+2　1	5　0

Diachrony of Present Participles and Gerunds Followed by *Not*

The quotations with the post-position of *not* appear in (64),[22] where those with negative intensifiers and *not* A *but* B construction have been omitted. The text categories whereby 45 examples of the post-positioned *not* occur are, according to BNC's own terminology, 'world affairs' (10 times); 'imaginative' (9 times), 'social science' (5 times); 'arts', 'belief and thought', 'leisure', 'speech recorded in business context' (3 times respectively); 'applied science', 'natural and pure science', 'speech recorded in educational context' (twice respectively); 'conversation', 'speech recorded in public context' (once respectively). It is evident that the post-positioned *not* occurs even in formal documents. (For detailed information on writers and sources of quotations of the post-positioned *not*, see pp. 319-322.)

(64) Examples of the post-position of *not* in BNC

    a. Simple participial Verb-*ing not*

      <be>

        1984 P. Norton, *The British polity*, BNC-J57, In this view, parties are seen as <u>being</u> <u>not</u> quite as central to formulation of public money as both reformers and the politicians themselves believe. <world affairs> | 1980 J. Lowerson, *A short history of Sussex*, BNC-CB6, Unlike many of those who followed him and profited from pirated editions of his works, Russell was not a quack and his treatments were not to be taken lightly, the firm physical and mental regimen he prescribed <u>being</u> <u>not</u> far from the modern practices of hydropathic establishments or the health clubs beloved of overweight executives. <world affairs> | 1989, *The Guardian, electronic edition of 1989-12-10: Foreign news pages*, BNC-A9J, Its significance lies in its double message: that the aim of the

---

[22] The following example is excluded from the list of examples in (64) and their tabulation (Table 35a) because it is a quotation from a document written in the remote past by an Elizabethan writer Thomas Nash(e) (1567-1601):

    1991 J. Litten, *The English way of death—the common funeral since 1450*, BNC-CD3, The process is satirically described by Nashe in the Anatomie of Martin Marprelate: Having bestowed his bowels in a ditch; and filled his hungry belly; with coal dust, for spice they could not bestow (his carrion <u>being</u> <u>not</u> worth it) and sawdust they could have none; they wrapped him in a blanket; for that all others are lapped in sheets

Chapter VI

Palestinian struggle is the establishment of Palestinian independence, and that this independence is regarded as being not at Israel's expense. <world affairs> | 1990 A. Maidment, *I remember, I remember*, BNC-B22, I wanted to have a go but being not yet seven was refused, however the sideshow gave me an idea. <leisure> | 1990 S. Farrow, and J. Farrow, *Madeira: the complete guide*, BNC-CA7, For example, between 1747 and 1751 the British physician Dr Thomas Heberden kept weather records which showed the excellence of the winter climate — pleasant between October and May, being not too humid and not too dry, with clean, dust-free air. <leisure> | 1990 P. Wiat, *The child bride*, BNC-CCD, Joan de Warenne being not of royal blood and not linked as you yourself are, Lady Anne, by a bond of marriage, I can see no virtue in such an arrangement. <imaginative> | 1991 N. Longmate, *Island fortress*, BNC-BNB, At all events a Council of War, called by Durand, decided that "the castle being not tenable, it is for His Majesty's service that it be abandoned"; <world affairs> | 1991 C. Willock, *Kingdoms of the East*, BNC-CK2, There are many species of "flying"; squirrels, but none of these is so well equipped for flight as the colugo, their gliding membranes being not nearly so extensive. <natural sciences> | 1991 D. Urwin, *The community of Europe*, BNC-CLR, This arrangement might well have been satisfactory, with some accommodation between the two sides being not too difficult to achieve, but for the rancour that had been aroused in recent years. <world affairs> | 1992 R. Alexander, *Policy and practice in primary education*, BNC-G1F, This was viewed by teachers as having the force of policy and therefore being not open to challenge. <social science> | *Gwynedd County Council tape 4: interview for oral history project*, BNC-HEM, So the actual So w why was it the fetching of etcetera, were thought of as being not so good? <speech recorded in leisure context> | *EIP meeting at Strensall Village Hall, day 3, afternoon session: public county council planning meeting*, BNC-HVK, we don't know what he's going to say about sites er which were at issue, or on the need for flexibility between the inner erm boundary of the greenbelt and the city, irrespective of course of what the inspector says, erm being not yet statutory adopted the County and Ryedale

Diachrony of Present Participles and Gerunds Followed by *Not*

will still have the opportunity to consider, reconsider there policies there, <speech recorded in public context>

<have>

1980 J. Lowerson, *A short history of Sussex*, BNC-CB6, That perceptive government spy, Daniel Defoe, said in the 1720s: Bramber hardly deserves the name of a town, having not above fifteen or sixteen families in it, and of them not many above asking you an alms as you ride by; <world affairs> | *Justice and Peace Group meeting*, BNC-G3U, That we're really talking about the re the reign of God, and how in fact God's plan is not in operation with people starving <pause> and people having <pause> not a future they c they can anticipate. <speech recorded in business context>

<know>

1992 C. Cookson, *The rag nymph*, BNC-CK9, They were out in the street now and Aggie, for once in her life, stood helpless, knowing not what to do. <imaginative>

<feel>

1987 D. L. Nuttall, P. S. Clift and R. McCormick, *Studies in school self-evaluation*, BNC-HNW, The degree of involvement in the reviews has generally been high, nearly half the teachers feeling very involved, a further third fairly involved, and only 5 per cent feeling not involved at all. <social science> | 1993 P. Wilson, *A healing fire*, BNC-HGD, Jenna just stared at him blankly, feeling not quite capable of absorbing this. <imaginative>

<look>

1990 P. Wiat, *The child bride*, BNC-CCD, Henceforth I shall take life as it comes, looking not to the future <imaginative> | 1993 B. Neil, *The possession of Delia Sutherland*, BNC-FPF, She sat on the tool-box, pressing her hat to her head, and looking not this time out to sea but at all that was passing and being left behind. <imaginative>

<wish>

1992 R. Elliot, *Lover's charade*, BNC-JY5, At last her conscience won out and she gave a tiny sigh, wishing not for the first time that she could, just occasionally, be a touch more ruthless. <imaginative>

Chapter VI

b. Simple gerundive Verb-*ing not*
<be>
1988 J. C. K. Cornwall, *Wealth and society in early 16th century England*, BNC-CTW, Besides being not untypical, 3 1/2 per cent was a fair enough share of the community's wealth for the fifty-two secular priests, who formed almost exactly the same proportion of the 1484 adult male inhabitants. <world affairs> | 1989 *Independent, electronic edition of 1989-10-14: Arts section*, BNC-A5E, Only a short while later these were accused (by Schiller amongst others) of being not worthy of him - "Fit only for the nursery, to use in connection with Noah's Ark" — but the truth is they are irresistible. <arts>

c. Compound participial passive *being not* + PP
1993 *Nucleic acids research* [periodical], BNC-K5R, For instance, among the 22 Arg residues 19 are coded by AGA, 1 by AGG, CGT and CGC, the codons CGA and CGG being not used at all; furthermore, triplets ending in A or T are preferred to those ending in C or G. <natural sciences>

d. Compound gerundive passive *being not* + PP
1992 W. Swann, T. Booth, M. Masterton and P. Potts, ed., *Policies for diversity in education*, BNC-CRS, Every one of these parents can recount stories of being not believed, not looked at, not spoken to: that is what dead people experience, if the dead have experiences. <social science>

e. Compound participial perfective *having not* + PP
1988 M. Batchelor, *Forty plus*, BNC-BLW, One or both of them may not wish to cope with parenting a second time round, having not long been released from the exhaustion and limitations of childcare on their own account. <belief and thought> | 1988 B. Cant and S. Hemmings, ed., *Radical records*, BNC-CF4, I wasn't involved in setting up the Group, having then not accepted my lesbian identity, but from what I could see there was a lot of resentful and suspicious comparison between the BWG and the LGWG. <social science> | 1989 M. Aspel, *In good company*, BNC-CH8, Having not gone outside my own area until that point I hadn't realized how good I

Diachrony of Present Participles and Gerunds Followed by *Not*

was. <arts> | 1989 F. Field, *Losing out: the emergence of a UK underclass*, BNC-FAF, One of the crucial changes brought about by Mrs Thatcher is the attitude of those who have made it and believe that others can do likewise, or, if they fail to do so, are judged as having not really tried. <social science> | 1990 *Keesings Contemporary Archives* [periodical], BNC-HKS, On March 11 former President Ahmed Ben Bella's party, the Movement for Democracy in Algeria (Mouvement pour la démocratie en Algérie), was legalized although Ben Bella himself remained in exile in Switzerland, the Algerian judicial authorities having not yet reached a decision on whether to drop charges against him. <world affairs> | 1991 B. Howell, *Dandelion days*, BNC-ACK, We held hands all the way through Live Aid, having not spoken to each other for a week, and then rushed off to the Post Office as soon as we could with our three pounds. <imaginative> | 1991 J. Spottiswoode, *Undertaken with love*, BNC-CES, The following Sunday, having not yet received an appointment card, I was certain, quite suddenly, that Nigel's pain was not muscular. <belief and thought> | 1991 G. Vesey, *Inner and outer*, BNC-CK1, Someone might say: surely he can imagine recognising (or having not recognised) the person. <belief and thought> | 1991 *Keesings Contemporary Archives* [periodical], BNC-HLB, On Sept. 9, Tajikistan became the 12th Soviet republic to declare independence (only the Russian Federation, Kazakhstan and Turkmenia having not done so). <world affairs> | 1991-1992 *Running* [periodical], BNC-CB4, Before you leave, double-check your bag has everything any marathon runner could ever need inside and as you arrive (calm and collected, having not lost your temper with the public transport system) do a little stretching and gentle jogging. <leisure> | 1992 *CD Review* [periodical], BNC-BMC, Having not heard either work for some years, I was pleasantly surprised to be reminded what a delightfully unaffected piece the Missa choralis, in particular, really is. <arts> | 1992 *31 Conversations Recorded by 'Martine' (PS0LK) between 12 and 20 March 1992 with 10 Interlocutors*, BNC-KD8, Having not done one I wouldn't know how they go about it <conversation> | 1993 *East Anglian Daily Times* [periodical], BNC-CFC, You are also misled yet again by newspaper reports, having not read the transcript. <world affairs> | 1993 J.

Chapter VI

Critchley, *The floating voter*, BNC-HNK, They were likely to make trouble, <u>having</u> <u>not</u> yet <u>come</u> to terms with the hurried departure of Mrs Thatcher following upon the events of November 1990. <imaginative> | 1993 J. Steele, *West of Bohemia*, BNC-JYF, Both she and Lubor had a glass of beer to go with it, and, <u>having</u> <u>not</u> <u>been</u> hungry, the meal went down much better than Fabia had anticipated. <imaginative> | *Tarmac Construction: training session*, BNC-JSA, Remember I asked you this morning to just <unclear> just after lunch to jot down what it was that you need to improve on just as you're setting the clock just say something like by the end of this talk I'd like you to congratulate me on having moved around a bit more <u>having</u> <u>not</u> <u>put</u> me hands in me pockets, whatever it might be. <speech recorded in business context> | *Computergram international* [periodical], BNC-CNM, Sun is still tinkering around with the Cypress Semiconductor Corp Ross Systems HyperSparc chip, <u>having</u> apparently <u>not</u> <u>found</u> a home for it yet: in benchmarks, the part outpaced the SuperSparc but by how much remains a mystery; <applied science> | *Britain and Europe - European art: radio programme*, BNC-KRS, What that exhibition in fact is doing is that it's not saying here's a new spirit in painting, it's saying that we the organizers, <u>having</u> <u>not</u> <u>bothered</u> to show you these things in the sixties and seventies, will now allow you to see them in the eighties, and we will pretend there's a new spirit because we think it's good for the art world to have new fashions, new movements, or at least something new going on that will produce some kind of emotional pressure. <speech recorded in educational context> | *Fox FM News: radio programme*, BNC-KRT, British Gas up four at two one four point five, British Telecom were down four at two hundred and sixty four, Goodhead Publishing Group unchanged at fifty-eight, Metal Box up one thousand two hundred, Morland Brewers unchanged at two hundred and seventy five and Oxford Instruments er ended the day unchanged at two hundred and seventy five and Oxford Instruments er ended the day at two three four, <u>having</u> er <u>not</u> <u>changed</u> their position. <speech recorded in educational context> | R. N. Alan, ed., *Gut: Journal of Gastroenterology and Hepatology* [periodical], BNC-HU2, The patients fasted at 0900 <u>having</u> <u>not</u> <u>taken</u> any drugs which affect gastric secretion or motility over the previous 10 days. <ap-

Diachrony of Present Participles and Gerunds Followed by *Not*

plied science>

f. Compound gerundive perfective *having not* + PP
British Rail quality assurance seminar, BNC-H47, Because it means
you can always criticize the individual, for either not having done
the job well enough or for having not done it quite the way you
thought it ought to be done. <speech recorded in business context>[23]

As shown above, tabulation of the data for the variations between
the post-position and the pre-position of *not* in these five corpora, presented in Tables 34a-c (pp. 134-135) and 35a-d (p. 136), reveals several findings of particular interest. First, the post-position of *not* tends to occur
more frequently in participles than in gerunds and in compound forms than
in simple forms. Second, although the frequency of the post-position of *not*
in all the forms and functions of the *ing*-form is low, with the possible exception of the compound participial perfective *having* + PP in Table 35d,
the post-position of *not* has not totally disappeared in Present-day English.
This seems to suggest that, out of the three grammar books in (61), the
statement in (61b) sounds appropriate, although the three grammatical
usages are based upon their own evidence. The description in (61c), even
though it was only to be expected from linguistic data, is over-generalised
considering the fact that the post-position of *not* is evidenced in Present-
day British English as represented in the BNC.

6.1.3. Previous Studies on the History of the Position of *Not* against *Ing*-
forms and Purpose of the Present Chapter

Few references to *ing*-forms followed by *not* can be detected in diachronic studies as well as in Present-day English grammar books. The former includes monumental studies devoted to more than one period of the
history of the English language written by linguistic historians such as
Jespersen (1905 [1972], 1931 [1970], 1940 [1970]), Trnka (1930 [1968]),

---

[23] It is interesting that, even in twentieth-century speech recorded in business contexts,
both "not having done" and "having not done" are used in their vicinity by the same
speaker.

144

Chapter VI

Poutsma (1919, 1923, 1926, 1928), Baugh (1951 [1976]), Mustanoja (1960), Partridge (1953b, 1969), Visser (1969, 1970, 1972, 1973), Barber (1976), Strang (1970), Araki and Ukaji (1984), Denison (1993, 1998) and Rissanen (1999) in chronological order; the latter includes those devoted to a particular period, writer or text written by historical linguists such as Schmidt (1900), Uhrström (1907), Sugden (1936), Franz (1939), Phillipps (1970) and Ando (1976).

To the best of the present author's knowledge, there are no more than four grammarians who have noticed and referred to this construction, as shown in (65): William Bullokar, Joseph Priestley, Johannes Söderlind and Akira Wada.

(65) References to the position of *not* against *ing*-forms in the history of English

a. The negatiu' not, iȝ commųn/y ſett after the v'erb or hiȝ ſýn of tenc', and be'fór a partic'ipl
(Bullokar 1586 [1971]: 141)

b. The negative particles are not well situated between the active participles of auxiliary verbs, and the passive participles of other verbs. *Which* being not *admitted into general use*, does not please the ear so well as *which* not being *admitted*. Having not *known, or not considered*; i.e. not having *known*.
(Priestley 1761 [1769]: 124-125)

c. 1683 J. Dryden, *The Vindication of the Duke of Guise*, 213, debates *coming not* by any Act to any issue
(Söderlind 1958 [1976]: 158 & n. 1)

d. 1598?/1599?/1600? T. Deloney, *Thomas of Reading*, 264, 7-9, in Mann, F. O., ed. (1912) *The Works of Thomas Deloney*, but himselfe being sore wounded, and faint with ouermuch bleeding, at length fell downe, *being not* able any longer to stand
(Wada 1975: 19)

Bullokar, an Elizabethan grammarian, states that the negative particle *not* usually occupies the pre-position of participles in (65a). In (65b), Priestley frowns at the usage of *being not* PP / *having not* PP because of

Diachrony of Present Participles and Gerunds Followed by *Not*

their cacophony and harsh sounds. In (65c), Söderlind draws the readers' attention to a single instance quoted from Dryden's play. In (65d), Wada describes, with respect to Thomas Deloney's English, that "the negative *not* stands after finite verbs or between the finite and non-finite verbs without a single exception", and that, in contrast, "the negative *not* stands before the non-finite forms", showing the quotation as the only exceptional example.

Here a question arises regarding whether Bullokar's and Priestley's statements can bear witness to Early and Late Modern English respectively. At this point, the rule in Present-day English may hold true for the time in which Bullolar and Priestley lived, and *ing*-forms followed by *not* seem to have been a very rare type of negative form. However, as provided later in Sections 6.2-6.4, a fairly large number of counterexamples occur in the texts and electronic corpora examined. Too many examples occurred to be regarded as a "rare" construction. The so-called 'unusual' type of participles or gerunds followed by *not* seem to have been overlooked by historical grammarians perhaps because this construction has been stigmatised simply as a slip of tongue or pen as hinted in (65a, b). When the position of the negative particle *not* versus the participial *ing*-form is considered, it becomes apparent that the descriptions in (65a, b) turn out to be overly generalised and even contrary to historical English facts. The construction of the post-positioned *not* was being used not only by ordinary citizens but also by the upper class or educated people of the time. The spread of this construction into a multitude of documents implies that it would be unfair to label this construction simply as an erroneous usage.

Thus the main purpose of this chapter is to clarify whether the rule in Present-day English stated in 6.1.2.1 above holds true of earlier English, or whether the use of post-positioned *not* in current English is a peripheral usage or even a mere misuse. If it is permitted to state a part of the conclusions here, the use of the post-position of *not* in Present-day English proves to be a fossil or residual in the discussions of Sections 6.2-6.4. What is insisted on in this chapter is that, in the Modern English period,

Chapter VI

especially in the 17th century, the post-position of *not*, particularly following participles, was used by many people and, accordingly, was no rare usage, even though less frequently than the pre-position of *not*. This means that the post-positioned *not* must have been a part of grammar in Modern, especially Early Modern, English. This construction seems to have escaped grammarians' notice in the history of English research. The extent to which this particular structure spread implies that it seems to have been far from an erroneous usage.

6.1.4. Texts and Electronic Corpora Examined, and Methodology in Collecting Examples

Texts and electronic corpora examined are listed on pp. 377-389. For the analysis of the English in LOB, FLOB, Brown and Frown corpora in 6.1.2.2., KWIC Concordance for Windows 4.7.0.4 was utilised as a lexical analysis software, as was Oxford WordSmith Tools 4.0 for BNC. For the analysis of the English in 17th- to 20th-century diaries and correspondence published in the form of a book in 6.2, a traditional methodology without the use of electronic software was conducted, collecting examples line by line, page by page. For the analysis of the English in CEECS, Lampeter and Newdigate in 6.3, collection of examples was double-checked through both KWIC Concordance for Windows 4.7.0.4 and Oxford WordSmith Tools, 4.0. For the collection of examples from Helsinki-DP and ARCHER 3.1, Oxford WordSmith Tools 5.0 was operated. Examples in the *OED²* on CD-ROM, Version 3.01 were compiled through *OED*'s advanced search function in 6.4. In all of the electronic corpus analysis, search words and context words were *-ing/-inge/-yng/-ynge* and *not/nott/nat/nought* respectively, permitting five other words or fewer to intervene. The methodology of collecting examples explained here is tabulated in Table 36:

Diachrony of Present Participles and Gerunds Followed by *Not*

Table 36   Methodology in Collecting Examples

Corpus	Lexical analysis software	Search words	Context words	Search horizons
Diaries & Correspondence	traditional methodology, a snail work, of collecting examples line by line, page by page			
LOB FLOB Brown Frown	KWIC Concordance for Windows 4.7.0.4.	*ing *inge *yng *ynge	not nott nat nought	L5 R5
BNC	Oxford Wordsmith Tools 4.0			
CEECS Lampeter Newdigate	Double check through both KWIC Concordance for Windows 4.7.0.4. and Oxford Wordsmith Tools 4.0			
Helsinki-DP ARCHER 3.1	Oxford Wordsmith Tools 5.0			
OED²	OED advanced search			

This example-compiling process was time- and energy-consuming because undesirable examples needed to be weeded out from raw software results. For example, Table 37 shows the frequency of the co-occurrence of *-ing(e)*, *-yng(e)* with *not(t)*, *nat*, *nought* in the *OED²*. This table indicates that, for instance, *-ing* and *not* co-occur in 36,704 examples, and *-inge* and *nott* in three examples.

Table 37   Co-occurrence of *-ing(e)* and *-yng(e)* with *Not(t)*, *Nat* and *Nought*— *OED²*

	not	nott	nat	nought
-ing	36,704	36	4662	195
-inge	476	3	33	23
-yng	976	12	132	85
-ynge	669	9	104	62

Nevertheless, some nouns and adjectives end in *-ing(e)* and *-yng(e)*, and the length of the sentences in the computer list obtained through the lexical analysis software can be too short to grasp the entire context. Accordingly, examples had to be scrutinised one by one by referring back to the citations shown directly under their definitions or even visiting the libraries for the original texts, in order to examine whether the example concerned

148

Chapter VI

included the target construction. The statistics of 2,572+84 in 6.4 were thus deduced. Every electronic corpus examined in this chapter has numerous raw lexical analysis software results, and the sieving process took more time than expected.

6.1.5. Criteria of Analysis—Inclusion or Exclusion of Examples

Criteria for what kind of examples deserve inclusion and analysis in 6.2-6.4 require delineation; statistics vary slightly or even greatly accordingly. They are presented in this section so that grammarians starting with different criteria may make adjustments to the statistics in this chapter according to their own criteria.

6.1.5.1. Inclusion

Grammarians may differ in judgment when faced with the example in (66), in which negated participles or gerunds may be construed with a negative intensifier such as superlative degree word + N, *a* (*single*)/*an*/*one* + N, (*in*) *the least* and *at all*. Since not only the post-positioned but also the pre-positioned *not* occurred in the texts and corpora examined, this construction needed to be taken into consideration, as already referred to under footnote 21 (pp. 133-134) in relation to (63b, c).

(66) 1607 R. C[arew] tr. *Estienne's World of Wonders* i. xxiv. 194 The poore gentlewoman . . speaking not a word, gaue him a twinch with a weeping eye. (*OED²*, s.v. twink, *n.*[1] 1) | 1679 H. Savile, L11, 94, instead of saying not a word of it, as I should have thought the best way, I am now fain to turn it into ridicule as the second best, | 1696 P. Ventris *Reports* I. 191 The Court inclined strongly for the Defendant, there being not the least negligence in him. (*OED²*, s.v. negligence, *n.* Add: [1.] d)

Although this accompaniment of negative intensifiers can be considered one of the factors which induce the post-position of *not*, this is not always the case. As shown in Table 38, in 130 volumes of 17th- to 20th-century diaries and correspondence, for instance, 3 examples with the simple participial *not* Verb-*ing* as against 11 with the simple participial Verb-*ing* not

Diachrony of Present Participles and Gerunds Followed by *Not*

have been encountered. Similarly, in the *OED²*'s citations, the table for which is omitted here, 4 examples with the simple participial *not* Verb-*ing* as against 12 with the simple participial Verb-*ing not* have been collected. In Sections 6.2-6.4, examples with negative intensifiers will be separated from general examples.

Table 38   Variations between Pre- and Post-position of *Not* Accompanied by Negative Intensifiers—17th- to 20th-century Diaries and Correspondence

a. Simple Participial Verb-*ing*

Period	Pre	Post
-1649		
1650-1699	say (1) see (1)	afford (1) be (3) find (1)
1700-1749		
1750-1799		be (1) have (1) leave (1)
1800-1849	be (1)	have (1) say (1)
1850-1899		have (1) take (1)
1900-1699		occupy (1)

b. Simple Gerundive Verb-*ing*

Period	Pre	Post
-1649		
1650-1699		say (1)
1700-		

Next, the judgement over the quotations in which negated participles or gerunds may be construed with correlative *not*-A-*but*-B will be clarified. Nobody would object to including examples of the type (67a, b), where two participial *ing*-forms are correlated by means of *not* and *but*. In particular, the 1534 and 1968 quotations are easy to deal with since *desyring* and *counting* are repeated after *but* respectively. In the *OED²*, for example, 44 examples with the simple participial *not* Verb-*ing* as against 1 with the simple participial Verb-*ing not*, and 3 examples with the simple gerundive *not* Verb-*ing* have been compiled. The examples with two *ing*-forms correlated by *not*-A-*but*-B are all included in the statistics in Sections 6.2-6.4.

Chapter VI

(67) a. 1534 More *Comf. agst. Trib.* iii. Wks. 1262/1 Not desyring to be
brought vnto ye peril of persecucion (for it semeth a proude high
mind to desyre martyrdom) but desyring helpe and strength of god,
if he suffer vs to come to the stresse. (*OED²*, s.v. stress, *n.* 2c) | 1553
T. Wilson *Rhet.* (1580) 14 [Certain orators] would so muche saie as
their witte would giue, not weighyng the state of the cause, but
mindyng the vaunt of their braine. (*OED²*, s.v. vaunt, *n.*[1] 1) | 1611
Bible *2 Macc.* ix. 22 Not distrusting mine health, but hauing great
hope to escape this sicknes. (*OED²*, s.v. distrust, *v.* 2b) | 1642 Fuller
Holy & Prof. St. iii. xxv. 229 Others . . not going through the porch
of humane Arts, but entring into Divinity at the postern, have made
good Preachers. (*OED²*, s.v. postern, *n. (a.)* 2a) | 1663 S. Pepys,
D10, IV 140, where I find it almost night and my wife and the Dan-
cing Maister alone above, not dancing but walking. | 1968 'O.
Mills' *Sundry Fell Designs* i. 9 This . . must be her eleventh protest
camp, not counting non-overnight demonstrations in Trafalgar
Square but counting the Aldermaston marches. (*OED²*, s.v. protest,
n. 5)

b. 1648 W. Jenkyn *Blind Guide* i. 14 Shining not like a sweetly influentiall star, but flashing like an angry bloody Comet. (*OED²*, s.v. influential, *a. (n)*, 1a)

However, some readers may frown at the present author for including
examples of the type in which the positions A and B in *not*-A-*but*-B construction are occupied by nominals, adjectivals, adverbials and prepos-
itionals. In (68a), for example, they may think that *not* negates the part
'from their uropygium', not 'growing'. If 'growing' were repeated after
'but', or 'but all up their backs' were not written, a different interpretation
would be plausible, i.e. that *not* is related to 'growing'. There seems to be
some truth in this interpretation. All of this thinking precludes the present
author from excluding examples of the type (68a) as those of local negation. Furthermore, if (68a) should be excluded, it follows that (68b)
should also be not included for consideration for the simple reason that it
contains *not*-A-*but*-B construction. When the fact that the type (68a) is a
variant of the type (68b) is considered, the type (68a) could not be excluded from the present analyses, even though the frequency of the type

Diachrony of Present Participles and Gerunds Followed by *Not*

(68a) is comparatively low. This is the reason why the quotations in which negated participles or gerunds may be construed with correlative *not-A-but*-B merit inclusion in this study. In the presentation of examples, however, those with the type (68a) are isolated from the general ones. In the *OED²*, for instance, 42 examples with the simple participial *not* Verb-*ing* as against 34 with the simple participial Verb-*ing not*, and 5 examples with the simple gerundive Verb-*ing not* have been collected. The accompaniment of *not-A-but*-B can be thought of as one of the factors which promote the post-position of *not*.

(68) a. 1771 G. White *Let.* in *Selborne* (1789) xxxv. 92 The trains of those magnificent birds [*sc.* peacocks] . . . growing not from their uropygium, but all up their backs. (*OED²*, s.v. uropygium) [*uropygium*: "the rump in birds"]

b. 1813 Bingley *Anim. Biog.* (ed. 4) II. 235 The brilliant train of the Peacock . . . not growing from the uropygium (or rump,) but upon the back. (Ibid.)

In the texts and corpora examined, the majority of the participles accompanied by *not* are used adverbially and occasionally adjectivally. Both usages are included in the statistics. With the adjectival use represented in (69), the negative particle *not* always precedes the *ing*-form. Examples are focussed on the following verbs: *exceed, surmount, breathe, depend, have, lead*, and *possess*, in this order of frequency.

(69) 1667 J. Milward, D6, 75, This day was read the bill for preventing fightings and disorders of seamen at their pay day; power was given to the officers of the Naval forces to punish any such disorders, by fining such as should fight and be disorderly, the fine not exceeding one pound,

In *willing to* + infinitive, *willing* is thought to be a participial adjective and, accordingly, *willing not to* + infinitive was excluded from the statistics. As *willing* in the constructions of *willing* + *that*-clause and *willing* sb *to* + infinitive is a present participle, a form of the verb *will*, however, examples with these structures were taken into consideration, as shown

Chapter VI

in (70). In all of the examples *not* occupied the position before the *ing*-form.

(70) 1699 J. Evelyn, D9, V 347, not willing any should persist in sinn, & be lost. | 1796 W. B. Stevens, D22, 351, when she inserted her last note into Jones's Letter, not willing that He should know the contents,

Most of the gerunds stand as the subject of a sentence, or the object of a verb or a preposition. Occasionally 'sentence- or clause-kernel' use (Söderlind 1958 [1976] 184) is encountered. Such examples as represented in (71) are included.

(71) 1786 J. Woodforde, D21, II 229, Sent Ben to Norwich this Morning after Newspapers &c. Mr. Cary not going this week.

The quotations in (72), in which the form of the subject of the *ing*-form is not in the nominative case *he*, are included in the statistics for the simple participial Verb-*ing*.

(72) 1736 J. Wesley, D17, 14, His not going so soon, I went to Ashley-Ferry on Thursday, | 1780 J. Woodforde, D21, I 296, he is going to leave the Ariadne, the Captain whose name is Squire and him not agreeing | 1799 J. Woodforde, D21, V 223, but his not being at home, William returned home to dinner

In documents not intended for publication, readers encounter unnatural usage. In (73), for instance, John Bruce, the editor of King Charles I's letters, correctly insists that *having* should be replaced with *hearing*. The present author adhered, however, to the original usage, so this example was included in the statistics for the simple participial *having*.

(73) 1646 King Charles, L2, 76, having [hearing?] yet not certainly neither from thee nor Ireland concerning it, I will not . . . engage myself in it before I know thy opinion,

In correspondence, the same letters are at times recorded in different correspondence. For instance, 1705 D. Defoe, L1, 321 reads "I was wholly ignorant of the design of that act, *not knowing* it had such a noble original" and 1705 D. Defoe, L14, 82 reads "I was wholly Ignorant of the De-

Diachrony of Present Participles and Gerunds Followed by *Not*

sign of that act, *Not knowing* it had Such a Noble Originall". Such examples were counted as one example and quoted with a single source text in 6.2. Similarly in the *OED*[2], the same citations can appear under different lemmas. For example, the citation "1664 Evelyn *Kal. Hort.* (1679) 33 [Plants] *not perishing* but in excessive Colds, . . Laurels, Cherry Laurel" appears under the four following lemmas: cherry, *n.* 10; cineraria; cold, *n.* 1d; and laurel, *n.*[1] 3a. The citation "1538 Starkey *England* I. iii. 84 The partys in proportyon *not agreyng* . . leue much enormyte . . in thys polytyke body" is quoted under the three lemmas: enormity 1; lend, *v.*[2] and monstrous, *a.* 2b. Such examples were also counted as one example respectively and quoted with one of the sources in 6.4.

In the analyses of electronic corpora in 6.3, the same examples as collected in 6.2 also appear as follows: two examples with the usage of the simple participial Verb-*ing* + *not* (the same examples as in D2 and D10), one example with the compound participial *having not* PP (the same as in L1), one example with the simple gerundive Verb-*ing not* (the same as in D2), three examples with the simple participial *not* Verb-*ing* (the same as in D10), and one example with the simple gerundive *not* Verb-*ing* (the same as in D10). As the duplication is slight, however, these examples were not excluded from the statistics for the electronic corpora so as not to disturb the harmony within the corpora.

6.1.5.2. Exclusion

In contrast to what has been stated, the quotations under the criteria in 6.1.5.2 have been excluded from the statistics in Sections 6.2-6.4.

First, quotations with local negation of *not*, apart from the construction in which negated participles or gerunds may be construed with a negative intensifier (pp. 148-149) and that with correlative *not*-A-*but*-B (pp. 149-151), were weeded out as undesirable. In (74), for example, it is the words modified by double lines, i.e. 'long' in (74a), 'to permit' in (74b), 'safe' in (74c), 'a little' in (74d), 'only her mistress' in (74e) and 'more (than sixty feet)' in (74f), not *ing*-forms, that are negated by *not*.

154

Chapter VI

(74) a. 1666 S. Pepys, D10, VII 203, he was not up – being <u>not</u> <u>long</u> since married;

b. 1673 H. Ball, L8, II 44, Mr. Seymour . . . cannot hold his place, because he is a Privy Councellor, the custome of the house being <u>not</u> <u>to permit</u> him to come to Court or beare any office without their leave dureing the time of its Session,

c. 1673 R. Yard, L8, I 143, the officers thinking it <u>not</u> <u>safe</u> to putt the articles lately published in execution, on this side of the water;

d. 1738 J. Wesley, D17, 33, Afterwards I . . . gave them a short but plain account of the state of the colony: an account, I fear, <u>not</u> <u>a</u> <u>little</u> differing from those which they had frequently received before,

e. 1797 A. Hughes, D20, 137, all the praise should go to the dear mistress who had done so much for her, bein [*sic*] <u>not</u> <u>only her mistress</u> but her dear respected friend;

f. 1850 T. H. Huxley, D35, 325, The fall was very pretty; much the same style of place as the Chamarelle, only not so grand, being <u>not</u> <u>more</u> than sixty feet, but then in compensation, there was a much larger body of water.

g. 1989 K. Miller, *Authors*, BNC-A05, this could well be an opinion that underlies the talk about his later books being <u>not</u> <u>nearly</u> <u>as</u> good <u>as</u> his earlier ones. <arts> | 1989 D. Wingrove, *Chung Kuo book one: the Middle Kingdom*, BNC-FRF, She laughed quietly, that same feeling she had had staring down at the cove through the trees — that sense of being <u>not</u> <u>quite</u> herself — returning to her. <imaginative> | 1993 G. Holtham, V. Joshi and D. Helm, *Oxford Review of Economic Policy*, BNC-FRN, Obviously the result is dependent on there being <u>not</u> <u>too</u> <u>much</u> differentiation at the upstream stage, <commerce>

The quotations in (75) also represent a kind of local negation; *not* does not negate the preceding *ing*-form but the following *to* + infinitive. This construction typically occurs with the following verbs and structures: *advise* / *beg* / *beseech* / *caution* / *encourage* / *exhort* / *hold* / *induce* / *persuade* / *petition* / *plead* / *pray* / *procure* / *promise* / *urge* / *warn* / etc. + Ob-

Diachrony of Present Participles and Gerunds Followed by *Not*

ject + *to*-infinitive; *affect* / *agree* / *appear* / *desire* / *determine* / *happen* / *intend* / *intend* / *mean* / *mind* / *pretend* / *resolve* / *suppose* / *try* / *vow* / *wish* / etc. + *to*-infinitive.[24]

(75) 1660 S. Pepys, D10, I 133, so that I sent for Mr. Pitts to come to me from the Vice-Admirall, entending not to have imployed Burr any more. | 1702 P. Skinner, L7, II 289, Beseeching Heaven not to cutt it shorter, | 1772 J. Wesley, D17, 374, Resolving not to shoot over their heads, as I had done the day before, I spoke strongly of death and judgment, heaven and hell. | 1825 H. Arbuthnot, D27, I 393, Lord Bathurst has written to him urging him not to retire, | 1827 W. E. Gladstone, D33, 118, wishing not to have a very long debate, kept me from speaking | 1830 T. Raikes, L44, 41, promising not to write again without something else to say,

According to the *OED²*, *ing*-forms as underlined in (76) had been no longer participles but transferred into prepositions/adjectives at the time when each document was written and, accordingly, they were not included in the statistics in Sections 6.2-6.4. The following *ing*-forms were also excluded: *according (to), againstanding, concerning, excluding, including, owing (to), touching; adjoining, aspiring, divertising, exhilarating, favouring, fitting, flattering, knowing, offending, officiating, provoking, satisfying, surmounting, wanting*, etc.

(76) 1611 Shakes. *Wint. T.* iv. iv. 747 They often giue vs (Souldiers) the Lye, but wee pay them for it with stamped Coyne, not stabbing Steele. (*OED²*, s.v. stamped, *ppl. a.* 2; stabbing, *ppl. a.* 1) | 1695 W. Gilpin, L12, 254, not withstanding all this dust I find he is not yet ready for Mr Howard; | 1697 Evelyn, D9, V 263, The severe frost & weather not relenting, and freezing with snow, againe kept us from Church: | 1751

---

[24] The closer relation of *not* to *to*-infinitive is most clearly revealed in the following sentences:

(i) 1664 S. Pepys, D10, V 224, I did desire not to have it at all | 1667 S. Pepys, D10, VIII 110, our maisters do begin not to like of their counsels in fitting out no fleet, but only squadrons

(ii) 1749 G. B. Dodington, D16, 18, the bulk of mankind, I say, not being taught to see, or rather being taught not to see it in that light, judged of it in gross,

156

Chapter VI

J. Wesley, D17, 197, We rode to Edinburgh; one of the dirtiest cities I had ever seen, not excepting Cölen in Germany. | 1873 A. C. Swinburne, L56, I 119, There are also other matters connected with Hotten about which I want your advice—books of mine in his hands, and papers *not* relating to this matter.

Examples of the negation of participles and gerunds collected from prose parts constitute the statistics in 6.2. Those collected from verse text are treated separately, as in (77).

(77) 1640 "A Dialogue between Two Zelots, concerning "Etc." in the Newe Oath", D4, 103, Thus they dranke on, not offering to parte, / Till they had sworne out the eleventh quart; | 1794 R. Southey, L42, 65, . . . To the distant shore / Where Freedom spurns Oppressions iron reign / I go: not vainly sorrowing to deplore / The long-loved friends I leave to meet no more, | 1800²W. Wordsworth, D24, 181, … and we two, / Conversing not, knew little in what mould / Each other's mind was fashioned;

On the contrary, in case of the *OED²* as a corpus, appropriate citations gathered not only from prose parts but also from verse text were all included in its statistics in 6.4. Here English translations, although they can be influenced by the original languages, were also included. Partly because of this reason, this study abstained from calculation of the percentage of the pre- and post-position of *not* and its figuration in the *OED²* even though the frequency of these cases are low.

A further problem arises with the quotations in (78) because of defects in the manuscripts, where additions within brackets are editorial. In the first quotation, for example, the editors feel it necessary to alter *from* into *not*. Indeed, their interpretation is correct, but it is still merely an educated assumption on the part of the editors; for example, *not* could be replaced by *no*, among other possibilities. Consequently, these quotations were excluded from the statistics in this chapter.

(78) 1667 S. Pepys, D10, 495, his greatest failure was (that I observed) from his not^e considering whether the Question propounded was his part to answer to or no, [*e* MS. 'from'] | 1683 NEWDIG 13, The Earl

Diachrony of Present Participles and Gerunds Followed by *Not*

of Conway the late Secretary of state on Thursday last treated his Matie Royall Highnesse & most of the Court at a sumptuous dinner butt the Marquis Hallifax was either not Invited or his occasions [not?] pmitting him to be prsent. | 1801 R. Southey, L42, 259, I have been expecting them since Friday—and growling at the lazy and uncivil trick of not [writing] to prevent expectation. | 1836 S. Palmer, L48, I 75, Mine, however, you will call a cracked fiddle, not have[ing] heard from me yet;

The quotation in (79) indicates that 'respecting' in the earlier editions of *North's Plutarch* was altered into 'suspecting' in 1656 edition, which was utilised in the *OED²*. In such cases, the quotations which the *OED²* judges the most authentic ('suspecting' in this particular example) were included in statistics.

(79) 1656 *North's Plutarch* 927 (*Epaminondas*) Not suspecting [*edd*. 1612, 1631 respecting] the dignity of an Ambassador, nor of his Country. (*OED²*, s.v. suspect, *v.* 6)

In the first two citations in (80), 'nought' is not used as a negative particle modifying 'delighting' and 'being' but as a part of a set phrase meaning 'nothing but', and therefore the two quotations were excluded from the statistics in 6.4. The third citation was also not included in the statistics for the following reasons: the status of 'witting' is ambiguous as to whether it is a participle or a gerund, and the meaning of 'nought' is unclear as regards whether it denotes 'not' or 'nothing'.

(80) 1591 Sylvester *Du Bartas* i. iv. (1641) 34/2 Brave-minded Mars . . Delighting nought but Battails, blood, and murder. *(OED²*, s.v. delight, *v.* 3) | 1592 Davies *Immort. Soul* Introd. v. 2 Which Ill being nought but a Defect of Good. (Ibid., defect, *n.* 1) | 1867 Bailey *Universal Hymn* 8 Witting nought. (Ibid., wit, *v.*[1] 6)

The quotation in (81) was excluded as it was a 19th-century English translation by J. Smith of a 17th-century French letter written by C. Morelli. This example is not included in the statistics.

(81) 1679 C. Morelli, L5, 83, all could agree in my not having been known

Chapter VI

at Lisbon as a priest, much less as a Jesuit.

The quotation in (82) was not included in the statistics because of the large-scale omission.

(82) 1701 J. Jackson, L7, II 195, I had been gone 'ere this from hence, had my companion used the same diligence as myselfe; but [Nakamura my companion] having not [Nakamura used the same diligence], I fear 'twill be Sunday before wee sett-out for Seville.

In contrast to Nakamura (1998a, c; 2000), English written by non-native speakers of English was excluded from the statistics, however proficient they might have been. For example, in Michael E. Hoare, ed., *The Resolution Journal of Johann Reinhold Forster, 1772-1775*, 4 Vols (London: The Hakluyt Society, 1982), Rev. Forster (1729-1798) used the pre- and post-position of *not* as in Table 39. He was a German Lutheran pastor, naturalist on Captain James Cook's second circumnavigation and author of *The Resolution Journal <ODNB>*. L19 is a collection of letters between Samuel Richardson and Johannes Stinstra (1708-1790). Stinstra was a Dutch Mennonite pastor and theologian famous for his translation of Richardson's *Clarissa and Sir Charles Grandison* into the Duch language <http://gameo. org/index.php?title=Stinstra,_Johannes_(1708-1790)>. In the letters written by Stinstra, only the pre-position of *not* was used as Table 39 shows.

Table 39   Use of Pre- and Post-Position of *Not* in Documents Written by Non-native Speakers of English

	Pre	Post
Compound Participial *having* PP	J. R. Forster (2)	J. R. Forster (1)
Compound Participial *being* PP	J. R. Forster (1)	J. R. Forster (1)
Simple Participial Verb-*ing*	J. R. Forster be (6); exceed, have, know (2); allow, attend, find, mention, reach, think, understand (1) J. Stinstra abstain, find, permit (1)	J. R. Forster have (2), be (1)
Simple Gerundive Verb-*ing*	J. R. Forster be, permit (2), see (1)	

Diachrony of Present Participles and Gerunds Followed by *Not*

In the *OED²*, citations are quoted from not only British English but also a number of varieties of English such as the English in the United States, Australia, Guyana, Jamaica, New Zealand, South Africa and Trinidad. The number of examples of the construction now in question collected from these varieties of English was small: eight examples from American English (83a) and one from New Zealand English (83b). In order to distinguish them and British English, they were excluded from the statistics in 6.4.[25]

---

[25] The first example in (83a) is a quotation from the definition of 'irreproachableness' in the first edition of N. Webster's *An American Dictionary of the English Language*. In its second edition, the definition was deleted, leaving the vocabulary entry only. In the third edition, 'Irreproachableness' was newly defined as "irreproachability", and this lemma was defined as "the quality or state of being irreproachable". By means of this use of 'irreproachable' in the definition, something of clumsiness stemming from the strings of 'being not Adjective' seems to have been avoided. Furthermore, a glance over the definitions of lemmas beginning with 'ir-' and 'un-' in the second and third editions of *Webster's International Dictionary* suggests that, when *being* is used in the definitions, simultaneous use of *being* and *not* seems to be deliberately shunned by rendering adjectives in the negative forms. In cases where *not* and *being* are inevitably used together, *not* precedes *being*, just in the same way as participle/gerunds of the other verbs are negated.

All of the other examples in (83a) represent American English. The writers, R. W. Emerson, N. Hawthorne, 'Mark Twain', more fully S. L. Clemens and H. J. Muller, are easily identified owing to the <http://plato.stanford.edu/entries/emerson/>, <*Britannica*>, <http://global.britannica.com/EBchecked/topic/610829/MarkTwain> and <http://www.sciencedirect.com/science/article/pii/S1383574212000488> respectively. The writers of 1890 *Century Illustrated Monthly Magazine* 127/2 and 1972 *Rolling Stone* 9 Nov. 10/2, however, have not been identified by the present author. The examples the nature of the sources of which I was not able to identify are 1838 Emerson *Addr., Cambridge (Mass.)* Wks. (Bohn) II. 195 and 1858 Hawthorne *Fr. & It. Jrnls.* II. 132. The unabbreviated title of the former source *Addr., Cambridge (Mass.)* is not shown among Emerson's writings in the *OED²*'s Bibliography. The same or similar title has not been discovered in the complete list of R. W. Emerson's works. Accordingly, relevant information on this source has not been collected yet. The latter source *Fr. & It. Jrnls* is not listed among N. Hawthorne's writings in the *OED²*'s Bibliography. Of all the lists there, this abbreviated title appears to have the closest resemblance to *Passages from the French and Italian note-books a*1864 (1871). As the year of publication is different between the two sources, however, the correct source of the example of 1858 Hawthorne *Fr. & It. Jrnls.* II. 132 is still

160

Chapter VI

Similarly, the four examples collected from the OED^2 and BNC in (83c) were excluded from the statistics. Jean Le Clerc (1657-1736) was born in Geneva, educated there (and also in France), became an encyclopaedist and biblical scholar, and left Geneva to break with scholastic Calvinism <http://global.britannica.com/EBchecked/topic/334368/Jean-Leclerc>. The sources of the quotations are *Memoirs of Emeric Count Teckely*, a translation of a biography and *Lives of the Primitive Fathers*, a translation of a religious book. Concerning Hans Gadow (1855-1928), the present author failed in gathering information except for the fact that he was a German zoologist. The source of the quotation is "Amphibia and Reptiles", a treatise on amphibious and reptiles, included in the eighth volume of *Cambridge Natural History* <http://www.biodiversitylibrary.org/bibliography/31361#/summary>. Penelope Lively (1933-) was born and reared in Cairo, moved to England at the age of twelve, studied at the University of Oxford, and became a novelist and children's writer <http://literature.britishcouncil.org/penelope-lively>, and the quotation is taken from a novel entitled *Passing on*.

(83) a. 1828 Webster, *Irreproachableness*, the quality or state of being not reproachable. (*OED²*, s.v. irreproachable, *a.*) | 1838 Emerson *Addr., Cambridge (Mass.) Wks.* (Bohn) II. 195 And finding not names and places . . but even virtue and truth foreclosed and monopolized. (*OED²*, s.v. foreclose, *v.* 6) | 1858 Hawthorne *Fr. & It. Jrnls.* II. 132 Men and horses, wading not overleg. (*OED²*, s.v. over- 31) | 1863 Hawthorne *Our Old Home, Haunts of Burns* II. 72 A bust of Burns . . looking . . not so warm and whole-souled as his pictures usually do. (*OED²*, s.v. whole, *a., n., adv., (int.)* D. Special Collocations and Combinations, 2d) | 1881 'Mark Twain' *Prince & Pauper* 137, I like not much bandying of words, being not overpatient in my nature. (*OED²*, s.v. over- 28a) | 1890 *Century Mag.* 127/2, I do not often see anybody outside of my servants, being not at all given

unclear.

The example in (83b) is quoted from *Here and Now: an Independent Monthly Review*, a publication in New Zealand. The year of publication is unstable: '1914' in the citation and '1949-' in *OED²*'s Bibliography.

Incidentally, the writers and nature of the sources have not been identified with some examples in 6.2-6.4, as clarified in 6.5.

Diachrony of Present Participles and Gerunds Followed by *Not*

to visiting. (*OED²*, s.v. outside, *n., adv.,* and *prep.* C. *adv.* 3b) | 1932 H. J. Muller in *Proc. 6th Internat. Congr. Genetics* I. 242 Since it has been found that there are reverse muta- tions of hypomorphic genes . . , we must regard the allelomorphs thereby resulting not as hypomorphic but as hypermorphic to their immediate progenitor genes. (*OED²*, s.v. hyper-, *prefix* IV.) | 1972 *Rolling Stone* 9 Nov. 10/2 Having not played for several months, Miles had lost the eternally fragile trumpeters' lip. (*OED²*, s.v. lip, *n.* 1d) [Nakamura *Rolling Stone*: a music magazine in the U.S.A.]

b. 1914?/1949? *Here & Now* (N.Z.) Oct. 30/3 The intangibles—the many local developments—being not reducible to statistics, the food of all bureaucracy, count for nothing. (*OED²*, s.v. intangible, *a.* and *n.* B. *n.*)

c. 1693 *Mem. Ct. Teckely* ii. 145 It having not been imagin'd that the Turks would leave behind them Comorra and Raab unattack'd. (*OED²*, s.v. unattacked, *ppl. a.*) | 1702 tr. *Le Clerc's Prim. Fathers* 27 Having not undertaken to take them off from this Opinion. (*OED²*, s.v. take, *v.* 85d) | 1901 H. Gadow in *Cambr. Nat. Hist.* VIII. viii. 303 Many of the Theromorpha reached a considerable size, massive skulls of one foot in length being not uncommon. *Note.* Cope, the inventor of this most appropriate name (Theromorpha, or 'beast-shaped' animals), soon changed it, unnecessarily, into Thero mora. (*OED²*, s.v. theromorph) | 1990 P. Lively, *Passing on*, BNC-G0Y, He left Helen and went to have a bath and in the cold steamy bathroom there came to him this vision of a distant unreal Helen looking — well, radiant was the unexpected word that came to mind — looking not her usual self at all in some frock that glowed and billowed and rustled as she came in at the front door late, pink-cheeked, a touch dishevelled and greeted by the stone wall of Dorothy's disapproval. <imaginative>

Examples with vague dating were excluded from the statistics. In ARCHER 3.1, for example, "16xx" and "18xx" represent the years 1600-1699 and 1800-1899 respectively. Table 40 (p. 162) indicates that during these periods four examples with the pre-position of *not* occur. As the periodisation of the present chapter is based on fifty years, such examples

Chapter VI

were not included in the statistics.

Table 40   Examples Collected from Broadly Dated Documents in ARCHER 3.1

16xx	Simple Participial V-*ing* —British English		
		Pre	Post
	be	2	0
18xx	Simple Gerundivel V-*ing* —British English		
		Pre	Post
	be	1	0
	Simple Participial V-*ing* —American English		
		Pre	Post
	know	1	0

ARCHER 3.1 is a good historical electronic corpus with consideration paid to American English as well; it contains American English documents written between 1750 and 1799, 1850 and 1899, and 1950 and 1999. Since the present chapter focuses essentially on British English, however, variations between the pre- and post-position of *not* in American English documents in this corpus are not shown in 6.3 but in this section as Tables 41-44 (pp. 163-164). A glance at the four tables shows that *not* should be regularly positioned before *ing*-forms as a whole. The only exception is the simple participial *having not* in (84), the writer of which is J. Rowe (1715-1787) who was born in Exeter, England, emigrated to Boston at an early age and became a successful and prominent Boston merchant <http://www.masshist.org/objects/cabinet/july2002/rowe.htm>.

(84) 1759 John Rowe, *Letters and diary of John Rowe: Boston merchant*, in ARCHER 3.1 1759rowe.x4a, It is a Long time since I had the pleasure to write you & <u>having</u> <u>not</u> a Line from you you'l please to excuse it.

Diachrony of Present Participles and Gerunds Followed by *Not*

Table 41   Variations between Pre- and Post-Position of *Not* in American English Documents in ARCHER 3.1—Simple Participial Verb-*ing* (Pre : Post)

	1726-1750	1751-1800	1801-1850	1851-1900	1901-1950	1951-
be		4 : 0	1 : 0	2 : 0		
care		2 : 0				
correspond				1 : 0		
depend				1 : 0		
dream				1 : 0		
get		1 : 0				
have		1 : 1				
impute		1 : 0				
keep		1 : 0				
kill		1 : 0				
know		4 : 0		1 : 0		
look				1 : 0		
notice		1 : 0				
permit		1 : 0				
put		1 : 0				
regard		1 : 0				
rise				1 : 0		
take		+1 : 0		1 : 0		
tend	1 : 0					
understand		1 : 0				
wish		1 : 0				
Total	1 : 0	21+1 : 1	1 : 0	9 : 0	0 : 0	0 : 0

Table 42   Variations between Pre- and Post-Position of *Not* in American English Documents in ARCHER 3.1—Simple Gerundive Verb-*ing* (Pre : Post)

	1726-1750	1751-1800	1801-1850	1851-1900	1901-1950	1951-
answer		1 : 0				
be		1 : 0		1 : 0		
dare to-inf				1 : 0		
discuss				1 : 0		
go		1 : 0				
play				1 : 0		
send		1 : 0				
speak				1 : 0		
stand				1 : 0		
subscribe		1 : 0				
write		2 : 0				
Total	-	7 : 0	-	6 : 0	-	0 : 0

Chapter VI

Table 43 Variations between Pre- and Post-Position of *Not* in American English Documents in ARCHER 3.1—Compound Participial Perfective *Having* PP and Passive/Perfective *Being* PP

	Perfective *have* PP		Passive *be* PP		Perfective *be* PP	
	Pre	Post	Pre	Post	Pre	Post
1726-1750			-			
1751-1800			3	0		
1801-1850			-			
1851-1900	2	0				
1901-1950			-			
1951-						

Table 44 Variations between Pre- and Post-Position of *Not* in American English Documents in ARCHER 3.1—Compound Gerundive Perfective *Having* PP and Passive/Perfective *Being* PP

	Perfective *have* PP		Passive *be* PP		Perfective *be* PP	
	Pre	Post	Pre	Post	Pre	Post
1726-1750			-			
1751-1800						
1801-1850			-			
1851-1900						
1901-1950			-			
1951-						

6.1.6. Principle of Presentation of Examples in Sections 6.2-6.4

As shown in (61b, c) and (65a, b) respectively, the post-position of *not* is regarded as of irregular usage in Present-day English and seems to have been avoided in Early and Late Modern English. Accordingly, its discovery and presentation will contribute to history of English research; therefore, the whole example of the post-positioned *not* is quoted in Chapter VI on the one hand. On the other hand, presentation of an unmarked form of the pre-position of *not* was restrained to reduce the page length of this chapter except for 6.2.1.3-6.2.1.5, where lexical, semantic and syntactic differ-

Diachrony of Present Participles and Gerunds Followed by *Not*

entiations are attempted between the pre- and post-position of *not*.

This chapter is a study based on the analyses of 914+10 examples of participles and gerunds followed by *not*, exhaustively and carefully compiled from 99 collections, 130 volumes of diaries and correspondence, Helsinki-DP, CEECS, Lampeter, Newdigate, ARCHER 3.1 and the *OED²* on CD-ROM, as well as LOB, FLOB, BNC, Brown and Frown.

6.2. Evidence from Seventeenth- to Twentieth-Century Diaries and Correspondence

In 6.2, the results of the analyses of the diachrony of *ing*-forms followed by *not* are presented, based upon the analyses of 99 collections, 130 volumes of diaries and correspondence written between the 17th and 20th centuries and those published in the form of books.

6.2.1. Variations between Pre- and Post-position of *Not* in Simple Participial Verb-*ing*

6.2.1.1. Examples of Simple Participial Verb-*ing Not*

Examples of the simple participial Verb-*ing not* that have been encountered in the examined texts are presented by periods in (85).

(85) Examples of the simple participial Verb-*ing not*
  < -1600>
    <be>
      1599 M. Hoby, D2, 68, After praier in the morninge, I, beinge not well, did heare Mr Rhodes read of Gyffard vpon the songe of Sallemon: | 1599 M. Hoby, D2, 71, after priuat praiers in the morning I, being not well, did walk a litle, and then eate my brecfast: | 1599 M. Hoby, D2, 84, and after, being not well, I slept a while and then reed a while, | 1599 M. Hoby, D2, 92, beinge not well, I did omitte my orderarie exercise of praier tell after supper: | 1600 M. Hoby, D2, 95, After I was vp I went to doe some beusenes about the house: after beinge not well, I did eate my breakfast: | 1600 M. Hoby, D2, 96, In the morninge I, beinge not well, was

Chapter VI

driuen, to the discomfort of my hart, with short praier and preperation to goe to church: | 1600 M. Hoby, D2, 98, then I went about the house and, beinge not verie well, did litle but satt with Mr Hoby twll 6: | 1600 M. Hoby, D2, 103, after, I went to supper, then to the lector, and, sonne after that, to bed, being not verie well in my head. | 1600 M. Hoby, D2, 106, after, walked abroad vith Mr Hoby, tooke order for supper, and then Came to my Chamber to rest, beinge not well, wher I talked with Mr Hoby tell supper time, | 1600 M. Hoby, D2, 111, after I Came home I went to diner, with short medetation, beinge not well: | 1600 M. Hoby, D2, 115, after the sarmon I Came to my lodging and lay downe, beinge not well, | 1600 M. Hoby, D2, 115, and, after, Came home and, beinge not well, I went to bed: | 1600 M. Hoby, D2, 121-122, vhen I had taken order for supper, I lay downe, being not well: | 1600 M. Hoby, D2, 128, after, I went to supper and then, being not well, I went to bed: | 1600 M. Hoby, D2, 133, and, after, beinge not well, I went to bed: | 1600 M. Hoby, D2, 136, emediatly after I went to bed and, when Mr Rhodes had praied with us, I rested, beinge before not well | 1600 M. Hoby, D2, 147, after publeck praers, beinge not Verie well, I went to bed | 1600 M. Hoby, D2, 148, I supper, then I went to publecke praers and so to bed, beinge not well | 1600 M. Hoby, D2, 152-153, after, I helped my mother to washe some fine linan, my Maide france beinge not able: | 1600 M. Hoby, D2, 153, beinge not well, I went to supper and so to bed

<1601-1625>

<be>

1601 M. Hoby, D2, 160, After priuat praier . . . I went about som busenes for Mr Hoby tell dinner tim: after, I spent it with him at my booke and at my work, he being not well, tell 5 a cloke, | 1601 M. Hoby, D2, 160, after, we Came home and then I, beinge not well, did sonne after supper goe to bed | 1601 M. Hoby, D2, 161, and, in the after none, Mr Hoby, my Mother, and my selfe, went to visitt some freindes who, beinge not at home, we retourned: | 1601 M. Hoby, D2, 163, and After I lay downe, being not well, when, after a litle sleepe, Mr fuller Came in, and he repeated to vs the substance of Mr Egerton Sarmon/ | 1601 M. Hoby, D2, 163, this day I, beinge not well, praied and reed in mine owne chamber, |

Diachrony of Present Participles and Gerunds Followed by *Not*

1601 M. Hoby, D2, 181, and after, I slept a whill, <u>being</u> <u>nott</u> well, |
1601 M. Hoby, D2, 188, This day I, <u>beinge</u> <u>not</u> well, kept att home
| 1605 M. Hoby, D2, 222, This day, hauinge care to rise in time, I
went to church, and so likewise in the after none, but not so profet-
ablye as I ought, <u>beinge</u> <u>not</u> well | 1625 J. Glanville, D3, 35, And
wee might heare / putt in and come out with more varietie of wynd
and weather, or if opportunitie were offered or need required
might march from hence by land to St Lucas, to assault and take it,
<u>being</u> <u>not</u> aboute 12 miles or a short daies March from St Mary
Port.

<1626-1650>

<be>

1627 W. Bedell, L1, 136, at my beeing with him at Drogheda this
sommer, he told me he did esteeme it ever for the translation sake
(<u>being</u> <u>not</u> the Vulgar, but according to the Hebrew verity). | 1641
J. Evelyn, D9, II 76, About midnight we weigh'd, and at 4 in the
morning <u>being</u> <u>not</u> far from Dover, we could not yet make the
Peere till 4 that afternoone, the wind proving contrary and driving
us Westward; but at the last we got on shore, being the afternoone
of Octob: 12th. | 1643 F. Cheynell, D5, 212, It is ye desire of y^e
Committee that the Souldiers should have a faire reward for their
magnanimous adventure, but the goods, horses, wagon, &c. <u>being</u>
<u>not</u> in the enemyes hand for ye space of 24 houres. they conceive
that the souldiers by ye law of Armes are not to make their owne
markets, they therefore intreat you . . . to moderate the buisnesse,

<find>

1648 R. Josselin, D8, 126, at London rid in a great shoure but I
was their before I was wett through, Dr Wright not at home, I came
downe and <u>finding</u> <u>not</u> the Dr by the way, came safe to Colne

<have>

1646 King Charles I, L2, 76, nevertheless, <u>having</u> [hearing?] yet
<u>not</u> certainly neither from thee nor Ireland concerning it, I will
not . . . engage myself in it before I know thy opinion, which I
desire thee to send with all possible speed

<return>

1639 J. Evelyn, D9, II 23, I went to Lewes, <u>returning</u> <u>not</u> till the

Chapter VI

26t: so it was the 8th of Octob. e're I went back to Oxon. (Cf. 1654 J. Evelyn, D9, III 95, I went to Lond, to visite many relations, & return'd not til the 12th, lying at the Temple:

<1651-1675>

<be>

1657 J. Evelyn, D9, III 186, Being not well, could not go to the Parish Church. | 1660 S. Pepys, D10, I 73, But he being not within, I went up, | 1660 S. Pepys, D10, I 168, After dinner into my cabin to cast my accounts up; and find myself to be worth near 100*l*, for which I bless Almighty God – it being more then I hoped for so soon; being, I believe, not clearly worth 25*l* when I came to tea, besides my house and goods. | 1661 S. Pepys, D10, II 114, But they being not come, we went over to the Wardrobe and there find that my Lord Abbot Mountagu being not at Paris, my Lord hath a mind to have them stay a little longer before they go. | 1662 S. Pepys, D10, III 44, And all the afternoon rumaging of papers in my chamber, and tearing some and sorting others till late at night, and so to bed - my wife being not well all this day. | 1662 S. Pepys, D10, III 93, I seated myself close by Mr. Prin; who, in discourse with me, fell upon what records he hath of the lust and wicked lives of the Nuns heretofore in England, and showed me out of his pocket one wherein 30 Nuns for their lust were ejected of their house, being not fit to live there, and by the Popes command to be put, however, into other Nunnerys. | 1662 S. Pepys, D10, III 167, it being not 7 a-clock yet, the doors were not open; | 1662 S. Pepys, D10, III 219, and so home again and to supper and to bed – being not quiet in mind till I speak with Piggott to see how his business goes, whose land lies mortgaged to my late uncle; | 1662 S. Pepys, D10, III 231, It is 30*l* damage to me for my joining with others in committing Field to prison, we being not Justices of the Peace in the City, though in Middlesex; | 1663 C. Lyttelton, L3, I 29, I was deeply engaged wth him upon a planting interest, whereby I had greate hope to have settled a good fortune, wch now is quite lost, I being not at leizure, by reason of my other employment, | 1663 C. Lyttelton, L3, I 33, if he recall my comission as Governor, I shall stay heere I thinke but a little while after, any other employ in this place being not worth the owninge, | 1663 S. Pepys, D10, IV 7, Up

Diachrony of Present Participles and Gerunds Followed by *Not*

pretty earely; that is, by 7 a-clock, it being not yet light before or then. | 1663 S. Pepys, D10, IV 132, but there being not a committee . . . I parted and went homeward, | 1663 S. Pepys, D10, IV 135, which he could not take the freedom to do face to face, it being not so proper as by me; | 1663 S. Pepys, D10, IV 147, They say that this way [i.e. of milling] is more charge to the King then the old way. But it is neater, freer from clipping or counterfeiting, the putting of the words upon the edges being not to be done (though counterfeited) without an engine of that charge and noise that no counterfeit will be at or venture upon. | 1663 S. Pepys, D10, IV 165, she going out of town today and being not willing to come home with me to dinner, I parted and home. | 1663 S. Pepys, D10, IV 196, "Why," says he, "in the sea-service it is impossible to do anything without them, there being not more then three men of the whole King's side that are fit to command almost;" | 1663 S. Pepys, D10, IV 205, and so to boat and home by water – I being not very forward to talk of his business; | 1663 S. Pepys, D10, IV 208, and so took upon himself the whole blame and desired their pardon, it being not to do any wrong to their fellow-member, but out of zeal to the King. | 1663 S. Pepys, D10, IV 272, and so my two ladies and I in Mrs. Turners coach to Mr. Povys, who being not within, we went in and there showed Mrs. Turner his perspective and volary and the fine things that he is building of now, | 1664 C. Lyttelton, L3, I 39, Lord Ch[ancellor] had occasion for to make use of some stone for his building which was prepared for Paul's, and, being not to be soe soone used for that end, he borrows it and undertooke to deliver the like quality at the time it could be employed. | 1664 S. Pepys, D10, V 7, My wife was not there, being not well enough nor had any great mind. | 1664 S. Pepys, D10, V 68, I am very free to tell my mind to him in the case, being not unwilling he should tell him again if he will, or anybody else. | 1664 S. Pepys, D10, V 119, Dined well with my wife at home, being myself not yet thorough well, making water with some pain; | 1664 S. Pepys, D10, V 132, my Lady being not well, kept her chamber. | 1664 S. Pepys, D10, V 166, This happened the 3rd of May last, being not before the day twelvemonth of his entering into his government there, | 1664 S. Pepys, D10, V

Chapter VI

240, <u>being</u> <u>not</u> very well, and other things advising me to the contrary, I did forbear going; | 1664 S. Pepys, D10, V 305, And by and by, I out of doors to look after the Flagon, to get it ready to carry to Woolwich. That <u>being</u> <u>not</u> ready, I stepped aside and found out Nellson, | 1665 S. Pepys, D10, VI 73, and then with Creed, my wife, and Mercer to a play at the Dukes of my Lord Orerey's, called *Mustapha* - which <u>being</u> <u>not</u> good, made Baterton's part and Ianthes but ordinary too, so that we were not contented with it at all. | 1665 S. Pepys, D10, VI 90, I am well prepared for it to bear it, <u>being</u> <u>not</u> clear whether it will be more for my profit to have it or go without it, | 1665 S. Pepys, D10, VI 91, Thence he and I out to Sir Phill. Warwickes; but <u>being</u> <u>not</u> up, we took a turn in the garden hard by, | 1665 S. Pepys, D10, VI 102 A fine seat, but a old-fashion house; and <u>being</u> <u>not</u> full of people, looks desolately. | 1665 S. Pepys, D10, VI 131, Up; to White-hall with Sir W. Batten (calling at Lord Ashlys, but to no purpose, by the way, he <u>being</u> <u>not</u> up) | 1665 S. Pepys, D10, VI 310, So it <u>being</u> <u>not</u> dinner time, I to the Swan, | 1666 J. Evelyn, D9, III 464, I gave my Bro: of *Wotton* a Visite, being^a myselfe^a also <u>not</u> well, & returnd the 4th, so as I entred into a Course of Steele, against the *Scorbut*: (Footnote: ^{a-a} Substituted for *who was*.) | 1666 S. Pepys, D10, VII 12-13, as also got him to find me a Taylor to make me some clothes, my own <u>being</u> <u>not</u> yet in Towne, nor Pym, my Lord Sandwiches tailor. | 1666 S. Pepys, D10, VII 97, I went forth and took him with me by coach to the Duke of Albemarle; who <u>being</u> <u>not</u> up, I took a walk with Balty into the park, | 1666 S. Pepys, D10, VII 120, I like not hers half so well as I thought at first, it <u>being</u> <u>not</u> so like, nor so well painted as I expected or as mine and my wife's are. | 1666 S. Pepys, D10, VII 127, and so home to settle some papers there, and so to bed, <u>being</u> <u>not</u> very well, having eaten too much Lobster at noon at dinner with Mr. Hollyerd, he coming in and commending it so much. | 1666 S. Pepys, D10, VII 166, I was not a little fearful of what she told me but now; which is, that her servant was dead of the plague – that her coming to me yesterday was the first day of her coming forth, and that she had new-whitened the house all below stairs, but that above stairs they are not so fit for me to go up to, they <u>being</u> <u>not</u> so. | 1666 S. Pepys, D10, VII 197, He tells

Diachrony of Present Participles and Gerunds Followed by *Not*

me he finds all things mighty dull at Court, and that they now begin to lie long in bed – it being, as we suppose, not seemly for them to be found playing and gaming as they used to be; | 1666 S. Pepys, D10, VII 251, "But why," say they, "would you say that without our leave, it being not true?" | 1666 S. Pepys, D10, VII 260, I avoided it – being not willing to imbark myself in money there where I see things going to ruine. | 1666 S. Pepys, D10, VII 273, This day, Mercer being not at home, but against her mistress order gone to her mother's, and my wife going thither to speak with W. Hewer, met her there and was angry; | 1666 S. Pepys, D10, VII 332, And so we broke up, and all parted – Sir W. Coventry being not very well, but I believe made much worse by this night's sad discourse. | 1666 S. Pepys, D10, VII 350, the King doth not look after his business himself, and thereby will be undone, both himself and his nations - it being not yet, I believe, too late, if he would apply himself to it, to save all and conquer the Duch; | 1667 S. Pepys, D10, VIII 63, we desire, unless better provided for with money, to have nothing more to do with the payment of tickets, it being not our duty; | 1667 S. Pepys, D10, VIII 114, She is pretty still, but had no mind to be vido, being not habilado as ella would be. | 1667 S. Pepys, D10, VIII 124, he being not well, I sent for a quart of claret and burnt it and drank, | 1667 S. Pepys, D10, VIII 365, though I am against it in my heart, she being not handsome at all | 1667 S. Pepys, D10, VIII 444, and therefore am content to take my wife's and maids' accounts as they give them, being not able to correct them, which vexes me; | 1667 S. Pepys, D10, VIII 578, By and by comes out my Cosen Roger to me, he being not willing to be in the House at the business of my Lord Keeling, | 1668 S. Pepys, D10, IX 133, and thence I alone to the Duke of York's House to see the new play called *The Man is the Maister*, where the house was, it being not above one a-clock, very full. | 1668 S. Pepys, D10, IX 350-351, The Duke of York told me how these people do begin to cast dirt upon the business that passed the Council lately touching Supernumerarys, as passed by virtue of his authority there, there being not liberty for any man to withstand what the Duke of York advises there; | 1668 S. Pepys, D10, IX 370, This evening comes Mr. Billup to me to read over Mr. Wren's al-

Chapter VI

terations of my draft of a letter for the Duke of York to sign, to the Board; which I like mighty well, they being not considerable, only in mollifying some hard terms which I had thought fit to put in. | 1669 S. Pepys, D10, IX 440, Thence home and there to dinner, and my wife in a wonderful ill humour, and after dinner I stayed with her alone, being not able to endure this life, and fell to some angry words together; | 1669 S. Pepys, D10, IX 492, which under their present wants of money is a place that disobliges most people, being not able to do what they desire to their lodgings. | 1669 S. Pepys, D10, IX 559, I did not meddle to say anything upon it, but let her go; being not sorry, because now we may get one that speaks French to [go] abroad with us. | 1669 S. Pepys, D10, IX 564, thus ends all that I doubt I shall ever be able to do with my own eyes in the keeping of my journall, I being not able to do it any longer, having done now so long as to undo my eyes almost every time that I take a pen in my hand; | 1671 J. Evelyn, D9, III 583, there being not a quorum of us, we rose & went home: | 1673 H. Ball, L8, I 163-164, Various reports goe already amongst the giddy multitude of the fight, which are so silly that 'tis needless to trouble your Excellency with them, but the greatest, and I feare the most true, is the story . . . that the Earle of Carlisle being not well at sea should have been aboard in his yacht, and hearing of the approach of the enemy and fearing to loose the sight of the battle, caused himselfe to be putt on board Sir John Holmes his ship, the first he could reach in so rough weather, and in quitting his yacht, being not nimble enough, should crush his legg between that and the ship, so as to breake his toes, which is the modestest report, | 1673 H. Ball, L8, I 187, there is nothing further done about it, more than that the woman being not dead, but only has lost her eye, | 1673 H. Ball, L8, I 193, This night people discourse as if the Prince was not to goe to sea againe, the French and he being not able to agree, | 1673 T. Povey, L8, II 6, I may only have the favour of preferencie, it being not unlikely that I may come up to those conditions which you may thinke fitt to propose to your successor. | 1675 J. Evelyn, D9, IV 66, This afternoone came Monsieur *Quierwill* & his Lady . . . to see Sir Rich: Bro: my F. in Law, with whom they were intimately acquainted in *Bretagne*, what time Sir

Diachrony of Present Participles and Gerunds Followed by *Not*

Richard was sent to *Brest*, to supervise his Majesties sea affaires during the later part of his Majesties banishment abroad: This Gent: house being not a mile from *Brest*; Sir *Richard* made an acquaintance there,

<come>

1660 S. Pepys, D10, I 234, My Lord came to town today; but coming not home till very late, I stayed till 10 at night; and so home on foot. | 1665 S. Pepys, D10, VI 125, Up, and expected long a new suit; but coming not, dressed myself in my late new black silk camelot suit; | 1668 S. Pepys, D10, IX 74, I think I have heard he did send it [= a letter] to my Lord Arlington's, and that there it lay for some hours, it coming not to Sir Ph. Honiwoods hand at Portsmouth till 4 in the afternoon that day, being about fifteen or sixteen hours in going; | 1669 S. Pepys, D10, IX 461, where we stayed, expecting her coming from church; but she coming not, I went to her husband's chamber in the Temple and thence fetched her, she having been there alone ever since sermon, | 1669 J. Evelyn, D9, III 534, In the afternoone, the Church was so crowded, that coming not so early, I could not approch to heare:

<consist>

1686 G. Etherege, L9, 36, I can hardly beleive the Emperor's Armie will be of the Number he mentions, the Auxillaries this yeare consisting not of above 27 thousand men.

<do>

1664 S. Pepys, D10, V 78, I to the office, where we sat all the morning; doing not much business through the multitude of counsellors, one hindering another | 1665 S. Pepys, D10, VI 75, Thence to Westminster-hall and up and down, doing not much;

<find>

1668 S. Pepys, D10, IX 14, but I finding him not there, nor the Duke of York within, I away by coach to the Nursery,

<have>

1651 R. Josselin, D8, 250, Rid to Redgewell, preached the lecture on Phil. 4.11. about content, which the lord in mercy learne mee, I have more than ordinary need, having not so much quiet, as I have had, | 1660 S. Pepys, D10, I 215, To bed, having not time to write

Chapter VI

letters; and endeed, having so many to write to all places that I have no heart to go about them. | 1663 S. Pepys, D10, IV 101, and so going out, met with Mr. Mount, my old acquaintance, and took him in and drunk a glass of wine or two to him and so parted, having not time to talk together; | 1663 S. Pepys, D10, IV 251, And so to a less house hard by, where we liked very well their Codlin tarts (having not time, as we entended, to stay the getting ready of a dish of peese); | 1665 S. Pepys, D10, VI 105, But that that troubles me most, is my Lord Arlington calls to me privately and asks me whether I had ever said to anybody that I desired to leave this imployment, having not time to look after it. | 1665 S. Pepys, D10, VI 322, I was fearful any accident might by death or otherwise defeat me, having not now time to change papers. | 1666 S. Pepys, D10, VII 5, So we had a great, but I a melancholy, dinner, having not her there as I hoped. | 1666 S. Pepys, D10, VII 101, so back, and called at Kirton's to borrow 10s to pay for my ruled papers – I having not money in my pocket enough to pay for them. | 1666 S. Pepys, D10, VII 414, Nay, Evens, the famous man upon the Harp, having not his equal in the world, did the other day die for mere want, and was fain to be buried at the almes of the parish | 1667 S. Pepys, D10, VIII 66, we are neglected, having not money sent us in time. | 1667 S. Pepys, D10, VIII 141, at such times as those I am at a great loss, having not confidence, | 1667 S. Pepys, D10, VIII 267-268, maisters of ships that we are now taking up do keep from their ships all their stores, or as much as they can, so that we can despatch them - having not time to appraise them nor secure their payment. | 1668 S. Pepys, D10, IX 306, but I did not lend her any, having not opportunity para hazer alieno thing mit her. | 1668 S. Pepys, D10, IX 361, He tells me that there is no way to rule the King but by brisknesse, which the Duke of Buckingham hath above all men; and that the Duke of York having it not, his best way is what he practises, that is to say, a good temper, | 1668 S. Pepys, D10, IX 403, My wife down by water to see her mother, and I with W Hewers all day together in my closet, making some advance in the settling of my accounts, which have been so long unevened that it troubles me how to set them right, having not the use of my eyes to help me. | 1669 S. Pepys, D10, IX 504, being

Diachrony of Present Participles and Gerunds Followed by *Not*

afeared to be seen with him (he <u>having</u> <u>not</u> leave yet to kiss the King's hand, but notice taken, as I hear, of all that go to him) I did take the pretence of my attending Tanger Committee to take my leave; | 1669 S. Pepys, D10, IX 527, her sister being gone to Portsmouth to her husband, I did stay and talk with and drink with Doll and hazer ella para tocar mi thing; and yo did the like para her, but <did> not the thing itself, <u>having</u> <u>not</u> opportunity enough; | 1674 S. Pepys, D11, 48-49, nothing which has yet or may further happen towards the rendering me more conspicuous in the world, has led or can ever lead to the admitting any alteration in the little methods of my private way of living; as <u>having</u> <u>not</u> in my nature any more aversion to sordidness than I have to pomp, | 1674 T. Derham, L8, II 138, My Lord's committee sitts still to little purpose, not haveing yet got through the first article, and now <u>haveing</u> <u>not</u> hopes to ruine him they are very slow in meeteing, and when they doe 'tis onely to adjourne;

<know>

1663 S. Pepys, D10, IV 22, Called at my brother's and find him sick in bed of a pain in the sole of one of his feet, without swelling; <u>knowing</u> <u>not</u> how it came, but it will not suffer him to stand these two days.

<meet>

1660 S. Pepys, D10, I 261, but <u>meeting</u> <u>not</u> Mr. Sheply there, I went home by water and Mr. Moore with me, who stayed and supped with me till almost 9 at night.

<need>

1663 S. Pepys, D10, IV 327, Thence rise with Sir G. Carteret, and to his lodgings and there discoursed of our frays at the table today, and perticularly of that of the contract and the contract of masts the other day, declaring my fair dealing and so <u>needing</u> <u>not</u> any man's good report of it or word for it,

<see>

1663 S. Pepys, D10, IV 291, To church, I alone, in the afternoon; and there saw Pembleton come in and look up, which put me into a sweat, and <u>seeing</u> <u>not</u> my wife there, went out again.

<write>

1668 S. Pepys, D10, IX 143, the girl writing not so well as she would do, cried, and her mistress construed it to be sullenness and so was angry, and I seemed angry with her too;

<Examples with a negative intensifier>

1667 S. Pepys, D10, VIII 433, Anon comes Sir W. Batten and his Lady, and Mr. Griffith their Ward, and Sir W. Penn and his Lady, and Mrs. Louther (who is grown, either through pride or want of manners, a fool, having not a word to say almost all dinner; | 1667 S. Pepys, D11, 30, And yet I must acknowledge, my Lord, that this is but the third, having no desire of disquieting your Lordship with bad news; and the times affording not one passage fit to be called good, from the hour I had the honour to see your Lordship last, to that of publishing of your Lordship's articles of peace with Spain: | 1668 S. Pepys, D10, IX 307, and so by water to the King's playhouse to see a new play, acted but yesterday, a translation out of French by Dryden called *The Ladys a la Mode*; so mean a thing, as when they came to say it would be acted again to- morrow, both he that said it, Beeson, and the pit fell a-laughing - there being this day not a quarter of the pit full.

<1676-1700>

<be>

1677 J. Evelyn, D9, IV 121, With Sir *Robert Clayton* to *Marden*, an estate he had lately bought of my *kindsman* Sir *John Evelyn* of *Godstone* in Surry: which from a despicable farme house Sir Robert had erected into a Seate with extraordinary expense: Tis seated in such a solitude among hills, as being not above 16 miles from Lond, seemes almost incredible, the ways also to it so winding & intricate: | 1679 S. Pepys, L6, 95-96, as he has more or less the reputation of an honest man I should reckon my selfe the more Safe in our negotiating with him, it being not enough in this age, and in the company I am fallen into, to have the innocence of a Dove, without some mixture of the Serpent's prudence. | 1679 S. Pepys, L6, 111, for what you mention concerning Will Hewer hee is, I thanke God very well, and one who from his heart wishes you soe, it being not (I assure you) from any want of kindness, that you

Diachrony of Present Participles and Gerunds Followed by *Not*

have not heard from him, <u>but</u> from his haveing at this time Some cares extraordinary of his owne, and his beleeveing you to have your full load of mine. | 1680 C. Lyttelton, L3, I 213, yesterday as I was passing ye ferry at Richm^d, my hors leapt over board wth mee on his back into ye river, . . . But, what wth ye flounsing of ye hors and my own endeavors, I soone was free; but then was so intangled wth a p^r of greate French bootes and many cloathes, I was not able to turn myself as I lay on my back; but yet kept myself above water, till Thom Brok leapt out of ye boate and pulld mee up, <u>being</u> then <u>not</u> out of my depth. | 1680 J. Evelyn, D9, IV 201-202, He was pleased also during this Conversation, to impart to me divers particulars of state relating to the present times; but being no greate friend to the D — was now laied aside; his integritie & abillities <u>being</u> <u>not</u> so sutable in this Conjuncture: | 1681 R. Josselin, D8, 632, shee checkt at his estate <u>being</u> <u>not</u> suitable to her porcon. | 1682 S. Pepys, D11, 145, You <u>being</u> <u>not</u> now to be come at, (the Council sitting,) I take this way of kissing your hands and placing this with you, | 1683 J. Evelyn, D9, IV 298, I went to *Lond*: about my E: *India stock*, which I had sold to the *Royal Society* for 750 pounds: it <u>being</u> <u>not</u> to be paied 'til the 25 of *Mar*: | 1683 S. Pepys, D11, 150, if . . . you shall give me any advice, I will endeavour to complete both this of yours and my own; <u>there</u> <u>being</u> <u>not</u> anything I know of extant in history, so much to the honour of our country, as this piece of Sir Thomas Reeves's; | 1683 S. Pepys, D11, 405, Dr. Trumbull and I did also prepare, for the Commissioners of the Survey, a letter for the Portuguese priests, on their difficulty of valuing lands and houses of their church, <u>being</u> <u>not</u> their own property, but their King's. | 1685 J. Evelyn, D9, IV 445, *Oates*, who had but two days before ben pilloried at severall places, & whip't at the Carts taile from New-gate to Algate; was this day placed in a sledge (<u>being</u> <u>not</u> able to go by reason of his so late scourging) & dragd from prison to Tyburn, & whip'd againe all the day, | 1686 P. Skinner, D11, 171-172, And further I desire Your Honours Excuse for the Weekness of so Greene a Youth, that <u>being</u> <u>not</u> capable of Expressing my Sence of Grattitude As I ought to your Honour, | 1688 S. Pepys, L6, 216-217, that which is to bee said further upon it <u>being</u> <u>not</u> so properly for hand-

Chapter VI

ling in a Letter, I shall respite it till Our meeting. | 1690 R. Davies, D13, 79, Then, Mr. Milbourn being not at home, I went and read prayers; | 1690 R. Davies, D13, 136, the Lord Ginkell being not there, we straight returned in search of him, and at length found him, on the left of all the army. | 1690 R. Davies, D13, 142, There were actually some of our men in the city, but were beaten out, being not seconded, it being not the King's order to storm the city, but only to attack the counterscarp; | 1693 J. Evelyn, D9, V 129, whether in commiseration of his youth, being not 18 years old, though exceedingly dissolute, or upon what other reason . . . 69 Lords acquitted him & onely 14: Condemn'd him. | 1698 H. Wanley, L1, 258, he was pleas'd to entertain so good an opinion of me at first sight, that he would needs have me dine with him, which I did; his lodgings being not two hundred yards from mine: | 1698 H. Wanley, L1, 261, the noise and hurry is such, that I shall find more disturbance there than any where clse; my business being not so much to transcribe a few lines from them, as to copy their several hands exactly. | 1698 J. Evelyn, D9, V 294-295, Mr. Stringfellow 7. Rom: 20, shewing that . . . a practical & universal obedience, this whole Chapter of St. Paule being not meant or applicable to the Apostle, but by a metaschematisme transferring figuratively what concerned the Jewes, who thought that the bare external observation of the Mosaic law, was alone sufficient, | 1698 J. Evelyn, D9, V 306, By this Text he reproved the popish doctrine of Purgatory . . . & prayer to Saints, there being not any one Text in Scripture for it; | 1699 J. Evelyn, D9, V 352, A young man in our Chapell on 6.1. Cor: 20: Concerning the indispensable necessity of sincerity & purity of body & life, as being not our owne, but the Lords who bought us: | 1699 J. Jackson, L7, I 236, Wee sett-out from Lyons on Thursday last, and arrived here yesterday-noon; where wee went immediately to church and saw the whole order of their devotion, and afterwards their diversions, they being not so nice observers of the Sabbath here as I thought they had been. | 1700 E. Halley, D14, 169, I take the Islands of Tristan d'acunha to bear N E 120 Leagues, and being not much out of my course I design to See and Discover them. | 1700 E. Halley, D14, 202, being not able to bear Saile, in Such Weather uncertain Winds and a high grown

Diachrony of Present Participles and Gerunds Followed by *Not*

Sea I was unwilling to runn any hazards, | 1700 J. Jackson, L7, II 97, Captain Man, whom I thought to have overtaken at Barcelona, I have mett with here, no less to my surprise than trouble; his demurr poor man, being not to his content or for his advantage.

<contain>

1685 J. Evelyn, D9, IV 456, He made no Speech on the Scaffold (which was on Towerhill) but gave a paper (containing not above 5 or 6 lines) for the King, in which he disclaimes all Title to the Crowne, accknowledges that the late King (his Father) had indeede told him, he was but his base sonn, & so desire'd his Majestie to be kind to his Wife & Children:

<examine>

1689 J. Evelyn, D9, IV 616-617, I din'd at the Admiralty, where was brought, a young Child . . . of the most prodigious maturity of memorie, & knowledge, for I cannot call it altogether memory, but [something more] extraordinary; Mr. Pepys & my selfe examining him not in any method, but [by] promiscuously questions, which required judgement and wonderfull discernement,

<have>

1683 J. Evelyn, D9, IV 331-332, This summer did we suffer 20 *French*-men of *Warr* to passe our Chanell towards the Sound, to help the Dane against the Swede, who had <abandoned> the <French> Interest; we having not ready sufficient to guard our Coasts, or take Cognizance of what they did; | 1700 S. Pepys, L7, II 55, having not convenience to open them as they ought to be here, I shall be driven to respite it till my house . . . shall be in a condition to receive me,

<know>

1680 B. St. Michel, L6, 166, being in a small wherry in open sea as low allmost as the Read-sand, and knowing not what to doe . . . and the winde freshening upon uss teribly, as the day before at East, at last on our totering resolutions, god sent uss passing by, a small Ketch bound to Margate

<Examples with a negative intensifier>

1678 S. Pepys, L6, 58, there can be nothing of that in this Case, there being not one Commander in the whole Fleet to whome I

Chapter VI

either really have, or have endeavoured to shew more reall Re-
spect then Captain Willshaw. | 1680 S. Pepys, L6, 148, I cannot
imagine why you should apprehend it needful for you to have the
King's Warrant for your coming into England, there being not the
least occasion I know of for it; | 1687 J. Evelyn, D9, IV 540, it was
very hard, and looked very unkindly, his Majestie . . . finding not
the least failor of duty in him during all his government of that
Kingdome: | 1691 H. Compton, L7, I 50, For being called to wit-
ness the title of a gentleman who has not wherewithal to reward
him, and being himself not worth a groat, he refused to keep back
his evidence, though he was offered a very considerable reward by
the other party which would have supported him all his life.

<1701-1725>

<amount>

1701 E. Halley, D14, 341, I humbly hope his Excellency my Ld
High Admirall will please to consider the smallness of my wages
in my late Channel cruise ammounting not to 50 li in the whole.

<be>

1702 P. Skinner, L7, II 289, your kindnesses to me have been soe
farr above my merritts that they are even above my gratitude, if
that were to be judged by words, being not capable to express it. |
1703 R. Gale, L7, II 304, Dr Stainforth was sensible of his mistake
at the very time, and therefore did not return it [= a bow], Mr
Halley's compliment being not due to him. | 1713 J. Swift, L16, II
616, being not very well, I dare not study much; | 1714 D. Defoe,
L14, 446, The Old Author Redpath Quarrell'd with his Printer
Hurt and Takes the Paper From him; Hurt Sets up for himself and
applyes himself and to a Certain Author to write it for him, but
being Not Able to get any One to Publish it, he lost ground. | 1714
J. Gay, L18, 31, The terms of politics being not so numerous as to
swell into a volume, especially in times of peace . . . I thought fit
to extract them in the same manner for the benefit of young practi-
tioners

<have>

1701 J. Jackson, L7, II 195, I had been gone 'ere this from hence,
had my companion used the same diligence as myselfe; but having

Diachrony of Present Participles and Gerunds Followed by *Not*

not, I fear 'twill be Sunday before wee sett-out for Seville | 1711 J. Swift, L16, I 253, I forgot to tell you that Mr. Harley askt me yesterday, how he came to disoblige the archbishop of Dublin? Upon which (having not his letter about me) I told him what the bishop had written to me on that subject, and desired I might read him the letter some other time. | 1714 D. Defoe, L14, 439, I presume I Need not Send The paper, haveing it not at hand. | 1714 H. Jolley, L17, 490, S^r haveing not elce thats materiall [I] shall beg leave to conclude & subscribe my self

<reach>

1701 J. Hudson, L1, 302, It may be in your way to persuade some of the Booksellers in London to what they are in some measure oblig'd; and I wissh you would try Smith & Walford for Cowper's Anatomy, and the Philosophical Transactions, our sett reaching not far, and being imperfect in the first Volumes.

<1726-1750>

<be>

1732 J. Wesley, L23, I 123-124, In March last he received a letter from you, which, being then not able to read, he desired me to read to him; | 1739 J. Wesley, L23, I 340, the elder people, being not so proper to be mixed with children (for we expect scholars of all ages, some of them grey-headed), will be taught in the inner room, either early in the morning or late at night, so as their work may not be hindered. | 1739 T. Gray, L26, I 113, the country round about is one great plain covered with vines, which at this time of the year afford no very pleasing prospect, as being not above a foot high. | 1750 J. Wesley, D17, 191, My brother being not yet able to assist, I had more employment to-day than I expected.

<1751-1775>

<be>

1765 J. Wesley, D17, 321, Being not yet able to ride, I returned in a chariot to London. | 1771 J. Wedgwood, L32, 102, I am now got well and go abroad again though I am not fond of doing so in frosty weather, being not so expert a footman as I have been,

<have>

Chapter VI

1759 W. Shenstone, L27, 369, Your *supplemental* stanzas to yᵉ g. Herdsman, must undoubtedly approach much nearer to what was yᵉ *orig: reading.* than those which I have substituted; having not yᵉ *final* words to direct me.

\<Examples with a negative intensifier\>

1760 W. Shenstone, L27, 402, I will return yᵉ old Ballad next Letter, having at present not a moments Leisure. | 1766 J. Wesley, D17, 325, They broke their windows, leaving not one whole pane with glass,

\<1776-1800\>

\<be\>

1778 J. Woodforde, D21, I 224, In the evening I took a walk and showed Mr. Pounsett and Jenny my Church etc., they being not at Church on Sunday as it rained much that day in the afternoon. | 1783 J. Woodforde, D21, II 112, I sent Ben on foot about 11 o'clock, he being not unwilling to go, | 1784 J. Woodforde, D21, II 154, I sent for Widow Greaves this morning to come to my House for a few Days to assist our Maids, they being not able to do much at present | 1785 J. Woodforde, D21, II 198, His Coachman being not able to drive on Account of his very lately breaking his Collar Bone, the Postillon drove with only 2 Horses | 1786 J. Woodforde, D21, II 259, Could not go to Church this morning being not well enough. | 1789 J. Woodforde, D21, III 146, I took a little Rhubarb and ginger going to bed to night, being not right well. | 1789 J. Woodforde, D21, III 83, He goes to School to Morrow by himself, his Brother Georges feet being not quite well yet from Chilblains. | 1790 J. Woodforde, D21, III 173, My Brother did not go to Church being not well. | 1792 J. Woodforde, D21, III 359, Mrs. Custance not at Church being not quite so well. | 1792 W. B. Stevens, D22, 48, Kitty Arden very copious in her account of Mrs. Dodsley's antipathy to her. She must console herself by considering it as a Compliment. For Mrs. Dodsley, being not dead to Personal Vanity, and having justly great Pretensions to Merit, cannot endure to be so completely eclipsed, especially by a Next Door Neighbour. Kitty's Ears are greedy of Praise. | 1798 H. More, L36, III 62, Returned from Bath in an improved state of health, as I thought; but health being doubtless not good for me, had a return of my head-

Diachrony of Present Participles and Gerunds Followed by *Not*

ache.

\<find\>

1798 J. Woodforde, D21, V 112, We walked up to Cary's this Morning and during our being out Mr. Custance came to the Parsonage and finding us not at home returned to Weston House.

\<have\>

1784 J. Woodforde, D21, II 157, I went to them and spoke with them, but they would not get of their Horses—having not time. | 1790 J. Woodforde, D21, III 202, the Weston House Family with Captain Beauchamp and his new Bride, sent word that they would drink tea with us in the Afternoon if not engaged, but we were obliged to put them off having not time to get ourselves trigged up, and also no white bread in House.

\<Examples with a negative intensifier\>

1782 J. Wesley, D17, 440, he totally missed his mark; having not the least conception of the persons whom he undertook to describe. | 1783 J. Woodforde, D21, II 61, The Barometer very low, and the Wind being very rough when I went up to my Chamber to go to bed, being not the lest sleepy, I lighted my Fire, and sat down and read the Life of Lewis 14 of France till after 2 o'clock in the morning and then went to bed, the Wind still high.

\<1801-1825\>

\<be\>

1802 D. Wordsworth, D24, 140, I had my breakfast in bed, being not quite well | 1802 D. Wordsworth, D24, 144, I breakfasted in bed, being not very well. | 1814 M. Todd, D31, 36, Remained most part of June and July in York, and perhaps should have spent a longer time but Mr B's health being not over good, the doctors recommended him to go to Cheltenham, so we left Old Ebor for London. | 1814 Princess of Wales, D26, 270, The second Prince of Orange is just arrived in London: he is of the same age as my daughter, and I should not be much surprised that this marriage would take place soon, as Princess Charlotte would certainly not be under obligation to leave her native country, [he] being not the successor, only the grandson. | 1815 G. Crabbe, L38, 190, If I were called upon to swear which I loved best & which I thought liked

Chapter VI

me, the Married Lady or the Single I wonder what I should say!—'Pray forbear to ask' I believe would be my Petition & if it were not granted: I should then say 'Give me time'—All this being not of myself alone, I commit to Miss Charter as my Friend & to her [X] Discretion— | 1817 P. Hawker, D29, I 154, The fishing has been so inferior this year that I have seldom gone out for a whole day; and, at last, I gave up keeping an account of what I caught, it being not worth it. | 1820 M. Todd, D31, 157, Luckily she discovered him in time to save him, the well being not very deep and nearly full of water.

<feel>

1814 M. Todd, D31, 35, There being no Packet Boat going to sail for England to-day and being very tired, as well as Mr B. feeling not very well, we dined early and retired to rest.

<Example with a negative intensifier>

1823 H. Arbuthnot, D27, I 215, Canning has this day written him an answer thanking him excessively for his letter & papers, hoping he will always continue to give him advice, but saying not one word upon the subject in debate.

<1826-1850>

<be>

1826 W. Blake, L39, 160, I also feel Myself weaker than I was aware, being not able, as yet, to sit up longer than six hours at a time;

<care>

1848 T. H. Huxley, D35, 143, He describes Hell like a practical *Times* reporter, sparing no detail however hideous and caring not how homely his comparisons may be so long as they are but apt.

<have>

1841 J. Clare, L46, 294, Having left the Forest in a hurry & not time to take my leave of you & your family but I intended to write & that before now but dullness & dissapointment prevented me for I found your words true on my return here having neither friends or home left but as it is called the 'Poet's Cottage' I claimed a lodging in it where I now am[26]

---

[26] In this zeugmatic example, 'having' is used both as a perfective auxiliary verb and a

Diachrony of Present Participles and Gerunds Followed by *Not*

<open>
1850 T. Carlyle, L49, I 691, I fled out of Wales, after 3 weeks or more, dumb, <u>opening</u> <u>not</u> my mouth;

<Examples with *not*-A-*but*-B construction>
1838 S. Palmer, L48, I 130, Here we stand like two little children, snubbing their noses flat, at the glass of a pastrycook's window— <u>longing</u> <u>not</u> for the pastry and sweetmeats of life <u>but</u> for that supply of simple wants which we cheerfully trust that Providence will give us, but for the attainment of which we must use all means.

<1851-1875>
<be>
1864 M. Arnold, L53, 227, it [= 'the present entire independence of middle class education'] <u>being</u> <u>not</u> in any way an official matter, the Council Office cannot complain of my treating it, as one of the public, without appearing to think our existing Education Department the least concerned. | 1868 M. Arnold, L53, 383, Ambleside <u>being</u> <u>not</u> possible, my next wish is Laleham, for which I . . . shall always have a home feeling. | 1874 F. Kilvert, D36, II 414, there is a free fishery in the Avon there and some good pike fishing, jack of 14 lbs <u>being</u> <u>not</u> uncommon.

<find>
1871 F. Kilvert, D36, I 391, Here I made a wrong turn and wandered up through more meadows into a wet green lane seeking Holditch Court but <u>finding</u> it <u>not,</u> till I came across a handsome boy sitting on a stile in a barley field, who set me right.

<have>
1861 S. Palmer, L48, II 635, You want something large enough to fill your heart, and imperishable enough to make it immortal like itself. That something is God. Having Him, you will possess all things; <u>having</u> Him <u>not,</u> you will be impoverished for ever.

<Examples with a negative intensifier>
1858 A. Tennyson, L50, 195, I answered this by acknowledging his book, <u>taking</u> <u>not</u> <u>the</u> <u>slightest</u> <u>notice</u> of his letter—a touch of satire, perhaps too fine for him to feel. | 1863 E. Buxton, D38, 80,

main verb.

Chapter VI

she had to come down in the train but having not a penny in her pocket she first had to go to the Brewery and borrow 5/- of the butler there, and then she came back to the station and walked up to our house in the pouring rain.

<Examples with *not*-A-*but*-B construction>

1852 A. Tennyson, L50, 53, I have only received your letter just now, being not at Twickenham but at this place where we have hired a house and stay till Christmas.

<1876-1900>

<be>

1885 C. L. Dodgson, L55, I 581, True, she hasn't yet reached the shy age: being not quite 10: she is a little actress . . . and . . . she has very nice manners,

<1900- >

<be>

1953 S. Spender, D41, 112, The whole city seemed covered in dust, and, being not fully awake, I started wondering whether an explosion had taken place before I realized that of course it was snow.

<Example with a negative intensifier>

1943 M. H. Macmillan, D40, 238, General Eisenhower, however, pointed out that to the contrary the other exiled Governments, occupying not an inch of their national territory, have declared war against Germany.

6.2.1.2. General Chronological Trends

Tabulation and figuration of the data for the variations between the pre-position and the post-position of *not* with regard to the simple participial Verb-*ing*, presented in Table 45 and Figure 5, indicates that, in the diaries and correspondence written during 1601-1625, 12 examples together with seven verbs in the form of *not* + Verb-*ing*, nine examples together with one verb in the form of Verb-*ing* + *not*, and during 1626-1650, 57 examples together with 37 verbs with the pre-positioned *not* and six examples together with four verbs with the post-positioned *not* have been encountered. In sum-

Diachrony of Present Participles and Gerunds Followed by *Not*

Table 45 Variations between Pre- and Post-position of *Not* with Simple Participial Verb-*ing*—Diaries and Correspondence

Period	Per 25 years				Per 50 years			
	Pre		Post		Pre		Post	
-1600	4	[3]	20	[1]	4	[3]	20	[1]
1601-1625	12	[7]	9	[1]	69	[40]	15	[4]
1626-1650	57	[37]	6	[4]				
1651-1675	550+6	[117+3]	100	[12]	839+7	[168+3]	135	[14]
1676-1700	289+1	[92]	35	[6]				
1701-1725	133+1	[52+1]	11	[4]	191+1	[67+1]	15	[4]
1726-1750	58	[28]	4	[1]				
1751-1775	76+1	[25+1]	5	[3]	246+1	[68+1]	21	[4]
1776-1800	170	[52]	16	[3]				
1801-1825	148	[53]	9	[3]	307+3	[98+2]	13+1	[7]
1826-1850	159+3	[65+2]	4+1	[5]				
1851-1875	121+4	[42+4]	7	[4]	146+4	[55+4]	8	[4]
1876-1900	25	[18]	1	[1]				
1901-1925	3	[3]	0	[0]	24	[20]	2	[2]
1926-	21	[18]	2	[2]				

Total varieties of verbs 292   Total number of examples 1,826+16 : 229+1

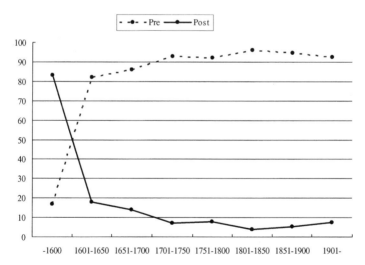

Figure 5 Variations between Pre- and Post-position of *Not* with Simple Participial Verb-*ing*—Diaries and Correspondence[27]

---

[27] The frequency of co-ordinated examples is not included in the calculation of percentage. For example, the frequency of the pre- and post-position of *not* during 1651-1700 is 839+7 and 135 respectively, and the percentage of the latter is com-

188

Chapter VI

mary, during the first half of the 17th century, the construction of *not* +
Verb-*ing* accounts for 69 examples together with 40 verbs, and that of
Verb-*ing* + *not* 15 examples together with four verbs.

Table 45 and Figure 5 present a completely different aspect in contrast to Tables 34a (p. 134) and 35a (p. 136) which represent the usage in
Present-day English. Table 45 and Figure 5 reveal that the post-position of
not was used to considerable extent until 1700, quite contrary to Bullokar's
statement in (65a) and that, after 1700, use of the participle followed by
not steadily waned until the present day. Needless to say, what the front of
Figure 5, i.e. the line for pre-1600, appears to be—a strikingly high frequency of the post-position of *not* accounting for over 80%—should not be
taken at face value. The reason is that these 20 examples are all of the verb
be, with which the post-position of *not* most predominantly occurred all
throughout the times, collected exclusively from Margaret Hoby's diary.
This percentage seems to reflect her idiosyncrasy, and should be discount-
ed, whereas the frequency of the post-position of *not* during 1651-1700 is
not necessarily distorted by the usage in Samuel Pepys's diary. It is true
that the examples gathered from his diary, which comprises the vastest number of words as a single text examined, accounts for the majority of those
during 1651-1675.[28] Almost all of the examples of the post-position of *not*
during 1676-1700, however, are compiled from the texts written by people
other than Pepys.

6.2.1.3. Verbs which Occured with Verb-*ing not*

In terms of lexical features, simple participial *ing*-forms followed by
not occurred most frequently with the verb *be*. As the seven pairs in (86)-
(92) show, however, it is evident that verbs occurring with the post-position of *not* were not restricted to the verb *be*: *come, do, find, have, know,
meet*, and *see* also occurred in this construction.

---

puted as $135 \div (839 + 135) \times 100$. The same applies to other figures.

[28] According to Robert C. Latham and William Matthews, the editors of D10, the total
word count of Pepys's diary is approximately 1.25 million words (D10, I, "Introduction", xli).

Diachrony of Present Participles and Gerunds Followed by *Not*

(86) a. 1660 S. Pepys, D10, I 310, he not coming, I went to my father's.
  b. 1669 S. Pepys, D10, IX 461, she coming not, I went to her husband's chamber

(87) a. 1668 S. Pepys, D10, IX 192, Which they not presently doing, they were all inflamed,
  b. 1665 S. Pepys, D10, VI 75, Thence to Westminster-hall and up and down, doing not much;

(88) a. 1661 S. Pepys, D10, II 154, he and I to the Dolphin but not finding Sir W. Batten there, we went and carried a bottle of wine to his house
  b. 1668 S. Pepys, D10, IX 14, but I finding him not there, nor the Duke of York within, I away by coach to the Nursery,

(89) a. 1662 S. Pepys, D10, III 269, not having time to do anything, I went toward my Lord Sandwichs
  b. 1660 S. Pepys, D10, I 215, To bed, having not time to write letters;

(90) a. 1661 S. Pepys, D10, II 169-170, he could not advise me to any thing therein, not knowing what the other hath done in the country,
  b. 1663 S. Pepys, D10, IV 22, Called at my brother's and find him sick in bed of a pain in the sole of one of his feet, without swelling; knowing not how it came, but it will not suffer him to stand these two days.

(91) a. 1666 S. Pepys, D10, VII 391, not meeting her, I home
  b. 1660 S. Pepys, D10, I 261, meeting not Mr. Sheply there, I went home

(92) a. 1667 S. Pepys, D10, VIII 102, not seeing her whom I love, I by water to White-hall
  b. 1663 S. Pepys, D10, IV 291, seeing not my wife there, went out again.

Table 46 (p. 190) shows the variety of verbs which took the post-position of *not*, and the historical transition of the variations between the two syntactic variants. From Table 46 it is evident that the post-position of *not* occurred with 25 varieties of verbs together with 229+1 examples, typically with a closed class of verbs: *be, have, know, come, do* and *find*,

Chapter VI

among other verbs. According to the *OED²*, all of the verbs in Table 46 came into verb-category before the mid-16th century. In other words, newly-born verbs never took the post-position of *not*. In this respect, the simple participle followed by *not* was less productive than the actual number of occurrences would indicate.

Table 46   Verbs Taking Post-Position of *Not* with Simple Participial Verb-*ing*—Diaries and Correspondence

Period	be		have		know		care		come		do	
	Pre	Post	Pre	Post	Pre	Post	Pre	Post	Pre	Post	Pre	Post
-1600	2	20	0	0	0	0	0	0	0	0	0	0
1601-1650	9	12	6	1	8	0	1	0	1	0	1	0
1651-1700	258+1	95	39	21	86	2	0	0	36	5	1	2
1701-1750	31	9	18	4	26	0	1	0	1	0	1	0
1751-1800	65	14	19	5	35	0	0	0	3	0	0	0
1801-1850	83	8	19	+1	38	0	3	1	2	0	1	0
1851-1900	32	4	10	2	22	0	0	0	0	0	+1	0
1901-	2	1	1	0	3	0	0	0	0	0	0	0

Period	find		meet		need		say		see	
	Pre	Post	Pre	Post	Pre	Post	Pre	Post	Pre	Post
-1600	0	0	0	0	0	0	0	0	0	0
1601-1650	1	1	0	0	0	0	1	0	1	0
1651-1700	28	2	9	1	0	1	1	0	10	1
1701-1750	9	0	2	0	0	0	0	0	0	0
1751-1800	2	1	1	0	0	0	1	0	0	0
1801-1850	4	0	1	0	0	0	0	1	4	0
1851-1900	3	1	0	0	0	0	0	0	0	0
1901-	0	0	0	0	0	0	1	0	0	0

Period	Other verbs which occurred once with the post-positioned *not* (the number with the pre-position of *not* being omitted)
-1600	
1601-1650	return
1651-1700	afford consist contain examine write
1701-1750	amount reach
1751-1800	leave
1801-1850	feel long open
1851-1900	take
1901-	occupy

6.2.1.4. Semantic Differences between Pre- and Post-position of *Not*

In terms of semantics, the pre-position and the post-position of *not* occurred in almost the same linguistic circumstances. In the three pairs of

Diachrony of Present Participles and Gerunds Followed by *Not*

not being and *being not* constructions in (93)-(95), the pre-position of *not* in (a) and the post-position of *not* in (b) are practically interchangeable with each other. As can be construed from the comparison of the two forms, there seems to be virtually no semantic difference between the two syntactic variants: the two constructions are not rooted in terms of the difference in extent of negation.[29]

(93) a. 1660 S. Pepys, D10, I 124, dinner <u>not being ready</u>, I went with Captain Hayward to the *Plimouth* and *Essex*,

b. 1664 S. Pepys, D10, V 305, That [=a flagon to be carried to Woolwich] <u>being not ready</u>, I stepped aside and found out Nellson,

(94) a. 1660 S. Pepys, D10, I 265, my Lord <u>not being up</u>, I went out to Charing-cross

b. 1666 S. Pepys, D10, VII 97, who <u>being not up</u>, I took a walk with Balty into the park.

(95) a. 1660 S. Pepys, D10, I 41, my Lady <u>not being within</u>, I spoke to Mrs Carter about it,

b. 1660 S. Pepys, D10, I 73, he <u>being not within</u>, I went up,

---

[29] As indicated in Chapter I, one of the merits of linguistically analysing diaries and letters is that we come across descriptions useful for understanding linguistic aspects of the time through real voices reflecting a writer's own view of the English language during his or her lifetime. As far as the usage now in question is concerned, Defoe's description shown below is interesting. In that quotation, he does not discuss the usage itself, but hints that there is a difference in connotation between *not being* + Adjective and *being un*-Adjective, although it is regrettable that Defoe is not referring to the difference between them and *being not* + Adjective.

1710 D. Defoe, L14, 287, I do Not pretend to be Able to Merit So Much Favor; yet the Meanest Capacity can allways do Something. There is a Difference between Not being Worthy, and being Unworthy. I hope I Need Not assure you Sir That I will slip no Opportunity of Service, but Sir It is wholly in your Self to make me Usefull, and as the Favor comes by your Intercession, So the Power of Serving Depends Upon your Assistance in Directing.

A question of the validity of *being not worthy*, and which of the two above this post-position of *not* was closer in meaning arouse my interest.

Chapter VI

6.2.1.5. Structural Differences between Pre- and Post-position of *Not*

In terms of structural features, as the three pairs in (96)-(98) indicate, the position of a participial phrase with regard to the superordinate clause is not a factor determining the choice of the two variants. Both the pre-position and the post-position of *not* can occupy the sentence-initial, sentence-medial and sentence-final positions. The two syntactic variants do not show complementary distribution.

(96) <s -*ing* (S)V>
    a. 1661 S. Pepys, D10, II 61, my wife <u>not</u> <u>being</u> <u>well</u>, she kept her chamber all this day.
    b. 1664 S. Pepys, D10, V 132, my Lady <u>being</u> <u>not</u> <u>well</u>, kept her chamber.

(97) <S -*ing* V>
    a. 1661 S. Pepys, D10, II 199, I <u>not</u> <u>being</u> <u>neat</u> in clothes . . . could not be so merry as otherwise and at all times I am and can be,
    b. 1665 S. Pepys, D10, VI 73, and then . . . to a play at the Dukes of my Lord Orerey's, called *Mustapha* - which <u>being</u> <u>not</u> <u>good</u>, made Baterton's part and Ianthes but ordinary too, so that we were not contented with it at all.

(98) <SV s -*ing*>
    a. 1663 S. Pepys, D10, IV 194, So late at my office and then home to supper - and to bed, my man Will <u>not</u> <u>being</u> <u>well</u>.
    b. 1662 S. Pepys, D10, III 44, all the afternoon rumaging of papers in my chamber and tearing some and sorting others till late at night, and so to bed - my wife <u>being</u> <u>not</u> <u>well</u> all this day.

With the participle *being*, there are many examples of the post-position as well as the pre-position of *not* in the texts examined, and the selection of the two variants does not depend on the parts of speech of the words linked with the copula *being*. Both of the variants can take adjective, adverb, noun and their equivalents as a complement.

Diachrony of Present Participles and Gerunds Followed by *Not*

6.2.1.6. Main Points with Respect to the History of the Negation of the Simple Participles

Based on the new historical facts shown in 6.2.1.1-6.2.1.5, the main points regarding the history of the negation of the simple participles are summarised in (99).

(99) a. From a historical perspective, the Verb-*ing not* structure was in its prime in the 17th century, and that it virtually ceased to be used towards the middle of the 18th century, except intermittently when combined with *be* and *have* as a main verb. Eventually, even these two verbs succumbed to the *not* Verb-*ing* structure by the end of the 18th century.[30]

   b. In terms of the variety of the verb, the post-positioned construction was employed with a closed class of verbs: *know, come, do, find*, among other verbs, not to say *be* and *have*. Verbs which came into the verb category from 1550 never took the Verb-*ing not* structure. The newly-born verbs were restricted to a major rule.

   c. Except in Hoby's diary, the negative particle *not* usually preceded the participial *ing*-form. The spread of the Verb-*ing not* structure into a number of corpora implies, however, that it would be unfair to label this construction simply as an erroneous usage. This usage was used by educated people as well, as shown later in 6.5.

   d. There seems to have been virtually no semantic and syntactic difference between the pre- and the post-position of *not*. The two variants did not show complementary distribution, and they were practically interchangeable with each other.

At this point, it is clear that it is not appropriate to stigmatise the usage of the post-positioned *not* as misuse, at least in the history of English. This doctrine of misuse should be abandoned and a revised theory on the

---

[30] This will make it possible to envisage the numerous uses of the *being not* structure in Late Middle English and Early Modern English. Historical studies with special regard to this usage in ME, however, do not seem to have been undertaken as yet.

Chapter VI

history of the negation of simple present participles should be put forward.

6.2.2. Reasons for the Post-position of *Not* in the Simple Participial Verb-*ing*

As has been demonstrated in 6.2.1.3-6.2.1.5 above, the supposition that the derivation of the Verb-*ing* + *not* construction can be attributed to semantic or structural factors, while seemingly reasonable, is not in fact true in this case. Therefore, alternatively, other internal and external reasonings have to be considered. In most cases, it is likely that language changes are ascribable not to a single but to multiple factors, intra- and extra-linguistic, and accordingly, attempts have been made to explain the derivation of the participial Verb-*ing* + *not* construction. Concerning the factors causing the simple participial post-position of *not*, however, only such intra-linguistic causes are proposed in 6.2.2.

6.2.2.1. Positional Freedom of *Not*

As an alternative to semantic or structural factors, the reasoning that the position of the negative particle *not* was free can be conceived. It is certain that, in Modern English, the negative particle *not* was fairly free in taking its position in a sentence. The usages in (100), which, except for High Church English, are not permitted or less acceptable in Present-day English, may confirm that, in some stages in the history of English, the negative particle *not* was permitted to take various positions, even in prose. In standard Present-day English, for example, *not* would stand between the auxiliary and the perfective *have* in (100a), between the auxiliary and the passive *be* in (100b), between the perfective *have/had* and the past participle in (100c, d) and between the auxiliary and the main verb in (100e). In (100f, g), *not* would be placed immediately after *had better/best*, and in (100h, i) directly before the *to*-infinitive. Such relative freedom and convenience may have exerted influence over the position of *not* with the simple participle.

Diachrony of Present Participles and Gerunds Followed by *Not*

(100) a. Aux *have _* PP

1800 G. Rose, L35, 275, I should really have not said even so much as this if I had not been desired to call to your recollection the situation of another.

b. Aux *be _* PP

1644 R. Symonds, D7, 152, The King consented; he required a passe, and the King denied, because he would be not seene to consent to his going.

c. *have/had* PP _

1766 J. Penrose, L25, 138, Fanny desires Mary to excuse her not writing this Post: she has had not Time, but hopes nothing will hinder her writing next Post. | 1792 W. B. Stevens, D22, 7, when I have known not where to look for Refuge, | 1815 C. S. M. Campbell, D26, 390, into which the spite and malice and sin of the Evil One have entered not;

d. *_ have* PP

1774 G. White, D18, 49, Swifts not have appear'd for these two evenings.

e. Aux V _

1791 J. Woodforde, D21, III 250, I . . . told her that I hoped she might repent not of what she was about to do. | 1797 A. Hughes, D20, 127, I fear I shall like not for her to go,

f. *had _ better/best*

1710 J. Swift, L16, I 98, whether he had not better stay till tomorrow.

g. *had better be _* PP

1757 T. Gray, L26, II 508, it had better be not understood at all.

h. *to*-infinitive _

1667 Pepys, D10, 80-81, the Duch are in very great straits, so as to be said to be not able to set out their fleet this year. | 1667 S. Pepys, D10, VIII 203, the fellow did think to have not had it discovered. | 1794 E. Darwin, L33, 266, but I believe them all to be not

Chapter VI

fever-producing, till they have been oxygenated. | 1818 D.
Wordsworth, L43, 153, the stillness seemed to be not of this world.

i. to _ infinitive
1815 M. Todd, D31, 105, Here we were obliged to show passports
and give half a paulo each to the Custom House Officers, to not
overhaul our baggage

This reasoning, however, is not thought to be positive. Under this reasoning, it is impossible to explain not only the fact that the post-position of *not*
was centred upon a group of verbs (Table 46 on p.190) but also the fact that
it scarcely ever occurred with the simple gerundive *ing*-form, even with the
same verbs, as shown in 6.2.2.4.3.[31]

6.2.2.2. Avoidance of Semantic Ambiguities

Another reasoning is based on the scope of negation; in (101), the
pre-positioning of *not* before *reaching* could lead to the negation of *being
imperfect* as well. This device for avoiding ambiguities may be effective in
clearly showing the scope of negation when more than one *ing*-form is coordinated.

(101) 1701 J. Hudson, L1, 302, and I wish you would try Smith & Walford
for Cowper's Anatomy, and the Philosophical Transactions, our sett
reaching not far, and being imperfect in the first Volumes.

This reasoning, however, applies to only one example: in the present texts
examined, 15 out of 16 coordinated sets of the simple participle take the
pre-positional *not*.

---

[31] *Never* was also fairly free in taking its position in a sentence; it was not restricted to
the slot immediately after auxiliaries. Quite a few examples of *never* Aux *have* PP,
never be/have PP, *never* Aux V, and *have* PP *never* can be evidenced in Mrs.
Arbuthnot (D27), Peter Hawker (D29), Ellen Buxton (D38), John Gay (L18),
Daniel Eaton (L20), Charles Lennox, 2nd Duke of Richmond (L22), Josiah Wedg-
wood (L32), William Blake (L39), Robert Southey (L42), Thomas Raikes (L44),
Robert Peel (L45), Edward FitzGerald (L49), Alfred Tennyson (L50) and Algernon
C. Swinburne (L56).

6.2.2.3. Seemingly Resultant Post-position of *not*

In (102), *having* is used sylleptically as an auxiliary and as a main verb left unexpressed. Its position as a main verb to be supplied could be either before or after '*not*' (*having not* time or *not having* time). Nevertheless, since 'Having' precedes '*not*' in the quotation, on the formal basis this example is included in the post-positioned *not*.

> (102) 1841 J. Clare, L46, 294, <u>Having</u> left the Forest in a hurry & <u>not</u> time to take my leave of you & your family

As indicated in 6.2.1.3-6.2.1.5 and 6.2.2.1-6.2.2.3, the supposition that the derivation of the Verb-*ing* + *not* construction can be attributed to semantic or structural factors apply only to a limited number of examples.[32]

6.2.2.4. The Most Plausible Explanation: Reflection of the Mode of Negation in Negative Declarative Sentences (RNDS theory)

In this section, what is regarded as the most plausible explanation for the promotion of the post-position of *not* is shown, together with statistics and graphs.

A glance over the verbs appearing in Table 46 above recalls the verb-group isolated with reference to another topic, that is, the verbs which continued to show aversion to the *do*-negative in the finite clause. They are the verbs in (103), Table 52 and Table 53 (pp. 227-228), in addition to *be*. Clearly these verbs and those in Table 46 roughly overlap with each other.

> (103) The Verbs which continued to show aversion to the auxiliary *do* in negative declaratives

---

[32] Neither is a phonological reasoning explicable to the derivation of the Verb-*ing* + *not* construction. In (ib) beautiful metre may be produced, but this is not always the case with other examples of this construction.

   (i) (= 86) a.   ` ´ ´ ` ` ´ ` ` ´ `

          he <u>not</u> <u>coming</u>, I went to my father's.

       b.   ` ´ ` ´ ` ´ ` ´ ` ` ´ `

          she <u>coming</u> <u>not</u>, I went to her husband's chamber

Chapter VI

a. know, care, doubt, mistake; wot(te), boot, trow, fear, list, skill; ask;
   question, say; come, deny, intend, speak, think; die, do, find, grieve,
   help, love, matter, move, see

(Nakamura 1988: 133)

b. Diaries: care, come, doubt, know, love, stay
   Correspondence: doubt, know, mistake, need, question (= 'doubt'),
   value

(Nakamura 1997: 114)

The post-position of *not* in participial *ing*-forms may be interpreted
as having mirrored the mode of negation in negative declarative sentences.
Participles such as *being not / having not / knowing not / caring not / coming not* must have reflected the finite form *I am not / I have not / He knows
not / She cares not / They come not*. Note the positional parallelism of *not*
between the finite verb phrase and the non-finite verb phrase of the present
participle. A series of secondary evidence supporting this theory of a *reflection of the mode of negation in *n*egative *d*eclarative *s*entences by the
post-position of *not* in participial *ing*-forms (RNDS theory) is shown
below in 6.2.2.4.1-6.2.2.4.3 (pp. 198-220).

6.2.2.4.1. Evidence Supporting the RNDS Theory: (1) High Percentage of
Post-position of *Not* in Compound Participial *Having* PP and *Being* PP

First, the above reasoning that the mode of negation of a participle
must have mirrored that of a finite clause is most applicable to those sentences in which the compound participle of perfective *having* + PP or pas-
sive/perfective *being* + PP occurs in the negative. The negative finite form
of such compounds requires that *not* should almost always come after *have*
or *be*.[33] Accordingly, the percentage of the compound participial *ing*-
forms followed by *not* is expected to be higher, since they have more verbal force in having tense, aspect or voice than the simple participial *ing*-
forms. This is exactly what Table 47 and Figure 6 demonstrate.

---

[33] The example (100d) is the possible exception.

Diachrony of Present Participles and Gerunds Followed by *Not*

Table 47   Variations between Pre- and Post-position of *Not* with Compound Participial *Having* + PP and *Being* + PP—Diaries and Correspondence

a. *Having* + PP

| Period | Perfective *having* + PP | | | |
| | Per 25 years | | Per 50 years | |
	Pre	Post	Pre	Post
-1600	0	0	0	0
1601-1625	1	1	7	4
1626-1650	6	3		
1651-1675	8	59	26	70
1676-1700	18	11		
1701-1725	11	12	21	12
1726-1750	10	0		
1751-1775	6	5	16	10
1776-1800	10	5		
1801-1825	18	1	36	3
1826-1850	18	2		
1851-1875	14	1	18	1
1876-1900	4	0		
1901-1925	0	0	2	0
1926-	2	0		
Total	126 : 100			

b. *Being* + PP

| Period | Passive/Perfective *being* + PP | | | |
| | Per 25 years | | Per 50 years | |
	Pre	Post	Pre	Post
-1600	0	1	0	1
1601-1625	2	1	8	4
1626-1650	6	3		
1651-1675	53+1	25	74+2	35
1676-1700	21+1	10		
1701-1725	15	8	25	10
1726-1750	10	2		
1751-1775	4	0	22+1	6
1776-1800	18+1	6		
1801-1825	12+1	0	22+1	0
1826-1850	10	0		
1851-1875	3	0	6	0
1876-1900	3	0		
1901-1925	0	0	0	0
1926-	0	0		
Total	157+4 : 56			

Chapter VI

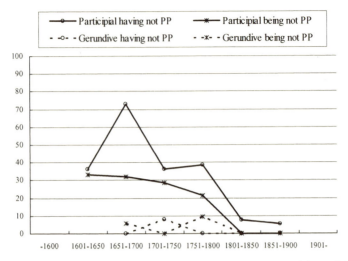

Figure 6 Transition of the Frequency of the Post-position of *Not* with Compound Participles and Compound Gerunds—Diaries and Correspondence

In Figure 6, the two upper bold lines represent the compound participles. The compound participles *having* + PP and *being* + PP continually maintain a higher percentage than the simple participle in Figure 5 above (p. 187) does. It is remarkable that the percentage of perfective *having not* + PP in the latter half of the 17th-century is over 70. These results can be attributed to the fact stated above on p. 198.

The compound perfective participial *having not* PP is exemplified in (104), and the compound passive/perfective participial *being not* PP in (105). In the latter, there seems to be no significant difference in frequency depending on the function of *be* PP whether it is passive or perfective.

(104) Examples of the compound perfective participial *having not* PP

<1601-1625>

1625 J. Glanville, D3, 65, Hereupon in the first place Itt was held noe matter of dishonor for us to quite the Towne upon good iudgement, haveing not yet engaged our selves by any battery against it,

Diachrony of Present Participles and Gerunds Followed by *Not*

nor breaking ground to entrenche ourselves before it.

<1626-1650>

1642-1645 Colonel Roe, D5, 19, they presently routed, haueing not drawne 40 together. | 1644 R. Symonds, D7, 64, By this time Colonel Goring, Generall of his Majesties horse, came to the King, having not heard of the enemyes march till 10 of the clock. | 1646 King Charles I, L2, 47, Having not heard from thee these last 3 weeks . . . my impatience hath made me find out this express to go unto thee . . . that I may have the more ways of hearing from thee.

<1651-1675>

1654 R. Josselin, D8, 651, Protector dissolved the Parliament in painted chamber, they having not made one act | 1660 S. Pepys, D10, I 3, This morning (we lying lately in the garret) I rose, put on my suit with great skirts, having not lately worn any other clothes but them. | 1660 S. Pepys, D10, I 5, There, having not eat anything but bread and cheese, my wife cut me a slice of brawn which I received from my Lady, which proves as good as ever I had any. | 1660 S. Pepys, D10, I 73, In the moening went to my Lord's lodgings, thinking to have spoke with Mr. Sheply, having not been to visit him since my coming to town. | 1660 S. Pepys, D10, I 151, At night, Mr. Pierce, Purser (the other Pierce and I having not spoke to one another since we fell out about Mr. Edwd:) and Mr. Cooke sat with me in my Cabbin and supped with me, and then I went to bed. | 1660 S. Pepys, D10, I 202, and so home to bed, having not been at my father's today. | 1660 S. Pepys, D10, I 205, After that to Westminster about my Lord's business, and so home - my Lord having not been well these [two] or three days. | 1660 S. Pepys, D10, I 219, Never since I was a man in the world was I ever so great a stranger to public affairs as now I am, having not read a newsbook or anything like it, or enquired after any news, or what the Parliament doth or in any wise how things go. | 1660 S. Pepys, D10, I 242, So we returned and landed at the Beare at the bridge-foot, where we saw Suthwark faire (I having not at all seen Bartlmew fayre); | 1662 S. Pepys, D10, III 209, I am also troubled for my journy which I must needs take suddenly to the Court at Brampton, but most of all for that I am not provided to understand my business, having not minded it a great while; | 1662 S. Pepys, D10, III 269, but the company not being ready, I did slip down to Wilkinsons and, having not eat anything today, did eat a mutton-pie and drank; | 1663 S. Pepys, D10, IV 66, where I find Mr. Moore got abroad and dined with me; which I was glad to see, he having not been able to go abroad a great while. | 1663 S. Pepys, D10, IV 105, and so home to talk with my father, and sup and to bed - I having not had yet one Quarter of an hour's leisure to sit down and talk with him since he came to towne. | 1663 S. Pepys, D10, IV 112, I did hear that the Queene is much grieved of late at the King's neglecting herm he having not supped once with her this Quarter of a year, and almost every night with my Lady Castkemayne, | 1663 S. Pepys, D10, IV 251, which I was sorry to see, it having not been hard for him to have got all the speech without booke. | 1663 S. Pepys, D10, IV 437-438, We had to dinner, my wife and I, a fine Turkey and a mince-pie, and dined in state, poor wretch, she and I; and have thus kept our Christmas together, all alone almost – having not once been out. | 1664 S. Pepys, D10, V 12, we fell in talk . . . of Musique, the the Universall Character – art of Memory – Granger's counterfeiting of hands – and other most excellent discourses, to my great content, having not been in so good company a great while. | 1664 S. Pepys, D10, V 19, and went home in a great shower of rain, it having not rained a great while before. | 1664 S. Pepys, D10, V 193, yet I bless God I am not conscious of any neglect in me that they are not done, having not minded my pleasure at all. | 1664 S. Pepys, D10, V 236, And so my wife and I abroad to the Kings play-house, she giving me her time of the last month, she having not seen any then; | 1665 S. Pepys, D10, VI 54, I sent the coach back for my wife, my Lord a second time dining at home on purpose to meet me, he having not dined once at home but those times, since his coming from sea. | 1665 S. Pepys, D10, VI 160, Thence back again by coach – Mr. Carteret having not had the confidence to take his lady once by the hand, coming or going; | 1665 S. Pepys, D10, VI 204, Up; and being ready, I out to Mr. Colvill the goldsmith's, having not for some days <been> [Nakamura Pepys's own addition] in the streets. | 1665 S. Pepys, D10, VI 227-228, coming out of the church, I met Mrs. Pierce, whom I was ashamed to see, having not been with her since

Diachrony of Present Participles and Gerunds Followed by *Not*

my coming to town – but promised to visit her. | 1665 S. Pepys, D10, VI 233, So I up; and after being trimmed . . . went to Sir J. Mennes, where I find all out of order still, they having not seen one another; | 1665 S. Pepys, D10, VI 240, and then to supper and to bed, my mind not being at full ease, having not fully satisfied myself how Captain Cocke will deal with me as to the share of the profits. | 1665 S. Pepys, D10, VI 278, his wife is come to town to see him, having not seen him since fifteen <weeks> ago, at his first going to sea last. | 1665 Earl of Sandwich, D11, 23, Havinge not heard from you of divers dayes, it was very good newes to mee to receive your letters, for I was in feare for you of the Infection. | 1665 J. Strype, L1, 183, That I have not yet wrote to Brother John-son is, because I have not been able to answer him in the particular of Subscription, having not had the opportunity of speaking either with the Proctor, or my Tutor; | 1666 S. Pepys, D10, VII 26, which I went further in inviting him to then I intended, having not yet well considered whether it will be convenient for me or no to have him here so near us. | 1666 S. Pepys, D10, VII 66, endeed I have been silent in my business of the office a great while and given but little account of myself, and least of all to him, having not made him one visit since he came to town from Oxford, | 1666 S. Pepys, D10, VII 71, after dinner comes my Uncle and Aunt Wright, the latter I having not seen since the plague – a silly, froward, ugly woman she is. | 1666 S. Pepys, D10, VII 93, The Bishop of Munster, everybody says, is coming to peace with the Dutch, we having not supplied him with the monies promised him. | 1666 S. Pepys, D10, VII 166, He had brought his family into a way of being great. But dying at this time, his memory and name . . . will be forgot in a few months, as if he had never been, nor any of his name be the better by it - he having not had time to coll[ect] any estate; but is dead poor rather then rich. | 1666 S. Pepys, D10, VII 323, and then to Colvill's, who I find lives now in Lymestreete – and with the same credit as ever – this fire having not done them any wrong that I hear of at all. | 1666 S. Pepys, D10, VII 355-356, Thence to my Lord Crews, and there dined and mightily made of, having not, to my shame, been there in eight months before. | 1666 S. Pepys, D10, VII 386-387, he hath promised to come and bring Madam Turner with him (who is come

Chapter VI

to town to see the City but hath lost all her goods of all kinds in Salsbury-Court, Sir Wm. Turner _having_ not _endeavoured_ in her absence to save one penny) to dine with me on Friday next | 1667 S. Pepys, D10, VIII 27, and to the New Exchange, there to take up my wife and Mercer, and to Temple Barr to my ordinary and had a dish of meat for them, they _having_ not _dined;_ | 1667 S. Pepys, D10, VIII 49, So to write a letter to my Lady Sandwich for him to carry, I _having_ not _writ_ to her a great while. | 1667 S. Pepys, D10, VIII 70, This evening, going to the Queen's side to see the ladies, I did find the Queene, the Duchess of Yorke, and another or two at Cards, with the room full of great ladies and men - which I was amazed at to see on a Sunday, _having_ not _believed_ it; | 1667 S. Pepys, D10, VIII 139, and then to supper and bed – _having_ not _had_ time to make up my accounts of this month at this very day, | 1667 S. Pepys, D10, VIII 162, Up, and to the office, where we sat all the morning; and (which is now rare, he _having_ not _been_ with us twice I think these six months) Sir G. Carteret came to us upon some perticular business of his office and went away again. | 1667 S. Pepys, D10, VIII 175, and so back, it raining a little; which is mighty welcome, it _having_ not _rained_ in many weeks, so that they say it makes the fields just now mighty sweet; | 1667 S. Pepys, D10, VIII 176, he cannot provide it any longer without money, _having_ not _received_ a penny since the King's coming in. | 1667 S. Pepys, D10, VIII 187, This noon I got in some coals at 23_s_ per chaldron, a good bargain I thank God, _having_ not _been put_ to buy a coal all this dear time, | 1667 S. Pepys, D10, VIII 356, It raining this day all day to our great joy, it _having_ not _rained_ I think this month before, so as the ground was everywhere as burned and dry as could be – and no travelling in the road or streets in London for dust. | 1667 S. Pepys, D10, VIII 368, the King hath declared that he did not get the child of which she is conceived at this time, he _having_ not as he says _lain_ with her this half year; | 1667 S. Pepys, D10, VIII 378, when I came home and find Mr. Good-groome my wife's singing-master there, I did soundly rattle him for neglecting her so much as he hath done, she _having_ not _learned_ three songs these three months and more. | 1667 S. Pepys, D10, VIII 430-431, Up, and all the morning at the office, where little to do but bemoan ourselfs under the want

Diachrony of Present Participles and Gerunds Followed by *Not*

of money – and endeed, little is or can be done for want of money, we having not now received one penny for any service in many weeks, and none in view to receive, saving for paying of some seamen's wages. | 1667 S. Pepys, D10, VIII 475, and did bring my gold, to my heart's content, very safe home, having not this day carried it in a basket but in our hands: | 1667 S. Pepys, D10, VIII 565, he was a man accused of treason by the House of Commons, and mercy was not proper for him, having not been tried yet, and so no mercy needful for him. | 1667 S. Pepys, D10, VIII 601, here I and my people did discourse of the Act for the accounts, which doth give the greatest power to these people, as they report that have read it (I having not yet read it; . . .), | 1668 S. Pepys, D10, IX 179, it being now about 9 a-clock at night, I heard Mercer's voice and my boy Tom's singing in the garden; which pleased me mightily, I longing to see the girl, having not seen her since my wife went; | 1669 S. Pepys, D10, IX 474, I thought this morning to have seen my Lord Sandwich before he went out of town, but I came half an hour too late; which troubles me, I having not seen him since my Lady Pall died. | 1669 S. Pepys, D10, IX 492, God knowing what my condition is, I having not attended and now not being able to examine what my state is of my accounts and being in the world, which troubles me mightily. | 1669 S. Pepys, D10, IX 522, and there hearing that *The Alchymist* was acted, we did go and took him with us, at the King's House; and is still a good play, it having not been acted for two or three years before; | 1669 S. Pepys, D10, IX 541, I saw him, and very kind; and I am glad he is so, I having not wrote to him all the time, my eyes endeed not letting me. | 1669 S. Pepys, D10, IX 551, which they having not done, he did give warrant to the Duke of York to direct Sir Jeremy Smith to be a Commissioner of the Navy in the room of Penn; | 1673 R. Yard, L8, I 74, he wanted nothing but men, which all endeavors possible have been used to raise, masters of vessells haveing not been exempted; | 1673 H. Ball, L8, I 158, This day came an expresse from our Fleete, but I haveing not seen the letter or received a perfect account of the condition it left them, I dare not tell your Excellency any more then that Mr. Richards told me they were then 6 leagues off of the Texell, and had done nothing further;

Chapter VI

<1676-1700>

1679 S. Pepys, L6, 66, this comes to tell you that I having not yet been able to obtain a Copy of the Affidavit made by Colonel Scot against mee (which I hoped to have had a day or 2 since) I am prevented in being able to draw out those Quaeries, which would be necessary for me to send to you out of it, relating to the Court of France, and Consequently cannot send you what I in my last promised to do by this post. | 1682 W. Hewer, L5, 137, Sir John Banks took very kindly my waiting on him with the Account you gave, he having not met with any, that was soe particular, | 1683 S. Pepys, L5, 163-164, 'T is with impatience . . . I have waited a change of weather, we having not had, till yesterday, one hour fair, to be able, for wind and rain, to look abroad since we came hither; | 1684 J. Evelyn, D9, IV 386, I was exceedingly drowsy this afternoone it being most excessively hot: we having not had above one or two considerable showres (& they stormes) these eight or nine moneths so as the trees lost their leafe like Winter, & many of them quite died for want of refreshment. | 1693 W. Gilpin, L12, 30, Your ships arrived here last week, how safely I know not, having not yet seen them. | 1694 J. Evelyn, L7, I 100, I speake not this by guesse, having not long-since examind him, after I had first read *Clemens Alexandrinus*, which you know is a booke of greate varietie; | 1696 J. Ray, L1, 201, For my own part I doe freely acknowledge myself altogether insufficient for such a task, having not seen the plants themselves, nor of many of them so much as dried Specimens, and of the rest having had but a transient view. | 1698 J. Lowther, L12, 628, Having not heard that you are under the same obligations you were the last election at Carlisle, I hope we may have your interest there for my son which both he and I doe earnestly desire, | 1700 S. Pepys, L7, I 317, which I am not without some apprehension of, our friends here having not thought fit to communicate to me these your letters or any other papers during my late illness, | 1700 S. Pepys, L7, II 26, Having not sped at Oxford, I shall apply my self to my friend Dr Shadwell at Paris for our two books of *Charity* there. | 1700 E. Halley, D14, 306, Since my last from St. Iago, which I hope came long since to Your hands, haveing not been able to fetch Madera by reason of the winds shifting upon me, I was

Diachrony of Present Participles and Gerunds Followed by *Not*

Obleged to putt into Ryo Jennero in Brasile to gett some Rumm for my Ships company, from whence I wrote you a letter which I suppose will not be in Engld: soe soon as this.

<1701-1725>

1704 W. Nicolson, D15, 258, The Bishop of St David's, haveing not assigned Errors his Writ was voted to Discontinue; and the At-tourney-General [Northey] directed to take out Judgement. | 1705 W. Nicolson, D15, 298-299, Young Lord Lonsdale brought in by Lord Wharton, Lord Weymouth haveing not been acquainted with his Design of comeing thither, | 1710 D. Defoe, L14, 300, I have been So Anxious About the Safe Conveying of My Letters, haveing Not had the honor of the Least hint from your Self, That I Convey This Enclosed by a Trusty Friend, | 1710 J. Swift, L16, I 22, got home early, and begun a letter to the *Tatler* about the corruptions of style and writing, &c. and having not heard from you, am resolved this letter shall go to-night. | 1710 R. Steele, L15, 264, I cannot pos-sibly come expecting Orders Here which I must overlook, and hav-ing not half done my other businesse at the Savoy. | 1711 J. Swift, L16, I 275, Parvisol has sent me a bill for fifty pounds, which I am sorry for, having not written to him for it, only mentioned it two months ago; | 1711 J. Swift, L16, I 330, I was tired with riding a trotting mettlesome horse a dozen miles, having not been on horse-back this twelve-month. | 1712 D. Defoe, L14, 389, The great floods have hindred my Travelling for Some Time, The like Rains, Especially on the border, haveing not been known a long Time. | 1714 H. Jolley, L17, 490, haveing not meet with that justice as I did expect, but complaints does but litle good here; so must do all in me lyes to beare these disappointm^ts with patience &c; | 1714 T. Hearne, L1, 355, the best part of the Description of Britain before Holinshed by Harrison is extracted from him, Harrison himself being a man but of indifferent judgement, and having not been a traveller. | 1714 T. Hearne, L1, 356, having not heard from him for almost two years together, I fear that he hath either forgot his Promise, or, at least, that his practise hath taken up so much of his time, that he hath not as yet found leisure; | 1717 J. Addison, L17, 353, Your letters of the 29th & 5th inst: have been put into my hands;

Chapter VI

but <u>having</u> <u>not</u> yet <u>had</u> an opportunity of receiving His Maj^{tys} directions upon them, I can at present only acknowledge the receipt of them.

<1751-1775>

1754 S. Richardson, L19, 86, I shall retouch Pamela . . . What I am now e{mp}loying myself about, is, <to collect> /in collecting/ the Sentiments of the first and last of ye th{ree} Pieces ({T}hose in Clarissa are already printed in the last Edition) and to print all containe{d} /in the/ Three i{n o}ne Pocket Volume, to serve as a kind of Vade Mecum to such as either have read, o{r}, <u>having</u> <u>not</u> <u>read</u>, can dispense w.th ye Stories, for the Sake of the Instruction aimed {to b}e given in them. | 1754 R. Dodsley, L24, 188, I have impatiently expected a Letter every Post last Week, but <u>having</u> <u>not</u> yet <u>receiv'd</u> any, begin to fear it must have miscarry'd. | 1764 J. Wesley, L23, 316-317, so I rested that night, <u>having</u> <u>not</u> quite <u>recovered</u> my journey from Shrewsbury to Roesfair. | 1767 J. Penrose, L25, 175, you are desired to send Word, whether Mr. Smith is sick, or has been sick, the Col. <u>having</u> <u>not</u> <u>heard</u> from him some time. | 1771 J. Woodforde, D21, I 105, Sister Jane took a vomit this evening by Dr. Clarke's order, she <u>having</u> <u>not</u> <u>been</u> right for some time—Bumps on her face etc.

<1776-1800>

1791 J. Woodforde, D21, III 319, Sent Briton this morning on foot to Mr. Du Quesnes with a Note, to enquire after him, <u>having</u> <u>not</u> <u>heard</u> from him since his return from Ely. | 1791 J. Woodforde, D21, III 323-324, Billy Bidewell brought my News and also a Letter from my Sister Pounsett, which I was very happy to receive, <u>having</u> <u>not</u> <u>had</u> one from her for many a Day owing to her being so long ill, | 1793 J. Woodforde, D21, IV 27-28, My Beer of late <u>having</u> <u>not</u> <u>been</u> clear and fine, so that I was willing to try some other scheme, | 1795 J. Woodforde, D21, IV 175, the Weather still continuing so very severe, and much Snow on the Ground, I thought too dangerous for me to venture to go into a damp Church and Walking upon Snow, <u>having</u> <u>not</u> <u>left</u> off my flannel lined second Gouty Shoes, therefore sent word to my Parishioners, that there would be no Service. | 1798 Bishop Porteus, L36, III 34, there have been evil

Diachrony of Present Participles and Gerunds Followed by *Not*

reports about you, which have alarmed and grieved us not a little, and indeed compelled me to write and inquire after you sooner than I otherwise should have done, having not yet struggled through that load of business which always overwhelms me on my first coming to town.

<1801-1825>

1801 D. Wordsworth, D24, 67, After dinner I felt myself unwell having not slept well in the night so, after we had put up the Book cases which Charles Lloyd sent us I lay down.

<1826-1850>

1827 J. Ruskin, L51, I 152, I have only a few minutes now to finish having not been able to escape sooner from my Customer. | 1838 S. Palmer, L48, I 187, We are still at La Cava; having not yet exhausted half its beauties;

<1851-1875>

1873 S. Palmer, L48, II 889, Who, having not seen their unfinished pictures would have supposed that some of the great Italians painted their flesh green?

(105) Examples of the compound passive/perfective participial *being not* PP

< -1600>

<Passive>

1587 J. Dee, D1, 25-26, afternone somwhat, Mr. Ed. Keley his lamp overthrow, the spirit of wyne long spent to nere, and the glas being not stayed with buks abowt it, as it was wont to be; and the same glas so flitting on one side, the spirit was spilled out, and burnt all that was on the table where it stode,

<1601-1625>

<Perfective>

1625 J. Glanville, D3, 69, the meeting of Captaines and Pursers was putt off to 8 a Clocke the next morning, My Lord Leiuteñnt being not yet retourned from this daie's March, nor expected till it should bee late at night.

Chapter VI

<1626-1650>

<Passive>

1630 J. Rous, D4, 52, They are in like manner to certifie the names of such men as being not qualified by lawe doe keepe chaplens in theire houses. | 1644 R. Josselin, D8, 20, he told mee separacion from the true church was lawfull in some cases; as being not rightly constituted;

<Perfective>

1630 J. Rous, D4, 55, The plague was sore at Cambridge this summer, so that there was no Sturbridge fayr; and in the beginning of this October . . . there was a commencement wherein many went out, doctors, bachelers of divinity, &c. at a cheape rate; the plague being not ceased there yet.

<1651-1675>

<Passive>

1660 S. Pepys, D10, I 151, I having spoke a word or two with my Lord, being not very well settled, partly through last night's drinking and want of sleep, I lay down in my gown upon my bed and sleep till the 4 a-clock gun the next morning waked me, which I took for 8 at night that night; | 1660 S. Pepys, D10, I 247, So to bed, after I had looked over the things my wife hath bought today; with which being not very well pleased, they costing too much, I went to bed in a discontent. | 1660 S. Pepys, D10, I 322, In the morning to Alderman Backwells for the Candle-sticks for Mr. Coventry; but they being not done, I went away; | 1662 S. Pepys, D10, III 265, my friends, partly being not so well acquainted with the Will, and partly I doubt not being so good wits as they . . . I was much troubled thereat; | 1663 S. Pepys, D10, IV 370, it was in no greater a matter, I being not at all concerned here. | 1663 S. Pepys, D10, IV 57, Thence home again by water presently; and with a bad dinner, being not looked for, to the office; | 1664 S. Pepys, D10, V 107, here I spoke with his kinswoman, he not being within, but did not hear her sing, being not enough acquainted with her | 1664 S. Pepys, D10, V 96, Being not known, some great person in the pew I pretended to and went in did question my coming in; | 1666 J. Milward, D6,

Diachrony of Present Participles and Gerunds Followed by *Not*

11, the House being not satisfied about the continuing this bill in the House, though laid aside for the present, it was out to the question whether the question should be put whether the bill should be cast out or not. | 1666 S. Pepys, D10, VII 120, I like not hers half so well as I thought at first, it being not so like, nor so well painted as I expected or as mine and my wife's are. | 1666 S. Pepys, D10, VII 309, being not burned, they stand still. | 1667 S. Pepys, D10, VIII 578, they will not agree to it, being not satisfied with that as sufficient, | 1667 S. Pepys, D10, VIII 588, it [= the Ceremony at Christmas Eve] being not begun, I to Westminster hall and there stayed and walked; | 1668 S. Pepys, D10, IX 276-277, so away to Coopers, where I spent all the afternoon with my wife and girl, seeing him make an end of her picture; which he did to my great content, though not so great as, I confess, I expected, being not satisfied in the greatness of the resemblance – nor in the blue garment; | 1672 C. Lyttelton, L3, I 100, They expect any day to heare the French and German armyes are ingaged, and I think there came some news of them to y^t purposse to night, wch being not told I suspect is none of ye best. | 1673 H. Ball, L8, II 20, It proves a mistake, which the merchants constantly affirmed last weeke, of the arrivall of our Virginia fleete at Kinsale, they being not yett heard of, and now only our Smirna fleete expected that putts us to any concerne. | 1674 G. Talbot L8, II 157, he hath cutt off the designe of all the factious bills that were in the forge, and prevented many new complaints which were begun to be opened to us by our friend my Lord O'Brian against the contract for and management of the revenue of Ireland by my Lord Ranelaugh there being not all this while one word spoken tending toward a supply to his Majesty for the strengthening of his Majesty's fleete,

<Perfective>

1661 S. Pepys, D10, II 114, But they being not come, we went over to the Wardrobe and there find that my Lord Abbot Mountagu being not at Paris, my Lord hath a mind to have them stay a little longer before they go. | 1661 S. Pepys, D10, II 3, That done, I left my friends and went to my Lord's; but he being not come in, I lodged the money with Mr. Sheply; | 1662 S. Pepys, D10, III 88, my father being not come, we walked home. | 1663 S. Pepys, D10, IV 30, After dinner walked to my Lord Sandwich and stayed with him in the chamber talking almost all the afternoon, he being not yet got abroad since his sickness. | 1664 C. Lyttelton, L3, I 40, His R[oyal] High[ness] went abroad the Swiftsure on Thursday last; the Charles wth ye rest of ye fleet being not then come to Portsmouth out of ye Downes, as they did yesterday morning; | 1666 S. Pepys, D10, VII 219, and I by appointment to attend the Duke of York at his closet. But being not come, Sir G. Carteret and I did talk together, | 1668 S. Pepys, D10, IX 391, So with W. Hewer by coach to Smithfield, but met not Mr. Pickering, he being not come; | 1673 H. Ball, L8, I 178, Sir Edward Spragg's will is not yet opened; Sir Joseph Sheldon his executor, with whom it was left, being not come up yet, but they report he is dead, worth but 5,000*l.* besides his jewells, | 1673 H. Ball, L8, II 21, I can heare nothing of the opening of the prizes, Mr. Charles Bennett being not yet returned from them;

<1676-1700>

<Passive>

1680 W. Hewer, L5, 103, they may putt and end to the Plott, and gett his Majestys gratious and generall Pardon, which being not well relished by the house, the debate ceased, | 1688 J. Evelyn, D9, IV 568-569, Coach to visite in the Citty, a Jolt (the doore being not fast-shut) flung her quite out of the Coach upon her back, in such manner, as the hind-wheles passed over both her Thighes a little above the knees: | 1689 J. Evelyn, D9, IV 640, Our Viccar on 6: Heb: Last 3 verses, shewing that the most godly men, though they had assured hope, yet they had not allways a presumptious Confidence of their Salvation: That assurance being not allways imparted to all alike, & that yet those who had that humble hope, were many times as certaine of Gods mercy, & perhaps upon better grounds, as the most confident: | 1690 R. Davies, D13, 124, the King's blue troop of guards soon supplied their place, and with them he charged in person and routed the enemy, and coming over the hill near Duleek appeared on our flank, and, being not known at first, made all our forces halt and draw up again in order, | 1690 R. Davies, D13, 142, There were

Diachrony of Present Participles and Gerunds Followed by *Not*

actually some of our men in the city, but were beaten out, <u>being</u> <u>not</u> <u>seconded</u>, it being not the King's order to storm the city, but only to attack the counterscarp; | 1698 J. Evelyn, D9, V 294-295, Mr. Stringfellow 7. Rom: 20, shewing that . . . a practical & universal obedience, this whole Chapter of St. Paule <u>being</u> <u>not</u> <u>meant</u> or applicable to the Apostle, but by a metaschematisme transferring figuratively what concerned the Jewes, who thought that the bare external observation of the Mosaic law, was alone sufficient,

<Perfective>

1680 Earl of Halifax, L11, 164, This King should have been here on Tuesday, but, taking St Omer in his way, will not be here till to morrow, to the great grief of my L^d of Oxford, who longs to be at home already, the jockeys <u>being</u> <u>not</u> yet <u>come</u>, and nobody taking a pipe with him. | 1680 W. Hewer, L5, 103, Katherine is taken very ill and has kept her bedd this 2 or 3 days, the Coachman <u>being</u> <u>not</u> yet <u>recovered</u> though it is hoped he is some what better than he was. | 1685 J. Evelyn, D9, IV 493, his Majestie deliverd *The Seale* to My L: *Tiveat* & my-selfe (the other Commissioner <u>being</u> <u>not</u> <u>come</u>) and then, gave us his hande to kisse: | 1687 G. Etherege, L9, 123, the Duke of Lorraine, who with a good body of the Army (all the Troops <u>being</u> <u>not</u> yet <u>arriv'd</u> at Barkan . . .) is already pass'd the Sarwitz and marches towards the Drave

<1701-1725>

<Passive>

1704 ?D. Defoe, L14, 24, a Generall shall be Indiffrent as to Success, his Own Fortunes <u>being</u> <u>Not</u> <u>Concern'd</u>. | 1704 W. Nicolson, D15, 263, A Crown of State made for the late King James's Queen. All these are now Viewed by Candles set with a Grate: Strangers <u>being</u> <u>not</u> <u>allowed</u> to take any nearer View, since Coll. Blood made so free as to carry off the Crown of State. | 1705 J. Evelyn, D9, V 589, as the Lords day none should think it enough to spend it in praying, or reading the service of the Church, & reading good Books or Sermons in the Closset, (<u>being</u> <u>not</u> <u>detained</u> by Indisposition, sicknesse &c) | 1709 R. Steele, L15, 258, Mr. Tryon and Mr. Water having desired to meet Me at three of Clock and the Gazette <u>being</u> <u>not</u> quite <u>finish'd</u> though now

Chapter VI

near Two I have not time to dine. | 1710 D. Defoe, L14, 292, Some Observations on the Conduct of the Parties on both Sides I shall Comunicate in My Next, being Not Sufficiently furnish'd for That work at So short Notice. | 1711 W. Nicolson, D15, 559, at his Earnest Intreaty, I did go in twice; being (at first) not well apprized of the Forms of the House, | 1712 W. Nicolson, D15, 703, Each half is made up of two, pasted together; the Art of printing on both sides, of the same, being not then discovered. | 1713 D. Defoe, L14, 405, The Excecution May not be Delay'd Meerly as an act of Clemency and Forbearance, the Certainty of its being Excecuted as well as the Reasons being Not known.

<1726-1750>

<Passive>

1741 J. Wesley, D17, 79, Being not suffered to go to church as yet [after a serious fever], I communicated at home.

<Perfective>

1744 Pelham, Thomas, 1st Duke of Newcastle, L22, 149-150, We are in great expectation of news from abroad, the Monday post, being not yet come in.

<1776-1800>

<Passive>

1784 J. Woodforde, D21, II 126, I stayed till 8 o'clock and it being then not finished I set of for home. | 1784 J. Woodforde, D21, II 167, About Noon, Charles Roupe with Nunn Davy, came here on horseback, to stay one Night with us—was not so well pleased with their Intentions at first of staying here all night, being not so well provided as I could wish to make things convenient for them and Horses—and especially as my House Maid Betty was very indifferent in a bad head ache. | 1785 J. Woodforde, D21, II 198, No Service again at Church this Day, it being not done.

<Perfective>

1783 J. Woodforde, D21, II 88, I rode to Honingham this morning and there read Prayers and Preached for Du Quesne he being not yet returned. | 1793 J. Woodforde, D21, IV 13, Mr. Custance not at Church being not returned from Sr Edmund Bacons at

Diachrony of Present Participles and Gerunds Followed by *Not*

Raveningham. | 1796 J. Woodforde, D21, IV 280, We did not go to Church this Morning, neither did Mr. Custance attend, he being not come home when we sent to Weston H. this Morning.

6.2.2.4.2. Evidence Supporting the RNDS Theory: (2) Low Percentage of Post-position of *Not* in Compound Gerundive *Having* PP and *Being* PP

Predictably, the weaker the verbal force is, the lower the percentage of the post-position of *not* becomes. Actually, as Table 48 and the two lower lines in Figure 6 (p. 200) show, even the compound forms of perfective *having* + PP or passive/perfective *being* + PP rarely took the post-position of *not* as gerundive use.

Table 48   Variations between Pre- and Post-position of *Not* with Compound Gerundive *Having* + PP and *Being* + PP—Diaries and Correspondence

a. *Having* + PP

Period	Perfective *having* + PP			
	Per 25 years		Per 50 years	
	Pre	Post	Pre	Post
-1600	0	0	0	0
1601-1625	0	0	2	0
1626-1650	2	0		
1651-1675	7	0	14	0
1676-1700	7	0		
1701-1725	3	1	23	2
1726-1750	20	1		
1751-1775	18	0	31	0
1776-1800	13	0		
1801-1825	39+1	0	59+1	0
1826-1850	20	0		
1851-1875	26	0	35	0
1876-1900	9	0		
1901-1925	0	0	5	0
1926-	5	0		
Total	169+1 : 2			

b. *Being* + PP

Period	Passive/Perfective *being* + PP			
	Per 25 years		Per 50 years	
	Pre	Post	Pre	Post
-1600	0	0	0	0
1601-1625	0	0	0	0
1626-1650	0	0		
1651-1675	11	0	16	1
1676-1700	5	1		
1701-1725	1	0	7	0
1726-1750	6	0		
1751-1775	2	1	19	2
1776-1800	17	1		
1801-1825	12	0	20	0
1826-1850	8	0		
1851-1875	2	0	10	0
1876-1900	8	0		
1901-1925	0	0	3	0
1926-	3	0		
Total	75 : 3			

The examples of the compound perfective gerundive *having not* PP appear in (106), and those of the compound passive/perfective gerundive *being not* PP in (107).

(106) Examples of the compound perfective participial *having not* PP

<1701-1725>
1713 J. Swift, L16, II 670, <u>Having</u> <u>not</u> <u>used</u> riding these 3 years, made me terrible weary; yet I resolve on Monday to sett out for Holyhead, as weary as I am. [= (60h)]

<1726-1750>
1727 A. Pope, L18, 71, You will enjoy that, and your own integrity, and the satisfactory consciousness of <u>having</u> <u>not</u> <u>merited</u> such graces from Courts as are bestowed only on the mean, servile, flattering, interested and undeserving.

(107) Examples of the compound passive/perfective gerundive *being not* PP

Diachrony of Present Participles and Gerunds Followed by *Not*

<1676-1700>

<Perfective>

1699 S. Pepys, L7, I 202, Between my comeing thus farr and the sealeing it, your 3d most unwellcome notice of your <u>being</u> <u>not</u> <u>gone</u> the 17th is come to hand. [= (60g)]

<1751-1775>

<Passive>

1775 J. Woodforde, D21, I 168, I went down to Sister Clarke's this morning and made her a visit, she is not at all pleased in <u>being</u> <u>not</u> <u>invited</u> to the Christening yesterday— [= (60f)]

<1776-1800>

<Passive>

1791 J. Woodforde, D21, III 249, I was rather out of temper this Aft. on Account of my Maid's (Nanny Kaye) Banns <u>being</u> <u>not</u> <u>published</u> this Afternoon by me,

6.2.2.4.3. Evidence Supporting the RNDS Theory: (3) Lowest Percentage of Post-position of *Not* in Simple Gerundive Verb-*ing*

It is as a matter of course that the simple gerund, which has the least connotation as a verb of all the *ing*-forms, seldom took the negative particle *not* after itself, as shown in Table 49 and its corresponding Figure 7 (p. 218). Out of 1,376+7 negative simple gerunds, the post-position of *not* occurred in only seven examples, six of *being* and one of *saying*, as shown in Table 50. These seven examples are shown in (108). In five out of them, the gerund has an explicit subject and conveys the meaning corresponding to a clause. In 1679 H. Savile, the close combination of *not* with a negative intensifier *a word* seems to strengthen the notion of negation.

Chapter VI

Table 49 Variations between Pre- and Post-position of *Not* with Simple Gerundive Verb-*ing*—Diaries and Correspondence

Period	Per 25 years				Per 50 years			
	Pre		Post		Pre		Post	
-1600	0	0	1	[1]	0	0	1	[1]
1601-1625	3	[3]	0	0	18	[14]	0	0
1626-1650	15	[12]	0	0				
1651-1675	221+1	[86]	2	[1]	397+1	[127]	4	[2]
1676-1700	176	[72]	2	[2]				
1701-1725	77	[42]	0	0	201+2	[77+1]	0	0
1726-1750	124+2	[54+1]	0	0				
1751-1775	132	[59]	1	[1]	259+1	[100]	2	[1]
1776-1800	127+1	[61+1]	1	[1]				
1801-1825	161	[82]	0	0	313+2	[120]	0	0
1826-1850	152+2	[69+2]	0	0				
1851-1875	100+1	[56]	0	0	149+1	[78]	0	0
1876-1900	49	[33]	0	0				
1901-1925	1	[1]	0	0	32	[20]	0	0
1926-	31	[19]	0	0				
Total varieties of verbs 299 Total number of examples 1,369+7 : 7								

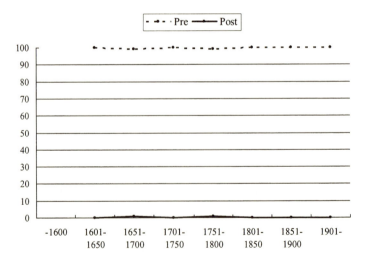

Figure 7 Transition of the Frequency of the Post-position of *Not* with Simple Gerundive Verb-*ing*—Diaries and Correspondence

Diachrony of Present Participles and Gerunds Followed by *Not*

Table 50 Verbs Taking Post-position of *Not* with Simple Gerundive Verb-*ing*—Diaries and Correspondence

Period	be Pre	be Post	have Pre	have Post	know Pre	know Post	care Pre	care Post	come Pre	come Post	do Pre	do Post
-1600	0	1	0	0	0	0	0	0	0	0	0	0
1601-1650	0	0	0	0	1	0	0	0	1	0	1	0
1651-1700	63	3	20	0	11	0	2	0	15	0	16	0
1701-1750	18	0	11	0	0	0	1	0	7	0	10	0
1751-1800	31	2	7	0	1	0	0	0	15	0	4	0
1801-1850	42	0	16	0	6	0	0	0	10	0	4	0
1851-1900	18	0	6	0	2	0	1	0	6	0	4	0
1901-	8	0	5	0	0	0	1	0	0	0	0	0

Period	find Pre	find Post	meet Pre	meet Post	need Pre	need Post	say Pre	say Post	see Pre	see Post
-1600	0	0	0	0	0	0	0	0	0	0
1601-1650	0	0	0	0	0	0	1	0	0	0
1651-1700	5	0	1	0	0	0	0	1	6	0
1701-1750	1	0	2	0	0	0	1	0	4	0
1751-1800	1	0	1	0	0	0	1	0	12	0
1801-1850	5	0	1	0	0	0	1	0	8	0
1851-1900	0	0	0	0	0	0	1	0	2	0
1901-	0	0	0	0	0	0	0	0	0	0

(108) Examples of the simple gerundive Verb-*ing not*

<be>

1599 M. Hoby, D2, 80, After priuat praier and breakfast I did read a whill for <u>beinge</u> <u>not</u> well, partly through myne owne folly, which I humble praie the Lord to pardon:

<1651-1675>

<be>

1660 S. Pepys, D10, I 226, many of my things are quite spoiled with mould, by reason of lying so long a-shipboard and my cabin <u>being</u> <u>not</u> tight. | 1673 H. Ball, L8, II 99, My Lady of Northumberland has miscarryed and is very ill this weeke, which is increased by her husband's <u>being</u> <u>not</u> yett free from his restraint.

<1676-1700>

<be>

1678 S. Pepys, L6, 58, For what you suspect of his <u>being</u> <u>not</u> soe

Chapter VI

well affected towards me (though that's noe new thing for me to meet with from Some Commanders);

<Example with a negative intensifier>

1679 H. Savile, L11, 94, instead of saying not a word of it, as I should have thought the best way, I am now fain to turn it into ridicule as the second best,

<1751-1775>

<be>

1767 J. Penrose, L25, 200, We concluded, that neither your Methleigh Jaunt, nor want of a Frank, nor it's being not regular Day of Writing, would have hindered you from acknowledging the Receipt of my Letter.

<1776-1800>

<bc>

1789 J. Woodforde, D21, III 94, When at last in great haste there came one—and the reason of its being not here before, was, that Raven at the Kings Head to whom I had sent a Note, had entirely forgot it.

6.2.2.5. Summary of Factors by which the Simple Participial Post-position of *Not* was Induced

As evidenced in 6.2.2.4, the verbal force of *ing*-forms had something to do with the position of the negative particle *not*. Those participles with verbal force, whether simple or compound, tended to share the mode of negation of finite verbs in declarative clauses. This twin relation between the finite and non-finite verb forms will perhaps explain the reason for the chronological similarity of obsolescence of post-position of *not* between the two. Once the negative type of *know not* loses its ground, the type of *knowing not* ought to become obsolete as well, since they are, as it were, in the same boat. Table 45 and its corresponding Figure 5 (p. 187) just verifies this speculation. The post-position of *not* often occurred during the time in which the *do*-less negative was the usual negative construction. Ever after the *do*-less negative was superseded by the *do*-negative in the

Diachrony of Present Participles and Gerunds Followed by *Not*

second half of the 17th century, however, the usage of Verb-*ing not* construction showed a gradual decrease, until at last it could only be detected sporadically by the middle of the 18th century except in the case of *be* and *have*, which are still averse to the *do*-negative.

6.2.2.6. Subsidiary Evidence Supporting the RNDS Theory: Further Features of the Verbs Most Frequently-occurring in Verb-*ing Not* Construction

The verbs most frequently occurring with the post-positioned *not*, namely verbs in Table 46, have further interesting traits, scarcely noticed in the other verbs. One is that they showed strong aversion to the auxiliary *do* which helped fix the word order in sentences beginning with negative adverbs such as *nor*, *little*, *neither*, and *never*. The other is that those verbs, the verb *have* in particular, resisted the auxiliary *do* in inverted conditional clauses, tag-questions, exclamatory sentences, coordination with another auxiliary and vicarious use.

6.2.2.6.1. Aversion to the Auxiliary *do* which Helped Fix the Word Order in Sentences Beginning with Negative Adverbs

On the Subject-Verb word order in Early Modern English, Bækken (1998: 267-281) states that, around 1700, sentence-initial negative adverbs such as *neither* and *nor* began to induce a high percentage of inversion with the aid of auxiliaries such as *can* and *do*, showing statistics as reproduced in Table 51 (p. 222). As Bækken's concern is about the correlation between kinds of adverbs and degree of inversion, she hardly ever comments on the counter-examples. But in fact, in such examples verbs significant from the present point of view can be found. The majority are, as shown in the right columns in Table 51, verbs which showed aversion to *do* in negative declaratives, in other words, verbs typically occurring in the simple participial Verb-*ing not* construction.

Chapter VI

Table 51   Rates of Subject-Verb Inversion according to Clause-initial
Adverbs—Bækken (1998: 267-281)

Clause-initial adverbs	1480-1530	1580-1630	1680-1730	Verbs not in Need of an Aid of an Auxiliary in Inversion
neither	100	100	93.9	go have know use
nor	15.8	75	99.1	care do fear have make need
never	33.3	28.6	50	hap mean
nevertheless	0	0	0	
only	0	0	0	
...				
little	-	100	-	know
...				

Similarly in the present texts examined, as shown in (109), the verbs *be*, *have*, *know*, *need* and a few verbs continued to show aversion to *do* in clauses beginning with negative adverbs *nor*, *neither*, *never*, *hardly*, *little*, *yet*, *no sooner* and *none*.

(109) <have>
1653 D. Osborne, L4, 114, I doe not think this is sence <u>nor</u> <u>have</u> <u>I</u> time to look it over. | 1673 R. Yard, L8, I 186 (nor have they) | 1674 T. Derham, L8, II 139 (nor have I) | 1697 J. Gale, L12, 380 (nor have wee) | 1697 J. Gale, L12, 452 (nor ... had I) | 1698 J. Lowther, L12, 531 (nor had he) | 1698 J. Lowther, L12, 552 (nor had my Lord L[onsdale]) | 1698 J. Gale, L12, 609 (nor have I) | 1687 B. St. Michel, L6, 207 (Nor have I) | 1700 S. Pepys, L7, I 285 (nor have I) | 1700 S. Pepys, L7, I 344 (Nor have I) | 1700 S. Pepys, L7, II 3, (nor had I) | 1700 J. Houblon, L7, II 14 (nor have I) | 1701 S. Pepys, L7, II 243 (Nor have either of you) | 1741 R. Hurd, L29, 52 (nor have I) | 1746 C. Lennox, L22, 227 (nor have I) | 1731 J. Wesley, L23, I 110 (Nor ... have I) | 1736 L23, I 201 (neither have they) | 1759 T. Gray, L26, II 631 (nor have I) | 1764 T. Gray, L26, II 838 (nor has he) | 1765 H. Walpole, L26, II 903 (nor have they) | 1769 T. Gray, L26, III 1056 (nor have I) | 1760 W. Shenstone, L27, 391 (nor has it) | 1760 W. Shenstone, L27, 393 (nor have I) | 1762 W. Shenstone, L27, 442 (Neither have you) | 1792 J. Wedgwood, L32, 335 (Nor have they) | 1794 E. Darwin, L33, 260, (nor have I) | 1795

Diachrony of Present Participles and Gerunds Followed by *Not*

R. Southey, L42, 90 (never had I) | 1797 R. Southey, L42, 144 (nor have I) | 1799 R. Southey, L42, 193 (nor have I) | 1801 R. Southey, L42, 247 (yet have we) | 1802 G. Rose, L35, I 515 (nor had he) | 1830 G. Crabbe, L38, 371 (nor ... have I) | 1858 A. Tennyson, L50, 194 (None have I) | 1866 A. Tennyson, L50, 438, (nor has he) | 1868 S. Palmer, L48, II 778 (nor have I) | 1844 E. FitzGerald, L49, I 439 (*nor has he; nor has not the other*) | 1880 E. W. Hamilton, D39, I 73 (Never had a Government) | 1880 E. W. Hamilton, D39, I 103 (nor has he)

<know>

1692 S. Pepys, L7, I 52, <u>Nor</u> <u>know</u> <u>I</u> any reason to disagree | 1693 J. Gale, L12, 76 (nor know wee) | 1696 W. Gilpin, L12, 333 (nor I know not) | 1697 J. Lowther, L12, 449 (nor know I) | 1698 J. Lowther, L12, 521 (neither knows he) | 1767 J. Penrose, L25, 198 (Nor know we)

<need>

1690 J. Evelyn, L7, I 29, <u>nor</u> <u>needs</u> <u>he</u> my comfort or counsel;

<do>

1673 R. Whitley, L8, II 76, <u>nor</u> <u>did</u> <u>we</u> any thing . . . that you would have bin pleased with the account of;

<Others>

1699 S. Pepys, L7, I 251, <u>nor</u> <u>send</u> <u>I</u> them now | 1700 J. Evelyn, L7, I 342, Vetruvius has said nothing of repaires, <u>nor</u> hardly <u>remember</u> <u>I</u> of any who repented not of an expense commonly greater than new-building, | 1701 S. Pepys, L7, II 176, <u>Nor</u> <u>fayles</u> <u>shee</u> . . . in returning all your remembrances of them in your letters, | 1701 J. Jackson, L7, II 231, <u>nor</u> <u>remains</u> <u>there</u> any temptation here to interpose between them. | 1738 J. Wesley, L23, I 239, <u>neither</u> <u>regard</u> <u>I</u> the contempt

Viewed in this manner, it seems to be reasonable to isolate that closed class of verbs in Table 46 as most frequently-occurring in Verb-*ing* + *not* construction.

Chapter VI

6.2.2.6.2. Resistance to the Auxiliary *do* in Inverted Conditional Clauses, Tag-questions, Exclamatory Sentences, Coordination with Another Auxiliary and Vicarious Use

The verbs typically used with the simple participial Verb-*ing not* also showed behaviour different from that of the other verbs as shown in (110)-(114), though concentrated on the verb *have* as far as the texts examined are concerned. They resisted the auxiliary *do* in inverted conditional clauses, tag-questions, exclamatory sentences, coordination with another auxiliary and vicarious use. Here again, there seems to be good reason to isolate that closed class of verbs in Table 46 as typically-occurring in Verb-*ing* + *not* construction.

(110) Aversion to the auxiliary *do* in inverted conditional clauses
    <have>
    1698 J. Lowther, L12, 532, The sill mentioned may probablely be very proper for stoneware but cannot be truly judged off without tryal, which Mr Dwight would be glad to make had he any of it at Fullham. | 1698 J. Gale, L12, 569 (had I) | 1739 J. Wesley, L23, 333 (had I) | 1760 W. Shenstone, L27, 393 (had I) | 1760 W. Shenstone, L27, 396 (had I) | 1762 E. Gibbon, L34, 128 (had we) | 1765 T. Gray, L26, II 860 (had I) | 1807 R. Southey, L42, 441 (had you) | 1828 G. Crabbe, L38, 337 (had I) | 1842 T. Carlyle, L49, I 348 (had I) | 1864 A. Tennyson, L50, 369 (had I) | 1869 A. Tennyson, L50, 536 (had I)

    <come>
    1878 G. Meredith, L54, 290, Come you to London on your way to the Continent, you must give us a visit.

(111) Aversion to the auxiliary *do* in tag-questions
    <have>
    1833 E. FitzGerald, L49, I 131, You have a good deal of leisure, have you not? | 1842 E. FitzGerald, L49, I 307, You have a bad habit of reading letters out, have you not? | 1872 F. Kilvert, D36, II 210, I asked . . . 'What do you do?' 'We go out hawking,' said the girl in a low voice. 'You have a beautiful voice.' 'Hasn't she?' interrupted the elder girl eagerly and delightedly. | 1879 G. Eliot, L52,

Diachrony of Present Participles and Gerunds Followed by *Not*

509, I have plenty to think of, have I not?

(112) Aversion to the auxiliary *do* in exclamatory sentences
<have>
1807 D. Wordsworth, L43, 82, Oh, what reason have we not to bless the Poets, our Friends and companions in solitude or sorrow, | 1807 D. Wordsworth, L43, 86 (oh! How much more delight have I . . !) | 1809 H. More, L36, III 315 (what bright spots have we . . !)

(113) Aversion to the auxiliary *do* in coordination with another auxiliary
1743 R. Hurd, L29, 122, I have not, nor can immediately have that warm Affection for him, I once had. | 1751 P. D. Stanhope, L21, 223, your dancing-master, who is at this time the most useful and necessary of all the masters you have or can have. [Cp. Auxiliary do is used with the other verbs as in "1751 P. D. Stanhope, L21, 243, my attention can, and does, from its centre extend itself to every profit of the circumference." | 1752 P. D. Stanhope, L21, 258, The Duke of Marlborough . . . had a manner, which he could not, and did not, resist.]

(114) Aversion to the auxiliary *do* in vicarious use (with so many examples having been encountered)
1693 H. Shere, L7, I 66, the Great King of France has not more thoughtfulness about his success against so many confederate foes than I have how you may hold out against the stone and the scurvy.

6.2.2.7. One Problem Involved with the RNDS Theory to be Rectified

Up to now attempts have been made to verify what is referred to as the RNDS theory as the most plausible explanation for the derivation and promotion of the Verb-*ing* + *not* construction. There may be a problem to be rectified, however: no example of *doubting not* has been collected, in spite of the fact that the verb *doubt* was one of the verbs which strongly resisted the acceptance of the auxiliary *do*.

Below will be shown the rivalry in frequency between the *do*-less and *do*-negative declaratives with the verbs listed in (103) as those which continued to show aversion to the auxiliary *do* in the texts examined. Table

Chapter VI

52 shows the situations with the verb *have*, and Table 53 and its corresponding Figure 8 those of the other verbs.[34]

From Tables 52 and 53 it is clear that the verb *have* has been the most averse to the *do*-negative; as far as the present corpus is concerned, it is not until 1787 that the verb *have* commenced to take the *do*-negative. The verbs, *care, come, do*, and *find*, which entered into the *do*-negative system much earlier and were less averse to it than *have*, were adherent to the simple negative until around the middle of the 18th century, as shown in Table 53, even in the very historical setting in which one verb after another finally capitulated to the *do*-negative. Thus, the following verbs prove to be the verbs which continued to be averse to the *do*-negative in the finite clause, as far as the mere percentage of the *do*-less form is concerned: *doubt, know, mistake, question, need, value* and *love* as well as *be* and *have*. If the RNDS theory is plausible, we ought to meet with the verb-*ing* + *not* constructions with these verbs. Unfortunately, no examples with *doubt, mistake, question, value* and *love* have been encountered in the texts examined, as Table 46 (p. 190) shows.

---

[34] Tables 52, 53 and Figure 8 are provisional. Until I complete the tables based on the years in which examples were written, please substitute them. The total number of examples towards the end of Table 53 admits of no doubt that the negative declarative sentences with the auxiliary *do* surpassed the simple negative sentences without *do* in frequency in the course of the 17th century. In Tables 3A and B of Nakamura (2000), where statistics are shown per text and verb, it is evident that the verb *know*, for example, began to predominantly accept the auxiliary *do* in the course of the second half of the 18th century. The verb *care*, earlier than *know*, accepted the *do*-negative. The verb *doubt* continued to take the simple negative in correspondence corpus even in the 19th century. This was mainly because of the idiomatic use *I doubt not* meaning as 'I am sure'. Regardless, Table 53 represents the linguistic situations in Modern English of what Ellegård calls verbs of '*know*-group' as well as a few commonly-used verbs. On the development of the auxiliary *do* itself, I would like to provide statistics per 25 or 50 years on another occasion.

Diachrony of Present Participles and Gerunds Followed by *Not*

Table 52 (Provisional)   Variations between *Do*-less and *Do*-negative Declaratives with *Have* in Diaries and Correspondence—Nakamura (2008c: 21)

	s	do	% do
16c	1	0	-
17c	38	0	0
18c	899	5	0.6
19c	614+2	5	0.8
20c	20	23	53.5

Note: 's' represents *do*-less simple negative declaratives, and 'do' those with *do*.

Table 53 (Provisional)   Variations between *Do*-less and *Do*-negative Declaratives with Verbs Termed "Verbs of Know-group" by Ellegård (1953) and Several Other Verbs in Diaries and Correspondence—Nakamura (2008c: 21-22)

	know		care		doubt		matter		mistake	
	s	do	s	do	s	do	s	do	s	do
16c	2	1	1	0	7	0	0	0	0	0
17c	762	182	33	19	234	60	10	0	6	4
18c	580	770+1	27	96	168	132	0	1	14	9
19c	369	936	33	131+2	76	39	9	35	14	2
20c	0	75	0	3	0	0	0	7	0	0

	come		do		find		meet		need	
	s	do	s	do	s	do	s	do	s	do
16c	1	0	0	0	1	0	0	0	0	0
17c	110	68	45	37+2	36	78	16	14	10	3
18c	30	174+1	6	34+1	15	86	2	22	10	7
19c	6	141	0	60+1	3	60	2	23	7	6+1
20c	0	9	0	10	0	4	0	0	0	4

	say		see		love		question		stay	
	s	do	s	do	s	do	s	do	s	do
16c	0	0	0	0	0	0	0	0	0	0
17c	13	21+2	34	99+2	19	28	25	14	42	27
18c	18	69+1	23	228+1	5	53	33	20	1	116+1
19c	13	81	5	254+3	8	33	0	0	1	18
20c	0	7	0	28	4	2	0	0	0	1

	value		ask		fear		deny		go	
	s	do	s	do	s	do	s	do	s	do
16c	0	0	0	0	0	0	0	0	0	0
17c	18	8	2	8	10	15+1	1	9+2	54	52
18c	8	8	1	21	2	16	0	8	6	228
19c	0	3+1	2	26	3	9	0	6	1	163+2
20c	0	0	0	4	0	1	0	0	0	17

	hear		let		like		make		mind	
	s	do	s	do	s	do	s	do	s	do
16c	1	0	0	0	0	0	0	0	0	0
17c	32	47+2	4	7	17	94	13	27+1	6	13+1
18c	4	64	0	9+2	22	186	4	72	1	16
19c	5	42+1	2	11	7	387+1	0	66	0	50
20c	0	3	0	2	0	30	0	11	0	9

	move		remember		sit		speak		stir	
	s	do	s	do	s	do	s	do	s	do
16c	0	0	0	0	0	0	0	1	0	0
17c	0	4	9	34	4	5	16	18+1	18	11+1
18c	1	5	0	72+1	5	17	10	28	1	13
19c	0	5	0	60+1	2	4	2	35	0	2
20c	0	1	0	9	0	0	0	2	0	0

	understand		Total number of examples	
	s	do	s	do
16c	0	0	19	12
17c	26	40	2,150	2,706+45
18c	5	98+1	1,177	6,642+62
19c	1	90+2	744	7,460+51
20c	0	16	10	783+6

Total varieties of verbs 1,102

Total number of examples 21,703+164

Diachrony of Present Participles and Gerunds Followed by *Not*

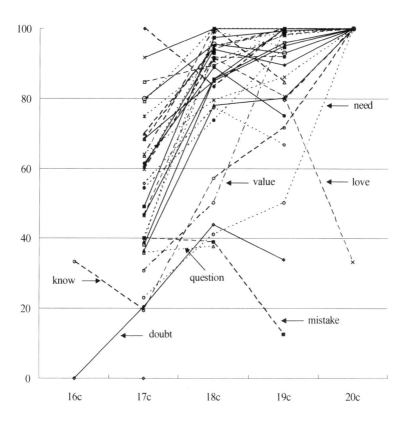

Figure 8 (Provisional) Frequency of *Do*-negative Declaratives with Verbs Termed "Verbs of Know-group" by Ellegård (1953) and Several Other Verbs in Diaries and Correspondence—Nakamura (2008c: 23)

Chapter VI

However, as Table 54 shows, even the frequency of pre-positioned *not* was extremely low with *mistake, question, value* and *love,* i.e. zero, twice, once, twice, respectively. Hence all that has to be done for the present is to find the *doubting not* construction. Fortunately, this construction can be found in the *OED[2]* on CD-ROM, even though in only two examples written in 1501-1550 and 1801-1850, as shown on pp. 299 and 304.

Table 54 Variations between Pre- and Post-position of *Not* with *Doubt, Mistake, Question, Value* and *Love*—Diaries and Correspondence

Period	doubt		mistake		question		value		love	
	Pre	Post	Pre	Post	Pre	Post	Pre	Post	Pre	Post
Total	25	0	0	0	2	0	1	0	2	0

6.2.3. Summary of Section 6.2

As indicated above, a diachronic investigation into the order of participles/gerunds and the negative particle *not* which occurred in 130 volumes of diaries and correspondence written mainly between the 16th and 17th centuries has been conducted in 6.2.1 and 6.1.2, where the ebb and flow of the simple participial Verb-*ing not* has been discussed in relation to that of the compound participial or gerundive *having/being not* PP as well as the simple gerundive Verb-*ing.*

Evidence suggests, in contradistinction to gerunds, which are less verbal, that participles favoured the post-position of *not*, whether simple or compound, in Early Modern English. The fact deserves special mention that, in the 17th-century texts, the perfective compound participial *having not* PP accounts for 69.2% (33 examples with the pre-position of *not* and 74 with the post-position of *not*), the passive/perfective compound participial *being not* PP 32.2% (82+2 vs. 39 examples), and the simple participial Verb-*ing* 14.2% (908+7 vs. 150 examples). Facts are contrary to the statements in the previous studies such as (65a). Here those statements that have been believed to be facts thus far have to be corrected and reexamined.

Through the investigation into the aforementioned diaries and cor-

Diachrony of Present Participles and Gerunds Followed by *Not*

respondence, the following examples were compiled:

	pre	post
Compound participial *having* PP	126	100
Compound participial *being* PP	157+4	56
Simple participial Verb-*ing*	1,826+16	229+1
Compound gerundive *having* PP	169+1	2
Compound gerundive *being* PP	75	3
Simple gerundive Verb-*ing*	1,369+7	7
Total	3,722+28	397+1

Based upon 4,119+29 examples compiled from aforementioned diaries and correspondence, comprising of 3,722+28 and 397+1 examples of the pre- and the post-position of *not* respectively, the points in (115), among other points, may be worthy of mention.

(115) a. 229+1 out of 2,055+17 examples of the negation of simple participial Verb-*ing* occurred with the post-position of *not*. The participial Verb-*ing not* structure was used with a closed class of verbs: *be, have*; *know, come, do, find*, among other verbs, and was in its prime in the 17th century. Towards the middle of the 18th century, however, the post-position of *not* virtually ceased to be used except intermittently when combined with *be* and *have*. Eventually, even these two verbs succumbed to the *not* Verb-*ing* structure by the end of the 18th century.

b. Newly-born verbs which came into the verb category in and after 1550 were put under a major rule which the vast majority of verbs observed, never taking the Verb-*ing not* structure.

c. There seems to have been virtually no semantic and syntactic difference between the pre- and the post-position of *not*. The two variants occurred under almost the same linguistic circumstances, and did not show complementary distribution. Apart from frequency, they were practically interchangeable with each other.

232

Chapter VI

d. Judging from the fact that the verbs occurring in the Verb-*ing not* structure and the verbs which were reluctant to take the *do*-negative in the finite clause overlapped with each other, it might be possible to confirm that the Verb-*ing not* construction was influenced by the *do*-less negative form of the verb occurring in the finite clause (e.g. *I am not a doctor / I have not a sister / I know not the news*). In actual fact, the extinction of the Verb-*ing not* construction around the mid-18th century followed less than a century after the decline of the *do*-less negative and in turn the regulation of the *do*-negative during the second half of the 17th century.

e. The simple participial Verb-*ing* has verbal force itself in being accompanied by an object and/or adverb, and the compound participial *having* PP and *being* PP has more verbal force in having tense, aspect and voice. Consequently, it quite naturally maintained much higher frequency of the post-position of *not* until the mid-18th century, regardless of Priestley's aversion in (65b).[35] In the entire text examined, 100 out of 226 examples of the negation of compound participial *having* + PP and 56 out of 213+4 examples of the negation of compound participial *being* + PP occurred with the post-position of *not*, as evidenced in Table 47 on p. 199.

f. Even the compound gerundive forms *having* PP and *being* PP had lower frequency of the post-position of *not* because of its less verbal nature, with 5 out of 249+1 examples. These five examples

---

[35] Priestley's statement in (65b) seems to represent his subjective aversion towards the popular use of the compound participial *having/being not* PP. From a different point of view, these constructions may have been in use regular enough to receive condemnation from Priestley. If the post-position of *not* had been infrequent and negligible, would he have taken the trouble to comment on this usage in his book? It is speculated that Priestley must have borne the same ill feeling towards this ongoing usage as J. Dryden did towards the dramatic increase of negative contractions in the second half of the 17th century in (20). Robert Lowth (1762 [1968]: 79) also showed aversion, with respect to the negative declarative form of *I not say*, to "the impropriety of placing the Adverb *not* before the Verb". The reason why they laid bare their irritation was that negative contractions rapidly gained popularity at that time (Tables 7, 8 and 10; details are shown in Nakamura 2011 and 2012b), and that, in contrast to the accepted theory, the form of *I not say* continued to be used even during the 18th century (Nakamura 2014).

Diachrony of Present Participles and Gerunds Followed by *Not*

occurred in 17th-18th century documents. The simple gerundive Verb-*ing*, which has the least verbal nature, had the lowest frequency of the post-position of *not*, with 7 out of 1,376+7 examples. These seven examples, six of which occurred with *be*, the verb most typicallly occurring with the simple participial Verb-*ing not*, and one with *say*, were collected from 17th-18th century documents.

g. Although the details are deferred to 6.5, the post-position of *not* was not owing to an idiosyncrasy of S. Pepys; this usage tended to come from the pens of a variety of people, ranging from the King, men of nobility and men of the cloth to men of literature. The texts in which this usage is often encountered are the diaries of M. Hoby, J. Evelyn, S. Pepys, J. Woodforde, and letters of C. Lyttelton (in L3) and H. Ball (in L8). The spread of the post-position of *not* structure into varieties of texts implies that it would be unfair to label this construction simply as a vulgar or erroneous usage; this usage was used by educated people and by people of high society.

To confirm the validity of what has been demonstrated on the basis of the analyses of diaries and correspondence in 6.2, the results of the research on five electronic corpora and those on the *OED²*'s citations are provided in 6.3 and 6.4 respectively.

6.3. Evidence from Electronic Corpora

In Section 6.3, results based upon the analyses of Helsinki-DP (c750-1710),[36] CEECS (1418-1680), Lampeter (1640-1740), Newdigate (1674-1692), and British English documents in ARCHER 3.1 (1650-1999) are provided not only to confirm whether the results in 6.2 stated in (115) above apply in these five corpora or not, but also to supplement the meagre amount of pre-1600 examples. The data for 6.3 show almost the same results as has been reached in 6.2, in terms of (i) the overall chronological

---

[36] Unlike other tables, periodisation of the Helsinki-DP per 50 or 25 years was not possible because the years in which the examples were written were not specified with some examples. I followed the corpus compilers' periodisation.

Chapter VI

trends, (ii) verbs or constructions which continued to take the post-position of *not*, and (iii) the tendency of the post-position of *not* to hardly ever occur with the gerund.

6.3.1. Variations between Pre- and Post-position of *Not* with Compound Participial *Having* PP

6.3.1.1. Helsinki Corpus (Diachronic Part)

In the Helsinki-DP, two examples with the compound participial *having* PP have been encountered, both of which have the post-position of *not*, as shown in Table 55. These two examples of the post-position of *not* appear in (116).

Table 55 Variations between Pre- and Post-position of *Not* with Compound Participial *Having* PP—Helsinki-DP

Period	Pre	Post
OE I-ME II -1350	0	0
ME III 1350-1420	0	0
ME IV 1420-1500	0	0
EModE I 1500-1570	0	0
EModE II 1570-1640	0	0
EModE III 1640-1710	0	2

(116) HC EModE III, 1665 J. Strype, *Original Letters of Eminent Letarary Men of the Sixteenth, Seventeenth, and Eighteenth Centuries*, 183, That I have not yet wrote to Brother Johnson is, because I have not been able to answer him in the particular of Subscription, <u>having not had</u> the opportunity of speaking either with the Proctor, or my Tutor; | HC EModE III, G. Fox, *The Journal of George Fox*, 80, you have-inge left out ye worde subject you have made mee uncapable of take-inge [THE WORD takeinge INTERLINEATED] ye oath: <u>haveinge not named</u> mee as a subject: soe not in a capacity of takeinge ior thou graunts It is not to bee tendred to any but ye kinges subjects. [George Fox (1624-1691), published 1694]

Diachrony of Present Participles and Gerunds Followed by *Not*

6.3.1.2. CEECS

In the CEECS, few examples have been encountered, and they are all of the pre-position of *not*, as Table 56 shows.

Table 56   Variations between Pre- and Post-position of *Not* with Compound Participial *Having* PP—CEECS

Period	Pre	Post
1417-1550	0	0
1551-1575	0	0
1576-1600	1	0
1601-1625	0	0
1626-1650	2	0
1651-1675	0	0
1676-1681	0	0
Total	3	0

6.3.1.3. Lampeter

The tabulation of the data for variations between the pre- and the post-position of *not* with compound participial *having* + PP in the Lampeter is presented in Table 57. This table suggests that the post-position of *not* was moderately used in the second half of the 17th century and the first half of the 18th century. Examples of the post-position of *not* appear in (117).

Table 57   Variations between Pre- and Post-position of *Not* with Compound Participial *Having* PP—Lampeter

Period	Pre	Post
1640-1650	0	0
1651-1675	2	3
1676-1700	3	0
1701-1725	1	3
1726-1740	0	0
Total	6	6

Chapter VI

(117) <1651-1700>

1666 J. Wallis, "An essay of Dr. John Wallis, exhibiting his hypothesis about the flux and reflux of the sea [...]" *Philosophical Transactions* 16, August 6, 1666, of this Epicylce, being little more than the Semidiameter of the Earth it self, or about 1 1/3 thereof (as is conjectured, in the *Hypothesis*, from the Magnitudes and Distances of the Earth and Moon compared;) and there having not as yet been observed any discernable *Parallax of Mars*, even in his neerest position to the Earth; it is very suspicious, that here it may prove so too. (Lampeter SciA) | 1669 R. Sherlock, *A sermon preached at a visitation, held at Warrington in Lancashire May 11, 1669*, he severely checks and reproves himself, that he had taken on him the Cure of other mens souls, having not sufficiently cared for and cured his own: (Lampeter RelA) | 1674 R. Hooke, *An attempt to prove the motion of the earth from observations [...]*, it is certain that it alwayes had the same position to the true Zenith, the Object Glass and Perpendiculars having not been in all that time removed out of the Cell, (Lampeter SciA)

<1701-1725>

1703 [C. Hore et al.], *A true and exact account of many great abuses committed in the victualling her Majesties Navy [...]*, And if so, they heard the Cause *Ex Porte*, against the Queen, as having not Examined my Evidence, as to the Embezelments of the Stores. (Lampeter LawA) | 1703 [C. Hore et al.], *A true and exact account of many great abuses committed in the victualling her Majesties Navy [...]*, a Report was given in to Your Royal Highnesses Council, that the said Stores were Extreamly Good, and fit for Her Majesties Service: Your Petitioner being assured of the Contrary, the said Surveyors having not Examined into all Her Majesties Stores, (Lampeter LawA) | 1703 [C. Hore et al.], *A true and exact account of many great abuses committed in the victualling her Majesties Navy [...]*, your Petitioner Replyed, who could their Honours give their Report, having not heard any Evidences since *February* last, to which the Board answer'd, it was no matter; (Lampeter LawA)

Diachrony of Present Participles and Gerunds Followed by *Not*

6.3.1.4. Newdigate

With the data tabulated for variations between the pre- and the post-position of *not* with compound participial *having* + PP in the Newdigate, a collection of newsletters written in the second half of the 17th century, Table 58 reveals that the post-position of *not* was frequently used at that time. Examples of *having not* + PP appear in (118).

Table 58   Variations between Pre- and Post-position of *Not* with Compound Participial *Having* PP—Newdigate

Period	Pre	Post
1674-1675	2	4
1676-1692	22	11
Total	24	15

(118) <1651-1700>

1674, From Spaine we heare that they were much supprised to receive noe good newes from fflanders the three Armys haveing not done any thinge Agst the Prince of Conde, (NEWDIG1) | 1674, ye seige of Grave advances but slowly the beseigers haveing not as yet made use of theire Cannon (NEWDIG1) | 1675, they have forborne farther meeting & from yarmth they tell us that hitherto ye Conventicles there have kept their word haveing not met since, (NEWDIG2) | 1675, The letters which came in yesterday from fflanders dated the 30 instant brought very little newes, the Prince of Orange nor Marshall d'Montmerency, haveing not made any remove since our last. (NEWDIG3) | 1678, The D of Lorrains army is Certainly In A very ill posture & In want of many things, Care haveing Not been taken to supply him with moneys & other Necesaries (NEWDIG7) | 1678, The treaty between the ffrench & spaniard haveing not yet been publicke I shall give you the most Materiall Articles (NEWDIG7) | 1680, The occasion is said to be that his Lordship Courting A yonge lady of A very honorable family & Related to mr seymour the late speaker & mr seymour haveing not done him that Right as his Lordship Exspected he meeting with mr seymour this day In whitehall gave him Exceeding High Language which being Retorted my Lord spit In his face & told him if he were A gentleman he knew what it meant (NEWDIG9)

Chapter VI

| 1680, mr Cornish lately Chose on of the Sheriffs hath Attended on the Ld Mayor & Aldermen offering them to seale A Bond to hold sheriffe provided they would declare him duely Elected he haveing not Recd the sacramt within 12 months (NEWDIG10) | 1681, Wee heare ye D of Norff is coming over hither from fflanders wth his whole ffamely intending to Reside here all this Winter, his Grace haveing not Inioyed his health perfectly (NEWDIG11) | 1682, yesterday the Company of Merchant Taylors who had 90 odd Livery men Shutt out of ye pole for the last Ld Major as haveing not taken the Oath (NEWDIG13) | 1684, His Maties messenger having not been able to gaine speech wth the duke of munmouth besides the legall notis left att More Parke has don ye same att ye cock pitt and att Mrs Roos [?] house where he useth to resort (NEWDIG15) | 1684, Mr Justice Withings declared that he was ready to give his opinion butt his breatheren having not given theirs differd itt (NEWDIG15) | 1684, The Society of London arrived on ye 5th at Cowes from Cadiz in 22 dayes ye master reports yt at his Comeing thence ye Ld Darthmouth was still at Tangier haveing not fully demolished itt but would finish itt in a short time, (NEWDIG15) | 1685, Last weeke the Ld Chancellor of Scotland &c set forwards for Edenbrough Those who Its said Came to oppose the Continuance of the Ld Chancellor in that office haveing not been able to effect anything (NEWDIG16) | 1685, This the Court overruled he haveing not surrendered himselfe but was taken & in fine A rule of Court was made for his Execution next ffriday (NEWDIG16)

6.3.1.5. CEECS, Lampeter and Newdigate Integrated

In terms of the periods covered, CEECS (1417-1681), Lampeter (1640-1740) and Newdigate (1674-1692) overlap each other. In order to supplement the low frequency in individual corpus, integrated statistics of these three corpora are shown in this section.

Table 59, into which Tables 56-58 are merged, reveals that the compound participial *having not* PP was frequently used in the second half of the 17th century.

Diachrony of Present Participles and Gerunds Followed by *Not*

Table 59   Variations between Pre- and Post-position of *Not* with Compound Participial *Having* PP—CEECS, Lampeter and Newdigate Integrated

Period	Pre	Post
1417-1550	0	0
1551-1575	0	0
1576-1600	1	0
1601-1625	0	0
1626-1650	2	0
1651-1675	4	7
1676-1700	25	11
1701-1725	1	3
1726-1740	0	0
Total	33	21

6.3.1.6. ARCHER 3.1

The tabulation of the data for variations between the pre- and the post-position of *not* with compound participial *having* + PP in the ARCHER 3.1 is presented in Table 60. This table indicates that the form of *having not* + PP may have been acceptable around 1700.

Table 60   Variations between Pre- and Post-position of *Not* with Compound Participial *Having* PP—British English Documents in ARCHER 3.1

Period	Pre	Post
1650-1700	1	2
1701-1750	3	1
1751-1800	0	0
1801-1850	1	1
1851-1900	3	0
1901-1950	0	0
1951-	0	0

Chapter VI

The examples of *having not* + PP are as follows:

(119) <1650-1700>
1678 Conway Letters: The Correspondence of Anne Viscountess Conway Henry More and Their Friends, 1642-1684, ARCHER 3.1 1678more.x2b, I HAVE forborne this good whyle from writing to your Ladiship partly because I thought it might be but a disturbance rather then a diversion, you being so very ill as I heard, and partly because I had no new occasion of writing, having not gone to London since my last writing unto you. | 1684 Will Briggs, "Two remarkable cases relating to vision", *Philosophical Transactions* 159, ARCHER 3.1 1684brig.m2b, it seems rather to depend on some of the Humours, tho I can't tell at present on which, having not had time since to consider of it.

<1701-1750>
1720 William Stukeley, *Diary, In The Family Memoirs of the Rev. William Stukeley M.D, etc.*, ARCHER 3.1 1720stuk.j3b, Sr. Is. Newton went to Oxford with Dr. Kiel, he having not been there before.

<1801-1850>
1827 Thomas Whitwell, *A Darlington Schoolboy's Diary*, ARCHER 3.1 1827whit.j5b, Our gymnastic apparatus having not yet come, we went with the French-teacher De Baste, to practise at his gymnasium where he teaches a number of young-men.

6.3.2. Variations between Pre- and Post-position of *Not* with Compound Participial *Being* PP

6.3.2.1. Helsinki Corpus (Diachronic Part)

In the Helsinki-DP, seven examples with the passive participial *being* PP have been encountered and, as shown in Table 61, all of them have the pre-position of *not*.

Diachrony of Present Participles and Gerunds Followed by *Not*

Table 61   Variations between Pre- and Post-position of *Not* with Compound Participial *Being* PP—Helsinki-DP

Period	Pre	Post
OE I-ME II -1350	0	0
ME III 1350-1420	0	0
ME IV 1420-1500	0	0
EModE I 1500-1570	0	0
EModE II 1570-1640	2	0
EModE III 1640-1710	5	0

6.3.2.2. CEECS

The tabulation of the data for variations between the pre- and the post-position of *not* with compound participial *being* + PP in the CEECS is presented in Table 62. This table indicates that the post-position of *not* was moderately used in the second half of the 17th century. Examples of the post-position of *not* appear in (120), in which (120a) and (120b) represent those of the passive and the perfective *being not* PP respectively.

Table 62   Variations between Pre- and Post-position of *Not* with Compound Participial *Being* PP—CEECS

Period	Pre	Post
1417-1550	1	0
1551-1575	0	0
1576-1600	0	1
1601-1625	0	0
1626-1650	1	0
1651-1675	1	3
1676-1681	0	0
Total	3	4

(120) a. Passive *being not* PP

<1551-1600>
1596 Queen Elizabeth I, Althogh I do not dout, as now I do

Chapter VI

perceaue, that you shuld think them now overstale for newes,
being by good espialz not made ignorant of our ennemis driftz,
(CEECS ROYAL1)

<1651-1700>
1659 J. Jones, This will likewise follow that ye Troopes coming
up here and ye incouradgem^t promised being not made good
unto them, They will fall foule upon ye Citie or att least upon
such as wilbee represented unto them as Adversaryes, (CEECS
JONES) | 1659 J. Jones, Your Lo^pps Troope being not Regiment-
ed, I have noething to direct me how their suffrages should be
taken (CEECS JONES)

b. Perfective being not PP

<1651-1700>
1660 King Charles II, I haue little to say to you, the post being
not yett arriued from England, which comes very vnseasonably,
(CEECS CHARLES)

6.3.2.3. Lampeter

In the Lampeter, the compound participial *being not* PP was used to
a more or less considerable portion until the end of the 17th century, as
Table 63 shows. Examples of *being not* PP appear in (121), in which the
examples are all in the passive use.

Table 63   Variations between Pre- and Post-position of *Not* with Compound Participial *Being* PP—Lampeter

Period	Pre	Post
1640-1650	0	1
1651-1675	0	2
1676-1700	7	4
1701-1725	3	1
1726-1740	1	0
Total	11	8

243

Diachrony of Present Participles and Gerunds Followed by *Not*

(121) <1601-1650>

1644 [H. Hammond], *Of Scandall [...]*, Or fourthly, unlesse that my absteining, or receding, or undoing what before I had done, be more likely to confirme him in his errour (which otherwise in time being not yeilded to, he may foresake) then to prevent or allay his causlesse anger and those effects of it. (Lampeter RelB)

<1651-1700>

1667 [J. Owen], *Indulgence and toleration considered: in a letter unto a person of honour*, they have any Community of Interest with such as being not concerned in Conscience with them; (Lampeter RelB) | 1674 R. Hooke, *An attempt to prove the motion of the earth from observations [...]*, from the uncertain and sudden variations of the Air or Atmosphere, either from heat and cold, from the thickness and thinness of Vapours, from the differing gravity and levity, from the winds, currents, and eddyes thereof, all which being not so well understood by what way, and in what degree, and at what time they work and operate upon the Air, must needs make the refraction thereof exceedingly perplext, (Lampeter SciA) | 1676 T. Guidott, *A discourse of Bathe, and the hot waters there. Also, Some Enquiries into the Nature of the water [...]*, the most perceptible taste is either acerbe or *austere*; which being not observed in these Waters, I have so much reason to judge *Alom* not predominant, as asserted here. (Lampeter SciB) | 1680 J. Hawles, *The English-mans right. A dialogue between a barrister at law and a jury-man. [...]*, they being not assured *it is so* from their own understanding, are *forsworn*, at least in *Foro Conscientiæ.* (Lampeter LawA) | 1692 H. Hody, *A letter from Mr. Humphrey Hody [...] concerning a collection of canons said to be deceitfully omitted in his edition of the Oxford treatise against schism [...]*, If a Presbyter shall in contempt of his Bishop, gather a separate Congregation, and erect another Altar, his Bishop being not condemn'd Not. (Lampeter RelB) | 1697 [J. Pollexfen], *England and East India inconsistent in their manufactures. [...]*, But this needs no answer here, it being not proposed that the *English* shall be Prohibited from bringing these Goods into *Europe*; (Lampeter EcA)

244

Chapter VI

<1701-1725>

1704 F. North, *An Argument of a Learned Judge in the Exchequer-Chamber upon a Writ of Error [...]*, I suppose the Wages of Parliament will not be mention'd for Damages, for in most Places they are only Imaginary, <u>being</u> <u>not</u> Demanded; (Lampeter LawB)

6.3.2.4. Newdigate

The tabulation of the data for variations between the pre- and the post-position of *not* with compound participial *being* + PP in the Newdigate is presented in Table 64. It is to be noted that the post-position of *not* occurred as frequently as the pre-position in this collection of newsletters written in the second half of the 17th century.

Table 64   Variations between Pre- and Post-position of *Not* with Compound Participial *Being* PP—Newdigate

Period	Pre	Post
1674-1675	3	3
1676-1692	24	24
Total	27	27

Examples of participial *being not* + PP appear in (122), in which (122a) and (122b) represent the passive and the perfective ones respectively.

(122) a. Passive *being not* PP

<1651-1700>

1675 On Saturday last Coll Lovelace was examind by ye comissers appoynted for yt purpose where hee gave ym ye reason of his absence when ye place was taken, but they <u>being</u> <u>not</u> well satisfyed therewth have adjournd themselves till Thursday, & in ye meane tyme will peruse his instructions & Comission for further light into yt buisness (NEWDIG2) | 1675, the beseigers [?] would hearken to no other proposalls than to take the Germans into service to sent the subjects of his Majesty of great Brittaine into England with their Armes & baggage & to have

Diachrony of Present Participles and Gerunds Followed by *Not*

the ffrench Prisoners of War which being not agreed to the beseigers, began on the 4 in ye morneing to play their Cannon againe upon the towne (NEWDIG3) | 1676, The Emperor has made answer to the addresse from severll parts of the Empire about sending his plentipotentiaryes to the treaty, that it was not yet necessary a maine point being not fully cleared whether the ffrench King would accept the mediation of the Pope or the Spanish that of Venice, (NEWDIG3) | 1676, They write from Holland that the disputes about Quarters in East ffreisland being not yet composed the States had held severall Conferences about it (NEWDIG3) | 1676, They had nothing from Rome about a new Election of a Pope the conclave being not shut up. (NEWDIG4) | 1678, Prance gives A sober account to the Councell of his Repeated Confession & denyall he being then not weaned from his Religion (NEWDIG7) | 1679, The late Indulgence granted that nation being not soe ffrankly Recd as Exspected is Countermanded (NEWDIG9) | 1679, The order for Doubling the Citty Guards being not yet put In Execution Tis thought may be deferred till the sitting of the parliamt (NEWDIG9) | 1682, he is expected to dine with the Artillery Company their feast being not observed the last yeare by reason of his absence (NEWDIG12) | 1683, Tis wrote from the Streights yt Admirall Herbert riding before Tripoly met wth sharpe weather being forced to slip & put to sea & ye James Galley being not afterward heard of tis feared she is cast away (NEWDIG13) | 1683, Which the Court took into Consideracon & being not altogeather sattisfyed in that objection sent Mr Justice Raymond to the Court of Common (NEWDIG13) | 1683, The Committee of 6 Aldrmen . . . sate yesterday att the Temple to have ye assistance of some Lawyers being a matter of weight importeing ye Surendr undr ye Citty Seale the office of mayor Sheriffe Aldermen Chamberlain &c to settle ye restrictions the Common Councill granted to his Matie to make them firme and Legall wch being then nott understood to imply a Surrender gives ye occasion of difficulty to performe itt. (NEWDIG15) | 1684, The E: India ship Suratt Merchant being not as yet heard of last night 45 L p C was given on her & Its feared shee is lost

Chapter VI

(NEWDIG15) | 1684, The said ship on the 26th Janry Came by Tangier & brought A pacquett from the Ld Dartmouth & sayes the Castle was then standing the demolishing of it being not then perfected (NEWDIG15) | 1685, The Conviction of Sr Samll Barnardiston being not Returned out of the Citty noe proceedings were had of him (NEWDIG16) | 1685, the Notingham Ryotters were fined vizt mr Sacheverill 500 Marks mr Gregory 300 mr Hutchinson 200 mr Charnell 100 mr Wilson 100 mr Turpin 100 mr Astlin being A Poor man 5 marks which 7 persons the Court said had noe occasion to be there being not Concerned in the old or new Charter (NEWDIG 16) | 1686, The Ld Brandon Gerrard Continues Prisoner in the Tower his Pardon being not Passed as was Reported (NEWDIG17)

b. Perfective *being not* PP

<1651-1700>

1674 the next day they all joyned & marched together against the enemy who lyes betweene Wassenheime & Saverne & Mounsieur de Crequi being not yet joyned wth them all endeavours are used to cut them of ffrom Grave of (NEWDIG1) | 1676, They tell us from Paris dat December the 30th that the day before many ships were released at St Germains the perticulars of which they did not give, the Secretary Marme being not then come thither, (NEWDIG 4) | 1678, at ostend there were 8 Companies of English foot . . . were Marched from there to Bruges under the Conduct of the Earle of Middleton the Rest of the men Being Not yet Arrived by Reason of the ill weather & Contrary winds, (NEWDIG6) | 1679, The Paris letters say the Dutch are not like to to shew their fine lyveries at publicke Entries the points of honour being not yet adjusted (NEWDIG7) | 1679, The fforreigne letters being not Come may Excuse the shortness of the letters (NEWDIG7) | 1679, His Maty being not yet Recovered of his Indisposition our feares doe still Continue (NEWDIG9) | 1682, but he will not goe till Munday being not perfectly recovered of his indisposicon. (NEWDIG12) | 1683, the Ld Ch Baron Mountague of ye Exchange was alsoe absent being not fully recovered of his late feavour & ague (NEWDIG14) | 1685, Our fforreign letters being not yet Come we have nothing more from Buda (NEWDIG 16) |

Diachrony of Present Participles and Gerunds Followed by *Not*

1689, Wee hear from Chester that the Campe Increases But the ships being not Come Abt Its not Certain when they will Embarke (NEWDIG19)

6.3.2.5. CEECS, Lampeter and Newdigate Integrated

As in 6.3.1.5, integrated statistics of those in CEECS, Lampeter and Newdigate are shown in this section. Table 65 below, into which Tables 62-64 are merged, reveals that the compound participial *being not* PP was used as frequently as *not being* PP in the second half of the 17th century.

Table 65 Variations between Pre- and Post-position of *Not* with Compound Participial *Being* PP—CEECS, Lampeter and Newdigate Integrated

Period	Pre	Post
1417-1550	1	0
1551-1575	0	0
1576-1600	0	1
1601-1625	0	0
1626-1650	1	1
1651-1675	4	8
1676-1700	31	28
1701-1725	3	1
1726-1740	1	0
Total	41	39

6.3.2.6. ARCHER 3.1

With the data tabulated for variations between the pre- and the post-position of *not* with compound participial *being* + PP in the ARCHER 3.1, Table 66 shows that the form of *being not* + PP occurred in only one example. The example with the passive use appears in (123)

Chapter VI

Table 66　Variations between Pre- and Post-position of *Not* with Compound Participial *Being* PP—British English Documents in ARCHER 3.1

Period	Pre	Post
1650-1700	4	0
1701-1750	2	1
1751-1800	1	0
1801-1850	4	0
1851-1900	1	0
1901-1950	0	0
1951-	0	0

(123) <1701-1750>

> 1735 *Read's Weekly Journal or British Gazetteer*, No. 531, ARCHER 3.1 1735rea2.n3b, they will afterwardds go to Guelderland, and pass some Time at Loo and Dieren; his Highness's making the Campaign <u>being</u> <u>not</u> yet absolutely <u>determined</u>.

6.3.3. Variations between Pre- and Post-position of *Not* with Simple Participial Verb-*ing*

6.3.3.1. Helsinki Corpus (Diachronic Part)

In the Helsinki-DP, examples of the post-position of *not* are observed during Early Modern English, as Table 67 and (124) show.

Table 67　Variations between Pre- and Post-position of *Not* with Simple Participial Verb-*ing*—Helsinki-DP

Period	Pre		Post	
OE I-ME II -1350	0		0	
ME III 1350-1420	6+1	[6+1]	0	
ME IV 1420-1500	12	[12]	1	[1]
EModE I 1500-1570	19	[17]	1	[1]
EModE II 1570-1640	13	[6]	5	[3]
EModE III 1640-1710	21	[18]	4	[2]

Diachrony of Present Participles and Gerunds Followed by *Not*

(124) <be>

HC ME IV, 1444 J. Bolton, "Petition concerning the Murder of Isabell, Wife of Roger Bakeler", 261, he gate hym a Chartre of pardon of yow of all maner tresons and felonies ye beyng not lerned of the forsaid horible felonies and treson the whiche Chartre ys allowed of Recorde. | HC EModE I, T. Mowntayne, *The Autobiography of Thomas Mowntayne*, 201, What sholde moufe yow for to handyll me after thys sharpe sorte as yow have done, so spytefullye, beynge here not yet iij dayes under your kepyng? | HC EModE II, 1599 M. Hoby, *Diary of Margaret Hoby*, 71, after priuat praiers in the morning I, being not well, did walk a litle, and then eate my brecfast: | HC EModE II, 1612 R. Coverte, *A Trve and Almost Incredible Report of an Englishman, 1612*, 12, Then we asked them, if there were any (Portugals) in the Iland, they said no, for they had banished them all because they would haue reliefe there perforce, and would make slaues of the people of the Iland, (which being not able to indure) they made continuall warres with them at their comming thither. | HC EModE II, *The Statutes of the Realm*, IV 852, And be it enacted also, That everie p~son being not of suche value w=ch= shall herafter dwell or inhabite in anye suche House so to be newe builded converted or devided as aforesaide, shall forfeyte for everie Moneth that he or she shall dwell or inhabite in the same, the some of Fyve Poundes. | HC EModE III, 1662 H. Oxinden, in *The Oxinden and Peyton Letters, 1642-1670*, 273, I have spoken with Sir Tho: Peyton twice and find him in such passions as I have no manner of hopes of his assistance; hee doth mee twice as much hurt as good; some bodie hath incensed Him very much against mee, you may quesse [*sic*_Nakamura?'guess'] who hath done it, the partie being not far from you. | HC EModE III, 1672-1681 J. Fryer, *A New Account of East India and Persia*, II 184, whereby I was encouraged to auspicate a more Coelestial Path might lead us to Getche, in the Turkish Language signifying a Goat Village; which was on Wheels, as the other, being not Twenty Miles distant; | 1672-1681 J. Fryer, *A New Account of East India and Persia*, I 188, nor do we read his stay in India was so long, to atchieve such Acts as these, this Place being not the only Instance of this nature; but more probable to be an Heathen Fane, or Idol-

Chapter VI

atrous Pagod, from the Superstitious Opinion they still hold of its
Sacredness:

<have>

HC EModE III, 1666 S. Pepys, *The Diary of Samuel Pepys*, VII
414, Nay, Evens, the famous man upon the Harp, having not his
equal in the world, did the other day die for mere want, and was
fain to be buried at the almes of the parish - and carried to his grave
in the dark at night, without one Linke,

<know>

HC EModE II, 1608 R. Armin, *A Nest of Ninnies*, 9, Here (quoth
he) - with that he shakes him by it, and sayes, I mistooke it before,
knowing not your eare from your hand, being so like one another.

<understand>

HC EModE II, 1614 Richard Hooker, Two Sermons upon Part of S.
Judes Epistle, 1614, 6, An instrument whether it be a pipe or harpe
maketh a distinction in the times and sounds, which distinction is
well perceived of the hearer, the instrumente it selfe vnderstanding
not what is piped or harped.

The verbs which occurred with the post-position of *not* are, as indicated in Table 68, *be*, *have*, *know* and *understand*, those which are referred
to as taking this construction in Table 46 (p. 190).

Table 68   Verbs Taking Simple Participial Verb-*ing Not*—Helsinki-DP

Period	be		have		know		understand	
	Pre	Post	Pre	Post	Pre	Post	Pre	Post
OE I-ME II -1350	0	0	0	0	0	0	0	0
ME III 1350-1420	0	0	1	0	1	0	0	0
ME IV 1420-1500	0	1	0	0	0	0	0	0
EModE I 1500-1570	1	1	1	0	3	0	0	0
EModE II 1570-1640	3	3	0	0	6	1	0	1
EModE III 1640-1710	1	3	1	1	3	0	0	0

6.3.3.2. CEECS

The tabulation of the data for variations between the pre- and the
post-position of *not* with simple participial Verb-*ing* in the CEECS is presented in Table 69. This table shows that the post-position of *not* was con-

Diachrony of Present Participles and Gerunds Followed by *Not*

siderably used in Early Modern English, although its frequency did not surpass that of the pre-position of *not*.

Table 69   Variations between Pre- and Post-position of *Not* with Simple Participial Verb-*ing*—CEECS

Period	Pre		Post	
1417-1500	9	[4]	1	[1]
1501-1525	5	[4]	0	0
1526-1550	1	[1]	1	[1]
1551-1575	0	0	0	0
1576-1600	16	[11]	6	[3]
1601-1625	9	[6]	7	[3]
1626-1650	19	[11]	3	[2]
1651-1675	13	[6]	5	[3]
1676-1681	0	0	0	0

The examples are as follows:

(125) <be>

> 1530? J. Foster, In my most humblyst wyse, I beyng not so bold as to appere before youre Lordshyp untyll your plesure ys knowyn, feere sett appartt, nede compellythe me to wrytt. (CEECS ORIGINA2) | 1582 M. Hutton, not onelie because it is contrarie to our statutes, whereunto we are all sworne, and shall be taken out of the livinge of the residenciaries, some being not well hable to spare it; but also because it doth open a window, (CEECS HUTTON) | 1586 F. Walsyngham, there weare not so many slayne as was otherwyse reported, the whole number being not above three or fower score, and of our people betwin thirty and forty taken and slayne, (CEECS LEYCESTE) | 1586 R. Dudley, 1st Earl of Leycester, I haue spoken this daie with the capten, whoe is secretlie stollen hether to me, being within a dayes iourney or litle more of their troupes, being not farr of Grave; he is as manlike a gentleman as euer I looked vppon, (CEECS LEYCESTE) | 1614 N. Bacon, Sweet Madam, W^{th}out circumstances I am her the same man as I parted from you,

Chapter VI

beinge not able to make my self more worthy of yo^e loue then before. (CEECS CORNWALL) | 1624 N. Bacon, I was desirous to haue seen you for a day at London, the journy being not much from Cambridge, wher I now am; (CEECS CORNWALL) | 1624 N. Bacon, neyther haue I hearde any thinge of yt since yo^e departure, being not able to com'end any thing concerninge that business but my many wishes for yo^e frutefull endeauors in the proceeding. (CEECS CORNWALL) | 1625 R. Mountague, But since it is, I understand by Mr. Cosin, his Majesty's pleasure to have them printed, if it please your Lordship my desire is to have them left out, as being not apperteynant to the mayne, unless your Lordship shall thincke otherwise, (CEECS COSIN) | 1638 Lady B. Harley, My good Ned - The last weake being not well, I could not inioye this contentment of rwiteing to you. (CEECS HARLEY) | 1652 J. Jones, the whole party left the carriadges, threw down theere armes and ranne to Co^{ll} Macffinnens howse being not farr off, except the L^t and six men, who it seemes stood and were slayne; the enemy pursued them to Macffinnins house to putt them all to the sword, but Mcffinnin being not soe unhospitable or barbarous as his neighbours would have him to bee, protested that himselfe and every man with him would dye in their own defense, unless they would accept of a Ransome for the men, (CEECS JONES)

<find>

1580$^?$ W. Fleetwood, My very good Lord, yesterday I sent your Lordship a Letter towchinge the admission of my Lord chieff Justice in to the Comen Place; but my man finding not your Lordship in the Court retorned the Letters to me agayne. (CEECS ORIGINA 3)

<have>

1497 E. Plumpton, Sir, I shewed to a gentleman . . . how that Kyng Richard . . . having you not in the favor of his grace, but utterly against you, caused them to have a parte of your lands by his award and ryall power, (CEECS PLUMPTON) | 1586 R. Dudley, 1st Earl of Leycester, my nephew Phillip told me he received a letter from him that you had sent him into Spayn, whereof I am hartly sorry, having greatly dysapointyd me, having not one to suply that place nowe, (CEECS LEYCESTE) | 1594 T. Matthew, But I send your

Diachrony of Present Participles and Gerunds Followed by *Not*

Lordship in liewe thereof (having not of myne owne to requite your Lordship's great favor therein) these included from your Lordship's verie good Lord and myne, the Lord Chamberlaine, and therwithall the predominant prelacie of this province. (CEECS HUTTON) | 1624 O. Naylor, He purposes to send it to London by Mr. Skippon to Mr. Blunt, about a fortnight hence, and having not acquaintance there to have a litle care of the comming forth of it, he intreated me to write to some about it, (CEECS COSIN) | 1624 O. Naylor, having not any newes to send you from this corner of the world, I commend you to God's protection, (CEECS COSIN) | 1642 King Charles I, I give you free leave to disobey my warants for issewing Armes; for what I have done in that, was in supposition that you had anew for your selfe and your frends; but having not, I confess Charity begins at home. (CEECS ORIGINA 3) | 1653 J. Jones, The lands I now hold as Tenant to yᵉ State . . . were wholy wast when I tooke them, haveing not within three myles of them neither wood, turfe, nor any other fuell, nor a River, (CEECS JONES) | 1661 Bishop J. Cosin, I wish you could, a month or 6 weeks hence, provide a private lodging of 3 or 4 rooms for me, and for your self, together with 3 or 4 servants, for to this number and privacy I must be forced to reduce my family, and to live with a little, having not much to spend, as I have hitherto done, (CEECS COSIN)

<succeed>

1624 O. Naylor, But that succeeding not, (which for myne owne part I allways thought the safest course for the peace of the College,) I cannot but wonder at this new intent that the fellowes will make choyce out of their owne foundation. (CEECS COSIN)

< Examples with a negative intensifier>

<be> 1644 King Charles I, Remember all courage is not in fyghting; constancy in a good cause being the cheefe, and the dispysing of slanderus tonges and pennes being not the least ingredient. (CEECS ORIGINA3)

<hear> 1653 J. Jones, Haveing all this while waited for some signification of the pleasure of them that are in authority with you, touching yᵉ late greate change in Governmᵗ and heareing not one syllable thereof, tending to require or direct such as serve you here, what to doe thereupon, wee have at last caused the inclosed

Chapter VI

paper to be publised [*sic*], (CEECS JONES)

The verbs which occurred with the post-position of *not* are, as shown in Table 70, specifically *be, have, find, hear* and *suceed*. The first three verbs are those which are referred to as typically taking this construction in Table 46 (p. 190). It is worthy of note that, with *be* and *have*, the post-position of *not* was more predominantly used in late 16th and early 17th centuries.

Table 70   Verbs Taking Simple Participial Verb-*ing Not*—CEECS

	be		have		know		find		hear		succeed	
	Pre	Post	Pre	Post	Pre	Post	Pre	Post	Pre	Post	Pre	Post
1417-1500	0	0	0	1	1	0	0	0	0	0	0	0
1501-1525	0	0	0	0	2	0	0	0	0	0	0	0
1526-1550	0	1	0	0	0	0	0	0	0	0	0	0
1551-1575	0	0	0	0	0	0	0	0	0	0	0	0
1576-1600	1	3	1	2	3	0	0	1	0	0	0	0
1601-1625	3	4	0	2	0	0	0	0	0	0	0	1
1626-1650	6	2	1	1	3	0	1	0	1	0	0	0
1651-1675	3	2	2	2	5	0	0	0	1	1	0	0
1676-1681	0	0	0	0	0	0	0	0	0	0	0	0

6.3.3.3. Lampeter

In the Lampeter, the post-position of *not* with the simple participial Verb-*ing* occurred frequently. As Table 71 shows, quite a few examples of the post-position of *not* were used in the second half of the 17th century and the first half of the 18th century, even though the frequency of Verb-*ing not* did not surpass that of the *not* Verb-*ing*.

Table 71   Variations between Pre- and Post-position of *Not* with Simple Participial Verb-*ing*—Lampeter

Period	Pre		Post	
1640-1650	19+1	[16+1]	7	[2]
1651-1675	27+1	[20+1]	7	[3]
1676-1700	62+3	[37+2]	13	[3]
1701-1725	26+1	[18]	5	[2]
1726-1740	28	[14]	2	[2]

Diachrony of Present Participles and Gerunds Followed by *Not*

As shown in Table 72, the verbs *be* and *have* were predominantly used with the post-position of *not* until 1700.

Table 72   Verbs Taking Simple Participial Verb-*ing Not*—Lampeter

	be		have		know		aim		build		claim		understand	
	Pre	Post	Pre	Post	Pre	Post	Pre	Post	Pre	Post	Pre	Post	Pre	Post
1626-1650	2	3	0	4	3	0	0	0	0	0	0	0	0	0
1651-1675	5	6	0	1	2	0	0	1	0	0	0	0	1	0
1676-1700	11	11	3	1	4	0	0	0	0	0	0	1	0	0
1701-1725	5+1	4	0	0	1	0	0	0	0	0	0	0	0	1
1726-1750	8	1	1	0	2	0	0	0	0	1	0	0	0	0

These 34 examples are presented in (126), where general examples are separated from those with so-called *not*-A-*but*-B construction. The slots A and B represent a noun phrase or *to*-infinitive or a prepositional phrase.

(126) a. <aim>

1659 Anon, *England's safety in the laws supremacy*, I purpose but favourably to touch upon them, as <u>aiming</u> <u>not</u> at exasperation, but recovering our selves into a better and more hopefull progress towards settlement. (Lampeter LawB)

<be>

1644 [H. Hammond], *Of Scandall [...]*, although they were Christian in the *positive* part, acknowledging so much as was answerable to the now-articles of the *Creed*. yet <u>being</u> <u>not</u> so in the *negative*, concerning the evacuating of the Judaicall law (but rather perswaded of the contrary) could no more eat *swines flesh*, then a meere Jew could do, (Lampeter RelB) | 1649 W. Prynne, *A Legall Vindication of the Liberties of England [...]*, they . . . searched the out-houses for Turkies, which they took from their eggs and young ones, Veal and Mutton <u>being</u> <u>not</u> good enough for them: (Lampeter LawB) | 1650 J. Cook, *A true relation of Mr. Iohn Cook's passage by sea from Wexford to Kinsale in that great storm [...]*, though he said he did well to be angry, even unto death, they <u>being</u> <u>not</u> words of express rebellion, but of a passionate spirit blinded with anger, therefore when he prayed unto thee out of the belly of Hell, he was mightily preserved. (Lampeter RelB) | 1652 Anon, *The Advocate*, It is by Trade, and the due ordering and governing of it, and by no other means, that Wealth

Chapter VI

and Shipping can either bee encreased, or upheld; and consequently by no other, that the power of any Nation can bee sus-
teined by Land, or by Sea: It beeing not possible . . . for anie Nation (having no Mines to supplie it self) to make it self powerful
in either of these (that is, either Monie, or Shipping) without
Trade, or a thorow Inspection into Trade, and the Cours of it.
(Lampeter EcA) | 1666 R. Holland, *Globe notes per R.H.*, the
Moon &moon;, or any other Planet being not in the Dragons
Head or Dragons taile or other stars being not in the Ecliptick, are
said to have Latitude so many degrees (Lampeter SciB) | 1669 R.
Sherlock, *A sermon preached at a visitation, held at Warrington
in Lancashire May 11, 1669*, And the generality of the flock being not wise enough to know what way to take; or whom most
securely to follow, they hereupon *heap to themselves Teachers
after their own Lusts*, (Lampeter RelA) | 1676 T. Guidott, *A dis-
course of Bathe, and the hot waters there. Also, Some Enquiries
into the Nature of the water [...]*, whereas if they did in this manner, as we say, follow their blows, they probably would not only
prevent arelapse, but set themselves in a way of perfect recovery
with one resolution, without many comings at several seasons,
being many times not so well at their second coming, as they
went away on their first season of bathing. (Lampeter SciB) |
1676 T. Guidott, *A discourse of Bathe, and the hot waters there.
Also, Some Enquiries into the Nature of the water [...]*, where the
Sulphur is separated, decocted, and precipitated; here not so, being not apart, but residing in a Salino-Sulphureous Salt, a piece of
whose Body, as we now have it, it seems to be. (Lampeter SciB) |
1678 Anon, *An exact account of the trials of the several persons
arraigned at the sessions-house in the Old-Bailey for London and
Middlesex [...]*, The Prisoner denied any hand in the Robbery, and
said, that she run away, because being not very rich, she was
afraid of a Prison, which they threatned her with. (Lampeter
LawB) | 1681 Anon, *The Trade of England Revived: And the
Abuses thereof Rectified, [...]*, notwithstanding the greatness of
this forfeiture, yet Trades men are continually obnoxious here-
unto; it being not possible to avoid it; (Lampeter EcA) | 1683 W.
Charleton, *Three anatomic lectures, concerning 1. The motion of*

Diachrony of Present Participles and Gerunds Followed by *Not*

the bloud through the veins and arteries; [...], Because the Orifices of the Capillary veins cannot continue always open and dilated; their consistence being not hard and bony, but membranose, soft and slippery; so that they are apt to be closed by conniving, and consequently to hinder the ingress of the bloud newly arrived. (Lampeter SciA) | 1692 [E. Settle], *The second part of the notorious impostor, compleating the history of the life, cheats, &c. of William Morrell, alias Bowyer, sometime of Banbury, Chirurgeon [...]*, This *Answer* being not the present point we must gain, our Squire (before prepared for a Reply) seem'd extreamly pleased with her for her Fidelity. (Lampeter MscB) | 1692 [E. Settle], *The second part of the notorious impostor, compleating the history of the life, cheats, &c. of William Morrell, alias Bowyer, sometime of Banbury, Chirurgeon [...]*, This wealthy Heiress he had married in very good Season, our Bridegroom truly being not over-rich, (the common Fate of great Wits,) for he had hardly Mony enough to pay for his Marriage. (Lampeter MscB) | 1697 Anon, *A Letter to a Friend, In Vindication of the Proceedings against Sir John Fenwick, by Bill of Attainder. [...]*, The reason is evident, because the other Witness was withdrawn; and according to the late Act, one, in the ordinary Course of Law being not sufficient, how clear soever the proof otherwise was; therefore without the Bill of Attainder it was *Impossible*. (Lampeter LawB) | 1698 W. Alingham, *A Short Account of the Nature and Use of Maps*, because the greatness of these inequalities have scarce any sensible proportion to the whole, the height of the highest Mountain being not 1/6000 part of its Diameter, which is inconsiderable; and therefore notwithstanding these small Irregularities, we may affirm the Earth to be round, or in form of a Globe, or Sphere. (Lampeter SciA) | 1708 J. Waller, *Religion and loyalty, or the reverence due both to Church and state, asserted in a sermon, [...]*, his Kingdom being not of this World; 'tis the Doctrine and example of our Saviour, the Apostles and the whole primitive Church, that we are obliged to submit to all Sufferings that we may meet with from the Temporal Power upon that account. (Lampeter RelA) | 1714 R. B., *Longitude to be found out with a new invented instrument, both by sea and land [...]*, And thus these Points of East and West

Chapter VI

being not absolute in any, respective in some, and not at all relating unto others, we cannot hereon establish so general Considerations, nor reasonably erect such immutable Assertions upon so
unstable Foundations. (Lampeter SciB) | 1720 R. Mead, *A short
discourse concerning pestilential contagion and the methods used
to prevent it.*, The keeping Men in *Quarentine* on board the Ship
being not sufficient; the only Use of which is to observe whether
any dye among them. (Lampeter SciA) | 1731 J. Davies, *An hum-
ble proposal for the increase of our home trade, and a defence to
Gibraltar [...]*, our Men of War could not prevent, it being not
safe to venture so close to the Land, (Lampeter EcB)

<have>

1643 H. Foster, *A True and exact relation of the marchings of the
two regiments of the trained bands of the city of London [...] As
also of the three regiments of the auxiliary forces [...] who
marched forth for the reliefe of the city of Glocester [...]*, where-
upon our red Regiment of the Trained, Band was constrained to
march halfe a mile further to get quarter, we were now in the Van
of the whole Army, having not so much as one Troope of Horse
quartered neer us: (Lampeter MscA) | 1643 H. Foster, *A True and
exact relation of the marchings of the two regiments of the
trained bands of the city of London [...] As also of the three regiments of the auxiliary forces [...] who marched forth for the reliefe of the city of Glocester [...]*, we were in great distraction,
having not any horse to send out as Scouts, to give us any intel-
ligence: (Lampeter MscA) | 1646 Commissioners of the Navy,
*The answer of the Commissioners of the Navie, to a scandalous
pamphlet, published by Mr. Andrewes Burrell*, In the next place,
he most desperately entred into the Port Holy-Island, the Castle
and Island being for the King; and having not above 100 men, he
first took the Town and the Island, and afterwards summoned the
Castle, and had it delivered to the use of the Parliament:
(Lampeter MscB) | 1649 W. Prynne, *A Legall Vindication of the
Liberties of England [...]*, they having not so much as a speaker
or Commons House til after the beginning of King *Edward* the
third his reign, (Lampeter LawB) | 1668 Anon, *The tryals of such
persons as under the motion of London-apprentices were tumul-*

Diachrony of Present Participles and Gerunds Followed by *Not*

tuously assembled [...], You that are now called, being moved through the Instigation of the Devill, and having not the Fear of God before your eyes, have withdrawn your Obedience to our Sovereigne Lord the King, (Lampeter LawA) | 1697 [J. Pollexfen], *England and East India inconsistent in their manufactures. [...]*, Jewels, Lead, Tin or Iron, though durable, yet having not those other qualifications, do not so well deserve to be esteemed Treasure. (Lampeter EcA)

<understand>

1712 F. Guybon, *An essay concerning the growth of empiricism; or the encouragement of quacks. [...]*, For what but the most dismal Execution upon the Lives, or the most dreadful Destruction of Mankind, can be expected from such a Prodigious Number of Men, who understanding not what they profess; may truly be said to be Qualified, as they are Licenc'd, to kill. (Lampeter SciA)

b. <Examples with *not*-A-*but*-B construction>

<be>

1659 Anon, *England's safety in the laws supremacy*, yet how contrary is our practice, our great business being not to further an establishment good for all, but to supplant one another: (Lampeter LawB) | 1684 R. Boyle, *Experiments and considerations about the porosity of bodies, in two essays*, For the Body of an Animal being not a rude and indigested lump of matter, but a curious engine, admirably framed and contrived for the exercise of several Functions as Nutrition, Generation, Sensation, and many differing local Motions, (Lampeter SciB) | 1684 [W. Assheton], *The royal apologie: or, an answer to the rebels plea [...]*, If it further be demanded, How *Birthright* doth Entitle to a Crown? 'Tis then truly replyed *That it is a Fundamental* Law *of* England, *That the Crown doth descend to the next in Blood;* England being not an *Elective* but an *Hereditary* Kingdom. (Lampeter PolA) | 1721 F. Hare, *Scripture vindicated from the misinterpretations of the Lord Bishop of Bangor: [...]*, But with respect to the *Christian* Religion, that being not to be confined to one People, but to be propagated to all Nations in which Governments were already settled, he sent his Son, (Lampeter RelB)

Chapter VI

<build>

1730 J. Henley, *Light in a candlestick, to all that are in the House: Or, the impartial churchman [...]*, For this Purpose, he is to consult all the Lights of Historians possible, neglecting none of either Party; weighing their Authentickness, their Honesty, their Knowledge of Persons and Incidents, and building, not upon *their* Opinions, Characters, Representations, and Reflexions, as *theirs*, but as *Facts* vouch'd by them; comparing them with one another, and passing a very slow, deliberate Sentence on the whole Comparison. (Lampeter RelB)

<claim>

1676 A. B., *A letter of advice concerning marriage*, His eldest Son he makes his Landlord of an interest wholly forreign and independent, able to borrow more pounds than himself can fairly shillings; and claiming not by descent, much less by his Father's bounty, but by even his own or his Mothers purchase, or at least the wise provision of his Parents on that side. (Lampeter MscA)

6.3.3.4. Newdigate

The tabulation of the data for variations between the pre- and the post-position of *not* with simple participial Verb-*ing* in the Newdigate is presented in Table 73. This table shows that, in the second half of the 17th century, the post-position of *not* was used to the extent that the use in studying the history of the English language cannot be overemphasised, in spite of the fact that its frequency did not take precedence over that of the pre-position of *not*.

Table 73   Variations between Pre- and Post-position of *Not* with Simple Participial Verb-*ing*—Newdigate

Period	Pre		Post	
1674-1675	21	[12]	9	[3]
1676-1692	192+1	[56+1]	34	[4]

The verbs which occurred with the post-position of *not* are primarily *be, have* and *know*, as shown in Table 74. These verbs are referred to as

Diachrony of Present Participles and Gerunds Followed by *Not*

typically taking this construction in Table 46 (p. 190).

Table 74   Verbs Taking Simple Participial Verb-*ing Not*—Newdigate

	be		have		know		lose		pass		understand	
	Pre	Post	Pre	Post	Pre	Post	Pre	Post	Pre	Post	Pre	Post
1674-1675	9	6	1	2	1	1	0	0	0	0	0	0
1676-1692	58	29	0	3	12	0	0	1	0	1	0	0

These 43 examples are presented in (127).

(127) a. <be>

1674, Into Plymouth are returned severall merchant men from abroad & into Whitby a vessell with corne wch sayes soe great a quantity of Corne is in these holes [?] that the King had sent orders to inspect the stores, that they maye not be unbearthed [?] this last year being not very hopefull (NEWDIG1) | 1674, Letters from Lisbonne tell us that ye Cortes have granted the Prince 800000 Cruzadoes per an for 3 yeares for defraying ye publique charges of ye Kingdome, but it being not to be raised in hast that Court have fallen a fresh upon ye buisness of ye Jews for procureing them a genell pardon, & ye priviledg of being Tryed for Judaisme as for other Crimes, ye Jesuites & ye nobillity favour ye designe but ye clergy & comunalty are very highly agst it, & have begd leave to send to roome [Rome?] by their agents to shew their reasons agst it. (NEWDIG1) | 1674, The Duke of Luxemburg being not farr from them (NEWDIG1) | 1674, they being not in a Capacity to pay leave themselves to the discretion of theire Conquerors (NEWDIG1) | 1674, Victualls grow very scarce in St Thome there being not then far about 2 Moneths left (NEWDIG2) | 1675, hee is shortly expected here, his buisness at Tripoly being not like to hold him many dayes. (NEWDIG2) | 1676 every Prince or State should provide for his own men, wch if they should persist in would be of all consequence the next Campagne it being not to be expected yt they should be early enough in the feild, if the troops should be soe farr divided. (NEWDIG4) | 1676, It seems that after all the Duke of Luxenburg will be forced to stand & look on, & see the place taken being not able to succor it The Germans haveing soe strongly

Chapter VI

fortified themselves. (NEWDIG4) | 1676, This in the mean time is certaine that the Prince has not men enough for such a seige his whole Army being not above 23 or 24000 men by which means the soldiers are at hard duty, (NEWDIG4) | 1676, the Diligent march of the Duke of Luxenburg . . . had broke the measure of the Duke of Lorraine, who still lay on the other side of Haguenaw, being not able to advance any farther by reason of the narrow lanes he must passe, (NEWDIG4) | 1678, The Committee Appointed to Examine what was due to the Army made their Report but the Charge of the Navy Being Not yet Ready to be brought In the house Adjourned (NEWDIG6) | 1679, That banishmt being not the punishmt the Law Inflicts upon those Crimes (NEWDIG 8) | 1679, the Kings forces that went hence to fight them are gone to sterling & durst not adventure to draw neer them till the Militia are all togather they being Not above 3000 men (NEWDIG8) | 1679, The Ld Bellasis is still in the Tower & there is like to Continue there being not yet any warrant to the Lieft of the Tower for hisdelivery [*sic*_Nakamura] (NEWDIG9) | 1679, The spanish Ambr being not at Wild house some Justices of Peace shut up the Chappell that Masse should not be said there (NEWDIG9) | 1679, on A sudden such A shower of water (it being not properly Raine because it was not by dropps) fell downe upon A Mountaine as if the Windowes of Heaven had been opened. (NEWDIG9) | 1681, A man & maid servant tis to be feared are burnt being not to be found (NEWDIG11) | 1681, The Com Councill sat not yesterday ye Ld Mayr being not well (NEWDIG11) | 1681, The Ld C Justice Replyed that they could take noe Cognizance of yt matter it being not before them, without his Maty speciall Comand (NEWDIG11) | 1681, noe true protestants Could be safe, the Mischeife being not to stop there, (NEWDIG11) | 1682, hee will as soone as opportunity prsents seize upon the Dukedome of Savoy yt Duke beeing now not Likely to Live and after that Geneva makeing his prtence the Right of the Duke of Loysons Prince Philliter who is imediate heire thereto his blindness incapable to Rule. (NEWDIG12) | 1682, Defaulters being not free and out of Towne Poled Sr Wm Prichard 76 and thise Defaulters for Sr tho Gould 28 and 2 poled twice (NEWDIG13) | 1683, Which the

Diachrony of Present Participles and Gerunds Followed by *Not*

Lawyers say is a Contradiction The Court of Chancery being not a place to determine any such poynt (NEWDIG13) | 1683, Tis said the K: of Spaine seemes now Inclined to hear to Termes of Peace finding his Allies unwilling to Joyne with him he being not sure of the Hollanders who are much divided Among themselves (NEWDIG15) | 1683, the Weather it seemes being not soe proper some of ye ships were very leaky & were in danger of founding in the sea (NEWDIG15) | 1684, he would forgive him ye whole upon his paying 1000 L towards ye building of Chelsea Colledge a condescension of a very great Mercy and wch ought to be acknowledged wth all thankfullness itt being not to be Imagined that when a man hath spitt out ye Venom of his Malice against a Peer of that high rancke he should Come off soe Easily as to lick himselfe whole wth his Tongue   (NEWDIG15) | 1684, the Lord Churchill will have the Honr of the Elephant Conferred on him which Prince George had before he had the Honr of the Garter being not much diferent from oures haveing A blew Ribbon A starr & An Elephant (NEWDIG15) | 1686, That on the 24th the Imperialists Sprung A mine under the Bastion in which was 36 C of Powder & 10000 men stood ready to make A Genll Assault but the mine being not far Enough under the Wall had A quite Contrary effect & Came out backwards Ruined their outlines & killed 200 Imperiallists & 100 Brandenburgers which Caused the Genll Assault to be deferred (NEWDIG17) | 1686, The Archbp of Canterbury was not at the opening of the Comission he being not well (NEWDIG17) | 1686, The Ld Ch: Justice being not yet well was not in Court this day (NEWDIG17) | 1686, This weeke the woman sold the necklace for 3000 L to A person of Honr to prsent the queen there being not the like to be bought (NEWDIG17) | 1688, The Coffe Indico &c they sold in Private Contract which being not Customary has much disgusted the Intended buyers at the Candle (NEWDIG18) | 1691, they Carried off Neare 2000 L and Leaft a Great Deale behind them being not able to Carry it off. (NEWDIG19)

\<have>

1674, it was thought it would soone be forcet to yeild it having not above 400 men in it (NEWDIG1) | 1675, be it further enacted

264

Chapter VI

by ye authority aforesd that from the time of passing this prsent
not all & every the Children hereafter to be begotten by any husband on a 2d wife the former being liveing & haveing not issue
shall be inheritable according to the Course at Comon law to such
husband as the said Children shall happen in priority of birth or
seniorty of age (NEWDIG3) | 1681, tis said yt his Matie has
made ye Dauphin Generalissimo, not without som prospect of the
taking it, wch is the Rather to be don thro the unexpectednes of
the Attaque amusing the world wth a Contrary course, they haveing not a Sufficient Garrison to make a defence nor cannot expect
assistance from the Empr before it be to late (NEWDIG11) | 1683,
being bereft of their Expectation as haveing not mischeife enough
for their money the rabble grew enraged and fell uppon pulling
downe the scaffolding (NEWDIG 14)

<know>

1675, They write from Legorne Ap: ye 15th that Capt Wettwang in
ye new Castle, knowing not of any Breach went directly to Tripo-
ly and sent his Boat wth his Leuit & a flagg of Truce, (NEWDIG
2)

b. < Examples with a negative intensifier>

<be>

1683, ye Spaniards will deliver Gibralterr, and Centa to them is
altogetherr fictitious, there being not ye least foundation for any
such discourse (NEWDIG15) | 1685, they question not but to
Carry the Place there being not the least Appearance of Reliefe
(NEWDIG16)

<have>

1682, The East India Company are in great payne for 3 of theire
Shipps from Suratt they haveing not the Least Intellige[nce of]
them (NEWDIG12)

<lose>

1685, Our fforeign letters all Confirme the seige of Buda was
Raised on the 1st Instant they haveing first sent away all their
sick & Wounded men being 8000 with their Heavy baggage &
then without any disturbance passed the danube to take winter
quarters in the Higher Hungary looseing not A man in their Re-

Diachrony of Present Participles and Gerunds Followed by *Not*

treat (NEWDIG16)
<pass>
1681, Two Second Rates wth a 100 men on Bord each, & a lesser
vessell wth 60 men on Board lye at the Mouth of Chatham River,
to Guard it, there passing not a Ship but they send their Boat on
Board to know whoe they are On ffriday Sr Maurice Eustace an
irish Gentleman had a hearing before the (NEWDIG11)

6.3.3.5. CEECS, Lampeter and Newdigate Integrated

As in 6.3.1.5 and 6.3.2.5, integrated statistics of those in CEECS,
Lampeter and Newdigate are shown in this section. Table 75 below, into
which Tables 69, 71 and 73 are combined, suggests that the simple participial Verb-*ing not* was used to a considerable degree in the 17th century,
despite the fact that it never exceeded the form of *not* Verb-*ing*.

Table 75   Variations between Pre- and Post-position of *Not* with Simple
Participial Verb-*ing*—CEECS, Lampeter and Newdigate Integrated

Period	Pre		Post	
1417-1500	9	[4]	1	[1]
1501-1525	5	[4]	0	0
1526-1550	1	[1]	1	[1]
1551-1575	0	0	0	0
1576-1600	16	[11]	6	[3]
1601-1625	9	[6]	7	[3]
1626-1650	38+1	[23+1]	10	[2]
1651-1675	61+1	[30+1]	21	[5]
1676-1700	254+4	[82+2]	47	[5]
1701-1725	26+1	[18]	5	[2]
1726-1740	28	[14]	2	[2]

Table 76 is a combination of Tables 70, 72 and 74. It is worthy of
note here that, as far as the verbs *be* and *have* are concerned, the post-position of *not* predominated over the pre-position around 1600 and was rare

Chapter VI

before the mid-18th century.

Table 76　Verbs Taking Simple Participial Verb-*ing Not*—CEECS, Lampeter and Newdigate Integrated

Period	be		have		know		find		hear		understand	
	Pre	Post	Pre	Post	Pre	Post	Pre	Post	Pre	Post	Pre	Post
1417-1500	0	0	0	1	1	0	0	0	0	0	0	0
1501-1550	0	1	0	0	2	0	0	0	0	0	0	0
1551-1600	1	3	1	2	3	0	0	1	0	0	0	0
1601-1650	11	9	1	6	6	0	2	0	1	0	1	0
1651-1700	86	53	6	9	24	1	7	0	2	1	1	0
1701-1740	13+1	5	1	0	3	0	0	0	0	0	0	1

Period	aim		build		claim		lose		pass		succeed	
	Pre	Post	Pre	Post	Pre	Post	Pre	Post	Pre	Post	Pre	Post
1417-1500	0	0	0	0	0	0	0	0	0	0	0	0
1501-1550	0	0	0	0	0	0	0	0	0	0	0	0
1551-1600	0	0	0	0	0	0	0	0	0	0	0	0
1601-1650	0	0	0	0	0	0	0	0	0	0	0	1
1651-1700	0	1	0	0	0	1	0	1	0	1	1	0
1701-1740	0	0	0	1	0	0	0	0	0	0	1	0

6.3.3.6. ARCHER 3.1

The tabulation of the data for variations between the pre- and the post-position of *not* with simple participial Verb-*ing* in the ARCHER 3.1 is presented in Table 77 per verbs. This table shows that, far less frequent than *not* Verb-*ing*, the form of Verb-*ing not* was moderately used around 1700 and was practically obsolescent before the mid-18th century. The verbs which occurred with Verb-*ing not* were *be* and *have* as (128) shows.

(128) a. <be>
　　　<1651-1700>
　　　ARCHER 3.1 1664bult.f2b, when the pleasant season Had invited his Mistress to return into the Country, not being able to indure her absence, whose only memory excited such troubles in his breast, he asked me, if I would accompany him to Coupava, that Castle being not far distant from Themira's: | 1664 ibid., In that condition you may guess, that being not the Master of my reason, I only talk what my extravagant imagination sug-

Diachrony of Present Participles and Gerunds Followed by *Not*

Table 77 Variations between Pre- and Post-position of *Not* with Simple Participial Verb-*ing*—British English Documents in ARCHER 3.1

	1650-1700	1701-1750	1751-1800	1801-1850	1851-1900	1901-1950	1951-
abate	1 : 0						
accept							1 : 0
allow		1 : 0					
appear	1 : 0						
attend				1 : 0			
be	7 : 5	3 : 3	1 : 1	3 : 1	1 : 1	1 : 0	2 : 0
bleed	1 : 0						
bury	1 : 0						
collapse						1 : 0	
come	1 : 0	1 : 0				1 : 0	
compear		1 : 0					
consider	1 : 0						
count						1 : 0	
dart						1 : 0	
do							1 : 0
doubt	2 : 0		1 : 0				
enquire							1 : 0
enter					1 : 0		
exceed	2 : 0	1 : 0	1 : 0				
extend				1 : 0			
feel					2 : 0		
find	2 : 0	1 : 0					
give	3 : 0						
have	3 : 0	3 : 1	1 : 0	1 : 0			1 : 0
heal			1 : 0				
imagine	1 : 0						
know	6 : 0	1 : 0	2 : 0			1 : 0	
leave	1 : 0						
lecture			1 : 0				
lend				1 : 0			
like	1 : 0	1 : 0			1 : 0		
meet	2 : 0						
mend			+1 : 0				
miss	1 : 0						
molest			1 : 0				
need					1 : 0		
omit		2 : 0					
permit	1 : 0	1 : 0					
question	1 : 0						
read						1 : 0	
rest	1 : 0						
rise				1 : 0			
see	1 : 0				1 : 0		
seem							1 : 0
stop						1 : 0	
suppose	1 : 0						
take							1 : 0
undermine							1 : 0
use	1 : 0						
want				2 : 0			1 : 0
Total	43 : 5	16 : 4	9+1 : 1	10 : 1	7 : 1	8 : 0	10 : 0

Chapter VI

gests, and that, which it may be, my Devoir would forbid me once to think on. | 1674 anon., *Brief Directions on How to Tan Leather*, ARCHER 3.1 1674ano1.s2b, The Figures of the naked Snails are omitted in this Specimen, being not material to that part of the design, which is . . . to give the Reader an exact view of Animal-shells, as well as of Fossils figured like Shells, | 1687 Richard Ferrier, *Journal of Major Richard Ferrier*, ARCHER 3.1 1687ferr.j2b, We there took up our old lodgins, it being not far from ye Messenger's & a civill house. | 1697 *The Post Man and Historical Account*, ARCHER 3.1 1697pos2.n2b, they [=the French Army] were afraid the Spanish Army would not be able to defend the Pass of Ostablrick; the same being not above 18000 men strong.

<1701-1750>

1722 Robert Cay, "An account of the manner of bending planks in his Majesty's Yard", *Philological Transactions* 32, ARCHER 3.1 1722cay-.s3b, The other Spot to the Northward, which appeared sometime after that marked B, being not quite so large, nor the Colours so intense, but the same way disposed, those next the Sun being red, the next yellow, and the rest white. | 1727 Mary Davys, "The Accomplished Rake; or Modern Fine Gentleman", ARCHER 3.1 1727davy.f3b, The footman followed and the lady had not gone far before she called a coach but the man being not near enough to hear the order where to go, as soon as the gentleman (which he took the lady for) was got in, he whipped up behind and the coach stopped at the Black Swan in Holborn, | 1743 ("written '1743' but almost certainly 1744") *The London Gazette*, ARCHER 3.1 1743lon1.n3b, There is great Sickness amongst the Spaniards there, and their Swiss Corps are not recruited, the Grievances of the Offciers being not yet redressed.

<1751-1800>

1778 Clara Reeve, *The Old English Baron: A Gothic Story*, ARCHER 3.1 1778reev.f4b, There were two doors on the further side of the room with keys in them; being not at all sleepy, he resolved to examine them;

Diachrony of Present Participles and Gerunds Followed by *Not*

<1851-1900>

1864 James Watson, "Observations on some new remedies", *Edinburgh Medical Journal* 9, ARCHER 3.1 1864wats.m6b, The flatulence continued pretty constant till a quarter past 8, when I again vomited slightly; the process though painful being not nearly so much so as at first. The clammy cold sweat continued, and the whole surface of my body felt benumbed.

<Examples with a negative intensifier>

1809 Richard Fenton, in J. Fisher, ed., *Tours in Wales*, ARCHER 3.1 1809fent.j5b, We proceeded to another elevation a little farther on; but in 5 Minutes found that it was only an old heap of Earth thrown up, when they were digging for Turf or making Peat land, there being not the least indication of burning, and the natural soil soon appearing. Near the first it seems are the limits of two Lordships, and it might have served as the Boundary mark.

b. <have>

<1701-1750>

1702 Anon., *The Adventures of Lindamira* [sic_Nakamura], *A Lady of Quality*, ARCHER 3.1 1702anon.f3b, I believe you agree with the opinion of most men that women are not capable of giving a rational answer, having not the advantage of learning and reading those authors that are so improving to the mind.

6.3.4. Variations between Pre- and Post-position of *Not* with Compound Gerundive *Having* PP

6.3.4.1. Lampeter

As shown in Table 78, only two examples of the compound gerundive *having* PP with the pre-positioned *not* occurred in the Lampeter. This frequency is too low to make a single comment.

270

Chapter VI

Table 78   Variations between Pre- and Post-position of *Not* with Compound Gerundive *Having* PP—Lampeter

Period	Pre	Post
1640-1650	0	0
1651-1675	0	0
1676-1700	0	0
1701-1725	2	0
1726-1740	0	0
Total	2	0

6.3.4.2. Newdigate

The compound gerundive *having* PP always took the pre-positioned *not* in the Newdigate, even though no more than four examples have been encountered, as shown in Table 79.

Table 79   Variations between Pre- and Post-position of *Not* with Compound Gerundive *Having* PP—Newdigate

Period	Pre	Post
1674-1675	1	0
1676-1692	3	0
Total	4	0

6.3.4.3. Lampeter and Newdigate Integrated

Table 80, into which Tables 78 and 79 are combined, shows that the compond gerundive *having* PP tended to take the pre-position of *not*.

Diachrony of Present Participles and Gerunds Followed by *Not*

Table 80   Variations between Pre- and Post-position of *Not* with Compound Gerundive *Having* PP—Lampeter and Newdigate Integrated

Period	Pre	Post
1417-1550	0	0
1551-1575	0	0
1576-1600	0	0
1601-1625	0	0
1626-1650	0	0
1651-1675	1	0
1676-1700	3	0
1701-1725	2	0
1726-1740	0	0
Total	6	0

6.3.4.4. ARCHER 3.1

As shown in Table 81, only two examples of the compound gerundive *having* PP occurred in the ARCHER 3.1, one with the pre-position and the other with the post-position of *not*. This frequency is too negligible to make a single comment. The only one example with the form of *having not* PP appears in (129).

Table 81   Variations between Pre- and Post-position of *Not* with Compound Gerundive *Having* PP—British English Documents in ARCHER 3.1

Period	Pre	Post
1650-1700	1	0
1701-1750	0	0
1751-1800	0	1
1801-1850	0	0
1851-1900	0	0
1901-1950	0	0
1951-	0	0

(129) 1791 Ann Radcliffe, *The Romance of the Forest*, in ARCHER 3.1 1791radc.f4b, She blamed herself for <u>having</u> <u>not</u> yet <u>mentioned</u> the

Chapter VI

discovery of the manuscript and chambers to La Motte, and resolved to delay the disclosure no longer than the following morning.

6.3.5. Variations between Pre- and Post-position of *Not* with Compound Gerundive *Being* PP

6.3.5.1. Lampeter

With a single exception in (130), the pre-position of *not* is the rule with the compound gerundive *being* PP in the Lampeter, as indicated in Table 82.

Table 82   Variations between Pre- and Post-position of *Not* with Compound Gerundive *Being* PP—Lampeter

Period	Pre	Post
1640-1650	1	0
1651-1675	0	0
1676-1700	2	1
1701-1725	3	0
1726-1740	0	0
Total	6	1

(130) 1679 H. Jones, *A sermon of Antichrist, preached at Christ-Church, Dublin. Novemb. 12. 1676,* But before this be shut up, one doubt is to be removed, *of the Empire being not yet taken out of the way*, which we now see in Being. (Lampeter RelA)

6.3.5.2. Newdigate

Only one example with the pre-position of *not* has been encountered in the Newdigate as follows:

Table 83   Variations between Pre- and Post-position of *Not* with Compound Gerundive *Being* PP—Newdigate

Period	Pre	Post
1674-1675	0	0
1676-1692	1	0
Total	1	0

Diachrony of Present Participles and Gerunds Followed by *Not*

6.3.5.3. Lampeter and Newdigate Integrated

Table 84 is a combination of Tables 82 and 83, and shows that the compound gerundive *being* PP tended to take the pre-position of *not*.

Table 84   Variations between Pre- and Post-position of *Not* with Compound Gerundive *Being* PP—Lampeter and Newdigate Integrated

Period	Pre	Post
1417-1550	0	0
1551-1575	0	0
1576-1600	0	0
1601-1625	0	0
1626-1650	1	0
1651-1675	0	0
1676-1700	3	1
1701-1725	3	0
1726-1740	0	0
Total	7	1

6.3.5.4. ARCHER 3.1

No more than two examples with the pre-position of *not* have been encountered in the ARCHER 3.1 as follows:

Table 85   Variations between Pre- and Post-position of *Not* with Compound Gerundive *Being* PP—British English Documents in ARCHER 3.1

Period	Pre	Post
1650-1700	0	0
1701-1750	0	0
1751-1800	1	0
1801-1850	1	0
1851-1900	0	0
1901-1950	0	0
1951-	0	0

Chapter VI

6.3.6. Variations between Pre- and Post-position of *Not* with Simple Gerundive Verb-*ing*

6.3.6.1. Helsinki Corpus (Diachronic Part)

As shown in Table 86, the pre-position of *not* is the rule with the simple gerundive Verb-*ing* in the Helsinki-DP, except for an example of the verb *be*, the same example collected from 1599 M. Hoby, D2, 80, in (108) on p. 219.

Table 86   Variations between Pre- and Post-position of *Not* with Simple Gerundive Verb-*ing*—Helsinki-DP

Period	Pre		Post	
OE I-ME II -1350	0		0	
ME III 1350-1420	0		0	
ME IV 1420-1500	0		0	
EModE I 1500-1570	2+1	[2+1]	0	
EModE II 1570-1640	4	[4]	1	[1]
EModE III 1640-1710	15+1	[14+1]	0	

6.3.6.2. CEECS

With a single exception with the verb *come* in (131), the pre-position of *not* is the rule with the simple gerundive Verb-*ing* in the CEECS, as indicated in Table 87.

(131) 1471? Wadehill, And yef ye may not come hider, þan þat ye wole find þe meane to my lord Chaunceler as to excuse my lord of <u>his comyng not</u> to London at þis time, like as my seid lord was wreten unto by a pryve seall (CEECS STONOR)

Diachrony of Present Participles and Gerunds Followed by *Not*

Table 87   Variations between Pre- and Post-position of *Not* with Simple
Gerundive Verb-*ing*—CEECS

Period	Pre		Post	
1417-1500	0	0	1	[1]
1501-1525	1	[1]	0	0
1526-1550	0	0	0	0
1551-1575	0	0	0	0
1576-1600	10	[6]	0	0
1601-1625	2	[2]	0	0
1626-1650	10	[7]	0	0
1651-1675	5	[5]	0	0
1676-1681	1	[1]	0	0

6.3.6.3. Lampeter

The tabulation of the data for variations between the pre- and the post-position of *not* with simple gerundive Verb-*ing* in the Lampeter is presented in Table 88. This table shows that the pre-position of *not* is the rule in case of simple gerundive *ing*-forms, which have least verbal force.

Table 88   Variations between Pre- and Post-position of *Not* with Simple
Gerundive Verb-*ing*—Lampeter

Period	Pre		Post	
1640-1650	9	[9]	0	0
1651-1675	19	[16]	0	0
1676-1700	20	[17]	0	0
1701-1725	27	[24]	0	0
1726-1740	4	[4]	0	0

6.3.6.4. Newdigate

It is evident from Table 89 that the pre-position of *not* is the rule with the simple gerundive Verb-*ing* in the Newdigate.

Chapter VI

Table 89   Variations between Pre- and Post-position of *Not* with Simple Gerundive Verb-*ing*—Newdigate

Period	Pre		Post	
1674-1675	9	[8]	0	0
1676-1692	101	[47]	0	0

6.3.6.5. CEECS, Lampeter and Newdigate Integrated

The statistics in Table 90, a combination of Tables 87-89, prove that the pre-position of *not* is the rule with the simple gerundive Verb-*ing*.

Table 90   Variations between Pre- and Post-position of *Not* with Simple Gerundive Verb-*ing*—CEECS, Lampeter and Newdigate Integrated

Period	Pre		Post	
1417-1500	0	0	1	[1]
1501-1525	1	[1]	0	0
1526-1550	0	0	0	0
1551-1575	0	0	0	0
1576-1600	10	[6]	0	0
1601-1625	2	[2]	0	0
1626-1650	19	[16]	0	0
1651-1675	33	[29]	0	0
1676-1700	122	[58]	0	0
1701-1725	27	[24]	0	0
1726-1740	4	[4]	0	0

Table 91 shows how the verbs which typically took the simple participial Verb-*ing* *not* behaved when they were used as the simple gerundive Verb-*ing*. Although the examples with the pre-position of *not* seldom occurred except for *come* and *be*, it is evident that the simple gerundive Verb-*ing* *not* was a rare construction.

Diachrony of Present Participles and Gerunds Followed by *Not*

Table 91   Verbs Taking Simple Gerundive Verb-*ing Not*—CEECS, Lampeter and Newdigate Integrated

Period	be		have		know		come	
	Pre	Post	Pre	Post	Pre	Post	Pre	Post
1417-1500	0	0	0	0	0	0	0	1
1501-1550	0	0	0	0	0	0	0	0
1551-1600	0	0	0	0	0	0	1	0
1601-1650	0	0	0	0	1	0	0	0
1651-1700	6	0	0	0	0	0	22	0
1701-1740	2	0	1	0	0	0	0	0

6.3.6.6. ARCHER 3.1

The tabulation of the data for variations between the pre- and the post-position of *not* with simple gerundive Verb-*ing* in the ARCHER 3.1 is presented in Table 92. This table shows that the pre-position of *not* is the rule with the simple gerundive *ing*-forms.

278

Chapter VI

Table 92　Variations between Pre- and Post-position of *Not* with Simple Gerundive Verb-*ing*—British English Documents in ARCHER 3.1

	1650-1700	1701-1750	1751-1800	1801-1850	1851-1900	1901-1950	1951-
answer					1 : 0		
attend				1 : 0			
be		2 : 0	4 : 0	3 : 0	1 : 0		
change							1 : 0
choose	1 : 0						
come							2 : 0
deal							1 : 0
differ	1 : 0						
discover	1 : 0						
disect					1 : 0		
dismember							1 : 0
do			1 : 0	1 : 0			
drink	1 : 0						
exceed			1 : 0				
find		1 : 0		2 : 0			
generate					1 : 0		
go				2 : 0		1 : 0	1 : 0
have				1 : 0	2 : 0		1 : 0
hear	1 : 0						
help							1 : 0
include					1 : 0		
keep							1 : 0
know	2 : 0		1 : 0				1 : 0
let							1 : 0
light				1 : 0			
make	1 : 0						1 : 0
offer							+1 : 0
pretend							1 : 0
produce					1 : 0		
remember						1 : 0	
revive				1 : 0			
run				1 : 0			
say							1 : 0
see	1 : 0	1 : 0		1 : 0			1 : 0
sleep							1 : 0
speak						1 : 0	1 : 0
stare							1 : 0
succeed			1 : 0				
take							1 : 0
tell						1 : 0	
use							1 : 0
visit						1 : 0	
vote					1 : 0		
wait		1+1 : 0					
write	4 : 0	1 : 0	1 : 0			1 : 0	
Total	13 : 0	6+1 : 0	9 : 0	14 : 0	9 : 0	6 : 0	20+1 : 0

6.3.7. Summary of Section 6.3

Through the analyses of Helsinki-DP, CEECS, Lampeter, Newdigate and ARCHER 3.1 corpora, the following number of examples were collected:

	pre	post
Compound participial *having* PP	41	27
Compound participial *being* PP	60	40
Simple participial Verb-*ing*	621+3	123
Compound gerundive *having* PP	7	1
Compound gerundive *being* PP	9	1
Simple gerundive Verb-*ing*	316+4	2
Total	1,054+7	194

These statistics show essentially the same results as has been reached in (115) in 6.2, including the chronological transition of the post-position of *not*, and verbs or constructions which continued to take the post-position of *not*. They also show almost the same tendency of the post-positioned *not* to hardly ever occur with the gerund, predominantly substantive *ing*-form. In the light of the fact that quite a few examples with the post-position of *not* were discovered even in such formal and serious writings as included in Lampeter Corpus and were written even by the educated, this construction was never a rare construction. Much less, it was not a slip of tongue or pen, in contradistinction to the statements of Bullokar and Priestley, referred to in (65a, b). In this respect, it may be asserted that a new objective evaluation of the usage should be given in the history of English.

6.4. Evidence from *OED²* on CD-ROM

In this section, analytical results of all of the citations in the *OED²* on CD-ROM, version 3.01 are presented. The functions of *ing*-forms in quotations not fully cited in the *OED²* can be ambiguous. For some, the function could be identified by examining the passages of their source-

280

Chapter VI

texts so far as they were available, yet for others it could not when they were particularly rare historical documents. Thus, the examples are categorised into those without ambiguity and prospective ones in both statistical tables and presentation of examples for as much preciseness as possible.[37]

6.4.1. Variations between Pre- and Post-position of *Not* with Compound Participial *Having* PP

6.4.1.1. Examples of Compound Participial *Having not* + PP

Examples of the compound participial *having not* + PP that have been encountered in the *OED²* are presented by periods below. Examples without ambiguity appear in (132) and prospective ones in (133).

(132) <1551-1600>

1594 Nashe *Terrors of Nt.* Wks. (Grosart) III. 251 He is a mettle-bruing Paracelsian, hauing not past one or two Probatums for al diseases. (*OED²*, s.v. probatum, 1a)

<1601–1650>

1606 in J. Nichols, *The progresses, processions and magnificent festivities of K. James the first*, (1828) II. 68 In so short a time to be accomplished, a most statelie Pageant, the workmen and plotters thereof having not past twelve dayes of respit after their first warning. (*OED²*, s.v. plotter, 2) | 1607 T. Walkington, *The optick glasse of humors* xiii. (1664) 138 He fell roundly to his victuals, having not eat any in a seven night before. (*OED²*, s.v. roundly, *adv.* 7)

<1651–1700>

---

[37] *OED²* is essentially a dictionary, not intended as a linguistic corpus. I still feel a sense of incongruity in regarding the frequencies of a construction and its variants gathered from citations as representing relative frequencies of the times. This is the reason why I presented only raw statistics of the pre- and post-position of *not* in 6.4, refraining from presenting their percentages and figuration. In my opinion, the chronological frequency transition of the two forms is shown abundantly in 6.2 and 6.3. It is exactly to evidence the fact that the post-position of *not* was undeniably used over times in the history of English that I conducted an examination of the whole citation in the *OED²*.

Diachrony of Present Participles and Gerunds Followed by *Not*

1659-60 Pepys *Diary* 1 Jan., I rose, put on my suit with great skirts, having not lately worn any other clothes but them. (*OED²*, s.v. skirt, *n.* 2b) | *a*1661 Fuller *Worthies* (1840) III. 306 Hitherto the English pale had been hide-bound in the growth thereof, having not gained one foot of ground in more than two hundred years. (*OED²*, s.v. hidebound, *a. (n.)* 3) | 1663 Butler *Hud.* i. ii. 47 They rode, but Authors having not Determined whether Pace or Trot (That is to say, whether Tollutation, As they do term 't, or Succussation) We leave it, and go on. (*OED²*, s.v. tolutation) | 1692 Luttrell *Brief Rel.* (1857) II. 530 They also brought off 50 wounded men, and divers of the dead with them, the enemy haveing not then stript the feild. (*OED²*, s.v. strip, *v.*¹ 3) | 1692 Wood *Life* (O.H.S.) III. 405 It rain'd and drisled most of the morning, having not rain'd, not to mention it, for a month. (*OED²*, s.v. mention, *v.* 1a)

<1701–1750>

1704 Luttrell *Brief Rel.* (1857) V. 501 Yesterday the lords adjourned . . having first discontinued the writt of error brought by Dr. Watson . . he having not assign'd errors in due time. (*OED²*, s.v. discontinue, *v.* 3a) | 1708 Lady Cave *Let.* in M. M. Verney *Verney Lett.* (1930) I. xiv. 266 Sir Thomas is glad to hear Col. Oughton is in the land of the living . . having not heard a word from him. (*OED²*, s.v. living, *ppl. a.* 2c) | 1726 Ayliffe *Parergon* 121 In those Times, the Bishops preach'd on the Steps of the Altar . . , having not as yet assum'd to themselves the Pride and State of a Throne. (*OED²*, s.v. throne, *n.* 1b)

<1801–1850>

1831 M. Edgeworth *Let.* 20 Jan. (1971) 473 A . . spoiled child of 30 whose mother and father having not been able to conceal from him that they think him the 8th wonder of the world have at last brought him to acquiesce in their opinion. (*OED²*, s.v. wonder, *n.* 1a)

(133) <1651–1700>

1656-7 Davenant *Rutland House* Dram. Wks. 1873 III. 226 She having not known . . the sufficient mystery of haut~gouts. (*OED²*, s.v. ‖ haut-goût, 3) | *a*1659 Osborn *Ess.* iii. Wks. (1673) 568 The Garden having not yet produced any Fruit so lateward. (*OED²*, s.v. lareward, *a.* and *adv.* 1) | 1698 Fryer *Acc. E. India & P.* 367 Having

Chapter VI

not saluted the Temple Twelve times since he began to Reign. (*OED²*, s.v. salute, *v.* 3)

<1751–1800>
1763 Swinton in *Phil. Trans.* LIV. 131 A pleonasmus or redundancy of מ having not been antiently uncommon. (*OED²*, s.v. pleonasm, 1b)

6.4.1.2. Chronological Trends

Tabulation of the data in (132) and (133) for variations between the pre- and the post-position of *not* with compound participial *having* + PP in the *OED²* is presented in Table 93. As *ing*-forms in quotations not fully cited in the *OED²* can be ambiguous as to their function, the examples without ambiguity (the upper statistics in each column) are separated from the prospective ones (the lower statistics). From Table 93, it is evident that the form of the post-position of *not* was moderately used, primarily between 1651 and 1750, and became obsolescent around mid-18th century.

Table 93   Variations between Pre- and Post-position of *Not* with Compound Participial *Having* PP—*OED²*

Period	Pre	Post	Period	Pre	Post
1301-1350	0	0	1651-1700	5	5
	0	0		4	3
1351-1400	0	0	1701-1750	2	3
	0	0		4	0
1401-1450	1	0	1751-1800	8	0
	0	0		6	1
1451-1500	0	0	1801-1850	5	1
	0	0		5	0
1501-1550	0	0	1851-1900	9	0
	0	0		5	0
1551-1600	0	1	1901-1950	2	0
	0	0		3	0
1601-1650	3	2	1951-2000	1	1
	2	0		0	0
			Total	36	13
				29	4

Diachrony of Present Participles and Gerunds Followed by *Not*

6.4.2. Variations between Pre- and Post-position of *Not* with Compound Participial *Being* PP

6.4.2.1. Examples of Compound Participial *Being not* + PP

Examples of the compound participial *being not* + PP collected from the *OED²* are presented below, classified into the unambiguous examples (134) and prospective ones (135).[38]

(134) <1501–1550>

    <Passive>

        1531 Elyot *Gov.* iii. xix, The stones beinge not surely couched and mortred, falleth a way. (*OED²*, s.v. couch, *v.*[1] 3b) | 1531-2 *Act 23 Hen. VIII*, c. 17 §1 No maner person . . [shall] winde . . any fleesse of wolle beinge not sufficiently riuered or wasshed. (*OED²*, s.v. river, *v.* 1) | 1540 in R. G. Marsden *Sel. Pl. Crt. Adm.*

---

[38] Although the underlined parts in the following appear to be passive *be* + PP, 'inbowed', 'fretted', 'vsed' and 'pleased' are all transferred into participial adjectives. Consequently, these examples were treated as the simple participial or gerundive Verb-*ing* + *not* forms.

    1552 Huloet, s.v. *Beame*, Beame of a rouffe, not beynge inbowed or fretted. (fretted, *ppl. a.*[2] 1) | 1632 Lithgow *Trav.* viii. 372 He succumb'd, and could not subsist, not beeing vsed to pedestriall trauayle. (subsist, *v.* 7b) | 1666 Pepys *Diary* 6 Aug., My wife in a chagrin humour, she not being pleased with my kindnesse to either of them. (chagrin, *a.* 1)

So were the following examples.

    not being accustomed to be disturbed (1748 *Anson's Voy.*) | not being accustomed to amorous blandishments (1750 Johnson) | being not as yet acquainted with the secret signification of a spowte (1582 N. Lichefield) | The book . . . not being sufficiently detailed for the technician (1909 *Athenæum*) | Not being geuen . . . To lerned iudgement (1556 J. Heywood) | being not at all given to visiting (1890 *Century Mag.*) | Not being . . . interested in snakeology (1882 C. C. Hopley) | not being . . . letted (1552 *Bk. Com. Prayer*) | not being entirely lost (1875 H. Walton) | The angle not being suited to either a right angled (normal) or half-normal bend (1901 Waterhouse) | Not being . . . unread in the authors (1790 Burke) | Rome . . . not being used to be brideled with the snaffle of such insolencie (1579 North) | The Duke . . being not vsed to meete with any rubs or confrontments (1611 Speed) | not being used to such heady Stuff (1712 Arbuthnot) | not being used to the difficult delivery of Bond (1881 *N.Y. Herald*).

Chapter VI

(1894) I. 91 The said shippe . . being not moryd came rydyng with thee floode by force. (*OED*², s.v. moor, *v.*¹ 1)

<Perfective>

1523 Wolsey in *St. Papers Hen. VIII*, VI. 189 That the lance-knygtes being not past with the Countie Felix 7000 pays, wer at Porte Sus la Sone. (*OED*², s.v. pay, *n.* 3b)

<1551–1600>

<Passive>

1565-6 *Child-Marriages* 136 To geve and bequethe vnto my Children, beinge not Maried, and not otherwise Competentlie preferred. (*OED*², s.v. prefer, *v.* 1c) | 1574 R. Scot *Hop Gard.* (1578) 52 The chynkes creuises, and open ioyntes of your Loftes being not close byrthed, will deuoure the seedes of them. (*OED*², s.v. berth, *v.*²) | 1586 J. Ferne *Blaz. Gentrie* 27 Poets and excellent musicions whose braines being not moysted with the iuyce of Bacchus . . be nothinge plenty nor facund. (*OED*², s.v. facund, *a.* 1) | 1586 J. Hooker *Giraldus's Hist. Irel.* in *Holinsh.* II. 134/2 In deciding of all matters he was vpright and iust, being not affectionated nor . . corrupted for anie mans pleasure. (*OED*², s.v. affectionated, *ppl. a.* 2) | 1593 Shakes. *3 Hen. VI*, i. ii. 23 An Oath is of no moment, being not tooke Before a true and lawfull Magistrate. (*OED*², s.v. true, *a. (n., adv.)* 4c) | 1598 Barret *Theor. Warres* IV. iv. 115 The which being not aduertised that they be any *supra* Round, he is bound to giue the word to none but only vnto the Sentinell. (*OED*², s.v. supra, *adv., (a.), prep.* B. *adj.*) | 1599 Hakluyt *Voy.* II. i. 134 For they saile away, being not once touched with the glaunce of a shot, and are quickly out of the Turkish canons reach. (*OED*², s.v. glance, *n.*¹ 1a)

<Perfective>

1576 Newton *Lemnie's Complex.* (1633) 218 Somewhat tart and sowrish, and as it is commonly tearmed, Ponticke: such a relish . . as is in a Grape . . being not as yet come to his perfect ripenesse and maturity. (*OED*², s.v. Pontic, *a.*¹ 2) | 1583 P. Stubbes *Anat. Abuses* Eij, The other contayneth neither length, breadth or sidenes (beeing not past a quarter of a yarde side) wherof some be paved. (*OED*², s.v. sideness, a)

Diachrony of Present Participles and Gerunds Followed by *Not*

<1601–1650>

<Passive>

1607 Topsell *Hist. Four-f. Beasts* (1658) 234 Hens do lay egges <u>being</u> <u>not</u> <u>troad</u> by a Cock. (*OED²*, s.v. tread, *v.* A. 3) | 1611 Shakes. *Cymb.* iv. iv. 10 Newnesse Of Clotens death (we <u>being</u> <u>not</u> <u>knowne</u>, not muster'd Among the Bands) may driue vs to a render Where we haue liu'd. (*OED²*, s.v. muster, *v.*[1] 2d) | 1617 Capt. Pepwell in *Lett. E. Ind. Comp.* (1901) V. 155 The muskets are generally naught, <u>being</u> <u>not</u> well <u>metalled</u>. (*OED²*, s.v. metal, *v.* 1) | 1617 Moryson *Itin.* iii. 74 The houses very seldome keepe out raine, the timbers <u>being</u> <u>not</u> well <u>seasoned</u>. (*OED²*, s.v. season, *v.* 4) | 1630 J. Taylor (Water P.) *Trav. Wks.* iii. 82/1 The fellow was hanged, who <u>being</u> <u>not</u> <u>choaked</u> . . did stirre his legges, and writhe and crumple his body. (*OED²*, s.v. crumple, *v.* 2) | 1646 Sir T. Browne *Pseud. Ep.* iv. xii. 218 <u>Being</u> <u>not</u> incontroulably <u>determined</u>, at what time to begin, whether at conception, animation, or exclusion. (*OED²*, s.v. incontrollable, *a.*)

<Perfective>

1638 Mede *Wks.* (1672) 835 My Sizer <u>being</u> <u>not</u> yet <u>come</u> with a candle, I will transcribe a passage of Eusebius. (*OED²*, s.v. sizar)

<1651–1700>

<Passive>

1653 R. G. tr. *Bacon's Hist. Winds* 364 Let the eighteenth Motion be the Motion of Trepidation, to which (as is understood by Astronomers) we give no great credit. . . In which bodies <u>being</u> <u>not</u> altogether well <u>placed</u> . . doe trepidate or agitate continually. (*OED²*, s.v. trepidate, *v.*) | *a*1661 B. Holyday *Juvenal* (1673) 211 He thinks it more unhappiness . . to die with a divided carcase, then with a whole one: . . the whole body <u>being</u> <u>not</u> usually so trivially <u>exposed</u> to scorn, as the head, when divided from the body. (*OED²*, s.v. trivially, *adv.* 1) | 1662 J. Chandler *Van Helmont's Oriat.* 69 Because the water which is brought into a vapour by cold, is of another condition, than a vapour raised by heat: therefore . . for want of a name, I have called that vapour, Gas, <u>being</u> <u>not</u> far <u>severed</u> from the Chaos of the Auntients . . (*OED²*, s.v. gas, *n.*[1] 1) | 1662 J. Davies tr. *Olearius' Voy. Ambass.*

Chapter VI

260 Their Inhabitants had water'd the Streets, which being not pav'd, . . the dust had otherwise . . annoy'd us. (*OED²*, s.v. water, *v.* 6d) | 1669 Sturmy *Mariner's Mag.* iv. viii. 218 This Rule will not be impertinent to this Place, being not named before. (*OED²*, s.v. name, *v.*[1] 6b) | 1671 Grew *Anat. Plants* i. App. (1682) 34 Cortical Thorns are such as those of the Rasberry Bush, being not . . propagated from the Lignous Body, but . . wholly from the Cortical and Skin. (*OED²*, s.v. cortical, *a.* 1a) | 1672 Eachard *Hobbs' State Nat.* 86 Roger has a vocal organ . . called a mouth, and being not muzled, gagg'd, or cop'd . . may stretch it as wide as he pleases. (*OED²*, s.v. cope, *v.*[5]) | 1686 Parr *Life Usher* 94 Which [treatises] being not set down in my Lord Primates own Words . . cannot be reckoned, being much enlarged by the Dr., as himself confesseth. (*OED²*, s.v. reckon, *v.* 4c)

<1701–1750>

<Passive>

1710 C. Shadwell *Fair Quaker Deal* i. 15 [Sailor speaks] Our Rogue of a Loblolly Doctor, being not satisfied with his two Pences, must have a Note for ten Months' Pay for every Cure. (*OED²*, s.v. loblolly, 4) | 1726 Leoni tr. *Alberti's Archit.* I. 94b, The air . . being not kept in motion either by Sun or Winds, wants its due concoction. (*OED²*, s.v. concoction, 2)

<1751–1800>

<Passive>

1753 N. Torriano *Gangr. Sore Throat* 51 Many Children sick of this Disease, to whom I could give no Help, being not called till the very Extremity. (*OED²*, s.v. extremity, 8) | 1766-87 Porny *Heraldry* Gloss. s.v., Cognisances were badges which subordinate officers, and even soldiers did bare on their Shields, for distinction sake, being not entitled to a Crest. (*OED²*, s.v. cognizance, -sance, 5)

<Perfective>

1768-74 Tucker *Lt. Nat.* (1834) I. 217 As to the unacquirableness of virtue, this somewhat resembles Whitfield's day of grace, which being not yet come or being once past, no man can attain to righteousness. (*OED²*, s.v. unacquirableness)

Diachrony of Present Participles and Gerunds Followed by *Not*

(135) < –1500>

    <Passive>

        1344 *Act 18 Edw. III, 1* Ceux qui mesnent les legnes par dela saunz estre cokettez ou saunz paier Custume. [*transl.* Those that transport Wooll <u>being</u> <u>not</u> <u>cocketted</u> or without Custome.] (*OED²*, s.v. cocket, *v.*[1])

    <1501–1550>

    <Passive>

        1531 Elyot *Gov.* iii. xix. (1880) II. 318 The colours <u>beynge</u> <u>nat</u> suerly <u>wrought</u>, . . by moystnesse of wether relenteth or fadeth. (*OED²*, s.v. relent, *v.*[1] 1b) | 1540-1 Elyot *Image Gov.* (1549) 113 <u>Beyng</u> <u>not</u> <u>instructed</u> in any occupacion or science, saulfe onely in feates perteynyng to warre. (*OED²*, s.v. save, quasi-*prep.* and *conj.*, 3) | 1546 *St. Papers Hen. VIII*, XI. 330 The matters . . <u>beyng</u> <u>not</u> before <u>disgrossed</u> <u>and</u> <u>brought</u> to a conclusion. (*OED²*, s.v. disgross, *v.* b)

    <1551–1600>

    <Passive>

        1562 *Act 5 Eliz.* v. §6 Any Herring, <u>being</u> <u>not</u> sufficiently <u>salted</u>, <u>packed</u> <u>and</u> <u>casked</u>. (*OED²*, s.v. cask, *v.*[1]) | 1578 Banister *Hist. Man* v. 70 The fift veyne, <u>being</u> <u>not</u> <u>depriued</u> of the felowshyp of an Arterie. (*OED²*, s.v. fellowship, *n.* 2) | 1581 J. Bell *Haddon's Answ. Osor.* 102b, His doctrine <u>being</u> <u>not</u> <u>straighted</u> within the boundes of Nature. (*OED²*, s.v. strait, *v.* 7) | 1594 *Ord. Prayer in Liturg. Serv. Q. Eliz.* (1847) 654 <u>Being</u> . . <u>not</u> any clearer <u>enlightened</u>, than by the dimmed glimpse of nature. (*OED²*, s.v. dimmed, *ppl. a.*)

    <1601–1650>

    <Passive>

        1613 Shakes. *Hen. VIII*, i. i. 59 <u>Being</u> <u>not</u> <u>propt</u> by Auncestry, whose grace Chalkes Successors their way. (*OED²*, s.v. prop, *v.*[1] 2) | 1632 J. Hayward tr. *Biondi's Eromena* 117 <u>Being</u> <u>not</u> <u>used</u> to contradict me. (*OED²*, s.v. contradict, *v.* b) | 1639 Fuller *Holy War* iv. xiii. (1640) 191 The shores there <u>being</u> <u>not</u> <u>shod</u> against the sea with huge high rocks. (*OED²*, s.v. shoe, *v.* 4) | 1642 Fuller

Chapter VI

Holy & Prof. St. i. ii. 5 Ill customs being not knockt, but insensibly scru'd into our Souls. (*OED²*, s.v. screw, *v.* 10b)

<1651–1700>

<Passive>

1660 *Bp. Hall's Rem. Wks., Life* 40 The drift whereof, being not well conceived by some spirits. (*OED²*, s.v. conceive, *v.* 9) | 1664 H. More *Myst. Iniq.* 95 This Infallible Judge being not appointed by God, and being unappointable by man. (*OED²*, s.v. unappointable, *a.*) | 1665 Glanvill *Sceps. Sci.* i. 3 The soul being not cloy'd by an unactive mass, as now. (*OED²*, s.v. cloy, *v.*¹ 6) | 1668 H. More *Div. Dial.* ii. I. 221 The Generations of men being not considerably scanted for all these four greedy devourers of them. (*OED²*, s.v. scant, *v.* 4a) | 1671 Glanvill *Disc. M. Stubbe* 31 Being not related to any Foundation in Oxford, but living there as a Commoner. (*OED²*, s.v. commoner, *n.* 6) | 1675 Baxter *Cath. Theol.* i. 107 Being not . . moved by him (as David to murder Urias, and to vitiate his wife). (*OED²*, s.v. vitiate, *v.* 3) | 1678 Cudworth *Intell. Syst.* i. iv. §36. 566 The humane soul of our Saviour Christ Himself . . being not partially appointed to that transcendent dignity of its hypostatick union, but by reason of its most faithful adherence to the divine word and wisdom in a pre-existent state. (*OED²*, s.v. hypostatic, *a.* 1) | *a*1687 Petty *Pol. Arith.* iv. (1691) 77 The said Ten being not concerned to increase their Territory. (*OED²*, s.v. concern, *v.* 9) | 1695 Ld. Preston *Boeth.* ii. 74 *note*, The Fierceness of the People being not wholly subdued. (*OED²*, s.v. fierceness, 1a)

<1701–1750>

<Passive>

1705 C. Purshall *Mech. Macrocosm* 186 Whose Particles being then not well Digested . . for want of Fermentation, and Inmastication. (*OED²*, s.v. inmastication) | 1722 *Hearne's Collect.* (O.H. S.) VII. 381 Wood-cutting being not so much used since ingraving came up. (*OED²*, s.v. wood-cutting, *n.* 1) | 1728 Rutty in *Phil. Trans.* XXXV. 630 The making of Tin-plates, or Lattin, as it is called, being not commonly practised in England. (*OED²*, s.v. latten, 2)

Diachrony of Present Participles and Gerunds Followed by *Not*

<Perfective>

1720 De Foe *Capt. Singleton* xvi. (1840) 271 Our beef and hogs . . being not yet all gone by a good deal. (*OED²*, s.v. deal, *n.*¹ 3b)

<1851–1900>

<Passive>

1856 Ruskin *Mod. Paint.* III. iv. xiii. §26 His ideas respecting all landscape being not uncharacteristically summed, finally, by Pallas herself. (*OED²*, s.v. uncharacteristically, *adv.*)

6.4.2.2. Chronological Trends

Tabulation of the data in (134) and (135) for variations between the pre- and the post-position of *not* with compound participial *being* + PP in the *OED²* is presented in Table 94 (p. 290). The upper statistics in each column represent those without ambiguity and the lower statistics prospective ones. It is worth noting that, as far as the citations in the *OED²* are concerned, the form of *being not* + PP continued to be used until the end of the 18th century and, during the 16th-17th centirues, more examples with the post-position of *not* were gathered than those with the pre-position of *not*.

6.4.3. Variations between Pre- and Post-position of *Not* with Simple Participial Verb-*ing*

6.4.3.1. Examples of Simple Participial Verb-*ing not*

Examples of the simple participial Verb-*ing not* that have been encountered in the *OED²* are presented in 50-year periods, classified into the unambiguous examples (136) and prospective ones (137).

(136) <1401–1450>

<decrease>

1413 Lydg. *Pylgr. Sowle* i. xv. (1859) 15 Thy grace alwey hath ben affluent, decrecyng nought . . though never so largely thou geue it. (*OED²*, s.v. affluent, *a.* and *n.* A. *adj.* 3)

Chapter VI

Table 94 Variations between Pre- and Post-position of *Not* with Compound Participial *Being* PP—*OED²*

Period	Pre	Post	Period	Pre	Post
1301-1350	0	0	1651-1700	6	8+2
	0	1		5	9
1351-1400	0	0	1701-1750	5	2
	0	0		2	4
1401-1450	0	0	1751-1800	3	4
	0	0		9	0
1451-1500	0	0	1801-1850	13	0
	0	0		7+1	0
1501-1550	2	4+2	1851-1900	12	0
	2+2	3+1		5	1
1551-1600	8+2	9+2	1901-1950	1	0
	2	4+2		2	0
1601-1650	3	7	1951-2000	4	0
	4	4		0	0
			Total	57+2	34+6
				38+3	26+3

<1501–1550>

<be>

c1530 More in *Fisher's Wks.* ii. 51 He should . . make it a matter of great conscience to cohabit with her, being not his lawfull wife. (*OED²*, s.v. cohabit, *v.* 2) | 1539 Elyot *Cast. Helthe* 29 The hunting of them [*sc.* deer] beinge not so pleasant, as the huntynge of other venery or vermyne. (*OED²*, s.v. venery¹, 2) | 1545 Brinklow *Compl.* iii. (1874) 14 What can the pore wyfe . . do witthall, being not culpable in the cryme? (*OED²*, s.v. culpable, *a.* (and *n.*) 1b) | 1548 Hall *Chron., Hen. VII* 3b, Beyng not hable to suffre the importunate heate, they cast away the shetes and all the clothes. (*OED²*, s.v. importunate, *a.* (*n.*) 2)

<know>

1548 Hall *Chron., Edw. IV* (1809) 292 He was a frayde to set ouer or to geue battayl, knowynge not to what parte his souldiers would enclyne. (*OED²*, s.v. set, *v.*¹ 150)

<1551–1600>

Diachrony of Present Participles and Gerunds Followed by *Not*

<be>

1553 T. Wilson *Rhet.* (1580) 222 Demosthenes beyng not able to pronounce the firste letter of that arte . . but would saie, for *Rhetorike, Letolike*, vsed to putte little stones vnder his tongue, and so pronounced, whereby he spake at length so plainly, as any manne in the worlde could doe. (*OED²*, s.v. pronounce, *v.* 5) | 1553 Eden *Treat. Newe Ind.* (Arb.) 22 Ye seuen starres called *Septentriones* (being not farre from *Vrsa maior* called charles wayne). (*OED²*, s.v. Septentrion, *n.* and *a.* A. *n.* 1 & Ursa, 2a). | 1557 Ld. Warton in Strype *Ann. Ref.* (1824) VII. 382 Our men being not of power to encounter them held them close from sparpling abroad to destroy the country. (*OED²*, s.v. sparpling, *vbl. n.*) | 1563 Golding *Cæsar* (1565) 119 The enemy being not able to withstand the violence of oure fotemen, . . toke them to flyght. (*OED²*, s.v. violence, *n.* 5) | 1564 Sparke in *Hawkins' Voy.* (Hakl. Soc.) 10 He espied another Island, . . and being not able . . to fetch it by night, went roomer untill the morning. (*OED²*, s.v. room, *adv.* 3. *Naut.* a) | 1565 Jewel *Reply Harding* 430 Simple folke, beinge not hable to discerne, what thinges they be in the Holy Scriptures, that are to be applied to the Inner Man, and what to the Vtter. (*OED²*, s.v. utter, *a.* 2b) | 1579 Fenton *Guicciard.* xv. (1599) 693 The City being not tenable . . it yeelded. (*OED²*, s.v. tenable, *a.* 2) | 1579-80 North *Plutarch* (1676) 624 Being not of authority . . to take the stern in hand, and govern the ship, he took himself to tricking the sails. (*OED²*, s.v. trick, *v.* 6) | 1581 G. Pettie *Guazzo's Civ. Conv.* iii. 145 Being not long since in an Aduocates studie, I heard [etc.]. (*OED²*, s.v. study, *n.* 8d) | 1582 N. Lichefield tr *Castanheda's Conq. E. Ind.* i. xxix. 72b, The Pilots (being not as yet acquainted with the secret signification of a spowte) . . thought the same to bee a signe of faire weather. (*OED²*, s.v. secret, *a.* and *n.* A. *adj.*1g) | 1597 Hooker *Eccl. Pol.* v. (1617) 198 Of two such euils, being not both euitable, the choice of the lesse is not euill. (*OED²*, s.v. evitable, *a.*) | 1598 Tofte *Alba* (1880) 21 Yet still (me thinkes) mine Ayme, being not base, I should deserue some little tynie Grace. (*OED²*, s.v. tiny, *a.* (*n.*) A. *adj.* a) | 1600 Holland *Livy* xxiv. xiii. 517 So Anniball contrariwise temporised, being not so readie now to credite the Nolanes. (*OED²*,

Chapter VI

s.v. temporize, *v.* 2)

<have>

1582 N. T. (Rhem.) *Jude* 19 These are they which segregate them selves, sensual, having not the Spirit. (*OED²*, s.v. segregate, *v.* 1a)

<With *not*-A-*but*-B construction>

1594 J. Dickenson *Arisbas* (1878) 62 That eye-Syren, alluring not with the sound, but at the sight. (*OED²*, s.v. eye, *n.*[1] 28) | 1600 Surflet *Country Farm* ii. lxvi. 414 The butterflies . . are forciblie kept within a narrow scantling, the pot it selfe being not wide, but narrow. (*OED²*, s.v. scantling, *n.* 3a)

<1601–1650>

<be>

1605 Bacon *Adv. Learn.* ii. xiv. §1 It is in proofe by Syllogisme; for the proofe being not immediate but by Meane: the Inuention of the Meane is one thinge [etc.]. (*OED²*, s.v. mean, *n.*[2] 4) | 1608 Willet *Hexapla Exod.* 461 So might the seruant be sold . . being not his owne man, but to be disposed of at the will of his master. (*OED²*, s.v. man, *n.*[1] 4l(*b*)) | 1611 Bible *Transl. Pref.* Therefore the Greeke being not altogether cleare, the Latine deriued from it must needes be muddie. (*OED²*, s.v. muddy, *a.* (and *n.*²) 6) | 1613 Purchas *Pilgrimage* vi. xi. 521 That is now rather become a Sep-ulcher of Sciences, then a Theater, there being not above five Students. (*OED²*, s.v. theatre, theater, *n.* 5a) | 1617 Moryson *Itin.* i. iii. i. 199 Who being not rich by patrimony, take these iourneys onely for experience, and to be inabled to that expence, doe con-dition this reasonable gaine. (*OED²*, s.v. condition, *v.* 2b) | 1622 F. Markham *Bk. War* iv. v. 138 A lieutenant of the late invented Drag-oones (being not aboue sixteene inch Barrell, and full Musquet bore). (*OED²*, s.v. dragoon, *n.* 1) | 1625 Bacon *Ess., Empire* (Arb.) 297 It being not possible for them to goe forward infinitely. (*OED²*, s.v. infinitely, *adv.* 2) | 1626 C. Potter tr. *Sarpi's Hist. Quarrels* 196 It sufficed . . to say they had many Reasons, being not able to particularize in any. (*OED²*, s.v. particularize, *v.* 2b) | 1630 Capt. Smith *Trav. & Adv.* 13 Being not able to rule his horse and defend himselfe, he was throwne to the ground. (*OED²*, s.v. rule, *v.* 3b) | 1639 S. Du Verger tr. *Camus' Admir. Events* 112 This pigeon being not of full age, could not contract it without the con-

Diachrony of Present Participles and Gerunds Followed by *Not*

sent of his mother. (*OED²*, s.v. pigeon, *n.* 3b) | 1639 Verger tr. *Camus' Admir. Events* To Rdr. avj, There be mindes which foyle in reading a history of great length, humane patience being not of any great extent. (*OED²*, s.v. foil, *v.*¹ 4c) | 1641 Abp. Williams *Sp.* in *Apol. Bishops* (1661) 89 Here I have fixt my Areopagus, and dernier resort, being not like to make any further appeal. (*OED²*, s.v. dernier, *a.* b) | 1650 Bulwer *Anthropomet.* xxiii. (1653) 452 Upon which a Quære might be raised. . . But this, as being not properly appertaining to our Designe, we shall wave it for the present. (*OED²*, s.v. waive, *v.*¹ 10a) | 1650 Fuller *Pisgah* ii. iv. 103 Here some Commentators being not able to quell, never raise this objection. (*OED²*, s.v. quell, *v.*¹ 2)

<bear>

1623 Cockeram 111, *Ebone*, a blacke tree, bearing not leafes nor fruit, being burnt, it yeelds a sweet smell. (*OED²*, s.v. ebon, *n.* and *a.* A. *n.* 2)

<care>

1627 E. F. *Hist. Edw. II* (1680) 9 Caring not what succeeds, so he may make it the Stair of his Preferment. (*OED²*, s.v. stair, *n.* 1d)

<have>

1611 Bible *Rom.* ii. 14 These [the Gentiles] hauing not the Law, are a Law vnto themselues. (*OED²*, s.v. law, *n.*¹ 16a) | *a*1617 Daniel *To Sir T. Egerton* 96 Having not this skill how to contend, Th' unnourish'd strife would quickly make an end. (*OED²*, s.v. unnourished, *ppl. a.*)

<hear>

1603 Shakes. *Meas. for M.* ii. iv. 4 Whilst my Inuention, hearing not my Tongue, Anchors on Isabell. (*OED²*, s.v. anchor, *v.* 4) | 1626 D'Ewes in Ellis *Orig. Lett.* Ser. i. III. 217 Others hearing not well what he saied hindred those by questioning which might have heard. (*OED²*, s.v. question, *v.* 3a)

<know>

1647 W. Browne *Polex.* 3iiija, Knowing not how to reward an action that was beyond all ballancing. (*OED²*, s.v. balancing, *vbl. n.* 4)

<like>

1633 G. Herbert *World* ii. in *Temple* 76 Then Pleasure came, who

Chapter VI

liking not the fashion, Began to make Balcones, Terraces. (*OED²*, s.v. balcony, 1)

<name>

1633 G. Herbert *Temple, Invitation* ii, Come ye hither all, whom wine Doth define, Naming you not to your good. (*OED²*, s.v. define, *v.* 7)

<see>

1610 Holland *Camden's Brit.* i. 260 Tirrell him seeing not Unwares him slew with dint of arrow shot. (*OED²*, s.v. unwares, *adv., n.,* and *a.* A. *adv.* 2)

<sort>

1650 Vaughan *Anthroposophia* 2 These Indeavours sorting not to my purpose, I quitted this Booke-businesse. (*OED²*, s.v. sort, *v.*¹ 7c)

<turn>

1646 F. Hawkins *Youth's Behav.* (1663) 24 Be attentive, turning not thine eyes here and there. (*OED²*, s.v. here, *adv.* 9b)

<vouchsafe>

1633 Ford *Broken H.* iv. i, A gallant man at arms is here; . . blunt and rough-spoken, Vouchsafing not the fustian of civility. (*OED²*, s.v. rough-spoken, *a.*)

< Examples with a negative intensifier>

1607 R. C[arew] tr. *Estienne's World of Wonders* i. xxiv. 194 The poore gentlewoman . . speaking not a word, gaue him a twinch with a weeping eye. (*OED²*, s.v. twink, *n.*¹ 1) | 1622 R. Hawkins *Voy. S. Sea* (1847) 238 This iland . . is a round humock, conteyning not a league of ground, but most fertile. (*OED²*, s.v. hummock, 1) | 1635 Jackson *Creed* viii. xxii. 252 The babes then did spel the Prophets meaning not amisse. (*OED²*, s.v. spell, *v.*² 2)

<With *not*-A-*but*-B construction>

1627 W. Bedell in *Lett. Lit. Men* (Camden) 136 For the translation sake (being not in the Vulgar, but according to the Hebrew verity). (*OED²*, s.v. verity, 2d.) | 1643 Sir T. Browne *Relig. Med.* i. §33. 73 There is in this Universe a Staire, or manifest Scale of creatures, rising not disorderly . . but with a comely method and proportion. (*OED²*, s.v. stair, *n.* 1e)

<1651–1700>

Diachrony of Present Participles and Gerunds Followed by *Not*

<be>

1651 Cleveland *Mixt Assembly* 35 Whose Members being not tallies, they'l not own Their fellows at the Resurrection. (*OED²*, s.v. tally, *n.*[1] 4a) | 1657 W. Coles *Adam in Eden* lxviii. 129 The tuberous and glandulous Cloggs being not much unlike those hard swellings. (*OED²*, s.v. glandulous, *a.*) | 1660 Stanley *Hist. Philos.* ix. (1687) 567/1 The Soul of the World God inkindled in the midst . . ; which (Soul) being not easily miscible, was not without difficulty contemperated. (*OED²*, s.v. miscible, *a.* (*n.*)) | 1662 Glanvill *Lux Orient.* iv. (R.), There being not a word let fall from them in disapproval of that opinion. (*OED²*, s.v. disapproval) | 1665 Hooke *Microgr.* 155 Microscopical seeds . . For first, though they grow in a Case or Hive often~times bigger then one of these . . being not above 1 / 32 part of an Inch in Diameter, whereas the Diameter of the Hive of them oftentimes exceeds two Inches. (*OED²*, s.v. hive, *n.* 5) | *a*1670 Hacket *Scrinia Reserata* (1693) ii. §159. 169 And therefore, my H. Lordships, here I have fixt my Areopagus, and dernier Resort, being not like to make any further Appeal. (*OED²*, s.v. Areopagus) | 1671 Wood *Life* (O.H.S.) II. 238 She not pleasing him, being not sportfull enough. (*OED²*, s.v. sportful, *a.* 2) | 1673 Temple *Observ. United Prov.* Wks. 1731 I. 38 This *Fond* being not sufficient in Times of War, is supplied by the States with whatever more is necessary from other *Fonds*. (*OED²*, s.v. fond, *n.* 3) | 1677 W. Hughes *Man of Sin* ii. v. 94 If the good Man blush'd, . . he may be pardon'd for this once, being not so squeamish often. (*OED²*, s.v. squeamish, *a., adv.,* and *n.* 7) | 1685 Baxter *Paraphr. N.T.* Matt. x. 11 Ministers being not heart-searchers, must pronounce God's Blessing on Men, on uncertainties. (*OED²*, s.v. heart-searching, *a.*) | 1698 Fryer *Acc. E. India & P.* 215 There are three sorts, one perfect Blue, and very hard. . . The second is perfect White, and very hard. . . The third, called Water-Saphires, are of small Esteem, being not so hard as the other, and commonly of a dead Waterish Colour. (*OED²*, s.v. sapphire, 1b)

<seem>

1668 Marvell *Corr.* Wks. 1875 II. 258 My Lord . . did wish [etc.]. . . Which, all circumstances considered, seeming not refus-

Chapter VI

able, my Lord Bellasis writ this letter. (*OED²*, s.v. refusable, *a.* 2)
<suffer>

1700 Dryden tr. *Ovid's Meleager & Atalanta* 33 Suff'ring not their yellow Beards to rear, He [*sc.* the wild boar] tramples down the Spikes, and intercepts the Year. (*OED²*, s.v. spike, *n.*¹ 1)
<value>

1663 Wood *Life* 15 June (O.H.S.) I. 476 A yong heire, who valuing not his father's labours, because of his ignorance, put most of his papers . . to infimous uses. (*OED²*, s.v. infimous, *a.*)

< Examples with a negative intensifier>

1696 P. Ventris *Reports* I. 191 The Court inclined strongly for the Defendant, there being not the least negligence in him. (*OED²*, s.v. negligence, *n.* Add: [1.] d)

<With *not*-A-*but*-B construction>

1655 Fuller *Ch. Hist.* iii. iv. §16 Iohn . . being . . not free, but feodary. (*OED²*, s.v. feudary, feodary, *n.* and *a.* B. *adj*). | 1678 Cudworth *Intell. Syst.* 451 The true Etymon of Jupiter . . being . . not Juvans Pater, but Jovis Pater. (*OED²*, s.v. etymon, 1)

<1701–1750>³⁹

<be>

*a*1708 Beveridge *Priv. Th.* i. (1730) 1 Being not capable of a reflexive act, they know it not. (*OED²*, s.v. reflexive, *a.* and *n.* A. *adj.* 2a) | 1742 Fielding *J. Andrews* i. xii, This the maid readily promised to perform, . . being . . not so squeamish as the lady. (*OED²*, s.v. squeamish, *a., adv.,* and *n.* 7) | 1747 *Gentl. Mag.* 208/ 1 His belly hangs low, being not far from the ground, as it sinks much in the middle. (*OED²*, s.v. sink, *v.* 3e)

<have>

1727-41 Chambers *Cycl.* s.v. *Rebate,* The merchants having not always wherewithal to pay for their goods in hand, by means of

---

³⁹ The year dated at the beginning of the citation "[W.] Beveridge, *Priv[ate] Th[oughts upon Religion (Private Thoughts upon a Christian Life)]* i. (1730)", which is quoted as the first of the examples during 1701-1750, suggests that this document dates from *a*1708, while the Bibliography defines the dating as 1661. All of the references I consulted such as *CHEL*, Vol. 9, 528 state that this document dates from 1709, a year after his death; therefore, I included this example among those dating from 1701-1750.

Diachrony of Present Participles and Gerunds Followed by *Not*

the rebatement, such as have, will find their account in it. (*OED²*, s.v. rebatement, 1) | 1748 Richardson *Clarissa* I. ii. 7 She was always thought comely, and comeliness . . having not so much to lose as beauty had, would hold, when that would evaporate. (*OED²*, s.v. comeliness, 1)

<reach>

1701 in *Lett. Lit. Men* (Camden) 302, I wish you would try . . the Philosophical Transactions, our sett reaching not far, and being imperfect in the first Volumes. (*OED²*, s.v. set, *n.*² 8c)

<1751–1800>

<be>

1774 Goldsm. *Nat. Hist.* (1776) III. 255 We will therefore call that animal of the panther kind, which is less than the panther, and with a longer tail, the ounce. . . The Ounce . . is much less than the pan- ther, being not, at most, above three feet and a half long. (*OED²*, s.v. ounce, *n.*² 2)

<1801–1850>

<like>

1819 Byron *Juan* i. clxxxvii, Juan . . liking not the inside, lock'd the out. (*OED²*, s.v. out, *n.* 2a)

<1851–1900>

<be>

1900 F. Litchfield *Pott. & Porc.* vii. 94 The ware is highly glazed, some of it being not unlike the brown Rockingham ware. (*OED²*, s.v. Rockingham)

<care>

1853 Trench *Prov.* (ed. 2) 136 The motto of some, who . . be- come utterly wretchless, caring not . . how much further they ad- vance. (*OED²*, s.v. wretchless, *a.* 1)

<extend>

1871 B. Stewart *Heat* §25 Between 0° and 100°, and for a range extending not too far beyond. (*OED²*, s.v. range, *n.*¹ 10b)

< Examples with a negative intensifier>

1857 Mrs. Gaskell *Let.* 28 Sept. (1966) 476 Only last week a let- ter to a little dressmaker, living not a mile off . . was returned to me by the Post Office. (*OED²*, s.v. little, *a., adv.,* and *n.* Add: [A.]

Chapter VI

[I.] [8.] c)

<With *not*-A-*but*-B construction>

1857 Kingsley *Two Y. Ago* I. v. 137 A little packet, <u>containing</u> <u>not</u> one five pound note, <u>but</u> four. . . The Mumpsimus men . . had 'sent round the hat' for him. (*OED²*, s.v. hat, *n.* 5b) | 1860 Ruskin *Unto this Last* iv. 126 As mere accidental stays and impediments <u>acting</u> <u>not</u> as wealth, <u>but</u> (for we ought to have a correspondent term) *as* 'illth'. (*OED²*, s.v. illth) | 1895 J. Denney *Stud. Theol.* ix. 223 A faith <u>standing</u> <u>not</u> in the wisdom of man <u>but</u> in the power of God. (*OED²*, s.v. stand, *v.* 72h) | 1898 *Westm. Gaz.* 2 May 5/2 One lady 'travels in balloons', it was said, <u>meaning</u> <u>not</u> that she soared aloft, <u>but</u> that she vended toyballoons to drapers and others. (*OED²*, s.v. travel, *v.* 2d)

<1901–1950>

<be>

1914 W. Raleigh *Let.* 5 Dec. (1926) II. 407 One has to think of public gains, the private gains <u>being</u> <u>not</u> very obvious except to . . armament syndicates. (*OED²*, s.v. armament, 5)

<With *not*-A-*but*-B construction>

1936 A. L. Haskell *Prelude to Ballet* 111 *Ballon*, <u>referring</u> <u>not</u> to the height of a jump <u>but</u> to the correct manner of landing in order to take off again (i.e. bounce). (*OED²*, s.v. ballon², 1)

<1951–2000>

<be>

1959 J. L. Austin *Sense & Sensibilia* (1962) vi. 61 In Berkeley's doctrine there are *only* ideas, in Kant's only *Vorstellungen* (things-in-themselves <u>being</u> <u>not</u> strictly relevant here). (*OED²*, s.v. vorstellung)

<*not*-A-*but*-B construction>

1985 G. T. Nurse et al. *Peoples Southern Afr.* ix. 226 Adam Kok's people, now sufficiently mictic to deserve the epithet Bastards (<u>signifying</u> <u>not</u> extramaritality <u>but</u> hybridity), were pushed northwards. (*OED²*, s.v. mictic, *a*).

(137) <1351–1400>

<With *not*-A-*but*-B construction>

1382 Wyclif *1 Pet.* v. 2 <u>Purueiynge</u> <u>not</u> constreynyngli [Vulg.

Diachrony of Present Participles and Gerunds Followed by *Not*

coacte, 1388 as constreyned], but wilfulli. (*OED²*, s.v. constrain-
ingly, *adv.*)

<1451–1500>

<dread>

*c*1475 *Harl. Contin. Higden* (Rolls) VIII. 445 Dredynge not sinis-
tralle fortune in batells. (*OED²*, s.v. sinistral, *a.* 1)

<1501–1550>

<be>

1539 Elyot *Cast. Helthe* 29 The hunting of them [*sc.* deer] beinge
not so pleasant, as the huntynge of other venery or vermyne.
(*OED²*, s.v. venery¹, 2)

<doubt>

*a*1548 Hall *Chron., Hen. VII*, 27 Doubting not to bring his ship to
the porte desired. (*OED²*, s.v. ship, *n.*¹ 3a)

<1551–1600>

<be>

1573 G. Harvey *Letter-bk.* (Camden) 40 Being not able to con-
iecture what purpose he should have in his hed. (*OED²*, s.v. con-
jecture, *v.* 3a) | 1585 T. Washington tr. *Nicholay's Voy.* i. xix. 22
The trenches of the Salaris beeing not passing 150. paces from
the Castle. (*OED²*, s.v. passing, *ppl. a.* (*adv.* and *prep.*) C. 1) |
1594 Shakes. *Rich. III*, iii. vii. 11 His resemblance being not like
the Duke. (*OED²*, s.v. resemblance, *n.*¹ 2a) | 1599 Nashe *Lenten
Stuffe* 32 Being not much behinde in the check-roule of his
Ianissaries and contributories, with Eagle~soaring Bulling-brooke.
(*OED²*, s.v. janizary, janissary, 3)

<have>

1590 Spenser *F.Q.* ii. vii. 14 And having not, complaine, and having it, upbrayd. (*OED²*, s.v. complain, *v.* 6a)

< Examples with a negative intensifier>

1590 *Tarlton's Newes Purgatorie* 1 Amongst the rest of whose
welwishers my selfe being not the least. (*OED²*, s.v. well-wisher)

<With *not*-A-*but*-B construction>

1587 Abp. Sandys *Serm.* (Parker Soc.) 448 Rude and indigested
platforms . . tending not to the reformation, but to the destruction
of the church of England. (*OED²*, s.v. indigested, *a.* 1b)

Chapter VI

\<1601–1650\>
　\<be\>

1604 Shakes. *Oth.* i. iii. 63 <u>Being</u> <u>not</u> deficient, blind, or lame of sense. (*OED²*, s.v. lame, *a.* 2b) | 1611 Speed *Hist. Gt. Brit.* ix. xvi, The Duke . . <u>being</u> <u>not</u> vsed to meete with any rubs or confront-ments. (*OED²*, s.v. confrontment, 1a) | 1613 Sherley *Trav. Persia* 3 The lesser Princes of Italy <u>being</u> <u>not</u> likely to endure the Churches so great encrease of Temporality. (*OED²*, s.v. temporal-ity, 1) | 1622 Bacon *Hen. VII*, 5 <u>Being</u> . . <u>not</u> very apprehensiue or forecasting of future Euents. (*OED²*, s.v. forecasting, *ppl. a.*) | 1623 Massinger *Dk. of Milan* ii. i, My brother <u>being</u> <u>not</u> by now to protect her. (*OED²*, s.v. by, *prep., adv.* B. *adv.* 1a) | 1632 J. Hayward tr. *Biondi's Eromena* 37 It <u>being</u> <u>not</u> lawfull for them, to commerce or trafficke without their patent of health, from the place whence they parted. (*OED²*, s.v. patent, *n.* 1c) | 1632 J. Hayward tr. *Biondi's Eromena* 63 There <u>being</u> <u>not</u> betweene us any cause of hostility. (*OED²*, s.v. hostility, 2) | 1633 T. Stafford *Pac. Hib.* i. ii. (1810) 39 Tyrone with his Hell-hounds <u>being</u> <u>not</u> farre from Corke. (*OED²*, s.v. hell-hound, 2) | 1635 J. Hayward tr. *Biondi's Banish'd Virg.* 97 It <u>being</u> <u>not</u> likely that shee should ever get a good looke of her Father. (*OED²*, s.v. look, *n.* 1b) | 1638 Wilkins *New World* (1707) ix. 67 There <u>being</u> <u>not</u> any Ab-surdity . . for which these Abusers of the Text will not find out an argument. (*OED²*, s.v. abuser¹, 1) | 1639 Du Verger tr. *Camus' Admir. Events* 12 <u>Being</u> <u>not</u> able any longer to beare the impetu-osity of his appetites. (*OED²*, s.v. impetuosity, b) | *a*1648 Ld. Her-bert *Hen. VIII* (1683) 435 Offenders . . <u>being</u> <u>not</u> able . . to . . fly from one lordship Marcher to another. (*OED²*, s.v. lordship, *n.* 7) | 1650 Howell *Giraffi's Rev. Naples* i. 20 The Bishop . . <u>being</u> <u>not</u> able to com himself to mingle speech with him. (*OED²*, s.v. mingle, *v.* 2d)

　\<have\>

1621 Bp. R. Montagu *Diatribæ* Introd. 32 <u>Hauing</u> <u>not</u> the gift of Prophesie, nor Intuitiue knowledge of what you would one day vndertake. (*OED²*, s.v. intuitive, *a.* (and *n.*) A. *adj.* 3c)

　\<like\>

1650 Weldon *Crt. Jas. I* 41 Salisbury <u>liking</u> <u>not</u> that any of Essex

Diachrony of Present Participles and Gerunds Followed by *Not*

his faction should come into play. (*OED²*, s.v. play, *n.* 4d)

<need>

1641 Milton *Reform.* 2 Faith needing not . . the Senses, to be either the Vshers, or Interpreters, of heavenly Mysteries. (*OED²*, s.v. usher, *n.* 2)

<shine>

1648 W. Jenkyn *Blind Guide* i. 14 Shining not like a sweetly influentiall star, but flashing like an angry bloody Comet. (*OED²*, s.v. influential, *a.* (*n.*) A. *adj.* 1a)

< Examples with a negative intensifier>

1625 in Foster *Eng. Factories India* (1909) III. 80 The Sultan suffaringe not a sticke to bee puld downe out of aney house. (*OED²*, s.v. stick, *n.*¹ 3b) | 1641 Wilkins *Math. Magick* ii. iv. (1648) 175 There being not the least contiguity or dependence upon any body. (*OED²*, s.v. contiguity, 1) | 1647 Clarendon *Hist. Reb.* i. §78 There being . . not the least Suspicion or Imagination that the Marriage would not Succeed. (*OED²*, s.v. suspicion, *n.* 3)

<With *not*-A-*but*-B construction>

1601 Bp. Barlow *Defence* 207 It being . . not the coaceruation of places, but the true alleadging, which supports the truth. (*OED²*, s.v. coacervation, 1) | 1606 Dekker *Sev. Sinnes* ii. (Arb.) 20 Marching not like a plodding Grasyer with his Droues before him, but like a Citty-Captayne. (*OED²*, s.v. grazier, 2) | 1613 Sir H. Finch *Law* (1636) 490 Being not diductory to bring any matter into plea or solemne action, but onely Commandatorie or Prohibitorie. (*OED²*, s.v. deductory, *a.* 1) | *a*1639 Wotton in *Reliq.* (1651) 484 Walking not like a Funambulus upon a Cord, but upon the edge of a rasor. (*OED²*, s.v. funambulus) | 1645 Tombes *Anthropol.* 11 The power of Pastors . . being . . not in a compulsory, but a directory way. (*OED²*, s.v. directory, *a.*)

<1651–1700>

<be>

1660 H. More *Myst. Godl.* x. ii. 496 They being not at leisure to perpend things to the bottom. (*OED²*, s.v. perpend, *v.* 1a) | 1667 Waterhouse *Fire Lond.* 28 Monies being not so flush with them. (*OED²*, s.v. flush, *a.*¹ 3a) | 1671 Wood *Life* (O.H.S.) II. 238 She

Chapter VI

not pleasing him, being not sportfull enough. (*OED²*, s.v. sportful, *a.* 2) | 1674 Grew *Anat. Plants* (1682) 228 [The atoms of] any fixed unodorable, or untastable Body . . being not able to make any Smell or Taste, unless they were first dissolved; that is to say, unpin'd one from another. (*OED²*, s.v. unpin, *v.* 2) | 1674 S. Jeake *Arith.* (1696) 89 Being not willing to spare so much time, or tumefie these Papers. (*OED²*, s.v. tumefy, *v.* 1b) | 1679 C. Nesse *Antid. agst. Popery* 38 Their worship being not . . terminative in the creature. (*OED²*, s.v. terminative, *a.* 2b) | *a*1682 Sir T. Browne *Tracts* (1684) 48 The Olive being not successfully propagable by Seed, nor at all by surculation. (*OED²*, s.v. propagable, *a.*) | 1684 *Scanderbeg Rediv.* v. 105 Being not above 15 or 16000 Men Effective. (*OED²*, s.v. effective, *a.* and *n.* 5a) | 1693 Pepys in *Lett. Lit. Men* (Camden) 213 This age being not very prolifique of customers for such a commodity. (*OED²*, s.v. prolific, *a.* 2b) | 1697 tr. *C'tess D'Aunoy's Trav.* (1706) 243 All that belong to the Inquisition being not subject to or tryable by any other Jurisdiction. (*OED²*, s.v. triable, *a.*[1] 1b)

<come>

1673 Hickeringill *Greg. F. Greyb.* 302 They coming not to church to see tumbling tricks and hocus juglings. (*OED²*, s.v. tumbling)

<find>

1690 Locke *Hum. Und.* iv. iii. §6 Finding not Cognition within the natural Powers of Matter. (*OED²*, s.v. cognition 2a)

<have>

*a*1691 Boyle *Hist. Air* (1692) 7 Having not the leisure to prosecute this discourse uninterruptedly. (*OED²*, s.v. uninterruptedly, *adv.*) | 1697 W. Dampier *Voy.* I. 117 They having not above 3 or 4 Hand-guns, the rest of them being arm'd with Lances. (*OED²*, s.v. handgun a.)

<sink>

1695 Woodward *Nat. Hist. Earth* ii. 75 That which had the least Gravity sinking not down till last of all, settling at the Surface of the Sediment. (*OED²*, s.v. settle, *v.* 18)

< Examples with a negative intensifier>

1665 J. Spencer *Prophecies* 114 There being not the least air of any promise of Prophecy made. (*OED²*, s.v. air, *n.*[1] A. 9) | 1700 T.

Diachrony of Present Participles and Gerunds Followed by *Not*

Brown *Amusem.* 127 Finding not a Penny to be screw'd out of the Prig. (*OED²*, s.v. screw, *v.* 5b)

<With *not*-A-*but*-B construction>

1651 Hobbes *Leviath.* ii. xxvi. 137 My designe being not to shew what is Law here, and there, but what is Law. (*OED²*, s.v. law, *n.*[1] 13) | 1653 Baxter *Chr. Concord* xviii. B2, The Ministerial power being not compulsive, . . but Nunciative, Swasory, and directive. (*OED²*, s.v. nunciative, *a.*) | 1655-60 Stanley *Hist. Philos.* (1701) 90/1 With a free contumacy proceeding not from Pride, but the greatness of his Mind. (*OED²*, s.v. contumacy, 1b) | 1664 H. More *Myst. Iniq.* 379 Lying not . . as the quarries of a Pavement, but as the scales of Fishes. (*OED²*, s.v. quarry, *n.*[3] 3) | 1667 Milton *P.L.* xi. 521 Disfiguring not Gods likeness, but thir own. (*OED²*, s.v. disfigure, *v.* 1) | 1672 Cave *Prim. Chr.* iii. v. (1673) 374 The medicinal vertue of Repentance, lying not in the duration, but the manner of it. (*OED²*, s.v. medicinal, *a.* and *n.* A. *adj.*1b) | 1684 *Comtempl. State Man* i. vii. (1699) 75 It being not then a suspicion, but an apparent certainty that Death will come. (*OED²*, s.v. certainty, 2) | 1684 H. More *Answer* xiv. 103 Which being not a final or total Ruine of Babylon, but, as it were, the Primity thereof. (*OED²*, s.v. primity, 2)

<1701–1750>

<be>

1704 Hearne *Duct. Hist.* (1714) I. 431 The Moselle . . being not capable of Ships of Burden. (*OED²*, s.v. capable, *a.* 1) | 1709 Hearne *Collect.* (O.H.S.) II. 197 He being not of great Birth, as appears from his arms. (*OED²*, s.v. great, *a., adv.,* and *n.* 13) | 1727 Swift *Gulliver* ii. viii, A sail, which he had a mind to make, being not much out of his course. (*OED²*, s.v. course, *n.* 11a)

< Examples with a negative intensifier>

1709 Hearne *Collect.* 11 Mar., Having not one dram of Learning. (*OED²*, s.v. dram, *n.*[1] 4)

<1751–1800>

<be>

1768-74 Tucker *Lt. Nat.* (1834) II. 486 The non-discernment, if owing to inability, being not a wickedness committed. (*OED²*, s.v.

Chapter VI

non-, *prefix* 1)
<find>

1765 C. Macaulay *Hist. Eng.* II. 232 <u>Finding</u> him <u>not</u> at so entire leisure to discipline their untowardness as in time of peace. (*OED²*, s.v. untowardness, 1)

<With *not*-A-*but*-B construction>

1771 G. White *Let.* in *Selborne* (1789) xxxv. 92 The trains of those magnificent birds [*sc.* peacocks] . . <u>growing</u> <u>not</u> from their uropygium, <u>but</u> all up their backs. (*OED²*, s.v. Uropygium) | 1773 Burke *Corr.* (1844) I. 427 <u>Writing</u> . . <u>not</u> in a desultory and occasional manner, <u>but</u> systematically. (*OED²*, s.v. desultory, *a.* (*n.*) A. *adj.* 2)

<1801–1850>

<attain>

1815 Southey *Roderick* viii. 15 His mother's after-guilt <u>attainting</u> <u>not</u> the claim legitimate he derived from her. (*OED²*, s.v. attaint, *v.* 11)

<be>

1831 *Fraser's Mag.* IV. 278 All this <u>being</u> <u>not</u> particularly new, and rather schoolboyish withal. (*OED²*, s.v. schoolboyish, *a.*)

<believe>

1839 Bailey *Festus* xix. (1848) 209 <u>Believing</u> <u>not</u> the aforetime unity Of the Divine and human. (*OED²*, s.v. aforetime, *adv.*)

<disturb>

1817 Shelley *Rev. Islam* ix. xxii, <u>Disturbing</u> <u>not</u> the leaves which are her winding~sheet. (*OED²*, s.v. winding-sheet, 1b)

<doubt>

1805 Wordsw. *Prelude* vi. 696 <u>Doubting</u> <u>not</u> that . . by no uncertain path . . Led, as before, we should behold the scene. (*OED²*, s.v. uncertain, *a.* 3b)

<eat>

1842 Tennyson *St. Sim. Styl.* 77 <u>Eating</u> <u>not</u>, Except the spare chance-gift of those that came To touch my body. (*OED²*, s.v. spare, *a.* and *adv.* 6c)

<pend>

1839 Bailey *Festus* xx. (1848) 256 Principles and doctrines <u>pending</u> <u>not</u> Upon the action of the poem here. (*OED²*, s.v. pend, *v.³* 2)

Diachrony of Present Participles and Gerunds Followed by *Not*

<With *not*-A-*but*-B construction>
1827 Whately *Logic* i. §1 (ed. 2) 22 The logician's object being not to lay down principles by which one may reason, but by which all must reason. (*OED²*, s.v. logician, 1)

<1851–1900>
<better>
1855 Tennyson *Will* ii, Bettering not with time. (*OED²*, s.v. with, *prep.*, (*adv.*, *conj.*) 16c)
< Examples with a negative intensifier>
1876 Mrs. Oliphant *Curate in Charge* II. ii. 34 The triumphant sunshine . . leaving not an inch even of the common high road unglorified. (*OED²*, s.v. unglorified, *ppl. a.*)
<With *not*-A-*but*-B construction>
1890 J. Martineau *Seat Author. Relig.* iv. ii. 394 The imitation being not homogeneous but homœogeneous with the original. (*OED²*, s.v. homœo-) | 1897 J. Hutchinson *Archives Surg.* VIII. 223 The patches . . being not a mere pigmentation, but distinctly a licheno-lupoid thickening. (*OED²*, s.v. licheno-)

6.4.3.2. Chronological Trends

Tabulation of the data in (136) and (137) for variations between the pre- and the post-position of *not* with simple participial Verb-*ing* in the *OED²* is presented in Table 95 (p. 306), in which the upper statistics in each column represent those of (136) and the lower statistics those of (137). Table 95 reveals that the forms of *not* Verb-*ing* and Verb-*ing* *not* occurred in 1,627+59 and 179 examples respectively, and that the latter form, the post-position of *not*, was frequently used primarily between 1551 and 1700.

Chapter VI

Table 95 Variations between Pre- and Post-position of *Not* with Simple Participial Verb-*ing*—*OED²*

Period	Pre		Post	
1301-1350	0	[0]	0	[0]
	0	[0]	0	[0]
1351-1400	9	[8]	0	[0]
	6+1	[5+1]	1	[1]
1401-1450	4	[3]	1	[1]
	9+1	[8+1]	0	[0]
1451-1500	13+2	[10+2]	0	[0]
	7+1	[7+1]	1	[1]
1501-1550	42+2	[31+2]	5	[2]
	40+2	[30+2]	2	[2]
1551-1600	98+7	[64+3]	16	[3]
	104+9	[74+6]	7	[3]
1601-1650	149+3	[89+3]	32	[16]
	115+5	[81+2]	25	[8]
1651-1700	126+4	[75+2]	17	[4]
	122+2	[75+2]	25	[9]
1701-1750	69+4	[37+3]	6	[3]
	40+2	[23+2]	4	[2]
1751-1800	49+1	[29+1]	1	[1]
	30+1	[22+1]	4	[4]
1801-1850	95+1	[48+1]	1	[1]
	59+1	[36+1]	9	[8]
1851-1900	160+3	[77+2]	10	[8]
	83+3	[59+2]	6	[5]
1901-1950	92	[42]	4	[3]
	11	[11]	0	[0]
1951-	90+4	[50+3]	2	[2]
	5	[5]	0	[0]

6.4.3.3. Verbs which Occured with Simple Participial Verb-*ing not*

The verbs which occur with the post-position of *not* in the *OED²*'s quotations are shown in Tables 96a-c. Table 96a represents the statistics for the verbs which typically take the post-position of *not* in the texts and electronic corpora examined in 6.2 and 6.3, Table 96b those for the other verbs and 96c those for the verbs which occur with negative intensifiers or *not*-A-*but*-B construction.

Table 96   Verbs Taking Simple Participial Verb-*ing not—OED²*

a. Verbs which Typically Take the Post-position of *Not* in the Texts and Electronic Corpora Examined in 6.2 and 6.3—*OED²*

	be		have		know		care		come		do	
	Pre	Post	Pre	Post	Pre	Post	Pre	Post	Pre	Post	Pre	Post
1301-1350	0	0	0	0	0	0	0	0	0	0	0	0
	0	0	0	0	0	0	0	0	0	0	0	0
1351-1400	0	0	2	0	1	0	0	0	0	0	0	0
	0	0	2	0	0	0	0	0	0	0	0	0
1401-1450	1	0	2	0	0	0	0	0	0	0	0	0
	0	0	2	0	0	0	0	0	0	0	0	0
1451-1500	2*[1]	0	2	0	0	0	0	0	0	0	0	0
	1	0	1	0	1	0	0	0	0	0	0	0
1501-1550	7	4	3	0	3	1	0	0	0	0	0	0
	3	1	2	0	1	0	0	0	0	0	0	0
1551-1600	12+1	13	4+1	1	6	0	1	0	1	0	0	0
	12	4	4	1	2	0	0	0	0	0	0	0
1601-1650	15	13	8	2	13	1	1	1	0	0	1	0
	8	13	6	1	3	0	4	0	0	0	0	0
1651-1700	22	11	7+1	0	7	0	2	0	0	0	1	0
	27	10	4	2	4	0	2	0	0	1	0	0
1701-1750	12	3	6	2	5	0	2	0	0	0	0	0
	15	3	1	1	2	0	1	0	0	0	0	0
1751-1800	13	1	2	0	1	0	0	0	0	0	1	0
	6	1	3	0	0	0	1	0	0	0	0	0
1801-1850	15	0	7	0	8	0	0	0	0	0	0	0
	14	1	2	0	3	0	1	0	1	0	0	0
1851-1900	33	3	6	0	2+1	0	1	1	0	0	0	0
	13	2	4	0	3	0	2	0	0	0	0	0
1901-1950	20	2	7	0	5	0	1	0	0	0	0	0
	2	0	0	0	1	0	0	0	0	0	0	0
1951-2000	12	1	6	0	2	0	0	0	0	0	0	0
	0	0	0	0	1	0	0	0	1	0	0	0

[1] One example with *not*-A-*but*-B construction is included here.

	doubt		find		meet		need		say		see	
	Pre	Post	Pre	Post	Pre	Post	Pre	Post	Pre	Post	Pre	Post
1301-1350	0	0	0	0	0	0	0	0	0	0	0	0
	0	0	0	0	0	0	0	0	0	0	0	0
1351-1400	0	0	0	0	0	0	0	0	0	0	1	0
	0	0	0	0	0	0	0	0	0	0	0	0
1401-1450	0	0	0	0	0	0	0	0	0	0	0	0
	0	0	0	0	0	0	0	0	0	0	0	0
1451-1500	0	0	0	0	0	0	0	0	0	0	0	0
	0	0	0	0	0	0	0	0	0	0	0	0
1501-1550	0	0	1	0	0	0	0	0	0	0	0	0
	2	1	1	0	0	0	0	0	0	0	0	0
1551-1600	3	0	0	0	0	0	0	0	0	0	1	0
	4	0	0	0	0	0	0	0	0	0	0	0
1601-1650	1	0	3	0	0	0	1	0	0	0	0	1
	2	0	2	0	0	0	2	1	0	0	0	0
1651-1700	1	0	3	0	0	0	0	0	0	0	1	0
	0	0	2	1	1	0	0	0	0	0	0	0
1701-1750	0	0	1	0	0	0	0	0	0	0	0	0
	2	0	0	0	0	0	0	0	0	0	0	0
1751-1800	0	0	0	0	0	0	0	0	0	0	0	0
	0	0	0	1	0	0	0	0	0	0	2	0
1801-1850	0	0	1	0	0	0	0	0	0	0	1	0
	0	1	1	0	0	0	0	0	0	0	0	0
1851-1900	0	0	2	0	1	0	0	0	0	0	0	0
	0	0	1	0	1	0	0	0	0	0	0	0
1901-1950	0	0	0	0	0	0	0	0	2*[2]	0	0	0
	1	0	0	0	0	0	0	0	0	0	0	0
1951-	1	0	0	0	0	0	0	0	0	0	0	0
	0	0	0	0	0	0	0	0	0	0	0	0

[2] One example with a negative intensifier is included here.

Diachrony of Present Participles and Gerunds Followed by *Not*

b. Other Verbs—*OED*[2]

1301-1400	
1401-1450	decrease 1
1451-1500	
	dread 1
1501-1600	
1601-1650	hear 2, bear 1, like 1, name 1, sort 1, turn 1, vouchsafe 1
	like 1, shine 1
1651-1700	seem 1, suffer 1, value 1
	sink 1
1701-1750	reach 1
1751-1800	
1801-1850	like 1
	attain 1, believe 1, disturb 1, eat 1, pend 1
1851-1900	extend 1
	better 1, look 1, wade 1
1901-	

c. Verbs which Occur with Negative Intensifiers or *Not*-A-*But*-B Construction—*OED*[2]

	With Negative Intensifiers	With *not* –A-*but* -B Construction (A, B ≠ V-*ing*)
1301-1350		
1351-1400		purvey 1
1401-1550		
1551-1600		allure 1, be 1
	be 1	tend 1
1601-1650	contain 1, mean 1, speak 1	be 1, rise 1
	be 2, suffer 1	be 3, march 1, walk 1
1651-1700	be 1	be 2
	be 1, find 1	be 4, disfigure 1, lie 2, proceed 1
1701-1750		
1751-1800		grow 1, write 1
1801-1850		be 1, find 1
1851-1900	live 1	act 1, contain 1, mean 1, stand 1
	leave 1	be 2
1901-1950		refer 1, result 1
1951-2000		signify 1

Chapter VI

From Tables 96a-c, it is evident that the post-position of *not* occurred typically with a closed class of verbs: *be, have*; *know, care, doubt, find*; *come, hear, like, need*, and *see*, among other verbs. These are the verbs already referred to in relation to Table 46 (p. 190), and the verbs which continued to take the form of Verb + *not* in the finite clause, as shown in (103) (pp. 197-198) and Tables 52-53 (pp. 227-228). The form of the participial Verb-*ing not* seems to have something to do with the mode of negation in the finite clause. The participial post-position of *not* with *doubt*, one of the verbs which showed aversion to the auxiliary *do*, is evidenced in two examples in (137) (pp. 299 and 304). Tables 96a-c suggest that quite a few verbs were permitted to concur with the post-position of *not*. Except for *act*, the earliest occurrences of the verbs in Tables 96a-c are all in and before 1500. In other words, newly-born verbs take the pre-position of *not*, to which category the majority of verbs belong.

6.4.4. Variations between Pre- and Post-position of *Not* with Compound Gerundive *Having* PP

With a single exception in (138), the pre-position of *not* is the rule with the compound gerundive *having* PP in the *OED²*, as indicated in Table 97.

(138) 1888 H. James in *Fortn. Rev.* May 651 M. Pierre Loti is a new enough talent for us still to feel something of the glow of exultation at his having not contradicted us, but [etc.]. (*OED²*, s.v. talent, *n.* 6d)

Diachrony of Present Participles and Gerunds Followed by *Not*

Table 97　Variations between Pre- and Post-position of *Not* with Compound Gerundive *Having* PP—*OED²*

Period	Pre	Post	Period	Pre	Post
1301-1350	0	0	1651-1700	2	0
	0	0		0	0
1351-1400	0	0	1701-1750	2	0
	0	0		0	0
1401-1450	0	0	1751-1800	4	0
	0	0		0	0
1451-1500	0	0	1801-1850	6	0
	0	0		0	0
1501-1550	0	0	1851-1900	9	1
	0	0		0	0
1551-1600	0	0	1901-1950	3	0
	0	0		0	0
1601-1650	0	0	1951-2000	1	0
	0	0		0	0
			Total	27	1
				0	0

6.4.5. Variations between Pre- and Post-position of *Not* with Compound Gerundive *Being* PP

No more than two examples with the post-position of *not* with the compound gerundive *being* PP have been encountered in the *OED²* as in (139). Otherwise the pre-position of *not* is the rule as indicated in Table 98.

(139) <1651–1700>

> *a*1685 Knatchbull *Annot. N. Test., Acts* xiii. 27 (1693) 133 The English Translator hath exprest the sence, but not Translated strictly to the words, which by reason of the Synchysis . . being not well distinguished, are not . . so rightly rendred as they ought. (*OED²*, s.v. synchysis, 1)

<1751–1800>

> 1773 *Cook's Voy.* (1784) II. iii. ix. 164 They speak of spirits being . . not totally divested of those passions which actuated them when

Chapter VI

combined with material vehicles. (*OED²*, s.v. vehicle, *n.* 4)

Table 98   Variations between Pre- and Post-position of *Not* with Compound Gerundive *Being* PP—*OED²*

Period	Pre	Post	Period	Pre	Post
1301-1350	0	0	1651-1700	3	1
	0	0		0	0
1351-1400	0	0	1701-1750	2	0
	0	0		0	0
1401-1450	0	0	1751-1800	2	1
	0	0		0	0
1451-1500	0	0	1801-1850	4	0
	0	0		0	0
1501-1550	0	0	1851-1900	9	0
	0	0		0	0
1551-1600	0	0	1901-1950	4	0
	0	0		0	0
1601-1650	1	0	1951-2000	4	0
	0	0		0	0
			Total	29	2
				0	0

6.4.6. Variations between Pre- and Post-position of *Not* with Simple Gerundive Verb-*ing*

The tabulation of the data for variations between the pre- and the post-position of *not* with simple gerundive Verb-*ing* in the *OED²* is presented in Table 99.[40]

---

[40] Referring to Blume, which I have not had an opportunity of reading because it does not seem to be listed in Jespersen's bibliography, Jespersen (1940 [1970]: 110) writes that the simple gerundive *not* Verb-*ing* began to occur from Elizabethan English with the earliest example quoted from Sir Philip Sidney. My statistics (Table 99) suggest that, however, this use dates from the first half of the 15th century.

Diachrony of Present Participles and Gerunds Followed by *Not*

Table 99　Variations between Pre- and Post-position of *Not* with Simple Gerundive Verb-*ing*—*OED²*

Period	Pre		Post	
1301-1350	0	[0]	0	[0]
	0	[0]	0	[0]
1351-1400	0	[0]	0	[0]
	0	[0]	0	[0]
1401-1450	2	[2]	0	[0]
	0	[0]	0	[0]
1451-1500	1	[1]	0	[0]
	0	[0]	0	[0]
1501-1550	7+1	[6+1]	0	[0]
	1	[1]	0	[0]
1551-1600	19	[19]	1	[1]
	0	[0]	0	[0]
1601-1650	55+4	[50+4]	1	[1]
	0	[0]	0	[0]
1651-1700	57+1	[50+1]	0	[0]
	0	[0]	0	[0]
1701-1750	47+3	[41+3]	1	[1]
	0	[0]	0	[0]
1751-1800	30	[26]	1	[1]
	0	[0]	0	[0]
1801-1850	61	[46]	1	[1]
	0	[0]	1	[1]
1851-1900	68+1	[51+1]	2	[2]
	0	[0]	0	[0]
1901-1950	47	[33]	1	[1]
	0	[0]	0	[0]
1951-2000	66+1	[45+1]	0	[0]
	0	[0]	0	[0]

Chapter VI

As shown in Table 99, the post-position of *not* has been collected in nine examples, in contrast to 461+11 examples with the pre-position of *not*. The table indicates that, in case of simple gerundive *ing*-forms, the pre-position of *not* was the rule throughout the entire history of English. Table 99 is contrastive to Table 95 (p. 306), which details the statistics for the simple participial Verb-*ing*.

Nine examples of the post position of *not* appear in (140). The verbs which occurred with the post-position of *not* are *be* (two examples), *interrupt*, *offer*, *travel* and *want* (one example respectively) in general examples, and *be*, *speak* and *swear* (one example respectively) in specific examples with *not*-A-*but*-B construction.

(140) General examples without ambiguity
    <1551–1600>
        1588 Parke tr. *Mendoza's Hist. China* 294 They shoulde haue a special care vnto their healthes, in <u>trauelling</u> <u>not</u> too fast but little and little. (*OED²*, s.v. little, *a.*, *adv.*, and *n.* 7c)
    <1601-1650>
        *a*1637 B. Jonson *Underw., to Browne*, See, that thou By <u>off'ring</u> <u>not</u> more sureties, than inow, Hold thyne owne worth unbroke. (*OED²*, s.v. unbroke, *ppl. a.* 1)
    <1701-1750>
        1731 Bailey, *Inarticulateness*, the <u>being</u> <u>not</u> articulate, indistinct, confused. (*OED²*, s.v. inarticulateness)
    <1851-1900>
        1876 Geo. Eliot *Dan. Der.* II. iv. xxxii. 298 He was affectionately directed by a precocious Jewish youth, who entered cordially into his <u>wanting</u> <u>not</u> the fine new building of the Reformed but the old Rabbinical school of the orthodox. (*OED²*, s.v. reformed, *ppl. a.* and *n.* A. *ppl. a.*1d)

    General prospective example
    <1801–1850>
        1823 Byron *Age of Bronze* xi, What is the simple standing of a shot, To listening long, and <u>interrupting</u> <u>not</u>? (*OED²*, s.v. stand, *v.* 52b)

Diachrony of Present Participles and Gerunds Followed by *Not*

Examples with *not*-A-*but*-B construction
1751 Jortin *Serm.* (1771) V. iii. 56 They took up a custom of <u>swearing</u> <u>not</u> by the Lord, <u>but</u> by other things. (*OED²*, s.v. by, *prep., adv.* A. *prep.* 2. a) | 1863 J. G. Murphy *Comm. Gen.* iii. 21 Moses <u>being</u> <u>not</u> the mere collector, <u>but</u> the composer of the documents contained in Genesis. (*OED²*, s.v. composer, 2) | 1945 *Mind* LIV. 58 The defenders of this view have recently been making quite a point of <u>speaking</u> <u>not</u> of 'a mind' and 'a body' <u>but</u> of a 'body-mind', seeking to emphasize by the hyphen in this compound word the monistic identity or inseparableness of the mental and bodily components. (*OED²*, s.v. body, *n.* 30)

6.4.7. Summary of Section 6.4

Through the analyses of the *OED²*, the following examples were collected:

	pre	post
Compound participial *having* PP	65	17
Compound participial *being* PP	95+5	60+9
Simple participial Verb-*ing*	1,627+59	179
Compound gerundive *having* PP	27	1
Compound gerundive *being* PP	29	2
Simple gerundive Verb-*ing*	461+11	9
Total	2,304+75	268+9

Based upon the above evidence, the following points (141a-e), among others, prove to be worthy of mention.

(141) a. The compound participial *having not* PP was used primarily between 1651 and 1750. During 1501-1700, more examples of the compound participial *being not* PP, which occurred mainly during 1501-1750, were evidenced than of *not being* PP.

    b. Many of the examples of the post-position of *not* with the simple participial Verb-*ing* were collected from the documents written in

Chapter VI

1551-1750. Post-positioned *not* concurred primarily with *be, have; know, care, doubt, find; come, hear, like, need* and *see*, verbs which showed aversion to the introduction of the auxiliary *do* in the finite clause. It was used with 33 (53 when the examples with negative intensifiers and *not*-A-*but*-B construction are included) varieties of verbs. These verbs are those which came into the verb category before 1500, except for *act*, the year of the first use of which is 1594 according to the *OED²*.

c. The gerund, whether compound *having/being* PP or simple Verb-*ing*, nearly always adopted the pre-position of *not* perhaps because of its less verbal nature.

d. The post-position of *not* was used by various people including people of nobility such as King, Queen, Earl, Duke, Viscount and Baron, the contributors to the King James's Version of the English Bible, and the upper class such as Lords. It was from the mouths of the aristocracy such as dukes and lords that Shakespeare had this usage uttered. The post-position of *not* was not the usage unique to a certain class, gender, generation or register. As shown later in 6.5, many of the users were affiliated with the University of Cambridge, University of Oxford, Gray's Inn, and Middle Temple, and were men of the cloth and people who left behind a reputation as great men of literature of the times. As far as the birthplaces of the users are concerned, the post-position of *not* was scattered throughout Britain and Ireland.

e. The examples with the post-position of *not* come from not only diaries, letters, literary works and travelogue, but also academic and formal prose in the fields of history, law, philosophy, religion, economics, politics, astronomy, botany, geography, mathematics, medicine, physics and science. Actually, this negative form was employed in various kinds of documents, whether formal or informal, academic or non-academic. The spread of the post-position of *not* structure into varieties of texts implies that it would be unfair to label this construction simply as a vulgar or erroneous usage.

Diachrony of Present Participles and Gerunds Followed by *Not*

6.5. Users of Post-position of *Not* and Nature of the Documents in which its Examples Occurred

With respect to 914+10 examples of participles and gerunds followed by *not*, their users and nature of the documents in which they occurred are elucidated in Section 6.5.

For some examples, however, it was not possible to collect information about their users. As to the citations in the *OED²* in particular, this was a tough task because names of authors and texts have quite a few abbreviations both in the citations and bibliography perhaps to meet the demands of the paper dictionary, and at times they are not listed in the bibliography. However by making extensive use of the *CDNB*, the *ODNB*, the *Britannica*, the *CHEL* and the official websites of reliable organisations and institutions, a large number of names of authors and texts were identified, yet not a few quotations still await identification. This holds true of the examples in Present-day English corpora. Many of them were written in the second half of the 20th century. Nevertheless their writers have not been recorded in reference books or websites above perhaps because they are still active. In spite of all this, however, names of both authors and texts of the majority of examples have been identified.

In the alphabetical list below, the user names of post-position of *not* and the nature of the documents in which its examples occurred are clarified according to the texts and electronic corpora examined: those from the LOB, FLOB, BNC, Brown and Frown dealt with in Section 6.1 are shown in 6.5.1, those from the diaries and correspondence (6.2) in 6.5.2, those from Helsinki-DP, CEECS, Lampeter, Newdigate and ARCHER 3.1 (6.3) in 6.5.3 and those from the *OED²* on CD-ROM (6.4) in 6.5.4. To show the geographical and chronological distribution of the users of post-position of *not* is attempted in 6.5.5, based on their birthplaces.

Each list consists of the user's family name, first name, lifetime, source and square brackets. Square brackets are separated by two vertical lines, on the left of which information on the user and on the right of which the genre or domain of the source is represented. Sources of these pieces of

Chapter VI

information are shown in angle brackets (<...>). With examples collected from diaries and correspondence, information of souces are omitted; they are shown on pp. 377-387. Information on users was limited to birthplaces, educational backgrounds and principal occupations. Even the educated can write ungrammatical or substandard sentences without a sense of style, while the uneducated can write in an ornate, refined and polished style, and therefore levels of education are no criterion of good or bad usage. It is thought, however, that they serve as a reference. Thus the information as to the writers' academic backgrounds and occupations was compiled. A glance over the users of the post-position of *not* indicates that this construction was noticeably employed by the educated, perhaps because, historically, documents written by ordinary citizens may not have been carefully stored.

Abbreviated degrees in the list are represented as follows:

BA: Bachelor of Arts	LLB: Bachelor of Laws
BD: Bachelor of Divility	LLD: Doctor of Laws
BL: Bachelor of Laws	MA: Master of Arts
BSc: Bachelor of Science	MB: Bachelor of Medicine
BTh: Bachelor of Theology	MD/DM: Doctor of Medicine
DCL: Doctor of Civil Law	MSc: Master of Science
DD: Doctor of Divinity	PhD: Doctor of Philosophy
DTh: Doctor of Theology	

6.5.1. LOB, FLOB, BNC; Brown, Frown (Section 6.1)

Out of the five corpora, LOB, FLOB, BNC, Brown and Frown, the post-position of *not* occurs in LOB, FLOB, BNC and Brown.

The example (142) quoted from the LOB is written in the narrative part of a novel by Victoria Gaul. To collect her personal information was beyond the scope of the present author's investigation.

(142) LOB: user unidentified
1961 Gaul, Victoria. [unidentified ‖ Category F (Popular lore), F29, "Ayrshire's Little Castle" run in *Scottish Field* <LOB, "List of Text

Diachrony of Present Participles and Gerunds Followed by *Not*

Samples">; narrative part of a novel]

In the FLOB, the post-position of *not* is used in the narrative part of a novel written by an educated novelist from South Africa.

(143) FLOB: both user and nature of source identified
Jacobson, Dan. *Hidden in the Heart.* [b. Johannesburg, grad. from Witwatersrand University; Professor at University College London, novelist who won the Somerset Maugham Award, etc. <http://litera ture.britishcouncil.org/dan-jacobson> || FLOB K14, narrative part of a novel]

The example in (144) quoted from the BNC is an example of recorded speech. To collect information further than this was beyond the scope of the present author's investigation.

(144) BNC: both user and nature of source unidentified
1992 *31 Conversations Recorded by 'Martine' (PS0LK) between 12 and 20 March 1992 with 10 Interlocutors.* [unidentified || BNC-KD8, recorded speech]

In (145), the nature of the documents are clear, but the users still await identification.

(145) BNC: user unidentified or unclear
1980 Lowerson, John. *A Short History of Sussex.* [unidentified || BNC-CB6, English history book]
1987 Nuttall, Desmons L., Philip S. Clift and Robert McCormick, *Studies in School Self-Evaluation.* [unidentified || BNC-HNW, social science textbook used for Open University]
1988 Batchelor, Mary. *Forty Plus.* [unidentified || BNC-BLW, belief and thought]
1988 Cornwall, J. C. K. *Wealth and Society in Early 16th Century England.* [unidentified || BNC-CTW, history of social science]
1989 Aspel, Michael. *In Good Company.* [unidentified || BNC-CH8, arts]
1989 Field, Frank. *Losing Out: the Emergence of a UK Underclass.* [unidentified || BNC-FAF, social science; the correct title seems

Chapter VI

not to be "... *a UK underclass*" but "... *Britain's Underclass*" according to other references]

1989 *The Guardian, Electronic Edition of 1989-12-10: Foreign News Pages.* [unidentified ‖ BNC-A9J, article on a world affairs section in a newspaper]

1989 *Independent, Electronic Edition of 1989-10-14: Arts Section.* [unidentified ‖ BNC-A5E, article on a arts section in a newspaper]

1990 Maidment, Arthur. *I Remember, I Remember: The Story of My Boyhood in Salisbury.* [unidentified ‖ BNC-B22, autobiography rather than 'leisure', terminology of the compiler]

1990 Farrow, Susan and John Farrow, *Madeira: the Complete Guide.* [unidentified ‖ BNC-CA7, leisure]

1990 Wiat, Philippa. *The Child Bride.* [unidentified ‖ BNC-CCD, narrative part of a novel]

1990, 1991 *Keesings Contemporary Archives.* [unidentified ‖ BNC-HKS, HLB, periodical on world affairs]

1991 Howell, Bette. *Dandelion Days.* [unidentified ‖ BNC-ACK, narrative part of a novel]

1991 Spottiswoode, Jane. *Undertaken with Love.* [unidentified ‖ BNC-CES, biography rather than 'belief and thought', terminology of the compiler]

1991 Vesey, Godfrey. *Inner and Outer* [unidentified ‖ BNC-CK1, essay on belief and thought]

1991 Willock, Colin. *Kingdoms of the East.* [unidentified ‖ BNC-CK2, book on natural sciences]

1991 Urwin, Derek W. *The Community of Europe.* [unidentified ‖ BNC-CLR, world affairs on politics and economy]

1991-1992 *Running.* [unidentified ‖ BNC-CB4, periodical on leisure]

1992 *CD Review.* [unidentified ‖ BNC-BMC, periodical on arts]

1992 Swann, Will, Tony Booth, Mary Masterton and Patricia Potts, ed., *Policies for Diversity in Education.* [unidentified ‖ BNC-CRS, book on social science]

1992 Alexander, Robin J. *Policy and Practice in Primary Education.* [unidentified ‖ BNC-G1F, book on social science]

1992 Elliot, Rachel. *Lover's Charade.* [unidentified ‖ BNC-JY5, narrative part of a novel]

1993 *East Anglian Daily Times.* [unidentified ‖ BNC-CFC, a period-

Diachrony of Present Participles and Gerunds Followed by *Not*

ical on world affairs]

1993 Neil, Barbara. *The Possession of Delia Sutherland*. [unidentified || BNC-FPF, narrative part of a novel]

1993 *Nucleic acids Research* [unidentified || BNC-K5R, periodical on natural sciences]

n.d. Alan, R. N., ed. *Gut: Journal of Gastroenterology and Hepatology*. [unidentified || BNC-HU2, periodical on applied science published by the British Medical Association]

n.d. *Britain and Europe - European Art: Radio Programme*. [unidentified || BNC-KRS, speech recorded in educational context]

n.d. *British Rail Quality Assurance Seminar*. [unidentified || BNC-H47, speech recorded in business context]

n.d. *Computergram International*. [unidentified || BNC-CNM, periodical on applied science]

n.d. *EIP Meeting at Strensall Village Hall, Day 3, Afternoon Session: Public County Council Planning Meeting*. [unidentified || BNC-HVK, speech recorded in public context]

n.d. *Fox FM News: Radio Programme*. [unidentified || BNC-KRT, speech recorded in educational context]

n.d. *Gwynedd County Council Tape 4: Interview for Oral History Project*. [unidentified || BNC-HEM, speech recorded in leisure context]

n.d. *Justice and Peace Group Meeting*. [unidentified || BNC-G3U, speech recorded in business context]

n.d. *Tarmac Construction: Training Session*. [unidentified || BNC-JSA, speech recorded in business context]

In (146), both the users of the post-position of *not* and nature of the documents in which its examples occurs are clear.

(146) BNC: both user and nature of source identified

Cant, Bob and Susan Hemmings, ed., *Radical Records*. [Bob Cant: Scottish journalist and writer, the author of *Footsteps and Witnesses* <http://www.lgbthistoryuk.org/wiki/index.php?title=Bob_Cant>; S. Hemmings: unidentified || social science]

Cookson [*née* Davies], Dame Catherine Ann (1906-1998). *The Rag Nymph*. [b. Durham; writer <*ODNB*> || descriptive part of a novel]

Critchley, Sir Julian Michael Gordon (1930-2000). *The Floating*

Chapter VI

Voter. [b. London; educated at Sorbonne and Oxford; Conservative MP for more than 30 years, supporter of former Prime Minister John Major; although he was wheelchair-bound and only able to write by using a portable word processor while lying on his side, he published many books <http://www.telegraph.co.uk/news/obi tuaries/1354889/Sir-Julian-Critchley.html + *ODNB*> ‖ political science]

Longmate, Norman. *Island Fortress.* [b. Berkshire; educated at Christ's Hospital and read modern history at Oxford; journalist in Fleet Street, producer of history programmes for the BBC, and for the BBC Secretariat, and writer of more than twenty books, mainly on the Second World War and on Victorian social history; Fellow of the Royal Historical Society <http://www.randomhouse.co.uk/ authors/norman-longmate> ‖ history book on world affairs]

Norton, Philip. *The British Polity.* [MA at the University of Sheffield, MA at the University of Pennsylvania, PhD at the University of Sheffield; Professor of Government at the University of Hull, Director of the Centre for Legislative Studies, Chairman of the House of Lords Select Committee on the Constitution, elevated to peerage as 'Lord Norton of Louth <http://www2.hull.ac.uk/fass/politics/staff/ professor-philip-norton.aspx> ‖ book on British political system]

Steele, Jessica. *West of Bohemia.* [b. Warwickshire; popular writer of romance novels <http://www.goodreads.com/book/show/9299588-west-of-bohemia> ‖ narrative part of a novel]

Wilson, Patricia (1929-). *A Healing Fire.* [popular writer of 53 romance novels <http://www.fantasticfiction.co.uk/w/patricia-wilson/> ‖ narrative part of a novel]

Wingrove, David. *Chung Kuo Book One: the Middle Kingdom.* [b. London; BA and MA at the University of Kent; science-fiction writer; <http://www.infinityplus.co.uk/misc/dw.htm> ‖ narrative part of a science fiction]

From the above list in (145)-(146), it seems to be evident that the post-position of *not* is used in academic writings such as books on social science/natural science/philosophy (23 examples) and in writings of the educated (5) as well as in recorded speech and in the narrative sections of novels.

Diachrony of Present Participles and Gerunds Followed by *Not*

6.5.2. Diaries and Correspondence (Section 6.2)

To collect information about the users in (147) was beyond the bounds of the present author's investigation.

(147) Diaries and correspondence: user unidentified
    1673 Ball, Henry. [unidentified ‖ letter]
    1674 Derham, Thomas. [unidentified ‖ letter]
    1714 Jolley, Henry. [Nothing is certain except that Jolley is Gulston Addison (Joseph Addison's brother)'s widow's brother <L17, p. 312, n. 1> ‖ letter]

In (148), however, both the users of the post-position of *not* and nature of the documents in which its examples occurred are clear.

(148) Diaries and correspondence: both user and nature of source identified
    Addison, Joseph (1672-1719). [b. Wiltshire; BA, MA, Fellow, University of Oxford; writer and politician <*ODNB*> ‖ letter]
    Arbuthnot, Harriet (1793-1834). [b. Lincolnshire; daughter of Henry Fane, MP of Fulbeck Hall (son of Thomas Fane, eighth Earl of Westmorland), and Anne, daughter of Edward Buckley Batson, banker; diarist <*ODNB*> ‖ diary]
    Arnold, Matthew (1822-1888). [b. Middlesex; educated at the University of Oxford; poet, writer, and inspector of schools; author of *Essays in Criticism, Culture and Anarchy* <*ODNB*> ‖ letter]
    Bedell, William (bap. 1572-1642). [b. Essex; BA, MA, Fellow, BD, University of Cambridge; Provost, Trinity College, Church of Ireland bishop of Kilmore and Ardagh <L1, p. 135 & n. + *ODNB*> ‖ letter]
    Blake, William (1757-1827). [b. London; studied at Royal Academy of Arts; engraver, artist and poet <*ODNB*> ‖ letter]
    Buxton, Ellen (1848- ?). [b. Leytonstone, then outside London; granddaughter of the leader of the campaign which led to the abolition of slavery <D38, "Introduction"> ‖ diary]
    Carlyle, Thomas (1795-1881). [b. Dumfriesshire; educated at the University of Edinburgh; author, biographer, historian, teacher of mathematics and translator of German literature <*ODNB*> ‖ letter]
    Cheynell, Francis (bap. 1608-1665). [b. Oxford; BA, MA, Fellow,

Chapter VI

BD, DD, University of Oxford; army chaplain and President of St John's College <D5, p. 212 + *ODNB*> ‖ letter in Appendix of D5]

Clare, John (1793-1864). [b. Northamptonshire; poet, farm labourer and naturalist <*ODNB*>] ‖ letter]

Colonel Roe. [little is known except for his name <D5, v> ‖ diary]

Compton, Henry (1631/2-1713). [b. Warwickshire; MA, University of Cambridge, MA, BD, DD, University of Oxford; son of the 2nd Earl of Northampton, court post of dean of the chapels royal, Bishop of Oxford and London <*ODNB*> ‖ letter]

Crabbe, George (1754-1832). [b. Suffolk; poet and Church of England clergyman <*ODNB*> ‖ letter]

Davies, Reverend Rowland (1649-1721) [b. Ireland; BA, MA, LLD, University of Dublin; Dean of Cork and Ross, vicar-general of Cloyne, chaplain to one of William III's regiments <*ODNB*> ‖ diary]

Dee, Dr John (1527-1609). [b. London; BA, MA, University of Cambridge, DD, University of Prague; mathematician, astrologer and antiquary <*ODNB*> ‖ diary]

Defoe, Daniel (1660?-1731). [b. London; writer, businessman; published more than 250 works such as "Robinson Crusoe" and "Moll Flanders" <*ODNB*> ‖ letter]

Dodgson, Charles Lutwidge [*pseud*. 'Lewis Carroll'] (1832-1898). [b. Cheshire; BA, MA, University of Oxford; author, mathematician and photographer who published "Alice's Adventures in Wonderland" and "Through the Looking Glass" under the name of Lewis Carroll, and who published "Euclid and his Modern Rivals" as a mathematician <*ODNB*> ‖ letter]

Dodsley, Robert (1704-1764). [b. Nottinghamshire; bookseller and writer of "Select Collection of Old Plays"; gave Samuel Johnson the idea for *Dictionary of the English Language* (1755) and, in collaboration with five other booksellers, published it <*ODNB*> ‖ letter]

Etherege, Sir George (1636-1691/2). [playwright and diploma; appointed as one of the forty gentlemen of the privy chamber-in-ordinary, who waited on the king, and was made secretary to the newly appointed (and knighted) ambassador to Turkey <*ODNB*> ‖ letter]

Evelyn, John (1620-1706). [b. Surrey; admitted to Middle Temple,

Diachrony of Present Participles and Gerunds Followed by *Not*

awarded a DCL by the University of Oxford; diarist and author of some 30 books on arts, forestry and religious topics; one of the virtuosi who formed the Georgical committee of what became the Royal Society in 1661 *<ODNB + Britannica>* || diary]

Gale, Roger (1672-1744). [b. Cambridgeshire; MA, University of Cambridge; regius professor of Greek at Cambridge and later dean of York, antiquary, the first vice-president of the Society of Antiquaries, treasurer of the Royal Society *<ODNB>* || letter]

Gay, John (1685-1732). [b. Devon; poet and playwright eminent for his *Beggar's Opera* and *Captives <ODNB>* || letter]

Gilpin, William (1724-1804). [b. Cumberland; BA, MA, University of Oxford; writer on art, biographer and headmaster *<ODNB>* || letter]

Glanville, Sir John (1585/6-1661). [Devon; studied at Lincoln's Inn, and called to the bar; DCL, University of Oxford; lawyer, king's serjeant at law and politician *<ODNB>* || voyage journal]

Gray, Thomas (1716-1771). [b. London; studied at Eton Colle; BL, University of Cambridge, educated at the Inner Temple; poet, literary scholar and professor of modern history at the University of Cambridge *<ODNB>* || letter]

Halley, Edmond (1656-1742). [b. London; MA, University of Oxford by command of the king; astronomer, orbit calculator, meteorologist, (geo)physicist, mathematician, on friendly terms with I. Newton, elected to the Royal Society at the age of 22; 'Halley's Comet' derives from his name <D14, Introduction, pp. 16-29 + *ODNB>* || voyage journal]

Hawker, Peter (1786-1853). [b. Hampshire; educated at Eton College; army officer and writer *<ODNB>* || diary]

Hearne, Thomas (bap. 1678-1735). [b. Berkshire; BA, MA, University of Oxford; Bodleian Library assistant, historian, antiquary and diarist; renowned as an editor of medieval chronicles *<Britannica + ODNB>* || letter]

Hewer / Ewers, William (1642-1715). [b. London; Commissioner of the Navy, Samuel Pepys's confidential and life-long friend <L5, 51 & n. 1 + *ODNB>* || letter]

Hoby [*née* Dakins], Margaret, Lady Hoby (bap. 1571-1633). [b. Yorkshire; educated in the household of Henry Hastings, 3rd Earl of

Chapter VI

Huntingdon, president of the council in the north; diarist *<ODNB>* || diary]

Hudson, John (1662-1719). [b. Cumberland; BA, MA, BD, DD, Fellow, University of Oxford; Bodleian Librarian and classical scholar *<ODNB>* || letter]

Huxley, Thomas Henry (1825-1895). [b. London; studied at Charing Cross Hospital, MB, University of London; biologist and science educationist who discovered a new membrane—a single layer of cells next to the human hair follicle, which is called 'Huxley's layer'; Fellow, and later President of the Royal Society *<ODNB>* || voyage journal]

Jackson, John. [Samuel Pepys's nephew and heir <L7, Vol. 2, 373> || letter]

Josselin, Ralph (1617-1683). [b. Essex; BA, MA, University of Cambridge; Church of England clergyman and diarist *<ODNB>* || diary]

Kilvert, Reverend (Robert) Francis (1840-1879). [b. Wiltshire; BA, University of Oxford; diarist; spent his life as a curate and vicar in remote regions of Wiltshire, Radnorshire and Herefordshire *<ODNB + D8, "Introduction", pp. 9-17>* || diary]

King Charles I (1600-1649). [b. Scotland; King of England, Scotland and Ireland *<ODNB>* || letter]

Lowther, John, 1st Viscount Lonsdale (1655-1700) [b. Westmorland; left without taking a degree at Oxford, and then studied at the Inner Temple, from which he was subsequently called to the bar; landowner, politician, vice-chamberlain in the new king's household, a privy councillor, lord lieutenant of Cumberland and Westmorland, and first lord of the Treasury and leader of the House of Commons *<ODNB>* || letter]

Lyttelton / Lit-, Sir Charles, 3rd Baronet (1629-1716). [b. Worcestershire; colonial governor, politician and governorship of Jamaica while it was a colony *<ODNB + L3, Vol. 1, pp. 11-12, 29>* || letter]

Macmillan, (Maurice) Harold, 1st Earl of Stockton (1894-1986). [b. London; studied at Eton Colle, matriculated at the University of Oxford but prevented from taking Greats because of his war service; prime minister *<ODNB>* || diary]

Milward, John. (1599-1670) [b. Derbyshire; parliamentary diarist;

Diachrony of Present Participles and Gerunds Followed by *Not*

commanded a foot regiment in the marquess of Newcastle's royalist army during the civil war <*ODNB*> ‖ diary]

Montagu, Charles, Earl of Halifax (1661-1715). [b. Northamptonshire; BA, MA, Fellow, University of Cambridge; politician <*ODNB*> ‖ letter]

Montagu / Mount-, Edward, 1st Earl of Sandwich (1625-1672). [b. Northamptonshire; aged ten, he was entered in the books of the Middle Temple, but never studied there; army and naval officer, diplomat and knight of the Garter <*ODNB*> ‖ letter]

More, Hannah (1745-1833). [b. near Bristol; writer and philanthropist <*ODNB*> ‖ letter]

Nicolson, William (1655-1727). [b. Cumberland; BA, MA, Fellow, University of Oxford; Church of Ireland bishop of Carlisle and Derry, antiquary <*ODNB*> ‖ diary]

Palmer, Samuel (1805-1881). [b. London; landscape painter and etcher <*ODNB*> ‖ letter]

Pelham, Thomas, 1st Duke of Newcastle upon Tyne and 1st duke of Newcastle under Lyme [Holles, Thomas Pelham-] (1693-1768). [b. Sussex; matriculated at the University of Cambridge but left before taking a degree; lord privy seal and prime minister, <*ODNB* + L22, xxxvii-xxxix*> ‖ letter]

Penrose, John (1713-1776). [b. Exeter; BA, University of Oxford; letter writer and Church of England clergyman <*ODNB*> ‖ letter]

Pepys, Samuel (1633-1703). [b. London; BA, MA, University of Cambridge; naval administrator, diarist and President of the Royal Society <*ODNB* + *Britannica*> ‖ diary, letter]

Pope, Alexander (1688-1744). [b. London; being invalid, educated in the hands of relatives and Catholic priests; poet, critic and religious humanist; establised the heroic couplet; eminent as the writer of *An Essay on Criticism* and *Rape of the Lock*, and as a translator of Homer's *Iliad* and *Odyssea* <*ODNB*> ‖ letter]

Porteus, Beilby (1731-1809). [b. York; BA, Fellow, DD, University of Cambridge; Bishop of Chester and London <*ODNB* + http://www.porteous.org.uk/beilby_porteus.html> ‖ letter]

Povey, Thomas (1613/4-*c*1705). [entered Gray's Inn; colonial entrepreneur and administrator <*ODNB* + L8, Vol. 2, p. 6 & n. 2> ‖ letter]

Chapter VI

Princess of Wales [= Princess Caroline of Brunswick-Wolfenbüttel] (1768-1821). [b. Brunswick; Queen of the United Kingdom of Great Britain and Ireland; consort of George IV <*ODNB*> || letter]

Ray / Wray, John (1627-1705). [b. Essex; BA, Fellow, MA, University of Cambridge; leading 17th-century English naturalist and botanist; theologian; Greek, mathematical and humanities lecturer at the University of Cambridge <*ODNB* + *Britannica*> || letter]

Rous, John (bap. 1584-1644). [b. Suffolk; BA, MA, University of Cambridge; diarist and Church of England clergyman <*ODNB*> || diary]

Ruskin, John James (1819-1900). [b. London; MA, University of Oxford; art critic and social critic <*ODNB*> || letter]

Savile, Henry (1642-1687). [b. Nottinghamshire; courtier and diplomat <*ODNB*> || letter]

Shenstone, William (1714-1763). [b. Shropshire; listed as a BA, University of Oxford, never claiming to have a degree; writer <*ODNB*> || letter]

Skinner, Peter. [son of Francis Skinner, whose sister married Lord Francis Butler of Wood Hal <D11, 89 & n. 1, 149 & n. 2> || letter]

Spender, Sir Stephen Harold (1909-1995). [b. London; poet, novelist and essayist <*ODNB*> || diary]

St. Michel, Balthasar. [Samuel Pepys's wife's brother, whose father is Alexandre le Marchant de St Michel, a French man of nobility <http://www.historytoday.com/richard-cavendish/pepys%E2%80%99s-marriage-elizabeth-de-st-michel; L6, 60> || letter]

Steele, Sir Richard (bap. 1672-1729). [b. Dublin; went up to Oxford but left without a degree; politician and writer who issued *Tatler* and *Spectator* <*ODNB*> || letter]

Stevens, William Bagshaw (1756-1800). [b. Berkshire; BA, Fellow (and MA, DD <*CDNB*>), University of Oxford; poet and diarist <*ODNB*> || diary]

Strype, John (1643-1737) [b. London; BA, MA, University of Cambridge; historian and biographer; editor of voluminous narratives and biographies of the Tudor period <*ODNB*> || letter]

Swift, Jonathan (1667-1745). [b. Dublin; BA, University of Dublin; writer and dean of St Patrick's Cathedral, Dublin; as a satirist, Swift has no equal in English literature for range, subtlety and power; J.

Diachrony of Present Participles and Gerunds Followed by *Not*

Dryden's cousin *<ODNB + Britannica>* ‖ letter]

Symonds, Richard (bap. 1617-1660). [b. Essex; royalist soldier and antiquary *<ODNB>* ‖ diary]

Talbot, Gilbert [ambassador to Denmark, M. P. for Plymouth, Master of the Jewel Office, courtier and knight <L8, II, 68 & n. 1> ‖ letter]

Tennyson, Alfred, 1st Baron Tennyson (1809-1892). [b. Lincolnshire; entered the University of Cambridge, but left without taking a degree; poet renowned for his "In Memoriam" and "Enoch Arden" *<ODNB>* ‖ letter]

Todd, Matthew (1791-1853). [b. Yorkshire; traveller <D31, 2-7> ‖ diary]

Wanley, Humfrey (1672-1726). [b. Coventry; Old English scholar, Bodleian librarian, antiquary and member of the F.S.A. *<ODNB>* ‖ letter]

Wedgwood, Josiah (1730-1795). [b. Staffordshire; master potter, fellow of the Royal Society and member of the F.S.A. *<ODNB>* ‖ letter]

Wesley / West-, John (1703-1791). [b. Lincolnshire; BA, Fellow, MA, University of Oxford; Church of England clergyman and a founder of Methodism *<ODNB>* ‖ diary, letter]

Woodforde, James (1740-1803). [b. Somerset; BA, MA, BD, University of Oxford; diarist and Church of England clergyman *<ODNB>* ‖ diary]

Wordsworth, Dorothy (1771-1855). [b. Cumberland; writer; William Wordsworth's sister *<ODNB>* ‖ diary, letter]

Yard, Robert (*c*1651-1705). [administrator and editor of the *London Gazette <ODNB>* ‖ letter]

From the list in (148) above, it seems to be evident that the postposition of *not* was used not only by people who were reputed as great men of literature of the times but also by King Charles I, Princess Caroline, and seven men of nobility such as earls and a duke. The list also indicates that 36 out of 72 persons graduated from the University of Cambridge, University of Oxford, Gray's Inn and/or Middle Temple, and that 16 out of 72 were men of the cloth who used High Church English.

Chapter VI

6.5.3. Helsinki Corpus (Diachronic Part), CEECS, Lampeter, Newdigate, ARCHER 3.1 (Section 6.3)

In this section, information on users of the post-position of *not* and the nature of the documents in which this negative form occurred in Helsinki-DP, CEECS, Lampeter, Newdigate and ARCHER 3.1 is presented. Information about previously mentioned people such as M. Hoby, S. Pepys and J. Strype is not repeated.

It was next to impossible to gather information on the writers of the post-position of *not* in the Newdigate, which is "valuable as primary-document sources, with much matter of intrinsic interest on the Stuart courts and those of most of Europe; on social, diplomatic, and military history; parliamentary news; commercial and maritime relations, particularly those with the colonies in North America and the Indies, West and East" (Introduction to the Newdigate). Even though it is speculated that the senders were respected people since most of the letters were addressed to Sir R. Newdigate, Warwickshire, information about them has not been collected, and accordingly the user information is not shown.

As with the examples in (149), to collect personal information of the writers was beyond the bounds of the present author's investigation.

(149) Five electronic corpora: user unidentified

    a. Helsinki-DP

        1444 Bolton, John. "Petition concerning the Murder of Isabell, Wife of Roger Bakeler". [unidentified || petition]

        1570-1640 (EModE II), *The Statutes of the Realm.* [unidentified || collection of English parliamentary acts until 1707]

        1612 Coverte, Robert. *A Trve and Almost Incredible Report of an Englishman That Travelled by Land Throw Many Unknowne Kingdomes.* [unidentified || travelogue]

    b. CEECS

        1471? Wadehill, Annys. (CEECS STONOR) [unidentified || letter]

        1497 Plumpton, Edward. (CEECS PLUMPTON) [unidentified || letter]

        1614, 1624 Bacon, Nathaniel. (CEECS CORNWALL) [uniden-

Diachrony of Present Participles and Gerunds Followed by *Not*

tified || letter]

1624 Naylor, Oliver. (CEECS COSIN) [unidentified || letter]

c. Lampeter

1643 Foster, Henry. *A True and Exact Relation of the Marchings of the Two Regiments of the Trained Bands of the City of London [...] As Also of the Three Regiments of the Auxiliary Forces [...] Who Marched Forth for the Reliefe of the City of Glocester [...].* [unidentified || tract on defence]

1646 Commissioners of the Navy. *The Answer of the Commissioners of the Navie, to a Scandalous Pamphlet, Published by Mr. Andrewes Burrell.* [Commissioner of the Navy, but unidentified || proclamation]

1652 Anon. *The Advocate.* [ananymous || economics/trade]

1659 Anon. *England's Safety in the Laws Supremacy.* [anonymous || law]

1668 Anon. *The Tryals of Such Persons as under the Motion of London-Apprentices Were Tumultuously Assembled [...].* [anonymous || law]

1676 B., A. *A Letter of Advice concerning Marriage.* [unidentified || essay]

1678 Anon. *An Exact Account of the Trials of the Several Persons Arraigned at the Sessions-House in the Old-Bailey for London and Middlesex [...].* [anonymous || law]

1681 Anon. *The Trade of England Revived: And the Abuses Thereof Rectified, [...].* [anonymous || economis/trade]

1697 Anon. *A Letter to a Friend, In Vindication of the Proceedings against Sir John Fenwick, by Bill of Attainder. [...].* [anonymous || letter on law]

1698 Alingham, William. *A Short Account of the Nature and Use of Maps.* [unidentified || science (geography)]

1703 [Hore, Charles et al.] *A True and Exact Account of Many Great Abuses Committed in the Victualling Her Majesties Navy [...].* [unidentified || law]

1708 Waller, John. *Religion and Loyalty, or the Reverence Due Both to Church and State, Asserted in a Sermon, [...].* [unidentified || religion]

Chapter VI

1712 Guybon, Francis. *An Essay concerning the Growth of Empiricism; or the Encouragement of Quacks. [...].* [unidentified ‖ medical science]

1714 B., R. *Longitude to be Found out with a New Invented Instrument, Both by Sea and Land [...].* [Nothing known except that the writer is a secretary to Francis Wheeler ‖ science (geography)]

1731 Davies, Joseph. *An Humble Proposal for the Increase of Our Home Trade, and a Defence to Gibraltar [...].* unidentified ‖ economics/trade]

d. ARCHER 3.1

ARCHER 3.1 1674ano1.s2b, anon., *Brief Directions on How to Tan Leather.* [anonymous ‖ science (tanning)]

ARCHER 3.1 1687ferr.j2b, Richard Ferrier, *Journal of Major Richard Ferrier.* [Nothing known except that the writer is a major ‖ diary]

ARCHER 3.1 1697pos2.n2b, *The Post Man and Historical Account.* [unidentified ‖ news]

ARCHER 3.1 1702anon.f3b, Anon., *The Adventures of Lindamira, A Lady of Quality.* [anonymous ‖ conversational part of a fiction]

ARCHER 3.1 1722cay-.s3b, Robert Cay, "An Account of the Manner of Bending Planks in his Majesty's Yard". [unidentified ‖ article in the *Philosophical Transactions*, the oldest scientific journal in the world <https://arts.st-andrews.ac.uk/philosophicaltransactions/brief-history-of-phil-trans/>]

ARCHER 3.1 1735rea2.n3b, *Read's Weekly Journal or British Gazetteer*, No. 531 [unidentified ‖ weekly journal]

ARCHER 3.1 1743lon1.n3b, *The London Gazette.* [unidentified ‖ the UK's official public record since 1665]

ARCHER 3.1 1827whit.j5b, Thomas Whitwell, *A Darlington Schoolboy's Diary.* [unidentified ‖ diary]

ARCHER 3.1 1864wats.m6b, James Watson, "Observations on Some New Remedies", *Edinburgh Medical Journal* 9. [unidentified ‖ medical journal]

With the examples in (150), however, both the users of the postposition of *not* and nature of the documents in which its examples occur are clear.

Diachrony of Present Participles and Gerunds Followed by *Not*

(150) Five electronic corpora: both user and nature of source identified

a. Helsinki-DP

Armin, Robert (1563-1615). *A Nest of Ninnies*. [b. Norfolk; actor and comic writer *<ODNB>* || novel]

Fox, George (1624-1691). *The Journal of George Fox*. [b. Leicestershire; founder of the Religious Society of Friends (Quakers) *<ODNB>* || journal posthumously published in 1694, 3 years after Fox's death, revised by the committee under the supervision of W. Penn *<ODNB>*]

Fryer / Fryar / Friar, John (d. 1733). *A New Account of East India and Persia*. [b. London; MB, MD, University of Cambridge; traveller, writer and fellow of the Royal Society *<ODNB>* || account of travels]

Hooker, Richard (1554-1600). *Of the Lawes of Ecclesiasticall Politie; the Sixth and Eighth Books ... Now Published According to the Most Authentique Copies*; "Two Sermons upon Part of S. Judes Epistle" [b. Exeter; MA, Fellow, University of Oxford; deputy professor of Hebrew, University of Oxford, theologian and philosopher *<ODNB>* || theological treatise; sermon]

Mountain / Mowntayne, Thomas (*c*1520-1573). *The Autobiography of Thomas Mowntayne*. [MA, University of Cambridge; religious activist *<ODNB>* || autobiography]

Oxinden / Oxen-, Henry (1609-1670) in *The Oxinden and Peyton Letters*. [b. Canterbury; BA, University of Oxford; admitted to Gray's Inn; gentry and 'letter-writer' *<ODNB>* || letter]

b. CEECS

Cosin, Bishop John (1595-1672). [b. Norwich; BA, MA, Fellow, BD, DD, Master of Peterhouse, University of Cambridge; Dean of Peterborough and Bishop of Durham *<ODNB>* || letter]

Dudley, Robert, 1st Earl of Leicester (1532/3-1588). [son of Duke of Northumberland, courtier and magnate, Queen Elizabeth's favourite, High Steward of ten boroughs and Chancellor of the University of Oxford *<ODNB>* || letter]

Fleetwood / Fletewoode, William (*c*1525-1594). [b. Lancashire; his name appears in the admissions register of the University of Oxford but he did not take a degree; educated at Middle Temple and

Chapter VI

was called to the bar; lawyer, recorder of London and antiquary <*ODNB*> ‖ letter]

Foster, Sir John (c1515-1602). [b. Northumberland; administrator and soldier <*ODNB*> ‖ letter]

Harley [*née* Conway], Brilliana, Lady Harley (bap. 1598-1643). [b. Netherlands with British parents; parliamentarian gentlewoman and letter-writer <*ODNB*> ‖ letter]

Hutton, Matthew (1529?-1606). [b. Lancashire; BA, MA, Fellow, BD, DD; Master of Pembroke Hall, regius professor of divinity, University of Cambridge; Dean of York <*ODNB*> ‖ letter]

Jones, John (c1597-1660). [parliamentarian army officer and regicide; he was a regularly attending commissioner at the trial of Charles I, and signed the King's death warrant <*ODNB*> ‖ letter]

King Charles II (1630-1685). [b. London; King of England, Scotland and Ireland <*ODNB*> ‖ letter]

Matthew, Tobie. (1544?-1628) [b. Bristol; BA, MA, BTh, DTh, University of Oxford; Dean and Bishop of Durham, and Archbishop of York <*ODNB*> ‖ letter]

Mountague / Montagu, Richard (bap. 1575-1641). [b. Buckinghamshire; BA, MA, BD, University of Cambridge; chaplain to James I, Bishop of Norwich, religious controversialist <*ODNB*> ‖ letter; religious treatise *Diatribæ on the First Part of the 'Late History of Tithes'*]

Queen Elizabeth I (1533-1603). [b. Kent; Queen of England and Ireland <*ODNB*> ‖ letter]

Walsingham (-syng-), Sir Francis (c1532-1590). [b. London or Kent; went up to the University of Cambridge but left without a degree; admitted to Gray's Inn; principal secretary and politician <*ODNB*> ‖ letter]

c. Lampeter

[Assheton, William (bap. 1642-1711).] *The Royal Apologie: or, an Answer to the Rebels Plea [...]*. [b. Lancashire; BA, MA, BD, DD, University of Oxford; Church of England clergyman <*ODNB*> ‖ politics]

Boyle, Robert (1627-1691). *Experiments and Considerations about the Porosity of Bodies, in Two Essays.* [b. Ireland; studied at Eton College, then tutored by a clergyman; natural philosopher and

Diachrony of Present Participles and Gerunds Followed by Not

chemist; published papers on physico-chemistry, morality and religion; leading member for the foundation of the Royal Society <*ODNB*> || medical science]

Charleton, Walter (1620-1707). *Three Anatomic Lectures, concerning 1. The Motion of the Bloud through the Veins and Arteries; [...].* [b. Somerset; DM, University of Oxford; physician-in-ordinary to Charles I and Charles II, and natural philosopher; published books on physiology, philosophy and antiquity <*ODNB*> || medical science]

Cook, Captain James (1728-1779). *A Voyage towards the South Pole and round the World in 1772-85.* [b. Yorkshire; explorer <*ODNB*> || voyage journal; the year "1772-85" should be modified into "1772-1775"]

Cook, John (bap. 1608-1660). *A True Relation of Mr. Iohn Cook's Passage by Sea from Wexford to Kinsale in That Great Storm [...].* [b. Leicestershire; went up to the University of Oxford but left without a degree; admitted to Gray's Inn; judge and regicide <*ODNB*> || religious tract, though the title may sound of a voyage journal]

Guidott, Thomas (1638?-1706). *A Discourse of Bathe, and the Hot Waters There. Also, Some Enquiries into the Nature of the Water [...].* [b. Hampshire; BA, MA, MB, University of Oxford; physician and writer <*ODNB*> || medical science]

[Hammond, Henry (1605-1660).] *Of Scandall [...].* [b. Surrey; BA, MA, Fellow, BD, DD, University of Oxford; Church of England clergyman and theologian, chaplain to James I, and Archdeacon of Chichester <*ODNB*> || religious tract]

Hare, Francis (1671-1740). *Scripture Vindicated from the Misinterpretations of the Lord Bishop of Bangor: [...].* [b. London; BA, Fellow, MA, DD, University of Cambridge; canon-residentiary of St Paul's and prebendary of Portpool in St Paul's Cathedral, and Bishop of Chichester <*ODNB*> || religious tract]

Hawles, Sir John (bap. 1645-1716). *The English-mans Right. A Dialogue between a Barrister at Law and a Jury-man. [...].* [b. Wiltshire; matriculated at the University of Oxford, and entered Lincoln's Inn, being called to the bar; lawyer and politician <*ODNB*> || frequently republished book on law]

Chapter VI

Henley, John (1692-1756). *Light in a Candlestick, to All that Are in the House: Or, the Impartial Churchman [...].* [b. Leicestershire; BA, MA, University of Cambridge; dissenting minister and eccentric; published books on eloquence, theology and grammar <*ODNB*> || religion]

Hody, Humphrey (1659-1707). *A Letter from Mr. Humphrey Hody [...] concerning a Collection of Canons Said to Be Deceitfully Omitted in His Edition of the Oxford Treatise against Schism [...].* [b. Somerset; BA, MA, BD, DD, Fellow, University of Oxford; Church of England clergyman and classical scholar, regius professor of Greek, University of Oxford <*ODNB*> || letter]

Holland, Richard (1596-1677). *Globe Notes.* [b. Lincoln; educated at Oxford, but appears not to have taken a degree; teacher of mathematics and geography at the University of Oxford <*ODNB*> || science (astronomy)]

Hookc, Robert (1635-1703). *An Attempt to Prove the Motion of the Earth by Observation.* [b. Isle of Wight; MA, University of Oxford (BA was not conferred); professor of geometry, University of Oxford; natural philosopher, Fellow of the Royal Society and inventor of wheel barameter <*ODNB*> || science (geophysics)]

Jones, Henry (1605-1682). *A Sermon of Antichrist, Preached at Christ-Church, Dublin. Novemb. 12. 1676.* [b. Ireland; BA, MA, Fellow, University of Dublin; Church of Ireland bishop of Meath <*ODNB*> || religion]

Mead, Richard (1673-1754). *A Short Discourse concerning Pestilential Contagion and the Methods Used to Prevent It.* [b. Middlesex; studied medicine at the University of Leiden; MD, University of Padua, DM, University of Oxford; physician to George II and collector of books and art; Fellow, Council and Vice-president of the Royal Society <*ODNB*> || medical science (prevention of epidemics)]

North, Francis, 1st Baron Guilford (1637-1685). *An Argument of a Learned Judge in the Exchequer-Chamber upon a Writ of Error [...].* [b. Cumberland; went up to the University of Cambridge, but left without a degree; began his legal education in the Middle Temple, and later was called to the bar; judge, politician and Lord Keeper of the Privy Seal <*ODNB*> || law]

Diachrony of Present Participles and Gerunds Followed by *Not*

[Owen, John (1616-1683).] *Indulgence and Toleration Considered: in a Letter unto a Person of Honour.* [b. Oxfordshire; BA, MA, DD, University of Oxford; theologian and Independent minister; Dean of Christ Church and Vice-chancellor, University of Oxford <*ODNB*> || anonymously published booklet advocating freedom of religion]

[Pollexfen, John (1636-1715).] *England and East India Inconsistent in Their Manufactures.* [b. Devon; merchant and political economist <*ODNB*> || economics/trade]

Prynne, William (1600-1669). *A Legall Vindication of the Liberties of England [...].* [b. Somerset; BA, Oxford; admitted to Lincoln's Inn and called to the bar; pamphleteer and lawyer <*ODNB*> || law]

[Settle, Elkanah (1648-1724).] *The Scond Part of the Notorious Impostor, Compleating the History of the Life, Cheats, &c. of William Morrell, alias Bowyer, Sometime of Banbury, Chirurgeon [...].* [b. Hertfordshire; left the University of Oxford without finishing his degree; playwright <*ODNB* + http://www.theodora.com/encyclopedia/s/elkanah_settle.html> || biography]

Sherlock, Richard (1612-1689). *A Sermon Preached at a Visitation, Held at Warrington in Lancashire May 11, 1669.* [b. Cheshire; MA, University of Dublin; Church of England clergyman <*ODNB*> || religion (sermon)]

Wallis, John (1616-1703). "An Essay of Dr. John Wallis, Exhibiting His Hypothesis about the Flux and Reflux of the Sea [...]". [b. Kent; BA, MA, University of Cambridge, MA, DD, University of Oxford; mathematician and cryptographer, Savilian professor of geometry, University of Oxford; published a grammar book; leading member of the foundation of the Royal Society <*ODNB*> || article running in *Philosophical Transactions*, the oldest scientific journal in the world]

d. ARCHER 3.1

Briggs, William (*c*1650-1704). "Two Remarkable Cases Relating to Vision", *Philosophical Transactions* 159, ARCHER 3.1 1684 brig. m2b [b. Norwich; BA, MA, MD, University of Cambridge; physician and oculist; physician-in-ordinary to William III <*ODNB*> ||

Chapter VI

medical article running in *Philosophical Transactions*, the oldest
scientific journal in the world]

Bulteel, John (1627-*c*1692). ARCHER 3.1 1664bult.f2b. [writer and
translator *<ODNB>* || fiction]

*Conway Letters: The Correspondence of Anne Viscountess Conway
Henry More and Their Friends*, ARCHER 3.1 1678more.x2b
[Anne Conway [*née* Finch], Viscountess Conway and Killultagh
(1631-1679): philosopher, daughter of Lord Heneage Finch, and
former speaker of the House of Commons *<ODNB>* || letter]

Davys, Mary (1674-1732). "The Accomplished Rake; or Modern
Fine Gentleman", ARCHER 3.1 1727davy.f3b [b. Ireland; novel-
ist and playwright *<ODNB>* || narrative part of a fiction]

Fenton, Richard (1747-1821), in J. Fisher, ed., *Tours in Wales*,
ARCHER 3.1 1809fent.j5b [b. Pembrokeshire; went up to the
University of Oxford, but left without a degree; began his legal
education in the Middle Temple, and later was called to the bar;
topographical writer and antiquary *<ODNB>* || travelogue]

Radcliffe [*née* Ward], Ann (1764-1823). *The Romance of the Forest*,
ARCHER 3.1 1791radc.f4b [b. London; pioneer of gothic novels
eminent for her *The Mysteries of Udolpho* and *The Italian <ODNB*
+ http://www.goodreads.com/author/show/43220.Ann_Radcliffe>
|| narrative part of a fiction]

Reeve, Clara (1729-1807). *The Old English Baron: A Gothic Story*,
ARCHER 3.1 1778reev.f4b [b. Suffolk; novelist and poet *<ODNB>*
|| narrative part of a fiction]

Stukeley, William (1687-1765). *Diary, in The Family Memoirs of
the Rev. William Stukeley M.D, etc.*, ARCHER 3.1 1720stuk.j3b
[b. Lincolnshire; MB, MD, University of Cambridge; antiquary,
natural philosopher, Fellow of the Royal Society and Fellow of
the Royal College of Physicians *<ODNB>* || diary]

The list in (149) and (150) indicates that, in terms of the nature of
sources, the post-position of *not* has been encountered even in official and
academic documents such as *Philological Transactions* (the oldest scientific journal in the world), *Edinburgh Medical Journal*, *The London Gazette*
(the UK's official public record since 1665) and books and articles in the
fields of astronomy, geography, jurisprudence, medicine, physics, politics

Diachrony of Present Participles and Gerunds Followed by *Not*

and religion. The list also shows that, in respect to the users, this negative form was used by the educated (4 / 5 / 17 / 3 examples in Helsinki-DP / CEECS / Lampeter / ARCHER 3.1) and men of the cloth (3 / 3 / 7 in Helsinki-DP / CEECS / Lampeter). In the CEECS, examples written by King Charles II and Queen Elizabeth I are evidenced. Six examples are used in novels. Two of them appear in conversation, which may remind one of rhetorical colouring of character's speech. Four of them, however, appear in narrative parts of novels.

6.5.4. *OED²* on CD-ROM (Section 6.4)

Sources of *OED²*'s quotations are usually specified in the beginning of citations. As stated already, however, sources have quite a few abbreviations both in the citations and bibliography sections perhaps to meet the demands as the paper dictionary, and at times the sources are not listed in the bibliography. The present section enquires into the users of the postposition of *not* in the *OED²* and the nature of the documents in which this negative form occurred. Information regarding previously mentioned people is not repeated.

First, examples in (151) represent the cases in which both the users and the nature of sources are unidentified.

(151) *OED²*: both user and nature of source unidentified

c1475 *Harl. Contin. Higden* (Rolls). [The abbreviated title appears to have the closest resemblance to "*Higden's Polychronicon* tr. 1432-50 (Rolls series 1865–86)". As the year of publication is different between the two sources, however, the correct source of the example of "*c*1475 *Harl. Contin. Higden* (Rolls)" is still unclear as is the writer.]

1523 Wolsey, in *State Papers Henry the Eighth*. ["St. Papers Hen. VIII", from which 544 citations are quoted in the *OED²*, seem to be official government documents; the details are unknown nonetheless, including the writer.]

1635 Jackson, *Creed*. [As this text is not recorded in the *OED²*'s Bibliography, to collect information regarding the user and nature of source is impossible.]

Chapter VI

*a*1617 Daniel, *To Sir T. Egerton.* [Though eight citations from letters written by 'Daniel' addressed to T. Egerton are quoted in the *OED²*, both 'Daniel' and source of text are unidentifiable.]

1632, 1635 Hayward, James. *Biondi's Eromena; or Love and Revenge* tr. 1632; *Biondi's Donzella Desterrada; or the Banish'd Virgin* tr. 1635. [No information regarding 'James Hayward' as a translator nor 'Biondi' as a writer nor titles of these translations have been collected from references nor websites.]

1641 Abp. John Williams, *Sp.* in *Apol. Bishops.* [Under 'Williams, Abp. John' nor 'Williams, Bp. John' nor three other persons under the name of 'Williams, John' in the *OED²*'s Bibliography, texts the abbreviated titles of which are '*Sp.*' or '*Apol. Bishops*' are not listed. Referring to the *ODNB*, the writer is most plausibly John Williams (1582-1650) [b. Wales; BA, MA, BD, DD, University of Cambridge; Archbishop of York]. With careful deliberation, however, this example was classified into (151) 'both user and nature of source unidentified'.]

1653 Baxter, *Chr. Concord.* [Works cited of seven persons under the name of "Baxter" in the *OED²*'s Bibliography do not include the above title or its similar title. The writer could be 'Richard Baxter', but this example was also classified into (151) as the reference to '*Chr(istian?) Concord*' cannot be encountered in the entry word 'Richard Baxter' in the *ODNB*.]

1696 P. Ventris, *Reports.* [Entry word "ventris, Edward" is positioned (between 'Fish, Simon' and 'Fisher, James' for unknown reasons) in the *OED²*'s Bibliography, but the heading 'Ventris, P.' is not itemised. In other citations, simply 'Ventris' is written as the author's name. Thus, the writer and source of text are both unidentified.]

1697 *C'tess D'Aunoy's Trav* tr. ['C'tess D'Aunoy', the writer of the original text, is thought to be Marie-Catherine Le Jumel de Barneville, Countess d'Au(l)noya, Freanch writer <*Britannica*>, but not merely the English translator but also nature of the text is unclear.]

1705 C. Purshall, *Mech. Macrocosm.* [This writer and text is not listed in the *OED²*'s Bibliography. No information has been collected from references nor websites.]

1857 Mrs. Gaskell *Let.* [Four persons of the name of 'Gaskell' are listed in the *OED²*'s Bibliography, but no useful information re-

Diachrony of Present Participles and Gerunds Followed by *Not*

garding the user and source has been collected from the list.]

1876 Mrs. Oliphant. [Eight citations are quoted from *Curate in Charge*, where the writer is simply "Mrs. Oliphant" and her first name is missing. There are two entries of the name of 'Oliphant' in the *OED²*'s Bibliography, but the list of their works cited does not include *Curate in Charge*. Thus, no information regarding this writer and source of her text has been collected from the *OED²* nor websites.]

1895 J. Denney, *Stud. Theol.* ['Denney' is not recorded in the *OED²*'s Bibliography. No relevant information regarding this writer and source has been collected from references nor websites.]

1945 *Mind* LIV. [No information regarding the writer and source has been collected from the *OED²*'s Bibliography nor websites.]

Regarding examples in (152), to collect the writers' personal information was beyond the bounds of the present author's investigation.

(152) *OED²* on CD-ROM: user unidentified

1344 *Act 18 Edw. III.* [unidentified ‖ English parliamentary legislation]

1523 Wolsey, in *State Papers* (during the Reign of) *Henry the Eighth.* [unidentified ‖ governmental official document]

c1530 More in Bishop John Fisher's *English Works.* [unidentified ‖ document written by a person named 'More' recorded in the works of Bp J. Fisher, BA, MA, University of Cambridge, Bishop of Rochester and cardinal <*ODNB*>]

1531-2 *Act 23 Hen. VIII* [unidentified ‖ English parliamentary legislation]

1540 Marsden, Reginald G., ed. *Select Pleas in the Court of Amiralty.* [unidentified ‖ pleas at a nautical court]

1546 *State Papers* (during the Reign of) *Henry the Eighth.* [unidentified ‖ governmental official document]

1562 *Act 5 Eliz.* [unidentified ‖ English parliamentary legislation]

1564 Sparke in Sir John Hawkins, *The (second) Voyage Made to the Coast of Guinea and the Indies of Nova Spania, Begun in 1564* (signed at end Iohn Sparke). [unidentified ‖ This text is a voyage journal. Whether the post-position of *not* was used in a narrative

Chapter VI

part or a dialogue or a quotation is unknown.]

1565-6 *Child-Marriages, Divorces, and Ratifications etc. in the Diocese of Chester, A.D. 1561-6.* (EETS OS) [unidentified || records of testimony at a court of law]

1582 Lichefield, Nicholas. *Lopez de Castanheda's First Booke of the Historie of the Discoverie and Conquest of the East Indias* tr. [unidentified || English translation of a book on politico-economics]

1582 *Rheims. The New Testament,* tr. in the English college of Rhemes. [unidentified || English translation of the Holy Bible]

1585 Washington, Thomas. *Nicolay's (N. de) Nauigations into Turkie* tr. [unidentified || English translation of travelogue; a discrepancy of the title of source is detected between the citation ('*Voy.*') and the Bibliography ('*Nauigations*').]

1606 Nichols, John. *The Progresses, Processions and Magnificent Festivities of K. James the First.* [unidentified || treatise on the King James I's reign]

1617 Pepwell, Capt. H. in *Lett. East India Company.* [unidentified || letter]

1625 Foster, William, ed. *The English Factories in India, a Calendar of Documents in the India Office, British Museum and Public Record Office.* [William Foster was an eminent historiographer who lived in the 19th-20th centuries. The user of the post-position of *not* in this early 17th-century example is unidentified. || book on historical politico-economics]

1653 G., R. *Bacon's Naturall and Experimentall History of Winds* etc. tr. [unidentified; simply written as 'G., R.' in the *OED²*'s Bibliography || English translation of Francis Bacon's Latin book on natural history]

1684 G., H. *Scanderbeg Redivivus, an Historical Account of the Life of .. John III, King of Poland.* [unidentified; simply written as 'G., H.' in the *OED²*'s Bibliography || book on Polish history]

1695 Preston, Viscount Richard Graham. *A. M. S. Boethius of the Consolation of Philosophy* tr. [unidentified except for his being a viscount || English translation of a Boethius' Latin book on philosophy entitled *De Consolatione Philosophiæ*]

1726 Leoni, James. *The Architecture of L. B. Alberti in Ten Books. Of Painting, in Three Books. And of Statuary, in One Book* tr. [uniden-

Diachrony of Present Participles and Gerunds Followed by *Not*

tified || English translation of a book on arts]

1728 Rutty in *Philosophical transactions of the Royal Society*. [The writer is assumed to be either John Rutty (1698-1775; b. Wiltshire; MD, University of Leiden; physician *<ODNB>*), or his cousin William Rutty (1687-1730; b. London; MB, MD, University of Cambridge; renowned physician, Fellow and Secretary of the Royal Society). To be precise, however, this example was classified into 152) 'user unidentified' || article in the *Philosophical Transactions*, the oldest scientific journal in the world]

1747 *Gentl. Mag.* [unidentified || monthly journal published in London between 1731 and 1907 <http://onlinebooks.library.upenn.edu/webbin/serial?id=gentlemans>]

1753 Torriano, N. *An Historical Dissertation on a Particular Species of Gangrenous Sore Throat.* [unidentified || book on medicine]

1766-87 Porny, Mark A. *The Elements of Heraldry.* [unidentified || book on heraldry]

1831 *Fraser's Magazine.* [unidentified || general interest magazine published in 19th-century London <http://onlinebooks.library.upenn.edu/webbin/serial?id=frasers>]

1898 *Westminster Gazette.* [unidentified || article dated 2nd of May in the newspaper *Westminster Gazette*]

1900 Litchfield, Frederick. *Pottery and Porcelain: a Guide to Collector.* [unidentified || introductory book for antiquaries]

With the examples in (153), sources are not clearly identified.

(153) *OED*^{2}: nature of source unidentified

1563 Golding, Arthur (1535/6-1606). *The Eyght Bookes of C. J. Cæsar* tr. [matriculated at the University of Cambridge but left without taking a degree; translator of Latin and French; half brother of the 16th Earl of Oxford's wife *<ODNB>* || No useful information regarding what kind of document was translated has been collected from references nor websites.]

1573 Harvey, Gabriel (1552/3-1631). *Letter-Book.* [b. Essex; BA, Fellow, MA, LLB, University of Cambridge, DCL, University of Oxford; scholar, writer and poet *<ODNB>* || This book is assumed to be correspondence, but the details are still unidentifiable.]

1638 Mede / Mead, Joseph (1586-1638). *Works.* [b. Essex; BA, MA,

Chapter VI

Fellow, BD, University of Cambridge; Hebraist, biblical scholar, historian, philologer, mathematician and botanist <*ODNB*> || Genre in which the example was used has not been identified.]

*a*1639Wotton, Sir Henry (1568-1639). *Reliquiæ Wottonianæ; or a Collection of Lives, Letters, Poems,* etc. [b. Kent; BA, University of Oxford; diplomat, Venetian Ambassador, writer, politician and poet <*ODNB*> || The document in which the post-position of *not* was used has not been identified.]

1651 Cleveland, John (bap. 1613-1658). *Mixt Assembly.* [b. Leicestershire; BA, MA, Fellow, University of Cambridge; Royalist poet <*ODNB* + http://venn.lib.cam.ac.uk/cgi-bin/search.pl?sur=&suro= c&fir=&firo=c&cit=&cito=c&c=all&tex=%22CLVT627J%22&sy e=&eye=&col=all&maxcount=50> || *Mixt Assembly* is not listed under the entry 'Cleveland' in the *OED²*'s Bibliography. Although this source has proved to be a collection of verses owing to *CHEL*, VII, 92, it is still uncertain whether the post-position of *not* occurs in verse part or prose part of the introduction to the book. Thus, this example was classified into (153) 'nature of source unidentified'.]

*a*1661 Holyday / Holi-, Barten (1593-1661). *D. J. Juvenalis and A. Persius Flaccus* tr. [b. Oxford; BA, MA, DD, University of Oxford; Church of England clergyman, chaplain to the King Chales I, archdeacon of Oxford, and poet <*ODNB*> || According to the *Britannica*, Decimus Junius Juvenalis (55/60?-*c*127) was a Roman satiric poet, and Aulus Persius Flaccus (34-62) an Italian Stoic poet. Accordingly, the source presently in question is likely to be an English translation of Latin poetics dealing with these two great poets. To be precise, however, this example was classified into (153) 'nature of source unidentified'.]

1731 Bailey, Nathan (bap. 1691-1742). [b. London; lexicographer and schoolmaster <*ODNB*> || The *OED²*'s example is quoted from a definition of a word. In the quotation, the year of publication is 1731. Nevertheless, no publication of this year is listed in the Bibliography. Perhaps the source of this example is either *An Universal Etymological English Dictionary* (1721 and many editions to 1800) or *Dictionarium Britannicum: or a More Compleat Universal Etymological English dictionary* 1730, 1736.]

Diachrony of Present Participles and Gerunds Followed by *Not*

In (154), however, both the users of the post-position of *not* and nature of the documents in which its examples occurred are identifiable.

(154) *OED²*: both user and nature of source identified

Austin, John Langshaw (1911-1960). *Sense & Sensibilia.* [b. Lancashire; studied at the University of Oxford; philosopher *<ODNB>* ‖ book on human perception]

Authorized Version of the English Bible. [English translation of the Christian Bible for the Church of England begun in 1604 and completed in 1611 under King James I's instructions to the learned translators <http://www.bible-researcher.com/kjvhist.html> ‖ English Bible]

Ayliffe, John (1676-1732). *Parergon Juris Canonici Anglicani.* [b. Hampshire; BA, MA, LLB, LLD, University of Oxford; lawyer and author *<ODNB>* ‖ academic article on religious law]

Bacon, Francis, Viscount St Alban (1561-1626). *Essayes.* [b. London; studied at the University of Cambridge and then at Gray's Inn; Lord Chancellor, politician, philosopher and lawyer knighted by the King James I *<ODNB>* ‖ essay on the subject of *Of the Advancement of Learning*; political history entitled *The Historie of the Raigne of King Henry the Seventh*]

Bailey, Philip James (1816-1902). *Festus.* [b. Nottingham; Bailey was matriculated at the University of Glasgow, then entered a member of Lincoln's Inn, but his legal studies were interrupted by his poetic pursuits; poet *<ODNB>* ‖ poem]

Banister (-nes-), John (1532/33-1599?). *The Historie of Man, Sucked from the Sappe of the Most Approved Anathomistes.* [b. Huntingdon; studied medicine at Oxford and received a licence to practise; surgeon *<ODNB>* ‖ book on medicine]

Barlow, William (1544-1625). *Defence of the Articles of the Protestant Religion.* [BA, University of Oxford; Church of England clergyman and natural philosopher *<ODNB>* ‖ religious prose]

Barret, Robert (*fl.* 1586?-1607). *The Theorike and Practike of Moderne Warres.* [soldier and author *<CDNB>*; the entry of Barret is deleted in *ODNB>* ‖ military treatise]

Baxter, Richard (1615-1691). *A Paraphrase on the New Testament* and *Catholick Theologie* [b. Shropshire; ejected minister and reli-

Chapter VI

gious writer; schoolmaster at Dudley; exceptionally prolific writer <*ODNB*> || religious prose]

Bell, James (d. 1606?). *Walter Haddon against Osorius*, tr. [b. Somerset; BA, Fellow, University of Oxford; rhetoric lecturer, translator and Reformer <*ODNB*> || translation of a religious prose]

Beveridge, Bishop William (bap. 1637-1708). *Private Thoughts upon Religion (Private Thoughts upon a Christian Life)*. [b. Leicestershire; BA, MA, DD, University of Cambridge; bishop of St Asaph, and prebendary of St Paul's Cathedral and Canterbury <*ODNB*> || religious prose]

Boyle, Robert (1627-1691). *The general history of the air*. [see pp. 334-335 || scientific prose]

Brinklow / -ke-, Henry (d. 1545/6). *Complaynt of Roderyck Mors*. [b. Berkshire; polemicist, controversialist and critic; wrote satires on society and religion under the pseudonym of 'Roderyck' or 'Roderigo Mors' <*ODNB*> || satire]

Brown, Thomas (bap. 1663-1704). *Fresny's Amusements Serious and Comical* tr. [b. Shropshire; BA, University of Oxford; satyrist, translator, fierce though entertaining and witty anti-Drydenist <*ODNB*> || translation of the satirical work]

Browne, Sir Thomas (1605-1682). *Certain Miscellany Tracts*; *Pseudodoxia Epidemica or Enquiries into Very Many Received Tenents*; *Religio Medici*. [b. Oxford; BA, MA, University of Oxford, MD, University of Leiden, DM, University of Oxford; physician and author <*ODNB*> || essays on plants, animals, languages, etc.; essays on mineral, vegetable, geography, etc.; self-portraited spiritual testament on religion as a physician, which was translated into Latin, Dutch, French and German <*ODNB*>]

Browne, William (1629/30-1678). *Le Roy's History of Polexander* tr. [b. Oxford; BA, Fellow, BD, Vice-president, University of Oxford; botanist <*ODNB*> || English translation of a book on botany]

Bulwer, John (bap. 1606-1656). *Anthropometamorphosis; Man Transformed, or the Artificial Changeling* etc. [b. London; medical practitioner and writer on deafness and on gesture; advocated concentration on lip reading in order to enable deaf mute people to communicate with others <*ODNB*> || treatise on the theme of the human body as a medium of communication <*ODNB*>]

Diachrony of Present Participles and Gerunds Followed by *Not*

Burke, Edmund (1729/30-1797). *Correspondence.* [b. Dublin; BA, University of Dublin; politician and author <*ODNB*> || letter]

Butler, Samuel (bap. 1613-1680). *Hudibras.* [b. Worcestershire; poet, clerk to a local magistrate and servant to the countesse of Kent <*ODNB*> || satirical poem]

Byron, George Gordon Noel, 6th Baron Byron (1788-1824). *The Age of Bronze*; *Don Juan.* [b. London; MA, University of Cambridge; poet <*ODNB*> || peoms; the former is not recorded in the *OED²*'s Bibliography]

Carew, Sir Richard, 1st Baronet (1579/80-1643?). *Estienne's World of Wonders* tr. [b. Cornwall; matriculated at the University of Oxford at the age of fourteen; admitted to the Middle Temple; medical experimenter and educationist <*ODNB*> || English translation of the work of R. Estienne, classicist affiliated with the University of Paris]

Cary [*née* Tanfield], Elizabeth, Viscountess Falkland (1585-1639). *The History of the Life, Reign, and Death of Edward II.* [b. Oxfordshire; daughter of a judge Lord L. Tanfield; writer and translator <*ODNB*> || politico-biography; in the *OED²*'s Bibliography, the author is shown only as "F., E.".]

Cave, William (1637-1713). *Primitive Christianity.* [b. Leicestershire; BA, MA, DD, University of Cambridge, DD, University of Oxford; Church of England clergyman, patristic scholar, chaplain in ordinary to Charles II and canon of Windsor <*ODNB*> || book on church history]

Chambers, Ephraim (1680?-1740). *Cyclopædia; or, an Universal Dictionary of Arts and Sciences.* [b. Westmorland; after apprenticeship to a map and globe maker in London, he became an encyclopaedist; translator of scientific treatises written in French <*ODNB*> || article in an encyclopaedia]

Chandler, John (1699/1700-1780). *Van Helmont's Oriatrike, or, Physick Refined* tr. [b. Bath; apothecary, Fellow of the Royal Society <*ODNB*> || translation of a medical book]

Clay, Reverend William Keatinge (1797-1867), ed. *Liturgical Services. Liturgies and Occasional Forms of Prayer Set Forth in the Reign of Queen Elizabeth.* [b. Cambridge; BD, University of Cambridge; liturgical scholar and antiquary <*ODNB*> || book on lit-

Chapter VI

urgy]

Cockeram, Henry (*fl.* 1623-1658). *The English Dictionarie, or an Interpreter of Hard English Words.* [lexicographer; author of the third dictionary of English following R. Cawdrey and J. Bullokar, and the first to bear the title of 'dictionary' <*ODNB*> ‖ definition in a dictionary]

Coles / cole, William (1626-1662). *Adam in Eden: or, Natures Paradise.* [b. Oxfordshire; BA, University of Oxford; botanist, <*ODNB*> ‖ book on botany]

Cudworth, Ralph (1617-1688). *The True Intellectual System of the Universe, wherein [...].* [b. Somerset; BA, MA, Fellow, BD, DD, University of Cambridge; Master of Clare College and Christ's College, and regius professor of Hebrew, University of Cambridge; philosopher and theologian <*ODNB*> ‖ philosophy]

Dampier, William (1651-1715). *A New Voyage round the World (Voyages and Descriptions, A Voyage to New Holland).* [b. Somerset; buccaneer and explorer <*ODNB*> ‖ voyage journal]

Davenant / D'Avenant, Sir William (1606-1668). *Declamations at Rutland House.* [educated at the University of Oxford; poet, playwright and theatre manager <*ODNB*> ‖ play]

Davies, John (1625-1693). *Olearius' Voyages and Travels of the Ambassadors Sent . . to the Great Duke of Moscovy. Whereto are Added the Travels of (J. A. de) Mandelslo from Persia into the East-Indies* tr. [b. Carmarthenshire; entered the University of Oxford but, because of the civil war, was relocated to the University of Cambridge; translator <*ODNB*> ‖ English translation of a voyage journal]

Defoe, Daniel (1660?-1731). [see above (93) ‖ novel titled *The Life, Adventures, and Pyracies of the Famous Captain Singleton*]

Dekker, Thomas (*c*1572-1632). *The Seuen Deadly Sinnes of London.* [of obscure origins; playwright and pamphleteer <*ODNB*> ‖ play]

D'Ewes, Sir Simonds, 1st Baronet (1602-1650). [b. Dorsetshire; went up to the University of Cambridge, but left without a degree; began his legal education in the Middle Temple, and later was called to the bar; diarist, antiquary, high sheriff of Suffolk, and author of "Journals of All the Parliaments during the Reign of Queen Elizabeth" <*ODNB* + L1, 164 & n.> ‖ letter]

Diachrony of Present Participles and Gerunds Followed by *Not*

Dickenson, John (*c*1570-1635/6). *Arisbas, Euphues amidst His Slumbers: or Cupids Journey to Hell.* [Nothing is known of Dickenson's early life, and he probably studied at Cambridge; author and government official <*ODNB*> || essay on poetry]

Dryden, John (1631-1700), in Sir Samuel Garth, ed. *Ovid's Metamorphoses. Translated by the Most Eminent Hands* (J. Dryden, J. Addison, L. Eusden, A. Mainwaring, S. Croxall, N. Tate, J. Gay, W. Congreve, and the editor) tr. [b. Northamptonshire; BA, University of Cambridge; poet, playwright, critic and author of "Essay of Dramatic Poesy" and "All for Love" <*ODNB*> || translation of Ovid's poetry]

DuVerger, Susan [Susan Du Vergeere; *née* Suzanne de la Vallée] (bap. 1610-1657/9). Camus' *Admirable Events Selected out of His Foure Bookes, Together with His Morall Relations* tr. [b. London; translator and author <*ODNB*> || English translation of moralistic French romance tales]

Eachard, John [*pseud.* 'T. B.'] (bap. 1637-1697). *Mr. Hobbs's State of Nature Considered, in a Dialogue between Philantus and Timothy.* [b. Suffolk; BA, Fellow, MA, DD, University of Cambridge; Master of St Catharine's College, and Vice-chancellor of the University of Cambridge <*ODNB*> || unique essay on human nature portrayed through a dialogue between a man who is a megalomaniac know-all afflicted by the fear and selfishness and a man who has intelligence, common sense and good humour <*ODNB*>]

Eden, Richard (*c*1520-1576). *A Treatyse of the Newe India* tr. [b. Herefordshire; BA, MA, University of Cambridge; translator <*ODNB*> || translation of part of book five of S. Münster's *Cosmographia* <*ODNB*>]

Edgeworth, Maria (1768-1849). *Letters from England 1813-1844.* [b. Oxfordshire; novelist and educationist <*ODNB*> || letter]

Evans, Marian [*pseud.* 'George Eliot') (1819-1880). *Daniel Deronda.* [b. Warwickshire; novelist eminent for his *The Mill on the Floss*, *Silas Marner* and *Middlemarch* <*ODNB*> || narrative part of a novel]

Elyot, Sir Thomas (*c*1490-1546). *The Boke Named The Gouernour*; *The Castel of Helth*; *The Image of Gouernance* [details regarding his education is unclear, except that he was admitted to Middle Temple; humanist, diplomat, writer and editor of a Latin-English

Chapter VI

dictionary *<ODNB>* ‖ treatise on monarchical political theory and the form of education appropriate for young men; summary of the teachings of the ancient Greek and Roman physicians for English men and women to understand and regulate their health; treatise on politics *<ODNB>*]

Fenton, Sir Geoffrey (c1539-1608). *The Historie of Guicciardini, conteining the Warres of Italie* tr. [translator and administrator in Ireland *<ODNB>* ‖ English translation of Francesco Guicciardini's treatise on political history *<ODNB>*]

Ferne, Sir John (c1560-1609). *The Blazon of Gentrie.* [b. Lincolnshire; called to the bar of the Inner Temple; administrator and writer on heraldry *<ODNB>* ‖ book on heraldry *<ODNB>*]

Fielding, Henry (1707-1754). *The History of the Adventures of Joseph Andrews.* [b. Somerset; studied literature at the University of Leiden, and entered the Middle Temple to begin preparing for the bar, to which he was admitted; author and magistrate; author of *Tom Jones* and *Amelia* *<ODNB>* ‖ narrative part of a novel]

Finch, Sir Henry (c1558-1625). *Law, or, a Discourse Thereof, in Foure Bookes.* [b. Kent; BA, University of Oxford; studied at Gray's Inn, and called to the bar; author and lawyer *<ODNB>* ‖ book on law]

Ford, John (bap. 1586-1639/53?). *The Broken Heart.* [b. Devon; very little is known about Ford's biography; matriculated at the University of Oxford; playwright *<ODNB>* ‖ play]

Fuller, Thomas (1607/8-1661). *A Pisgah-Sight of Palestine*; *The Church-History of Britain*; *The Historie of the Holy Warre*; *The History of the Worthies of England*; *The Holy State. The Profane State.* [b. Northamptonshire; aet. 13, Fuller entered the University of Cambridge; BA, MA, BD, MD, University of Cambridge; Church of England clergyman and prebend at Salisbury Cathedral *<ODNB>* ‖ all of the souces are religious prose]

Glanvill, Joseph (1636-1680). *A Further Discovery of M. Stubbe*; *Lux Orientalis, or an Enquiry into the Opinion of the Eastern Sages concerning the Præexistence of Souls*; *Scepsis Scientifica.* [b. Plymouth; BA, MA, University of Oxford; Church of England clergyman, rector of the abbey church in Bath and Fellow of the Royal Society *<ODNB>* ‖ treatise on religion]

Diachrony of Present Participles and Gerunds Followed by *Not*

Goldsmith, Oliver (1728?-1774). *A History of the Earth and Animated Nature.* [b. Ireland; BA, University of Dublin; author renowned for his novel *The Vicar of Wakefield* and *She Stoops to Conquer* <*ODNB*> || book on geophysics]

Grew, Nehemiah (bap. 1641-1712). *The Anatomy of Plants (The Anatomy of Plants Begun, the Anatomy of Roots,.. Trunks,.. Leaves,.. Flowers,.. Fruits* etc.). [b. Coventry; BA, University of Cambridge, MD, University of Leyden; botanist, physician, Fellow of the Royal Society and Honorary Fellow of the Royal College of Physicians <*ODNB*> || book on botany]

Hacket, John (1592-1670). *Scrinia Reserata a Memorial Offer'd to the Great Deservings of John Williams, Archbishop of York.* [b. London; BA, Fellow, MA, BD, DD, University of Cambridge; King James I's chaplain, Archdeacon of Bedford, and Bishop of London, Coventry and Lichfield <*ODNB*> || a study of the life of a public figure not quite of the highest importance <*ODNB*>]

Hakluyt, Richard (1552?-1616). *Diuers Voyages touching the Discouerie of Amerika.* [b. London; BA, MA, University of Oxford; prebendary of Bristol Cathedral, Archdeacon of Westminster, geographer, translator and editor of geographical literature <*ODNB*> || voyage journal]

Hall, Edward (1497-1547). *The Union of the Two Noble and Illustre Famelies of Lancastre and York.* [b. London; graduated BA in the University of Cambridge, and entered Gray's Inn; lawyer and historian <*ODNB*> || history of England (from the usurpation of Henry IV to the death of Henry VIII) <*ODNB*>]

Hall, Joseph (1574-1656). *The Shaking of the Olive Tree: The Remaining Works of J. H. With Some Specialities of Divine Providence in His Life, Noted by His Own Hand. Together with His Hard Measure, Written Also by Himself.* [b Leicestershire; BA, Fellow, MA, BD, DD, University of Cambridge; Bishop of Exeter and Norwich, Chaplain to the court of Prince Henry, religious writer and satirist <*ODNB*> || religious prose]

Haskell, Arnold Lionel David (1903-1980). *Prelude to Ballet.* [b. London; BA, University of Cambridge; ballet critic and director of the new Royal Ballet School <*ODNB*> || text on ballet; unrecorded in *OED*[2]'s Bibliography]

Chapter VI

Hawkins, Francis (1628-1681). *Youth's Behaviour: or, Decency in Conversation amongst Men* tr. [b. London; Jesuit; professor of holy scripture at the University of Liège; published two translations at the age of 10 and 13 *<CDNB + ODNB>* ‖ English translation of a French treatise on morality *<ODNB>*]

Hawkins / -kyns, Sir Richard (*c*1560-1622). *Observations in His Voiage into the South Sea 1593.* [b. Plymouth; naval officer, vice-admiral and captain of the queen's ship *Nonpareil <ODNB>* ‖ voyage journal]

Hearne, Thomas (bap. 1678-1735). *Remarks and Collections; Ductor Historicus; or a Short System of Universal History.* [b. Berkshire; BA, MA, University of Oxford; historian, Bodleian Library assistant, antiquary and diarist; historical scholarship today owes its greatest debt to Hearne's accurate editions of the sources of English history: annals, historical biographies, chronicles, and historical documents such as charters, chartularies, catalogues *<ODNB>* ‖ English history]

Herbert, Edward, 1st Baron Herbert of Cherbury and Castle Island (1582?-1648). *The Life and Reigne of King Henry the Eighth.* [b. Shropshire; matriculated at the University of Oxford; diplomat, philosopher and historian *<ODNB>* ‖ English history]

Herbert, George (1593-1633). *The Temple; Sacred Poems and Private Ejaculations.* [b. Wales; BA, Fellow, MA, University of Cambridge; Church of England clergyman and poet *<ODNB>* ‖ poem; the source at the beginning of the *OED²*'s citation is shown as "*Temple, Invitation*"]

Hickeringill / Hickhorn-, Edmund (bap. 1631-1708). *Gregory, Father Greybeard, with His Vizard Off.* [b. Yorkshire; BA, Fellow, MA, University of Cambridge; Church of England clergyman, religious controversialist and pamphleteer *<ODNB>* ‖ religious treatise]

Hobbes, Thomas (1588-1679). *Leviathan, or the Matter, Forme, and Power of a Commonwealth, Ecclesiasticall and Civill.* [b. Wiltshire; BA, University of Oxford; philosopher; gave lessons in mathematics to the young Prince Charles (future King Charles II); wrote his autobiography in verse *<ODNB>* ‖ book on political science]

Holland, Philemon (1552-1637). *Camden's Britain, or a Chorograph-*

Diachrony of Present Participles and Gerunds Followed by Not

icall Description of England, Scotland, and Ireland tr.; *Livy's Romane Historie* tr. [b. Essex; BA, Fellow, University of Cambridge, MA, University of Oxford, MD, University of Cambridge; translator admired by T. Fuller and R. Southey *<ODNB>* ‖ translations of books on topography and Roman history]

Hooke, Robert (1635-1703). *Micrographia, or Some Physiological Descriptions of Minute Bodies Made by Magnifying Glasses, with Observations and Inquiries Thereuon.* [b. Isle of Wight; MA, University of Oxford; professor of geometry at the University of Oxford; natural philosopher who has achievements on astronomy; advisor to I. Newton, inventor of a wheel barometer, a manometer, rain gauges, hygroscopes, etc., Fellow of the Royal Society *<ODNB>* ‖ treatise on microscopy]

Hooker [Vowell], John (*c*1527-1601) *The Irish Historie Composed by Giraldus Cambrensis* tr. [b. Exeter; went up to the University of Oxford, but left without a degree; antiquary and civic administrator *<ODNB>* ‖ translation of a book on Irish history]

Howell, James (1594?-1666). *Giraffi's Exact Historie of the Late Revolutions in Naples* tr. [b. Brecknockshire; BA, University of Oxford; historian and political writer *<ODNB>* ‖ translation of a book on Italian history]

Hughes, William (*c*1535-1600). *The Man of Sin: or a Discourse of Popery.* [b. Caernarvonshire; BA, Fellow, MA, BTh, University of Cambridge, BTh, DTh, University of Oxford, DTh, University of Cambridge; Bishop of St Asaph *<ODNB>* ‖ religious treatise]

Hutchinson, Sir Jonathan (1828-1913). *Archives of Surgery.* [b. Yorkshire; surgeon, President of the Royal College of Surgeons, president of most of the London medical societies, Fellow of the Royal Society *<ODNB>* ‖ periodical on surgery *<ODNB>*]

Hyde, Edward, 1st Earl of Clarendon (1609-1674). *The History of the Rebellion and Civil Wars in England.* [b. Wiltshire; completed his study at the University of Oxford, and then studied at the Middle Temple; barrister, politician, historian and privy councillor *<ODNB>* ‖ treatise on English political history]

James, Henry (1843-1916). [b. New York; dropped out of Harvard law school; novelist who played an active part in England and is renowned for his *Daisy Miller. <ODNB>* ‖ article contributed to

Chapter VI

the magazine *Fortnightly Review*]

Jeake, Samuel (1623-1690). *Logisticelogia, or Arithmetic Surveighed and Reviewed.* [b. Sussex; lawyer and nonconformist preacher *<ODNB>* || book on mathematics posthumously edited and published by his son *<ODNB>*]

Jenkyn, William (bap. 1613-1685). *The Blind Guide or the Doting Doctor.* [b. Suffolk; BA, MA, University of Cambridge; nonconformist minister *<ODNB>* || ?treatise on religion and morality]

Jewel, John (1522-1571). *A Replie unto M. Hardinges Answeare.* [b. Devon; BA, Fellow, MA, DD, Fellow, University of Oxford; Bishop of Salisbury *<ODNB>* || a booklet regarding the religious controversy between Protestant Jewel and Catholic Harding <https://uni versityofglasgowlibrary.wordpress.com/2013/03/22/the-develop ment-of-the-book-a-case-study-from-special-collections/>]

Jonson, Benjamin / Ben (1572-1637). *Underwoods, Consisting of Divers Poems.* [b. London; educated at the University of Cambridge; at the age of 46, MA, University of Oxford; poet and playwright eminent for his *Everyman in his Humour* and *The Alchemist*; friend of F. Bacon, J. Donne and W. Shakespeare *<ODNB>* || poem]

Jortin, John (1698-1770). *Sermons on Different Subjects.* [b. London; BA, MA, Fellow, University of Cambridge; ecclesiastical historian, literary critic and Archdeacon of London *<ODNB>* || sermons]

Kingsley, Charles (1819-1875). *Two Years Ago.* [b. Devon; studied at the University of London, and then moved to the University of Cambridge; Church of England clergyman, controversialist, amd regius professor of modern history at the University of Cambridge; novelist renowned for his *Westward Ho!* *<ODNB>* || narrative part of a novel]

Knatchbull, Sir Norton, 1st Baronet (1602-1685). *Annotations upon Some Difficult Texts in All the Books of the New Testament* tr. [studied at the University of Cambridge (BA) and the Middle Temple; Tory politician and biblical scholar *<ODNB>* || English translation of his authored Latin book on the Bible *<ODNB>*]

Lady Cave in *Verney Letters.* [daughter of John Verney, 1st Viscount Fermanagh (1640-1717) and wife of Sir Thomas Cave, 3rd Baronet <http://www.thepeerage.com/p2981.htm#i29806> || letter]

Locke, John (1632-1704). *An Essay concerning Humane Understand-*

Diachrony of Present Participles and Gerunds Followed by Not

ing. [b. Somerset; BA, MA, MB, University of Oxford; philosopher, praelector in Greek, praelector in rhetoric, and censor of moral philosophy, University of Oxford; Fellow of the Royal Society *<ODNB>* || book on philosophy]

Luttrell, Narcissus (1657-1732). *A Brief Historical Relation of State Affairs*. [b. London; received an MA, University of Cambridge, by royal mandate; studied at the Gray's Inn, and was called to the bar; annalist and book collector *<ODNB>* || chronicles (compiled from newsletters and newspapers) of contemporary events *<ODNB>*]

Lydgate, John (*c*1370-1449/50). *The Pylgremage of the Sowle*. [b. Suffolk; poet who wrote philosophical, scientific and historical poems; prior of Hatfield Regis *<ODNB>* || religious poem]

Macaulay (*née* Sawbridge), Catharine (1731-1791). *The History of England from the Accession of James I to That of the Brunswick Line*. [b. Kent; historian and political polemicist *<ODNB>* || book on English history]

Markham, Francis (1565-1627). *Five Decades of Epistles of Warre*. [b. Nottinghamshire; dropped out of the University of Cambridge; soldier *<ODNB>* || collection of letters regarding wars and honour *<ODNB>*]

Martineau, James (1805-1900). *The Seat of Authority in Religion*. [b. Norwich; entered Manchester College, York, to train for the ministry; Unitarian minister; Professor of mental and moral philosophy and logic, and Principal, Manchester College *<ODNB>* || book on religion]

Marvell, Andrew (1621-1678). *Correspondence*. [b. Yorkshire; BA, University of Cambridge; poet, satirist and politician *<ODNB>* || letter]

Massinger, Philip (1583-1640). *The Duke of Millaine, a Tragœdie*. [b. Salisbury; dropped out of the University of Oxford; playwright *<ODNB>* || conversational part of a play]

Milton, John (1608-1674). *Of Reformation touching Church Discipline in England; Paradise Lost*. [b. London; BA, MA, University of Cambridge; poet renowned for his "Lycidas", "Paradise Lost" and "Samson Agonistes", and polemicist *<ODNB>* || anti-prelatical pamphlet *<ODNB>*; epic poem]

More, Henry (1614-1687). *A Modest Enquiry into the Mystery of Iniq-*

Chapter VI

uity (second part Synopsis Prophetica; the Apology); *An Answer to ..
a Learned Psychopyrist; An Explanation of the Grand Mystery of
Godliness; Divine Dialogues.* [b. Lincolnshire; BA, MA, Fellow,
University of Cambridge; philosopher, poet, and theologian *<ODNB>*
|| booklets on religion; with the former booklet, a discrepancy can
be seen in the year of publication between in the citation ('1684')
and in the Bibliography ('1681 (1688)')]

Moryson, Fynes (1565/6-1630). *An itinerary ... containing his ten
yeeres travell through the twelve dominions of Germany, Bohmer-
land, Sweitzerland, Netherland, Denmarke, Poland, Italy, Turky,
France, England, Scotland, and Ireland. Divided into three parts.*
[b. Lincolnshire; BA, MA, Fellow, University of Cambridge; trav-
eller and writer *<ODNB>* || book composed of three heterogeneous
topics of travel journals, history of the Nine Years'War and essays
on the value and difficulties of travel *<ODNB>*]

Murphy, James Gracey (1808-1896). *A Critical and Exegetical Com-
mentary on Genesis.* [LLD, University of Dublin; Hebrew professor at the University of Belfast <https://archive.org/details/critical
exegeti00murp> || commentary on the Bible]

Nashe / Nash, Thomas (bap. 1567-1601). *Lenten Stuffe*; *The Terrors
of the Night, or, a Discourse of Apparitions.* [b. Suffolk; BA, Uni-
versity of Cambridge; writer *<ODNB>* || plays]

Ness, Christopher (1621-1705). *A Protestant Antidote against the Poy-
son of Popery.* [b. Yorkshire; BA, University of Cambridge; Inde-
pendent minister *<ODNB>* || religious prose]

Newton, Thomas (1544/5-1607). *Lemnie's Touchstone of Complex-
ions* tr. [b. Cheshire; studied at the University of Oxford and Cam-
bridge; translator and Church of England clergyman, *<ODNB>* ||
English translation of Latin book on medicine]

North, Sir Thomas (1535-1603?). *Plutarch's Lives of the Noble Gre-
cians and Romanes* tr. [b. London; it has been thought likely that
North attended the University of Cambridge, but his name does not
survive among the college records; studied at the Lincoln's Inn;
translator *<ODNB>* || English translation of French biography]

Nurse, G. T., et al., *Peoples Southern Afr.* [Trefor Jenkins [b. Wales;
studied medicine at the University of London and Westminster Hospital; professor of genetics, renowned for his research on DNA <http://

Diachrony of Present Participles and Gerunds Followed by *Not*

www.wits.ac.za/alumni/alumnirecognition/honorarydegreecitations/36
15/treforjenkins.html>] || book on genetics; the source book is not
shown in the *OED*[2]'s Bibliography; owing to the following website, it has proved to be G. T. Nurse, J. S. Weiner, and Trefor Jenkins,
The peoples of Southern Africa and their affinities (New York: Oxford University Press) <http://onlinelibrary.wiley.com/doi/10.1002/
ajhb.1310010414/abstract>]

Osborne, Francis (1593-1659). *A Miscellany of Sundry Essayes, Para-
doxes, and Problematicall Discourses, Letters and Characters.* [b.
Bedfordshire; master of the horse to the 3rd Earl of Pembroke;
writer famous for his *Advice to a Son* <*ODNB*> || essay]

Parke, Robert (*fl.* 1588-1589). *Mendoza's Historie of the Great and
Mightie Kingdome of China[, Etc.]* tr. [translator <*ODNB*> ||
English translation of Gonzales de Mendoza's account of China
<*ODNB*>]

Parr, Richard (1591/2-1644). *The Life of James Usher, Late Archbishop of Armagh.* [b. Lancashire; BA, Fellow, MA, BD, DD, University of Oxford; theologian and Bishop of Sodor and Man
<*ODNB*> || biography]

Pettie, George (*c*1548-1589). *Guazzo's Ciuile Conuersation* tr. [b. Oxfordshire; BA, University of Oxford; writer of romances <*ODNB*>
|| English translation of French translation]

Petty, Sir William (1623-1687). *Political Arithmetick, or a Discourse
concerning the Extent and Value of Lands, People, etc.* [b. Hampshire; studied medicine in the Netherlands and France; DM, University of Oxford; Vice-principal of Brasenose College, Professor
of anatomy, University of Oxford, natural philosopher and admin-
istrator in Ireland and Fellow of the Royal Society <*ODNB*> ||
book on political arithmetic]

Potter, Christopher (1590/91-1646). *Sarpi's History of the Quarrels of
Pope Paul V with the State of Venice* tr. [b. Westmorland; BA, MA,
Fellow, BD, DD, University of Oxford; college head and dean of
Worcester, and chaplain to the King Charles I <*ODNB*> || English
translation of Italian history written by Paolo Sarpi <*ODNB*>]

Purchas, Samuel (bap. 1577-1626). *Pilgrimage.* [b. Essex; BA, MA,
University of Cambridge, BD, University of Lambeth, BD, University of Oxford; geographical editor, compiler and Church of

Chapter VI

England clergyman *<ODNB>* ‖ compilation of travel literature; the title in the *ODNB* is *Purchas, His Pilgrimage <ODNB>*]

Raleigh, Sir Walter Alexander R. (1861-1922) *Letters.* [b. London; studied at the University of London (BA) and the University of Cambridge; professor of modern literature at the University of Liverpool; received honorary degrees from the University of Glasgow and Durham, and honorary fellowships from the University of Cambridge and Oxford *<ODNB>* + https://tspace.library.utoronto.ca/html/1807/4350/poet369.html> ‖ letter]

Richardson, Samuel (bap. 1689-1761). *Clarissa (Harlowe); or the History of a Young Lady.* [b. Derbyshire; printer and author *<ODNB>* ‖ narrative part of a novel]

Ruskin, John James (1819-1900). *Modern Painters; Unto This Last.* [b. London; MA, University of Oxford; art critic, social critic and reformer *<ODNB>* ‖ book on aesthetics; essay on politics and economics *<ODNB>*]

Sandys, Edwin (1519?-1588). *Sermons.* [b. present-day Cumbria; BA, MA, BTh, DTh, University of Cambridge; Master of St Catharine's College and Vice-chancellor, University of Cambridge, and Archbishop of York *<ODNB>* ‖ sermons]

Scott / Scot, Reginald (d. 1599). *A Perfite Platforme of a Hoppe Garden.* [b. Kent; educated at the University of Oxford, but he did not obtain a degree; writer on witchcraft *<ODNB>* ‖ the first practical treatise on hop culture in English *<ODNB>*]

Shadwell, Charles (*fl.*1692-1720). *The Fair Quaker of Deal, or, the Humours of the Navy, a Comedy.* [playwright *<ODNB>* ‖ play]

Shakespeare, William (1564-1616). *Measure for Measure*; *3 Hen. VI*; *Cymb.*; *Hen. VIII*; *The Tragedie of Othello, the Moore of Venice*; *The Tragedy of Richard the Third.* [b. Stratford upon Avon; at the King's New School, Shakespeare would have learned an immense amount of Latin literature and history, perhaps using the Latin-English dictionary; playwright and poet *<ODNB>* ‖ plays]

Shelley, Percy Bysshe (1792-1822). *The Revolt of Islam.* [b. Sussex; went up to the University of Oxford, but expelled; poet *<ODNB>* ‖ poem]

Sherley / Shir-, Sir Anthony, Count Sherley in the Nobility of the Holy Roman Empire (1565-1636?). *Relation of His Travels into*

Diachrony of Present Participles and Gerunds Followed by *Not*

Persia. [b. Sussex; BA, Fellow, University of Oxford; adventurer and diplomat in the Persian service <*ODNB*> || travelogue]

Smith, Captain John. *The True Travels, Adventures and Observations of Captaine J. Smith*. [adventurer, soldier, explorer and author; became a dominate force in the eventual success of Jamestown and the establishment of its legacy as the first permanent English settlement in North America <http://www.nps.gov/jame/learn/historycul ture/life-of-john-smith.htm> || travelogue]

Southey, Robert (1774-1843). *Roderick, the Last of the Goths*. [b. Bristol; admitted to but left the University of Oxford; poet and reviewer <*ODNB*> || epic]

Speed, John (1551/52-1629). *The History of Great Britaine*. [b. Cheshire; historian and cartographer <*ODNB*> || book on British history with its accompanying atlas <*ODNB*>]

Spencer, John (bap. 1630-1693). *A Discourse concerning Prodigies* 1663—Second ed. To which is added *a Short Treatise concerning Vulgar Prophecies* 1665. [b. Kent; BA, MA, BD, DD, Fellow, University of Cambridge; theologian, Hebraist and Master of Corpus Christi College and Vice-chancellor, University of Cambridge <http://venn.lib.cam.ac.uk/cgi-bin/search.pl?sur=&suro=c&fir=&fi ro=c&cit=&cito=c&c=all&tex=%22SPNR645J%22&sye=&eye= &col=all&maxcount=50 + *ODNB*> || treatise]

Spenser, Edmund (1552?-1599). *The Faerie Queene*. [b. London; BA, MA, University of Cambridge; poet and administrator in Ireland <*ODNB*> || poem]

Stafford, Sir Thomas (d. 1655). *Pacata Hibernia. Ireland Appeased and Reduced*. [b. Ireland; antiquary and editor of a history book on the wars of Ireland <*ODNB*> || record of war]

Stanley, Thomas (1625-1678). *The History of Philosophy*. [b. Hertfordshire; descendant of 3rd Earl of Derby; MA, University of Cambridge; poet and classical scholar who published poems and a series of translations from the Greek and Latin <*ODNB*> || philosophical history; a discrepancy can be seen in the year of publication between the citation and the Bibliography]

Stewart, Balfour (1828-1887). *An Elementary Treatise on Heat*. [b. Edinburgh; went to the University of St Andrews and the University of Edinburgh; physicist, meteorologist, Director of the Kew

Chapter VI

Observatory, Fellow of the Royal Society and professor of natural philosophy at University of Manchester <*ODNB*> ‖ textbook on physics <*ODNB*>]

Stubbes / Stubbs, Philip (*c*1555-*c*1610). *The Anatomie of Abuses.* [b. Cheshire; went up to the University of Cambridge but left; pamphleteer <*ODNB*> ‖ colourful diatribe against contemporary fashions, customs and pastimes <*ODNB*>]

Sturmy, Samuel (1633-1669). *The Mariners Magazine, or Sturmy's Mathematical and Practical Arts* etc. [b. Gloucester; writer on seamanship <*ODNB* + http://www.maa.org/publications/periodicals/convergence/mathematical-treasure-the-mariners-magazine> ‖ encyclopaedic book on the use of scales, the art of navigation, etc. <*ODNB*>]

Surflet, Richard. *Estienne and Liébault's Maison Rustique, or the Countrie Farme* tr. [practitioner in physic, oculist and translators of French wrtings on medicine and agriculture <http://europepmc.org/backend/ptpmcrender.fcgi?accid=PMC1138985&blobtype=pdf> ‖ translation of a French book on agriculture and hunting]

Swift, Jonathan (1667-1745). *Travels into several remote nations of the world, in four parts, by Lemuel Gulliver.* [see pp. 328-329 ‖ novel]

Swinton, John (1703-1777) in *Philosophical Transactions of the Royal Society.* [b. Cheshire; BA, MA, Fellow, University of Oxford; Church of England clergyman, orientalist, historian, antiquary and Fellow of the Royal Society <*ODNB*> ‖ article in *Philosophical Transactions*, the oldest scientific journal in the world]

Tarlton, Richard. (d. 1588) *Newes out of Purgatorie.* [b. Shropshire; English actor, ballad writer, favourite jester of Queen Elizabeth I, and the most popular comedian of his age <*Britannica*> ‖ a collection of comic stories; The title in the *OED²*'s citation concerned, *Tarlton's Newes Purgatorie*, can be misleading because the correct title seems to be 'Tarlton's *Newes out of Purgatorie*' <http://www.shakespeare-online.com/sources/merrysources.html>]

Taylor, John (1578-1653). *Works.* [b. Gloucestershire; dropped out of a grammar school; 'the Water Poet' <*ODNB*> ‖ collection of Taylor's works]

Taylor, Jeremy (bap. 1613-1667). *Contemplations of the State of Man in This Life, and in That Which Is to Come.* [b. Cambridge; BA, MA,

Diachrony of Present Participles and Gerunds Followed by *Not*

University of Cambridge, MA, University of Oxford; Church of Ireland bishop of Down and Connor, and religious writer *<ODNB>* || religious prose]

Temple, Sir William, Baronet (1628-1699). *Observations upon the United Provinces of the Netherlands.* [b. Ireland; left the University of Cambridge without taking his degree; diplomat, politician and author *<ODNB>* || essay on the workings of the Netherland's complex system of government *<ODNB>*]

Tennyson, Alfred, 1st Baron Tennyson (1809-1892). [b. Lincolnshire; left the University of Cambridge without taking a degree; poet eminent for his "In Memoriam" and "Enoch Arden" *<ODNB>* || poem; "St. Simeon Stylites" and "Will", from which the examples were quoted, are not listed in the *OED²*'s Bibliography]

Tofte / Tafte, Robert (bap. 1562-1619/20). *Alba. The Months Minde of a Melancholy Louer.* [b. London; poet, translator *<ODNB>* || poem]

Tombes, John (1602-1676). *Anthropolatria; or the Sinne of Glorying in Men.* [b. Worcestershire; BA, MA, BD, University of Oxford; clergyman and ejected minister *<ODNB>* || religious treatise]

Topsell, Edward (bap. 1572-1625). *The Historie of Foure-Footed Beasts.* [b. Kent; BA, MA, University of Cambridge; Church of England clergyman and author *<ODNB>* || animal-oriented allegory for human edification *<ODNB>*]

Trench, Richard Chenevix (1807-1886). *On the Lessons in Proverbs.* [b. Dublin; BA, MA, BD, University of Cambridge; Church of Ireland archbishop of Dublin, professor of divinity at the University of London and provider of the impetus that led to the *OED*. *<ODNB>* || lectures delivered before various Young Men's Societies, on the curiosities, interest, and uses of proverbs *<http://archive.spectator.co. uk/article/26th-february-1853/16/trench-on-the-lessons-in-proverbs-tins-little-book>*]

Tucker, Abraham (1705-1774). *The Light of Nature Pursued.* [b. London; studied at the University of Oxford; philosopher *<ODNB>* || book on philosophy]

Vaughan, Thomas (1621-1666). *Anthroposophia Theomagica; or a Discourse of the Nature of Man and His State after Death.* [b. Brecknockshire; BA, Fellow, University of Oxford; hermetic philosopher and alchemist *<ODNB>* || tracts on hermetic philosophy]

Chapter VI

Walkington, Thomas (*c*1575-1621). *The Optick Glasse of Humors, or, The Touchstone of a Golden Temperature.* [b. Lincolnshire; BA, MA, Fellow, BD, University of Cambridge, BD, University of Oxford, DD, University of Cambridge; Church of England clergyman and author *<ODNB>* || this book foreshadowed the literary culmination of the tradition in Burton's *Anatomy of Melancholy <ODNB>*]

Warton / Perfey, Robert (d. 1557) in John Strype, M. A., *Annals of the Reformation and Establishment of Religion, and Other Occurrences in the Church of England.* [of obscure origin; BTh, University of Cambridge; Bishop of Hereford *<ODNB>* || annals]

Waterhouse, Edward (1619-1670). *A Short Narrative of the Late Dreadful Fire in London.* [b. Middlesex; LLD *per literas regias*, University of Cambridge; heraldic writer and Fellow of the Royal Society *<ODNB>>* || narrative prose]

Weldon, Sir Anthony (bap. 1583-1648). *The Court and Character of King James.* [b. Kent; royal household official, local politician and reputed satirist *<ODNB>* || violently anti-Jacobean tract *<ODNB>*]

Whately, Richard (1787-1863). *Elements of Logic.* [b. London; BA, MA, Fellow, DD, University of Oxford; Church of Ireland archbishop of Dublin and philosopher *<ODNB>* || textbook on logic, originally recorded in the *Encyclopaedia metropolitana <ODNB>*]

Wilkins, John (1614-1672). *Mathematicall Magick; or, the Wonders that May Be Performed by Mechanicall Geometry;* ?*A discourse concerning a new world and another planet* / ?*The discovery of a world in the moone* [b. Northamptonshire; BA, MA, BD, DD, University of Oxford; theologian, natural philosopher, Bishop of Chester, Master of Trinity College, University of Cambridge, and leading member of the foundation of the Royal Society *<ODNB>* || treatise on mathematics; the latter source is unidentified in the *OED²*'s Bibliography]

Willet, Andrew (1561/2-1621). *Hexapla in Exodum.* [b. East Cambridgeshire; BA, MA, University of Cambridge, MA, Fellow, University of Oxford, BD, DD, University of Cambridge; Church of England clergyman and religious controversialist *<ODNB>* || sixfold commentarie upon the most divine Epistle of the Holy Apostle St. Paul to the Romanes <http://www.spurgeon.org/fsl/puritans.htm>]

Diachrony of Present Participles and Gerunds Followed by *Not*

Wilson, Thomas (1523/4-1581). *The Arte of Rhetorique.* [b. Lincoln-shire; Fellow, BA, MA, University of Cambridge, DCL, University of Ferrara, Italy, LLD, University of Oxford, LLD, University of Cambridge; administrator, privy councillor and humanist *<ODNB>* || book on rhetoric]

Wood, Anthony / Anthony à Wood (1632-1695). *Life, from 1632 to 1672, Written by Himself; Continued till 1695.* [b. Oxford; BA, University of Oxford; antiquary and historian *<ODNB>* || diary]

Woodward, John (1665/68-1728). *An Essay towards a Natural History of the Earth.* [b. Derbyshire; MD, University of Cambridge; physician, natural historian, antiquary, professor of physick at Gresham College and Fellow of the Royal Society *<ODNB>* || treatise]

Wordsworth, William (1770-1850). *The Prelude; or, Growth of a Poet's Mind.* [b. Cumberland; BA, University of Cambridge; awarded an honorary degree by the University of Durham and Oxford; poet *<ODNB>* || poem]

Wyclif / Wycliffe, John (d. 1384). *The First Epistle General of Peter.* ['northerner'; theologian, philosopher, and religious reformer; Fellow, Master of Balliol College, University of Oxford; translator into Middle English version of the English Bible *<ODNB>* || translation of 1 Peter in the New Testament into Middle English]

Based upon (152)-(154), the use of the post-position of *not* in the OED^2 can be summarised as follows. In terms of users, this construction was used by 10 peers, 1 peeress and 13 lords. (N.B. It was from individuals representing nobility such as the Duke of Buckingham, Brabantio, a Senator and Angelo, Deputy of Duke of Vincentio that Shakespeare had this usage uttered.) 105 users had well-educated backgrounds such as the University of Cambridge, University of Oxford, Lincoln's Inn and Middle Temple, and 39 individuals were clergymen. The post-position of *not* was employed by those who left behind a reputation as great men of literature of the times. With reference to nature of documents in which this construction occurred, the post-position of *not* was used in a wide range of documents, formal and informal, academic and non-academic, including parliamentary legislation, governmental documents such as *State Papers*, testi-

Chapter VI

mony and arraignments in nautical courts, books and treatise on laws; books on British history and political history, treatise on the reign of King James I, translations of books on the history of British politics and economics, chronicle, books on philosophy and philosophical history, textbooks on logic; books on medical science, mathematics, botany, ontogeny and (a textbook on) physics, treatises on hygiene and health, astronomy, the natural history of the earth, and in *Philosophical Transactions of the Royal Society*; English biblical translations, sermons, books on church history; articles in encyclopaedias, a definition in a dictionary, a textbook on ballet and a book on rhetoric. The extent to which this particular structure spread implies that the post-position *not* seems to have been far from an erroneous usage.

6.5.5. Geographical Distribution of Users of Post-position of *Not*

The birthplaces of the users of the post-position of *not* appear alphabetically in the list below, where '18-1 (2)', for example, represents that two examples occurred in the first half of the 18th century. People do not necessarily continue throughout their lives to use language they encounter in infancy, and there are some who leave their birthplaces. It is next to impossible to specify at which stage the users concerned acquired this usage. Therefore, their birthplaces were considered as an index.

Bedfordshire   17-2
Berkshire   16-1, 18-1 (2), 18-2, 20-2
Brecknockshire   17-1, 17-2
Bristol   18-2, 19-1
Buckinghamshire   17-1
Caernarvonshire   17-2
Cambridgeshire   16-2 (2), 17-1, 17-2, 18-1
Carmarthenshire   17-2
Cheshire   16-2 (2), 17-1, 17-2, 18-2, 19-2
Cornwall   17-1
Cumbria   16-2
Cumberland   17-2, 18-1 (3), 19-1 (2)

Diachrony of Present Participles and Gerunds Followed by *Not*

Derbyshire   17-2 (2), 18-2
Devonshire   16-2 (2), 17-1 (4), 17-2 (2), 18-1, 18-2, 19-2
Dorsetshire   17-1
Dumfriesshire   19-1
Durham   20-2
Essex   16-1, 16-2, 17-1 (5), 17-2 (3)
Gloucestershire   17-1
Hampshire   17-2 (2), 18-1, 19-1
Herefordshire   16-2, 17-2 (2)
Ireland   17-1, 17-2 (5), 18-1 (3), 18-2 (3), 19-2
Isle of Wight   17-2 (2)
Kent   16-2 (2), 17-1 (3), 17-2 (4), 18-2
Lancashire   16-2 (2), 17-2 (2), 20-2
Leicestershire   16-2, 17-2 (2), EModE III, 18-1 (2), 18-2
Lincolnshire   16-2 (2), 17-1 (2), 17-2 (2), 18-1 (3), 18-2, 19-1, 19-2 (2)
London   16-1, 16-2 (5), 17-1 (6), 17-2 (8), 18-1 (7), 18-2 (4), 19-1 (6),
    19-2 (3), 20-1 (3), 20-2 (3)
Middlesex   17-2, 18-1, 19-2
Norfolk   17-1, 17-2 (2), 19-2
Northamptonshire   16-2, 17-1 (2), 17-2 (3), 19-1
Northumberland   16-2, 17-1
North Yorkshire   18-2
Nottinghamshire   17-1, 17-2, 18-2, 19-1, 20-2
Oxfordshire   16-2 (2), 17-1 (4), 17-2 (4), 19-1
Pembrokeshire   19-1
Scotland   17-1, 19-2
Shropshire   16-2, 17-1, 17-2, 18-2
Somerset   16-2, 17-1, 17-2 (6), 18-1, 18-2
Staffordshire   18-2
Suffolk   15-1, 16-2, 17-1 (2), 17-2, 18-2, 19-1
Surrey   17-1, 17-2, 18-1
Sussex   17-1, 17-2, 19-1
Wales   17-1
Warwickshire   16-2, 17-1, 17-2, 19-2
West Midlands   17-2 (2)
Westmorland   17-2, 18-1
Wiltshire   17-1 (2), 17-2 (2), 18-1, 19-2

366

Chapter VI

Worcestershire   17-1, 17-2 (2)
Yorkshire   16-2, 17-1 (2), 17-2 (3), 19-1, 19-2

Based on the birthplaces above, the geographical and chronological distribution of users of the post-position of *not* can be illustrated as per the map on the next page. This map suggests that this usage was widely spread throughout Britain and Ireland in the history of the English language.

Diachrony of Present Participles and Gerunds Followed by *Not*

> A map showing users' instances of the post-position of *not* based on their birthplaces, in which '18-1 (2)', for example, represents that two examples occurred in the first half of the 18th century.

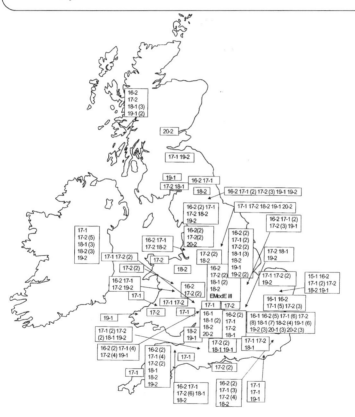

This copyright-free map was downloaded
from http://www.freemap.jp/item/europe/uk1.html.

Chapter VI

6.6. Summary of Chapter VI

Based upon the investigation of 99 collections, 130 volumes of diaries and correspondenc, Helsinki-DP, CEECS, Lampeter, Newdigate, ARCHER 3.1 and the *OED*[2] on CD-ROM, as well as LOB, FLOB, BNC, Brown and Frown, the following conclusions can be drawn:

a. The participial and gerundive *ing*-forms followed by *not* collected from Present-day English BNC, LOB, FLOB and Brown corpora are not mere slips of the pen or tongue, but residuals of earlier English. This construction was not necessarily 'rare' in the history of English.

b. Especially in Modern English, the participial or gerundive *ing*-forms followed by *not* were used widely by varied persons, including the nobility and the educated, throughout Britain and Ireland, and in varied documents, formal and informal, academic and non-academic.

c. The percentage of post-position of *not* was higher in the following order:

Perfective Participial *having not* PP /
Passive/Perfective Participial *being not* PP

>

Participial V-*ing not*

>

Perfective Gerundive *having not* PP /
Passive/Perfective Gerundive *being not* PP

≥

Gerundive V-*ing not*

It is evident that the more verbal force *ing*-forms assumed, the more frequently the post-position of *not* occurred, and that participial Verb-*ing not* typically occurred with not merely *be* and *have* but also with a closed class of verbs: *know, care, come, do, doubt,* and *find,* i.e. verbs which continued to show aversion to the auxiliary *do* in negative declaratives. These facts lead to speculation regarding the origin of the post-position of *not* that it has mirrored the mode of negation in negative declarative sentences.

Diachrony of Present Participles and Gerunds Followed by *Not*

d. The extent to which this particular structure spread implies that the post-position *not* seems to have been far from an erroneous usage. As shown in (61a-c) and (65a, b) respectively, it is an accepted theory that the post-position of *not* after *ing*-forms is not acceptable in Present-day English and was disliked in Modern English. It is likely, however, that this form may have been part of the grammar from the mid-16th to the mid-18th centuries, not an idiosyncrasy or mere slip of the pen.

Conclusion

Based upon primarily literary texts, historical English linguists have contributed to the description and explanation of both the stability of and change in the history of English. Even in the early 21st century, however, a considerable amount of evidence leading to the correction of historical English facts can be encountered from the reading of documents, such as private diaries and personal letters, which were not intended for publication.

In relation to such evidence, Chapter I has attempted to demonstrate the contribution the analyses of non-literary texts can make to the historical study of English, specifically by sorting linguistic data from such documents into the five following categories: (i) quotations indicating the initial phase of linguistic change, (ii) those showing linguistic conservatism, (iii) those filling in the chronologically awkward gap, (iv) those unveilling rare or unknown usages, and (v) those reflecting writers' own views of the English language during their lifetime. Based upon the compiled evidence, the necessity of the analysis of non-literary as well as literary texts and the indispensability of the traditional historical English linguistics as a complement, not a rival, to modern analyses have been demonstrated.

Out of the aforementioned five categories, category (iv) has been dealt with in detail in the subsequent chapters as it seems to be currently significant in the history of English research.

Chapter II has explored the diachrony of the usage of *he don't know*. Based on the diachronic analyses of *doesn't* and 3SG *don't* samples collected from not only 130 volumes of diaries and correspondence but also the *OED²*, the following conclusions have been derived. First, as far as written documents are concerned, the usage of 3SG *don't* was replaced by *doesn't* in the course of the second half of the 19th century. Second, it was accepted even in non-vulgar English until the end of the 19th century. *Doesn't* took more than 150 years before it became popular, despite its first written occurrence in 1674. Even the educated naturally resorted to the non-contracted form of *does not* or to 3SG *don't* until the wide acceptance of

Conclusion

doesn't around the mid-19th century. Third, no syntactic environments unique to 3SG *don't* were detected, except that 3SG *don't* occurred predominantly with the personal pronoun subject *he*/she/*it* and exclusively in declarative sentences. Fourthly, relative to the rise of *doesn't* around the mid-19th century, 3SG *don't* came to be stigmatised as a vulgar and informal usage, developing in that direction up to the early 20th century. It was then ultimately established at the vulgar or non-standard speech level, or current conversational grammar.

In American English, the usage of 3SG *don't* developed roots as a normal usage to the extent that it rose to the level of cultured speech in Southern dialects and the west part of the State of New York. Thus, it is thought that during the course of the second half of the 20th century *doesn't* was established in the United States, with the exception of those dialects. One of the reasons why Americans continued to resort to 3SG *don't* as a normal usage and consequently employment of *doesn't* was slow in acceptance in American English seems to be that *doesn't* was rarely used in British English until the mid-19th century, and accordingly, that this negative contraction was unnatural and unfamiliar to people who emigrated to the U.S. before that time.

Chapter III has discussed the diachrony of the passival progressive preceded by an animate or human subject. Although previous studies remark that its subject was practically and virtually expected to be [-animate], significant numbers of counter-examples have been presented. Accordingly, this usage was not as uncommon as has been believed. In fact, it was used by more diverse people, including the educated, and with more different verbs to the extent that it is not regarded as a mere idiosyncrasy or exception from around 1600 to 1820-50, when the passival progressive was superseded by the passive progressive. Animate or human nouns could be agentive surface subjects of this construction, at least in informal and common English. Although a distinct line can hardly be drawn between transitive and intransitive verbs, it is still an indisputable fact that the passival progressive with an animate or human subject occurred far more often than has been thought.

Conclusion

Related to this, the construction of the passival progressive followed by *by*-agent has been believed to be rare in the history of English; in previous studies only five examples have been collected. However, 14 more verbs together with 21 more examples have been discovered from the present texts examined. This usage was employed even by the educated and the upper echelon of society. Here also, the history of the passival progressive needs to be reconsidered.

Chapter IV has considered the diachrony of the participial progressive, such as *being going*. This usage, which first appeared in Middle English, has been believed to have been very rare throughout the history of the English progressive. In the 17th-19th centuries, however, it continued to be used in diaries and letters perhaps to convey dynamic connotation of the action in progress, plans or arrangements. For example, the form of *being* + Verb-*ing* occurred in 90+4 examples, written by 20 different individuals. This form proves to be not necessarily rare.

Chapter V has elucidated the diachrony of *seem* meaning 'to pretend'. This usage is thought to be uncommon in Present-day English, as the notion is not clearly defined in contemporary dictionaries, nor is it in the definitions of *seem, v.*[2] in the *OED*[2]. This meaning, however, is defined in large-scale American dictionaries such as *Webster's International Dictionary*, *The Century Dictionary* and *The Random House Dictionary*, and the *OED*[2]'s *seem*-derivatives—such as *seemer*, *seeming*, *seemingly* and *seemingness*—have the concept pertaining to active, deliberate show or pretence. It is a natural question why the verb *seem* in the *OED*[2] does not have the meaning 'to pretend', whereas some of its derivatives have the sense of 'pretence'. This chapter has attempted to unravel this mystery.

Evidence suggests that the verb *seem* as an active verb referring to deliberate show on the part of the agent subject originated in Elizabethan English, and continued being used in not only Early but also Late Modern English. This usage appeared in quite a few examples and was used even by the educated. In the course of the 19th century this usage became obsolescent, and the verb *seem* came to be restricted only to the modern use in which it describes the effect on our perceptions of appearances, at

374

Conclusion

least in Britain, while in American English it has or seems to have survived since its immigration. The usage of *seem* meaning 'to pretend' is thought to be one of the cases in which past British English usages are retained in American English.

All of these facts naturally and easily account for some *seem*-derivatives pertaining to the 'gene' of pretence. Even after the "parent", that is, the verb *seem*, finally abandoned this sense, the "children", namely primary derivatives, and the "grandchildren", secondary derivatives, retained the DNA, that is the sense of deliberate pretence. *Seemer, seeming, seemingly* and *seemingness* are, as it were, fossils. The aforementioned facts also explain the route of the development of *seem* 'pretend', which appears to still be in use to this day in present-day American English.

Chapter VI has attempted to modify earlier views on the diachrony of present participles or gerunds followed by *not*. This construction has been believed to be rare throughout the history of the English language. Nonetheless, the fact has been demonstrated that the participial or gerundive *ing*-forms followed by *not* were used widely by various persons, including the nobility and the educated, throughout Britain and Ireland, and in varied documents, formal and informal, academic and non-academic, especially in Modern English. It is likely that the post-position of *not* may have been part of the grammar from the mid-16th to the mid-18th centuries, not an idiosyncrasy or mere slip of the pen. The fact has also been clarified that the more verbal force *ing*-forms assumed, the more frequently the post-position of *not* occurred, and that the participial Verb-*ing not* typically occurred with verbs which continued to show aversion to the auxiliary *do* in negative declaratives. These facts have led to speculation regarding the origin of the post-position of *not* that it must have reflected the mode of negation in negative declarative sentences. Even though what has been substantiated above will not upset previous theories of English grammar, the idea of the history of English participial and gerundive negation has to be re-envisioned.

As presented above through five case studies, the emphasis has been laid on the necessity of the analysis of non-literary texts, especially docu-

Conclusion

ments not intended for public viewing or official use, such as private diaries and personal letters. At the common and informal speech level, as reflected in private diaries and personal letters, linguistic phases different from those which are shown in studies carried out based upon the analyses of literary language can be detected. (Here, the construction of participial and gerundive negation is exceptional, since the post-position of *not* was used in formal and academic writings as well as informal and non-academic ones.)

The present monograph may have provided readers with some new and enlightening theoretical ideas. However, although the results of the investigation conducted in this monograph will not disprove established theories on the English grammar system, they are far from being negligible. What has been done in this monograph is to have these rare usages, which have remained unnoticed, see the light of day by providing an abundance of evidence. What has been insisted on is the necessity of such analyses of non-literary as well as literary texts. Uncovering more hidden historical facts is one of the most important aims of historical linguistics and linguists because the explanation of linguistic changes presupposes comprehensive and thorough analyses of synchronic data of succeeding stages. An enormous amount of text remains unanalysed.

As demonstrated in this monograph, what are believed to have been 'rare' or 'unknown' usages are in fact not necessarily misuses, but elements of grammar in the past. It is hoped that these new discoveries will contribute to, or stir a controversy in, the historical study of the English language. This monograph concludes with the repeated emphasis upon the necessity of correcting and dispelling misunderstandings over historical linguistic facts.

Texts and Electronic Corpora Examined

(The years within angle brackets represent the time

covered by the texts and corpora examined)

Chapter I: D1-D42 and L1-L69 in A
Chapter II: D1-D41 and L1-L58 in A; B; D
Chapter III: D1-D42 and L1-L69 in A
Chapter IV: D1-D42 and L1-L69 in A
Chapter V: D1-D42 and L1-L69 in A
Chapter VI: D1-D41 and L1-L58 in A; C; D

A. Diaries and Correspondence

[The diaries and correspondence examined are all private diaries and personal letters, except for the following: D4 (John Rous), D12 (Thomas Cartwright) and D13 (Rowland Davies). From their entries, these three diaries cannot be regarded as 'private'. Nevertheless, they were included in the present texts examined so as to compensate for a chronological gap, as alternative contemporary texts were not available. Some texts consist of a mixture of diaries and letters. In such cases, they were classified into D(iaries) or L(etters) depending on which domain is predominant in terms of page length. In Robert G. Howarth, ed. (1932) *Letters and the Second Diary of Samuel Pepys*, J. M. Dent, London, inasmuch as the first 379 pages consist exclusively of letters and the rest of the text of entries for diaries 1683-1684, the former was labelled as L5 and the latter as D11 in the list below. In D9, John Evelyn (1620-1706) began to record daily events from around 1640 though his diary starts from 1620. The first 20 pages or so naturally take the form of reminiscences based upon the notes which he began to keep at the age of eleven (*ODNB*). It is confirmed that the whole entry in D28 (Peter Laurie) is memoirs based on a separate diary, because of the following passage "D28, 36 [2 October 1823], Thursday . . . and then went through all the duties which are detailed in Letts diary kept daily by me and not worth repeating in this book". To avoid clumsiness in quoting examples from D9 and D28, their dating adheres to the year shown in the texts.]

Texts and Electronic Corpora Examined

Diary [Diarist (Lifetime) Editor. *Title*. Etc. <Period Covered>

D1 [Dee, John (1527-1608)] Halliwell, James O., ed. (1842 [1968]) *The Private Diary of Dr. John Dee*, Camden, Rpt., Johnson Reprint, New York. <1577-1601>

D2 [Hoby, Margaret (1571-1633)] Meads, Dorothy M., ed. (1930) *Diary of Lady Margaret Hoby, 1599-1605*, George Routledge & Sons, London. <1599-1605>

D3 [Glanville, John (1586-1661)] Grosart, Alexander B., ed. (1883 [1965]) *The Voyage to Cadiz in 1625, Being a Journal Written by John Glanville*, Camden, Rpt., Johnson Reprint, New York. <1625>

D4 [Rous, John (1584-1644)] Green, Mary A. E., ed. (1856 [1968]) *Diary of John Rous*, Camden, Rpt., Johnson Reprint, New York. <1625-1642>

D5 [Roe, secretary of John Birch (1616-1691)] Webb, Thomas W., ed. (1873 [1965]) *Military Memoir of Colonel John Birch*, Camden, Rpt., Johnson Reprint, New York. <1642-1645>

D6 [Milward, John (1599-1670)] Robbins, Caroline, ed. (1938) *The Diary of John Milward*, Cambridge University Press, London. <1666-1668>

D7 [Symonds, Richard (1617-?1692)] Long, Charles E., ed. (1859 [1968]) *Diary of the Marches of the Royal Army during the Great Civil War; Kept by Richard Symonds*, Camden, Rpt., Johnson Reprint, New York. <1644-1645>

D8 [Josselin, Ralph (1617-1683)] Macfarlane, Alan, ed. (1976) *The Diary of Ralph Josselin 1616-1683*, Oxford University Press, London. <?1643-1683>

D9 [Evelyn, John (1620-1706)] de Beer, Esmond S., ed. (1955) *The Diary of John Evelyn*, 6 Vols, Clarendon Press, Oxford. <1640-1706>

D10 [Pepys, Samuel (1633-1703)] Latham, Richard and William Matthews, eds (1970-1983) *The Diary of Samuel Pepys*, 11 Vols, University of California Press, Berkeley and Los Angeles. <1660-1669>

D11 [Pepys, Samuel (1633-1703)] Howarth, Robert G., ed. (1932) *Letters and the Second Diary of Samuel Pepys*, J. M. Dent, London. [Part of a diary p. 379-] <1683-1684>

D12 [Cartwright, Thomas (1634-1689)] Hunter, Joseph, ed. (1843 [1968]) *The Diary of Dr. Thomas Cartwright*, Camden, Rpt., John-

Texts and Electronic Corpora Examined

son Reprint, New York. <1686-1687>

D13 [Davies, Rowland (1649-1721)] Caulfield, Richard, ed. (1857 [1968]) *Journal of the Very Rev. Rowland Davies*, Camden, Rpt., Johnson Reprint, New York. <1689-1690>

D14 [Halley, Edmond (1656-1742)] Thrower, Norman J. W., ed. (1981) *The Three Voyages of Edmond Halley in the Paramore 1698-1701*, The Hakluyt Society, London. <1689-1690>

D15 [Nicolson, William (1655-1727)] Jones, Clyve and Geoffrey Holmes, eds (1985) *The London Diaries of William Nicolson, Bishop of Carlisle, 1702-1718*, Clarendon Press, Oxford. <1702-1718>

D16 [Dodington, George B. (1691-1762)] Carswell, John and Lewis A. Dralle, eds. (1965) *The Political Journal of George Bubb Dodington*, Clarendon Press, Oxford. <1749-1762>

D17 [Wesley, John (1703-1791)] Parker, Percy L., abridg., Hughes, Hugh P., intro., Birrell, Augustine, apprec. (1902) *John Wesley's Journal*, Isbister, London. <1735-1790>

D18 [White, Gilbert (1720-1793)] Greenoak, Francesca, ed. (1988) *The Journals of Gilbert White*, Vol. 2, Century, London. <1774-1783>

D19 [Staniforth, Thomas (1735-1803)] Hext, Jean, ed., Rowse, Alfred L., foreword. (1965) *The Staniforth Diary: A Visit to Cornwall in 1800*, D. Bradford Barton, Truro. <1800>

D20 [Hughes, Anne (? -?)] Croucher, Michael, foreword. (1937 [1980]) *The Diary of a Farmer's Wife, 1796-1797*, Rpt., Allen Lane, London. <1796-1797>

D21 [Woodforde, James (1740-1803)] Beresford, John, ed. (1924 [1981]) *The Diary of a Country Parson: The Reverend James Woodforde*, 5 Vols, Rpt., Oxford University Press, Oxford. <1758-1802>

D22 [Stevens, William B. (1756-1800)] Galbraith, Georgina, ed. (1965) *The Journal of the Rev. William Bagshaw Stevens*, Clarendon Press, Oxford. <1792-1800>

D23 [Sheridan, Betsy (1758-1837)] LeFanu, William, ed. (1960) *Betsy Sheridan's Journal: Letters from Sheridan's Sister, 1784-1786 and 1788-1790*, Eyre & Spottiswoode, London. <1784-1790>

D24 [Wordsworth, Dorothy (1771-1855)] Moorman, Mary, ed., Darbishire, Helen, intro. (1958 [1991]) *Journals of Dorothy Wordsworth*, The Alfoxden Journal 1798, The Grasmere Journals 1800-1803, 2nd ed., Rpt., Oxford University Press, Oxford. <1798-1803>

Texts and Electronic Corpora Examined

D25 [Skinner, John (1772-1839)] Coombs, Howard and Peter Coombs, eds (1930 [1971]) *Journal of a Somerset Rector, 1803-1834, John Skinner, A. M. Antiquary, 1772-1839, Parochial Affairs of the Parish of Camerton*, Revised and Enlarged ed., Kingsmead, Weston-super-Mare. <1803-1834>

D26 [Campbell, Charlotte S. M. (1775-1861)] Steuart, Archibald F., ed. (1908) *The Diary of a Lady-in-Waiting*, Vol. 1, John Lane, The Bodley Head, London. <1810-1815>

D27 [Arbuthnot, Harriet (?1793-1834)] Bamford, Francis and the Duke of Welllngton, eds (1950) *The Journal of Mrs. Arbuthnot, 1820-1832*, Vol. 1, Macmillan, London. <1820-1825>

D28 [Laurie, Peter (1778-1861)] Shepherd, Elizabeth, ed. (1985) *The Journal of Sir Peter Laurie*, Costello, with the Saddlers' Company, Tunbridge Wells. <?1823-1859>

D29 [Hawker, Peter (1786-1853)] Payne-Gallwey, Ralph, intro, McKelvie, Colin L., new foreword (1893 [1988]) *The Diary of Colonel Peter Hawker, 1802-1853*, 2 Vols, Rpt., Greenhill Books, London. <1802-1853>

D30 [Watkin, Absalom (1787-1861)] Watkin, Alfred E., ed. (1920) *Absalom Watkin: Extracts from His Journal 1814-1856*, T. Fisher Unwin, London. <1814-1856>

D31 [Todd, Matthew (1791-1853)] Trease, Geoffrey, ed. (1968) *Matthew Todd's Journal: A Gentleman's Gentleman in Europe 1814-1820*, Heinemann, London. <1814-1820>

D32 [Greville, Henry W. (1801-1872)] Byng, Alice, ed. (1883-1905) *Leaves from the Diary of Henry Greville*, Vols 1 & 2, ed. by Viscountess Enfield, Vols 3 & 4, ed. by Countess of Strafford, Smith, Elder, & Co., London. <1832-1872>

D33 [Gladstone, William E. (1809-1898)] Foot, Michael R. D., ed. (1968) *The Gladstone Diaries*, Vol. 1, Clarendon Press, Oxford. <1825-1832 >

D34 [Darwin, Charles (1809-1882)] Keynes, Richard D., ed. (1988) *Charles Darwin's Beagle Diary*, Cambridge University Press, Cambridge. <1831-1836>

D35 [Huxley, Thomas H. (1825-1891)] Huxley, Julian, ed. (1935) *T. H. Huxley's Diary of the Voyage of H. M. S. Rattlesnake*, Chatto and Windus, London. <1846-1850>

Texts and Electronic Corpora Examined

D36 [Kilvert, Francis (1840-1879)] Plomer, William, ed. (1938-40 [1980])
Kilvert's Diary: Selections from the Diary of the Rev. Francis Kilvert,
3 Vols, Rpt., Jonathan Cape, London. <1870-1879>

D37 [Hawker, James (1836-1921)] Christian, Garth, ed. (1961) *James
Hawker's Journal: A Victorian Poacher*, Oxford University Press,
London. <1904-1905>

D38 [Buxton, Ellen (1848-1892)] Creighton, Ellen R. C., arrang. (1967)
Ellen Buxton's Journal, 1860-1864, Geoffrey Bles, London. <1860-
1864>

D39 [Hamilton, Edward W. (1847-1908)] Bahlman, Dudley W. R., ed.
(1972) *The Diary of Sir Edward Walter Hamilton, 1880-1885*, Vol.
1, Clarendon Press, Oxford. <1880-1882>

D40 [Macmillan, Harold. (1894-1986)] Macmillan, Harold (1984) *War
Diaries: Politics and War in the Mediterranean, January 1943-
May 1945*, Macmillan, London. <1943-1945>

D41 [Spender, Stephen H. (1909-95)] Goldsmith, John, ed. (1992)
Stephen Spender: Journals 1939-1983 (Corrected paperback edition), faber and faber, London. <1939-1983>

D42 [Gregory, Isabella A. (1852-1932)] Murphy, Daniel J., ed. (1978)
Lady Gregory's Journals, Vol. 1, Colin Smythe, Gerrards Cross.
<1916-1925>

Correspondence [Main provenance / correspondent (Lifetime)] Editor.
Title. Etc. <Period covered>

L1 [Eminent Literary Men] Ellis, Henry, ed. (1843 [1968]) *Original
Letters of Eminent Literary Men of the Sixteenth, Seventeenth, and
Eighteenth Centuries*, Camden, Rpt., Johnson Reprint, New York.
<15..-1799>

L2 [King Charles I (1600-1649)] Bruce, John, ed. (1856 [1968]) *Charles
I. in 1646: Letters of King Charles the First to Queen Henrietta
Maria*, Camden, Rpt., Johnson Reprint, New York. <1646-1647>

L3 [Family of Hatton] Thompson, Edward M., ed. (1878 [1965])
*Correspondence of the Family of Hatton, Being Chiefly Letters Ad-
dressed to Christopher First Viscount Hatton, A.D. 1601-1704*, Vol.
1, Camden, Rpt., Johnson Reprint, New York. <1601-1680>

L4 [Osborne, Dorothy (1627-1695)] Smith, George C. M., ed. (1928
[1968]) *The Letters of Dorothy Osborne to William Temple*, Rpt.,

Oxford University Press, Oxford. <1652-1657>

L5 [Pepys, Samuel (1633-1703)] Howarth, Robert G., ed. (1932) *Letters and the Second Diary of Samuel Pepys*, J. M. Dent, London. [Part of letters: pp. 1-375] <Lett., 1655-1703>

L6 [Pepys, Samuel (1633-1703)] Heath, Helen T., ed. (1955) *The Letters of Samuel Pepys and His Family Circle*, Clarendon Press, Oxford. <1663-1692>

L7 [Pepys, Samuel (1633-1703)] Tanner, Joseph R., ed. (1926) *Private Correspondence and Miscellaneous Papers of Samuel Pepys, 1679-1703*, 2 Vols, G. Bell & Sons, London. <1679-1703>

L8 [Williamson, Joseph] Christie, William D., ed. (1874 [1965]) *Letters Addressed from London to Sir Joseph Williamson*. 2 Vols, Camden, Rpt., Johnson Reprint, New York. <1673-1674>

L9 [Etherege, Sir George (?1635-1691)] Bracher, Frederick, ed. (1974) *Letters of Sir George Etherege*, University of California Press, Berkeley and Los Angeles. <1670-1689>

L10 [Russell, Rachel (1636-1723)] Sellwood, Thomas, ed. (1748 [1773]) *Letters of Lady Rachel Russell, From the Manuscript in the Library at Woburn Abbey, To Which Is Prefixed An Introduction Vindciating the Character of Lord. Russell against Sir John Dalrymple, &c.*, 2nd ed., Edward and Charles Dilly, London. <1679-1718>

L11 [Savile, Henry (1642-1687)] Cooper, William D., ed. (1858 [1968]) *Savile Correspondence: Letters to and from Henry Savile*, Camden, Rpt., Johnson Reprint, New York. <1661-1689>

L12 [Lowther, John (1642-1706)] Hainsworth, David R., ed. (1983) *The Correspondence of Sir John Lowther of Whitehaven, 1693-1698: A Provincial Community in Wartime*, Oxford University Press, London. <1693-1698>

L13 [Newton, Sir Isaac (1642-1727)] Hall, Alan R., and Laura Tilling, eds (1975) *The Correspondence of Isaac Newton*, Vol. 5, Cambridge University Press, Cambridge. <1709-1713>

L14 [Defoe, Daniel (?1659/?61-1731)] Healey, George H., ed. (1955) *The Letters of Daniel Defoe*, Clarendon Press, Oxford. <1703-1730>

L15 [Steele, Richard (1672-1729)] Blanchard, Rae, ed. (1941) *The Correspondence of Richard Steele*, Oxford University Press, Oxford. <?1684-1725>

L16 [Swift, Jonathan (1667-1745)] Williams, Harold, ed. (1948) *Jonathan*

Texts and Electronic Corpora Examined

Swift: Journal to Stella, 2 Vols, Clarendon Press, Oxford. <1710-1713>

L17 [Addison, Joseph (1672-1719)] Graham, Walter, ed. (1941) *The Letters of Joseph Addison*, Clarendon Press, Oxford. <1695-1719>

L18 [Gay. John (1685-1732)] Melville, Lewis (1921) *Life and Letters of John Gay (1685-1732): Author of "The Beggar's Opera"*, Daniel O'Connor, London. <1714-1732>

L19 [Richardson, Samuel (1689-1761)] Slattery, William C., ed. (1969) *The Richardson-Stinstra Correspondence and Stinstra's Prefaces to Clarissa*, Southern Illinois University Press, Carbondale and Edwardsville. <1752-1756>

L20 [Eaton, Daniel (1698-1742)] Wake, Joan and Deborah C. Webster, eds (1971) *The Letters of Daniel Eaton to the Third Earl of Cardigan, 1725-1732*, Dalkeith Press, Kettering. <1725-1732>

L21 [Stanhope, Philip D., Fourth Earl of Chesterfield (1694-1773)] Roberts, David, ed. (1992) *Lord Chesterfield: Letters*, Oxford University Press, Oxford. <1728-1772>

L22 [Lennox, Charles, 2nd Duke of Richmond (1701-1750)] McCann, Timothy J., ed. (1984) *The Correspondence of the Dukes of Richmond and Newcastle, 1724-1750*, Sussex Record Society, Lewes. <1724-1750>

L23 [Wesley, John (1703-1791)] Telford, John, ed. (1931 [1960]) *The Letters of the Rev. John Wesley, A. M., Sometime Fellow of Lincoln College, Oxford*, Vol. 1, Rpt., The Epworth Press, London. <1721-1741>

L24 [Dodsley, Robert (1703-1764)] Tierney, James E., ed. (1988) *The Correspondence of Robert Dodsley, 1733-1764*, Cambridge University Press, Cambridge. <1733-1764>

L25 [Penrose, John (1713-1776)] Mitchell, Brigitte and Hubert Penrose, eds (1983) *Letters from Bath, 1766-1767, by the Rev. John Penrose*, Alan Sutton, Gloucester. <1766-1767>

L26 [Gray, Thomas (1716-1771)] Toynbee, Paget, and Leonard Whibley, eds, Starr, Herbert W., correct. (1935 [1971]) *Correspondence of Thomas Gray*, 3 Vols, Clarendon, Rpt., Oxford University Press, Oxford. <1734-1771>

L27 [Shenstone, William (1714-1763)] Mallam, Duncan, ed. (1939) *Letters of William Shenstone*, University of Minnesota Press, Minneapolis. <1736-1763>

L28 [Pierce, Eliza (? -1776)] Macdonald, Violet M., ed. (1927) *The Letters of Eliza Pierce, 1751-1775, with Letters from Her Son Pierce Joseph Taylor, a Schoolboy at ETON*, Frederick Etchells & Hugh Macdonald, London. <1751-1771>

L29 [Hurd, Richard (1720-1808)] Brewer, Sarah, ed. (1995) *The Early Letters of Bishop Richard Hurd, 1739-1762*, Boydell Press, Woodbridge. <1739-1762>

L30 [Smith, Adam (1723-1790)] Mossner, Ernest C. and Ian S. Ross, eds (1977) *The Correspondence of Adam Smith*, Clarendon Press, Oxford. <1740-1790>

L31 [Percy, Thomas (1729-1811)] Brooks, Cleanth, ed. (1977) *The Correspondence of Thomas Percy & William Shenstone*, Yale University Press, New Haven & London. <1757-1763>

L32 [Wedgwood, Josiah (1730-1795)] Finer, Ann and George Savage, eds (1965) *The Selected Letters of Josiah Wedgwood*, Cory, Adams & Mackay, London. <1762-1795>

L33 [Darwin, Erasmus (1731-1802)] King-Hele, Desmond, ed. (1981) *The Letters of Erasmus Darwin*, Cambridge University Press, Cambridge. <1749-1802>

L34 [Gibbon, Edward (1737-1794)] Norton, Jane E., ed. (1956) *The Letters of Edward Gibbon*, Vol. 1, Cassell and Company, London. <1750-1773>

L35 [Rose, George (1744-1818)] Harcourt, Leveson V., ed. (1860) *The Diaries and Correspondence of the Right Hon. George Rose: Containing Original Letters of the Most Distinguished Statesmen of His Day*, Vol. 1, Richard Bentley, London. <1782-1802>

L36 [More, Hannah (1745-1833)] Roberts, William, ed. (1834) *Memoirs of the Life and Correspondence of Mrs. Hannah More*, Vols 3 and 4, 2nd ed., R. B. Seeley and W. Burnside, London. <1785-1828>

L37 [Burns, Robert (1759-1796)] Johnson, Reginald B., ed. (1928) *The Letters of Robert Burns*, John Lane the Bodley Head, London. <1781-1796>

L38 [Crabbe, George (1751-1832)] Faulkner, Thomas C., ed. (1985) *Selected Letters and Journals of George Crabbe*, Clarendon Press, Oxford. <1781-1832>

L39 [Blake, William (1757-1827)] Keynes, Geoffrey, ed. (1956 [1980])

Texts and Electronic Corpora Examined

The Letters of William Blake, with Related Documents, 3rd ed., Clarendon Press, Oxford. <1795-1829>

L40 [Cobbett, William (1762-1835)] Cole, George D. H., ed. (1937) *Letters from William Cobbett to Edward Thornton, Written in the Years 1797 to 1800,* Oxford University Press, London. <1797-1800>

L41 [Rogers, Samuel (1763-1855)] Barbier, Carl P., ed. (1959) *Samuel Rogers and William Gilpin: Their Friendship and Correspondence,* Oxford University Press, London. <1796-1803>

L42 [Southey, Robert (1774-1843)] Curry, Kenneth, ed. (1965) *New Letters of Robert Southey,* Vol. 1, Columbia University Press, London. <1792-1810>

L43 [Wordsworth, Dorothy (1771-1855)] Hill, Alan G., ed. (1981 [1985]) *Letters of Dorothy Wordsworth,* Rpt., Clarendon Press, Oxford. <1787-1838>

L44 [Raikes, Thomas (1778-1848)] Raikes, Harriet, ed. (1861) *Private Correspondence of Thomas Raikes, with the Duke of Wellington and Other Distinguished Contemporaries,* Richard Bentley, London. <1812-1847>

L45 [Peel, Sir Robert (1788-1850)] Peel, George, ed. (1920) *The Private Letters of Sir Robert Peel,* John Murray, London. <1810-1846>

L46 [Clare, John (1793-1864)] Tibble, John W. and Anne Tibble, eds (1951) *The Letters of John Clare,* Routledge & Kegan Paul, London. <1817-1860>

L47 [Martineau, Harriet (1802-1876)] Sanders, Valerie, ed. (1990) *Harriet Martineau: Selected Letters,* Clarendon Press, Oxford. <1819-1874>

L48 [Palmer, Samuel (1805-1881)] Lister, Raymond, ed. (1974) *The Letters of Samuel Palmer,* 2 Vols, Clarendon Press, Oxford. <1814-1881>

L49 [FitzGerald, Edward (1809-1883)] Terhune, Alfred M. and Annabelle B. Terhune, eds (1980) *The Letters of Edward FitzGerald,* Vol. 1, Princeton University Press, Prnceton. <1830-1850>

L50 [Tennyson, Alfred (1809-1892)] Lang, Cecil Y. and Edgar F. Shannon, Jr., eds (1987) *The Letters of Alfred Lord Tennyson,* Vol. 2, Clarendon Press, Oxford. <1851-1870>

L51 [Ruskin, John (1819-1900)] Burd, Van A., ed. (1973) *The Ruskin Family Letters: The Correspondence of John James Ruskin, His*

Wife, and Their Son, John, 1801-1843, Vol. 1, Cornell University Press, London. <1801-1837>

L52 [Eliot, George (1819-1880)] Haight, Gordon S., ed. (1985) *Selections from George Eliot's Letters*, Yale University Press, New Haven/London. <1836-1880>

L53 [Arnold, Matthew (1822-1888)] Russell, George W. E., collect. and arrang. (1895) *Letters of Matthew Arnold: 1848-1888*, Vol 1, Macmillan, London. <1848-1868>

L54 [Meredith, George (1828-1909)] Meredith, William M., ed. (1912) *Letters of George Meredith*, Vol. 1, 2nd ed., Constable, London. <1844-1881>

L55 [Dodgson, Charles L. (1832-1898)] Cohen, Morton N., ed. (1979) *The Letters of Lewis Carroll*, Vol. 1, Oxford University Press, New York. <c1837-1885>

L56 [Swinburne, Algernon C. (1837-1909)] Gosse, Edmund and Thomas J. Wise, eds (1918) *The Letters of Algernon Charles Swinburne*, Vol. 1, William Heinemann, London. <1858-1877>

L57 [Ritchie, Anne T. (1837-1919)] Ritchie, Hester, ed. (1924) *Letters of Anne Thackeray Ritchie, With Forty-two Additional Letters from her Father William Makepeace Thackeray*, The Ryerson Press, Toronto. <1837-1919>

L58 [Wilde, Oscar F. O. W. (?1854/?56-1900)] Hart-Davis, Rupert, ed. (1985 [1988]) *More Letters of Oscar Wilde*, Rpt., Oxford University Press, Oxford. <?1876-1900>

L59 [R. Oxenden ~ A Committee of Parishioners at Godmersham] Sheppard, J. B., ed. (1877 [1965]) *Christ Church Letters: A Volume of Mediaeval Letters Relating to the Affairs of the Priory of Christ Church Canterbury*, Camden, Rpt., Johnson Reprint, New York. <1334-15..>

L60 [King James VI (1566-1625)] Bruce, John, ed. (1849 [1968]) *Letters of Queen Elizabeth and King James VI of Scotland*, Camden, Rpt., Johnson Reprint, New York. <1582-1603>

L61 [Johnson, Samuel (1709-1784)] Hill, George B., ed. (1892) *Letters of Samuel Johnson*, 2 Vols, Harper & Brothers, New York. <1731-1784>

L62 [Montagu, Elizabeth (1720-1800)] Montagu, Matthew, publish. (1809) *The Letters of Mrs. Elizabeth Montagu*, Pt I, 2 Vols, W.

Texts and Electronic Corpora Examined

Bulmer, London. <1734-1744>

L63 [Sheridan, Richard B. (1751-1816)] Price, Cecil, ed. (1966) *The Letters of Richard Brinsley Sheridan*, Vols 1 & 3, Clarendon Press, Oxford. <1766-1816>

L64 [Austen, Jane (1775-1817)] Chapman, Robert W., ed. (1932 [1979]) *Jane Austen's Letters to Her Sister Cassandra and Others*, Rpt., Oxford University Press, Oxford. <1796-1817>

L65 [Dickens, Charles (1812-1870)] Storey, Graham, Kathleen Tillotson and Nina Burgis, eds (1988) *The Letters of Charles Dickens* (The Pilgrim Edition), Vol. 6, Clarendon Press, Oxford. <1850-1852>

L66 [Pater, Walter (1839-1894)] Evans, Lawrence, ed. (1970) *Letters of Walter Pater*, Clarendon Press, Oxford. <1859-1905>

L67 [Wilde, Oscar F. O. W. (?1854/?56-1900)] Hart-Davis, Rupert, ed. (1979) *Selected Letters of Oscar Wilde*, Oxford University Press, Oxford. <1875-1900>

L68 [Gissing, George (1857-1903)] Gissing, Algernon & Ellen Gissing, collect. (1927) *Letters of George Gissing to Members of His Family*, Constable, London. <1868-1903>

L69 [Galsworthy, John (1867-1933)] Garnett, Edward, ed. (1934) *Letters from John Galsworthy: 1900-1932*, Charles Scribner's Sons, London. <1900-1932>

B. Electronic British English texts, consisting of a heterogeneous mixture of 260 different documents such as biographies, dramas, essays, journals, letters, novels, speeches, travelogues, treatises, etc., randomly selected and downloaded from the websites of the following universities and organisations in October 2005 and July 2006. Here the present author would like to express to these university and organisation websites a great debt of gratitude. Their on-line electronic texts were very useful, saving the present author much time in compiling examples before drawing up Table 10.

Texts and Electronic Corpora Examined

McMaster University (http://socserv2.socsci.mcmaster.ca/)	Project Gutenberg (http://www.gutenberg.org/)
Rutgers University in Newark (http://andromeda.rutgers.edu/)	University of Michigan (http://www.hti.umich. edu/)
University of Oregon (http://darkwing.uoregon.edu/)	University of Pennsylvania (http:// digital.library.upenn.edu/)
University of Toronto (http://eir.library.utoronto.ca/)	University of Virginia (http://etext.lib.virginia.edu/)
York University, Canada (http://psychclassics.yorku.ca/)	

C. Electronic Corpora

a. The four following corpora included in Hofland, Knut, Anne Lindebjerg and Jørn Thunestvedt (1999) *ICAME Collection of English Language Corpora*, 2nd ed., The HIT Centre, University of Bergen:

(i) [LOB] Johansson, Stig, in collaboration with Geoffrey N. Leech and Helen Goodluck (1978) *The Lancaster-Oslo/Bergen Corpus of British English, for Use with Digital Computers*, Department of English, University of Oslo. <1961>

(ii) [FLOB] Hundt, Marianne, Andrea Sand and Rainer Siemund (1998) *The Freiburg-LOB Corpus of British English*, Englisches Seminar, Albert-Ludwigs-Universität Freiburg. <1991-1992>

(iii) [Brown] Francis, W. Nelson and Henry Kucera (1964 [1979]) *A Standard Corpus of Present-Day Edited American English, for Use with Digital Computers*, Revised and Amplified Edition, Department of Linguistics, Brown University. <1961>.

(iv) [Frown] Hundt, Marianne, Andrea Sand and Paul Skandera (1999) *The Freiburg-Brown Corpus of American English*, Englisches Seminar, Albert-Ludwigs-Universität Freiburg. <1991-1992>

b. [BNC] *British National Corpus* (2000), World Edition, SARA Version 0.98, Humanities Computing Unit of Oxford University on Behalf of the BNC Consortium, Oxford. <Mostly 1984-1994>

c. ARCHER 3.1 (adhering to ARCHER User Agreement, Part 1, April 2014, "6. How to cite ARCHER")

Texts and Electronic Corpora Examined

ARCHER 3.1 = A Representative Corpus of Historical English Registers version 3.1. 1990–1993/2002/2007/2010/2013. Originally compiled under the supervision of Douglas Biber and Edward Finegan at Northern Arizona University and University of Southern California; modified and expanded by subsequent members of a consortium of universities. Current member universities are Bamberg, Freiburg, Heidelberg, Helsinki, Lancaster, Leicester, Manchester, Michigan, Northern Arizona, Santiago de Compostela, Southern California, Trier, Uppsala, Zurich. Examples of usage taken from ARCHER were obtained under the terms of the ARCHER User Agreement (available on the Documentation page of the ARCHER website, http://www.manchester. ac.uk/archer/). <1650-1999>

d. The four following corpora included in Hofland, Knut, Anne Lindebjerg and Jørn Thunestvedt (1999) *ICAME Collection of English Language Corpora*, 2nd ed., The HIT Centre, University of Bergen:

(i) [CEECS] Sociolinguistics and Language History Project Team (1998) *Corpus of Early English Correspondence Sampler*, Department of English, University of Helsinki. <1418-1680>

(ii) [Helsinki-DP] Rissanen, Matti, *et al.* (1991) *The Helsinki Corpus of English Texts: Diachronic Part*, Department of English, University of Helsinki. < -1710>

(iii) [Lampeter] Schmied, Josef, Claudia Claridge and Rainer Siemund (1998) *The Lampeter Corpus of Early Modern English Tracts*, Real Centre, University of Chemnitz. <1640-1740>

(iv) [Newdigate] Hines, Philip, Jr., ed. (1994) *Newdigate Newsletters, Numbers 1 through 2100 (3 January 1673/4 through 11 June 1692)*. <1674-1692>

D. [*OED²*] Simpson, John A. and Edmund S. C. Weiner (2002) *The Oxford English Dictionary, Second Edition, on CD-ROM, Version 3.1*, Oxford University Press, Oxford.

Works Cited

[*AHD³*] Soukhanov, Anne H., *et al.*, eds (1969 [1992]) *The American Heritage Dictionary of the English Language*, 3rd ed., Houghton Mifflin, Boston.

Ando, Sadao (1976) *A Descriptive Syntax of Christopher Marlowe's Language*, University of Tokyo Press, Tokyo.

Araki, Kazuo, and Masatomo Ukaji (1984) *Eigoshi IIIA* [*History of English IIIA*] (Eigoshi Taikei [Outline of English Linguistics], 10), Taishukan, Tokyo.

Aronstein, Ph. (1918) "Die periphrastische Form im Englischen," *Anglia* 42, N. F. 30, 1-84.

Bækken, Bjørg (1998) *Word Order Patterns in Early Modern English, with Special Reference to the Position of the Subject and the Finite Verb*, Novus Press, Oslo.

Barber, Charles (1976) *Early Modern English* (The Language Library), André Deutsch, London.

Baugh, Albert C. (1951 [1976]) *A History of the English Language*, 2nd ed., Rpt., Routredge & Kegan Paul, London.

Bergeder, Fritz. (1914) *Die periphrastische Form des englischen Verbums im 17 Jahrhundert*, C. A. Kæmmerer & Co., Halle.

Biber, Douglas, Stig Johansson, Geoffrey Leech, Susan Conrad, and Edward Finegan (1999) *Longman Grammar of Spoken and Written English*, Pearson Education, Harlow.

Bloomfield, Morton W. and Leonard Newmark (1963) *A Linguistic Introduction to the History of English*, Alfred A. Knopf, New York.

Bolinger, Dwight (1979) "The Jingle Theory of Double-ing," in David J. Allerton, Edward Carney and David Holdcroft, eds, *Function and Context in Linguistic Analysis: A Festschrift for William Haas*, 41-56, Cambridge University Press, Cambridge.

Brainerd, Barron (1989 [1993]) "The Contractions of *not*: a Historical Note," *Journal of English Linguistics* 22, 176-196.

[*Britannica*] The On-line Version of the *Encyclopædia Britannica* (http://www. britannica.com/).

Bullokar, William (1586 [1971]) "Booke at Large, Bref Grammar and

Pamphlet for Grammar," with Explanatory Remarks by Takanobu Otsuka, in Takanobu Otsuka, gen ed., *A Reprint Series of Books Relating to the English Language*, Vol. 1, Nan'un-do, Tokyo, 5-164.

[*CDNB*] Lee, Sidney, preface (1903 [1979]) *The Dictionary of National Biography, Founded in 1882 by George Smith, The Concise Dictionary*, Part 1, 2nd ed., Rpt., Oxford University Press, Oxford.

[*CHEL*] Ward, Adolphus W. and Alfred R. Waller, eds (1911, 1912) *The Cambridge History of English Literature*, Vols. 7 and 9, Cambridge University Press, Cambridge.

[*COD¹⁰*] Pearsall, Judy, *et al.*, eds (1911 [1999]) *The Concise Oxford Dictionary*, 10th ed., Oxford University Press, Oxford.

Curme, George O. (1931) *Syntax* (Maruzen Asian Edition), D. C. Heath, Boston; Maruzen, Tokyo.

Denison, David (1993) *English Historical Syntax: Verbal Constructions* (Longman Linguistics Library), Longman, London.

Denison, David (1998) "Syntax," in Suzanne Romaine, ed., *The Cambridge History of the English Language*, Vol. 4 (1776- 1997), Cambridge University Press, Cambridge, 92-329.

Ellegård, Alvar (1953) *The Auxiliary Do: The Establishment and Regulation of Its Use in English* (Gothenburg Studies in English II), Almqvist & Wiksell, Stockholm.

Franz, Wilhelm (1939) *Die Sprache Shakespeares in Vers und Prosa*, Max Niemeyer, Halle.

Huddleston, Rodney, and Geoffrey K. Pullum (2002) *The Cambridge Grammar of the English Language*, Cambridge University Press, Cambridge.

Jespersen, Otto (1905 [1972]) *Growth and Structure of the English Language*, 9th ed., Basil Blackwell, Oxford.

Jespersen, Otto (1931 [1970]) *A Modern English Grammar on Historical Principles*, Part IV, Rpt., George Allen & Unwin, London.

Jespersen, Otto (1940 [1970]) *A Modern English Grammar on Historical Principles*, Pat V, Rpt., George Allen & Unwin, London.

Kubota, Yasuo (1970) "The Use of the Auxiliary *Do* in Dryden's Essays and Letters," *Tributaries* 2, 11-50.

[*LDCE⁵*] Mayor, Michael, *et al.*, eds (1978 [2009]) *Longman Dictionary of Contemporary English*, 5th ed., Rpt., Pearson Education, Harlow.

Lowth, Robert (1762 [1968]) "A Short Introduction to English Grammar," with Explanatory Remarks by Toshio Gunji, in Takanobu Otsuka, gen ed., *A Reprint Series of Books Relating to the English Language*, Vol. 13, Nan'un-do, Tokyo, 15-113.

Mair, Christian (2006) *Twentieth-Century English: History, Variation, and Standardization*, Cambridge University Press, Cambridge.

Matthews, William, comp. (1950 [1984]) *British Diaries: An Annotated Bibliography of British Diaries Written between 1442 and 1942* (California Library Reprint Edition), Rpt., University of California Press, Berkeley and Los Angeles.

Mencken, Henry L. (1919 [1977]) *The American Language: An Inquiry into the Development of English in the United States*, 4th ed., One-Volume Abridged Edition, Alfred A. Knopf, New York.

Mossé, Fernand (1938) *Histoire de la forme périphrastique être + participe présent en germanique*, Part II, C. Klincksieck, Paris.

Mustanoja, Tauno F. (1960) *A Middle English syntax*, Part I, Société Néophilologique, Helsinki.

[*MWCD¹²*] Mish, Frederick C., *et al.*, eds (1898 [2013]) *Merriam-Webster's Collegiate Dictionary*, 12th ed., Merriam-Webster, Springfield.

Nakamura, Fujio (1986) "*Oxford English Dictionary* and Samuel Pepys's 'Diary': Possible Antedatings and Postdatings (1)," *Mulberry* (English Literary Society of Aichi Prefectural University) 35, 161-171.

Nakamura, Fujio (1988) "A Word on the Regulation of the Auxiliary *Do*: Samuel Pepys's 'Diary' as a Test Case," *Mulberry* 37, 113-145.

Nakamura, Fujio (1989) "*The House is Building* Gata Activo-passive Progressive no Rekishi [On the Historical Development of the Activo-passive Progressive: *The House Is Building*]," Datasheets Presented at the Symposium of the Sixth Annual Meeting of Modern English Association, Daito-Bunka University, Japan, May 1989.

Nakamura, Fujio (1991) "*The House is Building* Gata Activo-passive Progressive no Rekishi [On the Historical Development of the Activo-passive Progressive: *The House Is Building*]," in Shuji Chiba, *et al.*, eds, *Gendai Eigogaku no Shoso: Ukaji Masatomo Hakushi Kanreki Kinen Ronbunshu* [*Aspects of English Linguistics and Philology: Festschrift Offered to Dr Masatomo Ukaji on His Sixtieth Birthday*], Kaitakusha,Tokyo, 121-143.

Nakamura, Fujio (1997) "Regulation of Negative Declarative Sentence with Auxiliary *Do*: Historical Facts Applicable as Subsidiary Evidence,"

Mulberry 46, 109-133.

Nakamura, Fujio (1998a) "Nikki Shokan Shiryou wa Kataru [Significance of Linguistic Analyses of Particular Text Types Such as Private Diaries and Personal Letters]," Datasheets Presented at the Symposium of the 15th Annual Meeting of Modern English Association, Kyoto University of Foreign Studies, Japan, May 1998.

Nakamura, Fujio (1998b) "A Word on the History of the English Passive Progressive," Datasheets Presented at the Tenth International Conference on English Historical Linguistics, University of Manchester, UK, Aug. 1998.

Nakamura, Fujio (1998c) "The Extinction of Participial *Being/Having/Knowing Not*: Further Evidence Confirming the Regulation of the Negative Declarative Sentence with Auxiliary *Do*," in Masahiko Kanno, Gregory K. Jember and Yoshiyuki Nakao, eds, *A Love of Words: English Philological Studies in Honour of Akira Wada*, Eihosha, Tokyo, 245-266.

Nakamura, Fujio (2000) "The Rise and Fall of the Construction of *Being/Having/Knowing Not*, in Connection with the Establishment of the Negative Declarative Sentence with the Auxiliary *Do*," Datasheets Presented at the Eleventh International Conference on English Historical Linguistics, University of Santiago de Compostela, Spain, Sept. 2000.

Nakamura, Fujio (2001) "A History of the Interrogative *do* in Seventeenth to Nineteenth-Century Diaries and Correspondence," Datasheets Presented at the First International Conference on the English Language in the Late Modern Period 1700-1900, University of Edinburgh, UK, Aug.-Sept. 2001.

Nakamura, Fujio (2002) "A Word on the Concurrence of Animate/Human Subject and the Passival Progressive," in Jacek Fisiak, ed., *Studies in English Historical Linguistics and Philology: A Festschrift for Akio Oizumi* (Studies in English Medieval Language and Literature, 2), Peter Lang, Frankfurt am Main, 307-326.

Nakamura, Fujio (2003a) "Contribution of Non-literary Texts to History of English Research," Datasheets Presented at the International Symposium on the Creation and Practical Use of Language Texts, Graduate School of Letters, University of Nagoya, Japan, June 2003.

Nakamura, Fujio (2003b) "Contribution of Non-literary Texts to History of English Research," in Masachiyo Amano, ed., *Creation and Practical*

Works Cited

Use of Language Texts (21st Century COE Program, International Conference Series, 2), Graduate School of Letters, University of Nagoya, 67-77.

Nakamura, Fujio (2005) "*Not* Kouchigata Genzai-bunshi no Seisui: Jo-doshi *Do* no Hattatsu no Saranaru Kenshou [The Rise and Fall of the Present Participle with Post-positioned *Not*: Another Phase of History of the Auxiliary *Do*]," Datasheets Presented at the Twenty-second Annual Meeting of the Modern English Association, University of Chiba, Japan, May 2005.

Nakamura, Fujio (2007a) "*Not* Kouchigata *Ing*-kei no Seisui: Jo-doshi *Do* no Hattatsu no Kakureta Sokumen (1) 16-20 Seiki Nikki Shokan Shiryou wo Konkyo ni [The Ascent and Demise of Participles/Gerunds Followed by *Not*: Demonstrating Another Phase in the History of the Auxiliary *Do*: (1) Evidence from 16th- to 20th-century Diaries and Correspondence]," *Bulletin of the Faculty of Letters, Aichi Prefectural University* 55, 41-86.

Nakamura, Fujio (2007b) "Uncovering of Rare or Unknown Usages: Contribution of Non-Literary Texts to History of English Research," Guest Lecture Datasheets Presented at the University of Helsinki, Finland, March 2007.

Nakamura, Fujio (2007c) "*How Do You?*: Jo-doshi *Do* wo Mochiinai Kouteigimonbun ni Tsukawareta Doshi no Shuusoku (Jou) [*How do you*: Historical Convergence of Verbs Used in the Affirmative Interrogatives without the Auxiliary *Do* (First Half)]," *The Rising Generation* 153/4, 42-45, Kenkyusha, Tokyo.

Nakamura, Fujio (2007d) "*How Do You?*: Jo-doshi *Do* wo Mochiinai Kouteigimonbun ni Tsukawareta Doshi no Shuusoku (Ge) [*How do you*: Historical Convergence of Verbs Used in the Affirmative Interrogatives without the Auxiliary *Do* (Second Half)]," *The Rising Generation* 153/5, 42-45, Kenkyusha, Tokyo.

Nakamura, Fujio (2007e) "Uncovering of Rare or Unknown Usages: A History of *Seem* Meaning 'to Pretend'," Datasheets Presented at the Fortieth Annual Meeting of the Societas Linguistica Europaea, University of Joensuu, Finland, Aug. 2007.

Nakamura, Fujio (2008a) "*Not* Kouchigata *Ing*-kei no Seisui: Jo-doshi *Do* no Hattatsu no Kakureta Sokumen: (2) *OED*^{2} on CD-ROM wo Konkyo ni

Works Cited

(Jou) [The Ascent and Demise of Participles/ Gerunds Followed by *Not*: Demonstrating Another Phase in the History of the Auxiliary *Do*: (2) Evidence from the *OED*[2] on CD-ROM (First half)]," *Bulletin of the Faculty of Letters, Aichi Prefectural University* 56, 45-63.

Nakamura, Fujio (2008b) "*Not* Kouchigata *Ing*-kei no Seisui: Jo-doshi *Do* no Hattatsu no Kakureta Sokumen: (3) CEECS, Lampeter, Newdigate Corpus wo Konkyo ni [The Ascent and Demise of Participles/Gerunds Followed by *Not*: Demonstrating Another Phase in the History of the Auxiliary *Do*: (3) Evidence from *CEECS, Lampeter* and *Newdigate* Corpora]," *Mulberry* 57, 63-98.

Nakamura, Fujio (2008c) "Uncovering of Rare or Unknown Usages: a History of Participles/Gerunds Followed by *Not*," Datasheets Presented at the Fifteenth International Conference on English Historical Linguistics, University of Munich, Germany, Aug. 2008.

Nakamura, Fujio (2008d) "Judou Shinkoukei no Doshi no Kakusan, Nou-Judou Shinkoukei no Doshi no Shuusoku [Historical Diffusion/Convergence of Verbs Used in the Passive/Passival Progressive]," *The Rising Generation* 153/12, 46-49, Kenkyusha, Tokyo.

Nakamura, Fujio (2009) "*Not* Kouchigata *Ing*-kei no Seisui: Jo-doshi *Do* no Hattatsu no Kakureta Sokumen (4) *OED*[2] on CD-ROM wo Konkyo ni (Ge) [The Ascent and Demise of Participles/Gerunds followed by *Not*, Demonstrating Another Phase in the History of the Auxiliary *Do*: (4) Evidence from the *OED*[2] on CD-ROM (Second half)]," *Mulberry* 58, 63-105.

Nakamura, Fujio (2010) "Uncovering of Rare or Unknown Usages: A History of *Seem* Meaning 'to Pretend'," in Merja Kytö, John Scahill and Harumi Tanabe, eds, *Language Change and Variation from Old English to Late Modern English: A Festschrift for Minoji Akimoto* (Linguistic Insights, 114), Peter Lang, Frankfurt/M, 217-238.

Nakamura, Fujio (2011) "A History of Negative Contractions," Datasheets Presented at the Historical English Word-Formation and Semantics, Academy of Management, School of English, Warsaw, Poland. Dec. 2011.

Nakamura, Fujio (2012a) "Hiteiji Shukuyaku no Rekishi wo Meguru Mondaiten [Unravelling Mysteries Surrounding a History of Negative Contractions]," Datasheets Presented at the 29th Annual Meeting of Modern English Association, Aoyama Gakuin University, Japan, May

Works Cited

2012.

Nakamura, Fujio (2012b) "The Period of Establishment of Tag-questions," Datasheets Presented at the 17th International Conference on English Historical Linguistics, University of Zurich, Switzerland, Aug. 2012.

Nakamura, Fujio (2012c) "A Correlation between the Establishment of Negative Contractions and the Development of Their Related Idioms: with Special Reference to *Can't Help* V-*ing* and Its Variants," Datasheets Presented at the 45th Annual Meeting of the Societas Linguistica Europaea, University of Stockholm, Sweden, Sept. 2012.

Nakamura, Fujio (2012d) "San-ninsho Tansuu Shugoni Koousuru *Don't* no Rekishi: *He Don't Care* kara *He Doesn't Care* he [A History of the Third Person Singular Present *Don't*: Transition from *He Don't Care* to *He Doesn't Care*]," *Mulberry* 61, 23-44.

Nakamura, Fujio (2013) "A History of the Third Person Singular Present *Don't*: Transition from *He Don't Know* to *He Doesn't Know*," Datasheets Presented at the Fifth International Conference on Late Modern English, University of Bergamo, Italy, August 2013.

Nakamura, Fujio (2014) "Negative Declarative 'I not say' in Modern English," Datasheets Presented at the 47th Annual Meeting of the Societas Linguistica Europaea, Adam Mickiewicz University, Poland, Sept. 2014.

Nakamura, Fujio (2015a) "*Not* Kouchigata *Ing*-kei no Seisui: Jo-doshi *Do* no Hattatsu no Kakureta Sokumen (5) ARCHER Corpus wo Konkyo ni [The Ascent and Demise of Participles/Gerunds Followed by *Not*, Demonstrating Another Phase in the History of the Auxiliary *Do*: (5) Evidence from ARCHER]," *Mulberry* 64, 31-50.

Nakamura, Fujio (2015b) "Diachrony of the Third Person Singular Present *Don't*: Transition from *He Don't Know* to *He Doesn't Know* (2)," *Mulberry* 65, 1-23.

Nakamura, Fujio (2015c) "Doushi ni Zenchi sareru Hite-Fukushi *not* no Rekishi [A History of Negative Particle *Not* Preceded by Verbs]," Datasheets Presented at the Symposium of the 32nd Annual Meeting of Modern English Association, Aichi Gakuin University, Japan, June 2015.

Nakamura, Fujio (2015d) "Diachrony of Present Participles and Gerunds Followed by *Not*," Datasheets Presented at the 45th Poznan Linguistic Meeting, Adam Mickiewicz University, Poland, Sept. 2015.

Works Cited

[*OALD⁸*] Turnbull, Joanna, *et al.*, eds (1948 [2010]) *Oxford Advanced Learner's Dictionary of Current English*, 8th ed., Oxford University Press, Oxford.

[*ODNB*] The On-line Version of the *Oxford Dictionary of National Biography* (http://www.oxforddnb.com/).

[*OED²*] Simpson, John A. and Edmund. S. C. Weiner (2002) *Oxford English Dictionary, Second Edition, on CD-ROM Version 3.1.*, Oxford University Press, Oxford.

Olsson, Yngve (1961) *On the Syntax of the English Verb with Special Reference to Have a Look and Similar Complex Structures*, Flanders, Göteborg.

Ota, Akira (1954 [1980]) *Kanryo-kei, Shinko-kei [Perfect Form, Progressive Form]*, 24th ed., Kenkyusha, Tokyo.

Partridge, Astley C. (1948 [1953a]) "The Periphrastic Auxiliary Verb 'do' and Its Use in the Plays of Ben Jonson," *Modern Language Review* 43, 26-33 [Reproduced in *Studies in the Syntax of Ben Jonson's Plays*, Bowes & Bowes, Cambridge].

Partridge, Astley C. (1953b) *The Accidence of Ben Jonson's Plays*, Bowes & Bowes, Cambridge.

Partridge, Astley C. (1964) *Orthography in Shakespeare and Elizabethan Drama: a Study of Colloquial Contractions, Elision, Prosody and Punctuation*, Arnold, London.

Partridge, Astley C. (1969) *Tudor to Augustan English: A Study in Syntax and Style from Caxton to Johnson* (The Language Library), André Deutsch, London.

Phillipps, Kenneth C. (1970) *Jane Austen's English* (The Language Library), André Deutsch, London.

Poutsma, Hendrik (1919) "Participles," *English Studies* 1, 129-140.

Poutsma, Hendrik (1923) *The Infinitive, the Gerund, and the Participles of the English Verb*, P. Noordhoff, Groningen.

Poutsma, Hendrik (1926) *A Grammar of Late Modern English*, Part II, Section II, P. Noordhoff, Groningen.

Poutsma, Hendrik (1928) *A Grammar of Late Modern English*, Part I, First Half, P. Noordhoff, Groningen.

Priestley, Joseph (1761 [1769] [1971]) "The Rudiments of English Grammar, Adapted to the Use of Schools; with Notes and Observations, for the Use of Those Who Have Made Some Proficiency in the Language,"

Works Cited

with Explanatory Remarks by Kikuo Yamakawa, in Takanobu Otsuka, gen ed., *A Reprint Series of Books Relating to the English Language*, Vol. 14, Nan'un-do, Tokyo, 9-137.

Quirk, Randolph, Sydney Greenbaum, Geoffrey Leech and Jan Svartvik (1985) *A Comprehensive Grammar of the English Language*, Longman, London.

Rissanen, Matti (1999) "Syntax," in Roger Lass, ed., *The Cambridge History of the English Language*, Vol. 3 (1476-1776), Cambridge University Press, Cambridge, 187-331.

Rydén, Mats (1979) *An Introduction to the Historical Study of English Syntax*, Almqvist & Wiksell International, Stockholm.

Schäfer, Jürgen (1980) *Documentation in the O.E.D*, Clarendon Press, Oxford.

Scheffer, Johannes (1975) *The Progressive in English*, North-Holland, Amsterdam.

Schmidt, Alexander (1875 [1971]) *Shakespeare-Lexicon: A Complete Dictionary of All the English Words, Phrases and Constructions in the Works of the Poet*, Vol. 2, 6th ed., Revised and Enlarged by Gregor Sarrazi, Walter de Gruyter, Berlin and Leipzig.

Schmidt, Fredrik (1900) *Studies in the Language of Pecock*, Almqvist & Wiksells, Upsala.

Söderlind, Johannes (1951 [1973]) *Verb Syntax in John Dryden's Prose*, Part I, Rpt., Kraus Reprint, Nendeln.

Söderlind, Johannes (1958 [1976]) *Verb Syntax in John Dryden's Prose*, Part II, Rpt., Kraus Reprint, Nendeln.

Strang, Barbara M. H. (1970) *A History of English*, Methuen, London.

Sugden, Herbert W. (1936) "The Grammar of Spenser's *Faerie Queene*," Supplement to *Language* 22, Linguistic Society of America, Philadelphia.

Trask, Robert L. (1995 [2004]) *Language: The Basics*, 2nd ed., Routledge, London & New York.

Trnka, Bohumil (1930 [1968]) *On the Syntax of the English Verb from Caxton to Dryden*, Rpt., Kraus Reprint, Nendeln.

Uhrström, Wilhelm (1907) *Studies on the Language of Samuel Richardson*, Almqvist & Wiksell, Upsala.

Visser, Fredericus Th. (1969) *An Historical Syntax of the English Language*,

Works Cited

Part III, First Half, E. J. Brill, Leiden.

Visser, Fredericus Th. (1970) *An Historical Syntax of the English Language*, Part I, E. J. Brill, Leiden.

Visser, Fredericus Th. (1972) *An Historical Syntax of the English Language*, Part II, E. J. Brill, Leiden.

Visser, Fredericus Th. (1973) *An Historical Syntax of the English Language*, part III, Second Half, E. J. Brill, Leiden.

Wada, Akira (1975) "Word-order of the Negative *Not* in Thomas Deloney's English," *Eigo to Eibei-Bungaku* [*English and English-American Literature*] 9, 15-33.

Warner, Anthony R. (1995) "Predicting the Progressive Passive: Parametric Change within a Lexicalist Framework," *Language* 71/3, 533-557.

Wright, Joseph, ed. (1905 [1981]) *The English Dialect Dictionary, Being the Complete Vocabulary of All Dialect Words Still in Use, or Known to Have Been in Use during the Last Two Hundred Years*, Vol. 5, Henry Frowde, Amen Corner, E. C., London, Rpt., Senjo, Tokyo.

Index

Index entries are intended to be helpful rather than exhaustive. References are by page number.

Name Index

Primary Source

Addison, Joseph 15, 207, 323, 383

Arbuthnot, Harriet 17, 39, 43, 92, 104, 155, 184, 196, 283, 323, 380

Arnold, Matthew 90, 107, 185, 323, 386

Austen, Jane 17, 84, 92, 387

Ball, Henry 83, 106, 154, 172, 205, 211, 212, 219, 233, 323

Blake, William 17, 184, 196, 323, 384

Burns, Robert 92, 384

Buxton, Ellen 185, 196, 323, 381

Campbell, Charlotte S. M. 195, 380

Cartwright, Thomas 377, 378

Clare, John 39, 43, 184, 197, 324, 385

Crabbe, George 183, 223, 224, 324, 384

Darwin, Charles 84, 380

Darwin, Erasmus 21, 222, 384

Davies, Rowland 101, 178, 212, 324, 377, 379 378

Defoe, Daniel 48, 81, 92, 102, 105, 152, 180, 181, 191, 207, 213, 214, 289, 324, 348, 382

Dickens, Charles 7, 9, 15, 22, 51, 52, 54, 55, 78, 80, 81, 387

Dodgson, Charles L. 9, 22, 40, 42, 43, 186, 324, 386

Dodington, George B. 102, 155, 379

Dodsley, Robert 208, 383

Eaton, Daniel 107, 196, 383

Eliot, George 80, 224, 314, 349, 386

Etherege, Sir George 173, 213, 324, 382

Evelyn, John 6, 22, 77, 85, 89, 92, 101, 102, 105, 107, 152, 153, 155, 167, 168, 170, 172, 173, 176, 177, 178, 179, 180, 206, 212, 213, 223, 233, 324, 377, 378

FitzGerald, Edward 106, 196, 223, 224, 385

Gay, John 180, 196, 325, 383

Gibbon, Edward 107, 224, 384

Gladstone, William E. 155, 380

Glanville, John 100, 167, 200, 209, 325, 378

Gray, Thomas 1, 19, 22, 37, 38, 43, 92, 181, 195, 222, 224, 325, 383

Gregory, Isabella A. 82, 89, 381

Greville, Henry W. 42, 87, 88, 380

Halley, Edmond 178, 180, 206, 325, 379

Hamilton, Edward W. 8, 9, 223, 381

Hawker, James 40, 43, 381
Hawker, Peter 83, 85, 92, 105, 106, 184, 196, 325, 380
Hoby, Margaret 16, 165-167, 188, 193, 219, 233, 249, 274, 325, 378
Hughes, Anne 17, 18, 39, 43, 82, 154, 195, 379
Hurd, Richard 105, 222, 225, 384
Huxley, Thomas H. 2, 61, 154, 184, 326, 380
Johnson, Samuel 50, 103, 283, 386
Josselin, Ralph 84, 107, 167, 173, 177, 201, 210, 326, 378
Kilvert, Francis 9, 21, 22, 42, 82, 85, 185, 224, 326, 381
King Charles I 152, 167, 201, 253, 326, 329, 357, 381
King Charles II 242, 334, 339, 352
King James I 316, 342, 345, 351, 364
Laurie, Peter 377, 380
Lennox, Charles 196, 222, 383
Lowther, John 17, 92, 206, 222, 223, 224, 326, 382
Lyttelton, Charles 37, 43, 168, 169, 177, 211, 212, 233, 326
Macmillan, Harold 186, 326, 381
Martineau, Harriet 9, 385
Meredith, George 39, 40, 43, 106, 224, 386
Milward, John 100, 151, 210, 326, 378
More, Hannah 110, 182, 225, 288, 301, 303, 327, 384
Newton, Sir Isaac 240, 325, 353, 382
Nicolson, William 102, 207, 213, 214, 327, 379
Osborne, Dorothy 2, 6, 7, 222, 381

Palmer, Samuel 19, 39, 43, 88, 157, 185, 209, 223, 327, 385
Peel, Sir Robert 17, 196, 385
Penrose, John 195, 208, 220, 223, 327, 383
Pepys, Samuel 1, 4-7, 14-16, 19, 22, 78, 80, 84, 92, 95-102, 106, 107, 113, 114-122, 130, 150, 154-156, 168-177, 179, 180, 188, 189, 191, 192, 195, 201-206, 210-212, 217, 219, 222, 223, 233, 250, 281, 283, 302, 325-328, 377, 378, 382, 393
Raikes, Thomas 155, 196, 385
Richardson, Samuel 48, 158, 208, 297, 358, 383
Roe 201, 324, 378
Rose, George 195, 223, 384
Rous, John 100, 210, 328, 377, 378
Ruskin, John 19, 39, 43, 209, 289, 298, 328, 358, 385
Savile, Henry 101, 105, 148, 217, 220, 328, 382
Shenstone, William 182, 222, 224, 328, 383, 384
Sheridan, Betsy 38, 43, 379
Sheridan, Richard B. 19, 50, 81, 387
Skinner, John 82, 84-86, 92, 105, 380
Skinner, Peter 155, 177, 180, 328
Smith, Adam 22, 100, 384
Southey, Robert 17, 156, 157, 196, 223, 224, 304, 353, 359, 385
Spender, Stephen H. 186, 328, 381
Stanhope, Philip D. 22, 121, 122, 225, 383
Steele, Richard 5, 20, 207, 213, 328, 382
Stevens, William B. 21, 122, 152,

Index

182, 195, 328, 379

Swift, Jonathan 20, 131, 180, 181, 195, 207, 216, 303, 328, 360, 382

Swinburne, Algernon C. 106, 156, 196, 386

Symonds, Richard 195, 201, 329, 378

Tennyson, Alfred 185, 186, 196, 223, 224, 304, 305, 329, 361, 385

Todd, Matthew 183, 184, 196, 329, 380

Watkin, Absalom 82, 380

Wedgwood, Josiah 8, 84, 181, 196, 222, 329, 384

Wesley, John 106, 152, 154-156, 181-183, 208, 214, 222, 223, 224, 329, 379, 383

White, Gilbert 151, 195, 304, 379,

Wilde, Oscar F. O. W. 21, 22, 386, 387

Woodforde, James 8, 9, 18, 38, 39, 43, 85, 86, 89, 92, 103-107, 130, 152, 182, 183, 195, 208, 214, 215, 217, 220, 233, 329, 379

Wordsworth, Dorothy 82, 100, 104, 183, 196, 209, 225, 329, 379, 385

ARCHER 3.1 xxiv, 129, 137, 146, 161, 162-165, 233, 239, 240, 247, 248, 266-269, 271, 273, 277-279, 317, 330, 332, 337-339, 368, 388,

389, 397

BNC Corpus 131, 132, 135-143, 146, 147, 154, 160, 161, 165, 317, 318-322, 368, 388

Brown Corpus 131-135, 146, 147, 165, 317, 318, 368, 388

CEECS Corpus 129, 146, 147, 165, 233, 235, 238, 239, 241, 242, 247, 250-254, 265, 266, 274-277, 279, 317, 330, 331, 333, 334, 339, 368, 389, 396

FLOB Corpus 31, 131-135, 146, 147, 165, 317, 318, 319, 368, 388

Frown Corpus 131, 132, 134, 135, 146, 147, 165, 317, 318, 368, 388

Helsinki-DP 129, 146, 147, 165, 233, 234, 240, 241, 248-250, 274, 279, 317, 330, 333, 339, 368, 389

Lampeter Corpus 129, 146, 147, 165, 233, 235, 236, 238, 239, 242-244, 247, 254-260, 265, 266, 269-273, 275-277, 279, 317, 330-332, 334-337, 339, 368, 389, 396

LOB Corpus 31, 131-135, 146, 147, 165, 317, 318, 368, 388

Newdigate Corpus 129, 146, 147, 165, 233, 237-239, 244-247, 260-266, 270, 271, 272, 273, 275-277, 279, 317, 330, 368, 389, 396

Secondary Source

AHD³ 109, 123, 391

Akimoto, M. 396

Amano, M. 394

Ando, S. 391

Araki, K. and M. Ukaji 144, 391

Aronstein, Ph. 80, 391

Bækken, B. 221, 222, 391

Barber, C. 26, 144, 391

Baugh, A. C. 78, 144, 391
Bergeder, F. 98, 99, 391
Biber, D., S. Johansson, G. Leech, S. Conrad, and E. Finegan 74, 389, 391
Bloomfield, M. W. and L. Newmark 74, 391
Bolinger, D. 100, 391
Brainerd, B. 26, 27, 391
Britannica 159, 160, 317, 325, 327-329, 340, 344, 360, 391
Bullokar, W. 144, 145, 188, 279, 348, 391
Chiba, S. 393
CDNB 317, 328, 346, 352, 392
CHEL 296, 317, 344, 392
COD¹⁰ 109, 123, 392
Curme, G. O. 10, 99, 131, 392
Denison, D. 8, 9, 74, 78, 79, 91, 92, 144, 392
Ellegård, A. 226, 227, 229, 392
Fisiak, J. 394
Franz, W. 144, 392
Gunji, T. 392
Huddleston, R., and G. K. Pullum 131, 392
Jember, G. K. 394
Jespersen, O. 15, 26, 81, 93, 95, 99, 106, 143, 312, 392
Kanno, M. 394
Kytö, M. 396
Kubota, Y. 20, 392
LDCE⁵ 37, 46, 55, 58, 59, 62, 68, 69, 109, 123, 133, 392
Lowth, R. 232, 392
Mair, C. 126, 393
Matthews, W. 3, 110, 393

Mencken, H. L. 74, 75, 393
Mossé, F. 15, 16, 393
Mustanoja, T. F. 144, 393
MWCD¹² 110, 123, 393
Nakamura, F. 1, 5-12, 14-16, 18, 20, 25-30, 32-36, 42, 45, 56, 64, 69, 73, 77, 80, 90, 97, 103, 109, 129, 158, 161, 198, 202, 226, 227, 229, 232, 249, 262, 269, 393-397
Nakao, Y. 394
OALD⁸ 37, 46, 48, 49, 50, 52, 54, 55, 57, 67, 68, 69, 110, 123, 398
ODNB 2, 21, 42, 43, 158, 317, 321-329, 333-338, 340, 341, 343-363, 377, 398
OED² 1, 3, 4-6, 8, 14, 15, 17, 20, 21, 26, 28, 30-32, 37, 44-74, 80, 82, 83, 85-87, 89, 90, 109-112, 122, 124, 126, 127, 129, 133, 146-151, 153, 155-157, 159-161, 165, 190, 230, 233, 279-307, 309-317, 339-345, 347, 352, 357, 360-363, 368, 371, 373, 389, 396-399
Olsson, Y. 92, 398
Ota, A. 98, 398
Otsuka, T. 392, 399
Partridge, A. C. 14, 26, 43, 73, 144, 398
Phillipps, K. C. 144, 398
Poutsma, H. 8, 18, 78, 80, 90, 91, 95, 106, 144, 398
Priestley, J. 144, 145, 232, 279, 398
Quirk, R., S. Greenbaum, G. Leech and J. Svartvik. 131, 399
Rissanen, M. 78, 79, 144, 389, 399
Rydén, M. xxiv, 2, 399
Scahill, J. 396

405

Index

Schäfer, J. 4, 5, 399
Scheffer, J. 93, 95, 106, 399
Schmidt, A. 113, 127, 399
Schmidt, F. 144, 399
Söderlind, J. 6, 79, 99, 144, 145, 152, 399
Strang, B. M. H. 144, 399
Sugden, H. W. 144, 399
Tanabe, H. 396
Trask, R. L. 74, 399

Trnka, B. 143, 399
Uhrström, W. 144, 399
Ukaji, M. 393
Visser, F. Th. 7, 10, 13, 14, 16, 78-80, 81, 92, 95, 106, 144, 399, 400
Wada, A. 144, 145, 394, 400
Warner, A. R. 17, 400
Wright, J. 113, 127, 400
Yamakawa, K. 399

Word, Phrase and Subject Index

be busy (in) + Verb- *ing* 15, 16
be busy to-infinitive 14, 15
be coming to-infinitive as a quasi-auxiliary 18-20
be near Verb-*ing* 4, 6
being not PP
    gerundive passive 130, 135, 136, 140, 200, 215-217, 230-232, 272, 311, 312, 368
    gerundive perfective 130, 215-217, 230-232, 368
    participial passive 130, 136, 140, 198-200, 209-214, 241-246, 248, 283-289, 368
    participial perfective 130, 198-200, 209-215, 242, 246, 247, 284-286, 289, 368
causative *do* 2
do not need to-infinitive 4, 7
do-less affirmative interrogative sentences 14
Dryden's aversion to the sudden increase of negative contractions 20
electronic corpora examined 146-

148
factors in which the post-position of *not* was induced 148, 151, 194-198, 220, 221
geographical distribution of users of *ing*-form + *not* 317, 364-368
gerundive progressive
    being coming 107
    being groveling 107
    being standing 107
    being translating 107
have could 2
having not PP
    gerundive 131, 133, 135, 136, 143, 215, 216, 231, 232, 269-272, 279, 310, 311, 315, 316, 368
    participial 130, 135, 136, 140-143, 198-209, 230-232, 234-240, 279, 280-282, 315, 368
in order to-infinitive 5
lexical analysis software 146-148
local negation of *not* 132, 148-151, 153-155
negative contractions

Index

the earliest written occurrence 28
occurrences in 17th- to 20th-century diaries & letters 28, 29
occurrences in the *OED²*'s citations 28, 30, 31
period and chronological order of the establishment of negative contractions 33-35
negative declarative *I not say* 14, 397
non-counterfactual *would have* PP 1, 2
parenthetic *I doubt* 1, 2
participial adjective *lowering* 5
participial progressive *being* Verb-*ing*
being advancing 101
being altering 96
being approaching 101
being beginning 95, 97
being brewing 103
being coming 102
being cutting 102
being discoursing 101
being dressing 96, 97, 103, 104
being expecting 101
being finishing 96
being going 95-97, 101-104
being hearing 102
being hedging 103
being laying 95
being leaving 101
being making 95
being mending 103
being painting 103
being paying 95
being preparing 102, 103, 105
being reading 102
being repairing 104

being returning 101-103
being rising 100
being sending 96
being sitting 96
being speaking 96
being standing 101
being stepping 102
being striking 95
being taking 101
being talking 103
being waiting 101
being writing 102
participial progressive *having been* Verb-*ing* 97, 98, 100, 105, 106
passival progressive *be* + V-*ing* with animate/human subject
annoint 80, 91
asserve 80, 91
bait 85, 86, 91
breed 81, 84, 91
bring 81, 91
carry 78, 80, 81, 91
change 84, 91
draw 84, 91
educate 78, 81-83, 91
enlist 86-88, 91
exhibit 81, 91
fat 82, 85, 86, 91
gather 84, 91
hang 88, 89, 91
harness 81, 91
hatch 84, 91
haul 81, 91
indulge 86-88, 91
levy 81, 91
muster 86-88, 91
need 81, 91

Index

nurse 82, 86, 91
plague 82, 86, 91
pour 86-88, 91
put 81-84, 91
rear 81, 91
send 80, 85, 91
shape 81, 91
swear 81, 91
take 81, 91
train 84, 91
transfer 81, 91
wean 82, 89, 91
whip 80, 91
woo 81, 91
passive progressive 4, 7, 10-13, 77, 90, 93, 372, 393, 394
positional freedom of *not* 194-196
present participles/gerunds followed by *not*
target constructions 129-131
use in Present-day English 131-143
results of analyses of diaries & correspondence 230-233
results of analyses of Helsinki-DP, CEECS, Lampeter, Newdigate & ARCHER 3.1 279
results of analyses of citations in the *OED²* on CD-ROM 315, 316
progressive of *have* "drink, eat, etc" / *have* + action noun 16-18
progressive of *have* + O + Adjectival/Adverbial/V-*ing* 16-18
progressive with passive/causative/modal *have* 4, 7-9
references to the position of *not* against *ing*-forms

in Present-day English 131, 132
in the history of English 143-145
RNDS theory 197, 198, 215, 217, 221, 225, 226
seem 'to pretend'
quotations noticed by Latham & Matthews, editors of D10 114-116.
quotations discovered by Nakamura 117-122
significance of the uncovering of *seem* 'to pretend' in Modern English 123-126
seemer, seeming, seemingly and *seemingness* with the concept of active, deliberate show or pre- tence 110, 111, 119, 120
semantic difference between participial *not* Verb-*ing* and Verb-*ing* *not* 190, 191
Stevens' linguistic self-introspection of why *will* + *not* is not contracted into *win't* 21, 22
structural differences between participial *not* Verb-*ing* and Verb-*ing* *not* 192
syntactic variants having both progressive & passive sense 10-13, 77
third person singular present *don't*
examples in 17th- to 20th-century diaries & letters 35-44
examples in the *OED²*'s citations 44-73
one of the reasons why employment of *doesn't* was postponed in American English 74-76

use of *kine* as a litmus test distinguishing older generations from younger generations 21

users of *ing*-form + *not* and text categories in which this usage occurred

ARCHER 3.1 332, 337, 338, 339

BNC 319-322, 339

CEECS 330, 331, 333, 334, 339

FLOB 319

Helsinki-DP 330, 333, 339

Lampeter 331, 332, 334-337, 339

LOB 318

OED² 339-364

17th- to 20th-century diaries & letters 323-329

Verb-*ing not*

gerundive

being not 140, 219, 220, 314, 315

caring not 133

coming not 274

interrupting not 314

missing not 133

offering not 314

saying not 220

speaking not 315

swearing not 315

travelling not 314

wanting not 314

participial

acting not 298

affording not 176

alluring not 292

aiming not 255

amounting not 180

attaining not 304

bearing not 293

being not 137-139, 144, 165-173, 176-186, 249-253, 255-259, 261-264, 266, 268, 269, 290-305

believing not 304

bettering not 305

building not 260

caring not 184, 293, 297

claiming not 260

coming not 144, 173, 302

consisting not 173

containing not 179, 294, 298

decreasing not 289

disfiguring not 303

disturbing not 304

doing not 173

doubting not 299, 304

dreading not 299

eating not 304

examining not 179

extending not 297

feeling not 139, 184

finding not 167, 173, 180, 183, 185, 252, 302-304

growing not 304

having not 139, 167, 173-176, 179-186, 190, 250, 252, 253, 258, 259, 263, 264, 269, 292, 293, 296, 297, 299, 300, 302, 303

hearing not 182, 253, 254, 293

knowing not 139, 175, 179, 190, 250, 264, 290, 293

leaving not 305

lying not 303

liking not 293, 294, 297, 300, 301

Index

living not 297
longing not 185
looking not 139
losing not 264, 265
marching not 301
meaning not 294, 298
meeting not 175
naming not 294
needing not 175, 301
occupying not 186
opening not 185
passing not 265
pending not 304
proceeding not 303
purveying not 298, 299
reaching not 181, 297
referring not 298
returning not 167
rising not 294
saying not 184
seeing not 175, 294
seeming not 295, 296
shining not 301
signifying not 298
sinking not 302
sorting not 294
speaking not 294
standing not 298

succeeding not 253
suffering not 296, 301
taking not 185
tending not 299
turning not 294
understanding not 250, 259
valuing not 296
vouchsafing not 294
waking not 301
wishing not 139
writing not 176, 304
Verb-*ing not* + negative intensifier
   133, 137, 148, 149, 153, 176, 179,
   182-186, 217, 220, 253, 264, 269,
   294, 296, 297, 299, 301-303, 305,
   307, 309, 316
Verb-*ing not* + correlative *not*-A-*but*- B
   137, 149-151, 153, 185, 186, 255,
   259, 260, 292, 294, 296, 298, 299,
   301, 303-305, 307, 309, 314-316
verbs which continued to show aversion to the auxiliary *do* in negative declaratives 197, 198, 221,
   222, 225-229, 310, 316, 368, 374
whereabout with the locality sense 5
Wilde's apprehension of his use of
   the auxiliary *will* and *shall* 21, 22

Fujio Nakamura

Born 5 Feb. 1956	Yasuijuku, Tottori, Japan
Mar. 2016	D. Litt., Hiroshima University
Sept. 1993–Sept. 1994	Visiting Scholar, Faculty of English and Darwin College, University of Cambridge
Aug.–Sept. 2007	Visiting Fellow, University of Bristol Language Centre
Apr. 2001–Present	Professor, Aichi Prefectural University

Fujio Nakamura has taught at Aichi Prefectural University since 1981 and is now Professor of English philology and linguistics. His research area is English historical syntax and morphology. His most recent academic publications include "Uncovering of rare or unknown usages: A history of *seem* meaning 'to pretend'", in Merja Kytö, John Scahill and Harumi Tanabe, eds (2010) *Language Change and Variation from Old English to Late Modern English: A Festschrift for Minoji Akimoto* (Linguistic Insights, 114), Peter Lang, Frankfurt/M, 217–238; "A history of negative imperatives: Transition from Verb + *not* to *do not* Verb", in Minoji Akimoto and Mitsuru Maeda, eds (2013) *Grammaticalization and Constructionalization*, Hituzi Syobo, Tokyo, 287–328 (written in Japanese); "Affirmative imperative *do* in Modern English: With special reference to its accelerators and syntactic patterns", in Ken Nakagawa, Editor in Chief (2014) *Studies in Modern English: The Thirtieth Anniversary Publication of the Modern English Association*, Eihōsha, Tokyo, 185–201. For further details of F. Nakamura's educational and academic history, please refer to http://researchmap.jp/read0020179/?lang=english.

UNVEILLING 'RARE' USAGES
IN THE HISTORY OF ENGLISH

2016 年 10 月 20 日　印　刷　　　　2016 年 10 月 31 日　発　行

著　　者 ⓒ 中 村 不 二 夫

発 行 者　佐 々 木　元

製作・発行所　株式会社 英 宝 社

〒101-0032　東京都千代田区岩本町 2-7-7
☎[03]（5833）5870　Fax[03]（5833）5872

ISBN 978-4-269-77054-6 C1082
［印刷・製本：モリモト印刷株式会社］

本書の一部または全部を、コピー、スキャン、デジタル化等での無
断複写・複製は、著作権法上での例外を除き禁じられています。本
書を代行業者等の第三者に依頼してのスキャンやデジタル化は、た
とえ個人や家庭内での利用であっても著作権侵害となり、著作権法
上一切認められておりません。